The Gun Digest® Book of
ASSAULT WEAPONS

Jack Lewis

Published by

700 East State Street • Iola, WI 54990-0001
715-445-2214 • 888-457-2873
www.krause.com

Our toll-free number to place an order
or obtain a free catalog is 800-258-0929.

The views and opinions of the author expressed herein are not necessarily
those of the publisher, and no responsibility for such views will be assumed.

In regard to the mechanical and safety aspects of the guns covered in this book, it
is assumed that the guns are in factory original condition with the dimensions of
all parts as made by the manufacturer. Since alteration of parts is a simple matter,
the reader is advised to have any guns checked by a competent gunsmith. Both the
author and publisher disclaim responsibility for any accidents.

Library of Congress Catalog Number: 85-73744

ISBN: 0-87349-658-2

Edited by Kevin Michalowski
Designed by Ethel Thulien

Printed in U. S. A.

TABLE OF CONTENTS

ABOUT THE AUTHORS

JACK LEWIS, who created this series of books on assault weaponry, was editor/publisher of Gun World magazine for 37 years. He has lost track of the number of books he and his staff produced over the years. He long ago lost track of the number of full-auto weapons he has fired in his continuing research.

Lewis is the author of more than 6000 published magazine articles. He also wrote and produced the first five earlier editions of this book. He currently lives in Hawaii, where he writes magazine articles and novels – when not on the firing range.

A veteran of World War II, Korea and Vietnam, he is a decorated, retired Marine Corps lieutenant colonel. His fascination with selective-fire weaponry dates back some six decades to his days as a private first class machine gunner.

DAVID E. STEELE has studied weapons and martial arts since childhood. He has been a UCLA varsity fencer, a U.S. Army infantryman and a police instructor. He holds a bachelor of arts degree in sociology and a master of science degree in police administration, as well as five teaching credentials. His master's degree thesis was on SWAT team tactics.

Steele has worked for one county, two state and three federal law enforcement agencies, including U.S. Customs. He was supervisor of the Police Weapons Center project in Washington, D.C., testing police equipment and writing tech manuals. For the past 15 years, he has been a criminal investigator for the State of California. He has authored three books and published more than 500 articles on firearms, combat knives and self-defense subjects.

INTRODUCTION

The longer we, the authors, look at what is happening in the world of military armament, the more we realize that some things change but little.

More than 200 years ago, in the French & Indian War, the guerilla tactics learned from American Indians were used against the French by American colonists. During the Revolutionary War, colonists used these same hit-and-move-on tactics against the British.

More recently, our own troops in Iraq have suffered casualties from bypassed enemy bands and even from civilian guerrillas or soldiers dressed as civilians. We have smart bombs, not-so-smart bombs and all sorts of modern technology at our command. But unless we – and others – at war resort to civilization-ending nuclear warfare, the final cleanup and dirty work are going to be done by the men armed with a rifles, machine guns and other small arms.

The effort to improve infantry weapons continues unabated around the world. In this country, for example, Alliant Techsystems headquartered in Anoka, Minn., is deep into development of an infantry rifle that will fire a cartridge that literally seeks out human targets, exploding like a grenade or mortar shell when in close proximity to what is considered an enemy.

All of which brings us to an experience by Jack Lewis that took place in 1984 just before he retired as a Marine Corps lieutenant colonel. He was assigned to a major exercise with the 1st Marine Division in the desert near 29 Palms, Calif. One of the Los Angeles newspapers sent a young female reporter to view the exercise.

Our co-author squired her around the desert to observe what was going on in the simulated combat situation. At noon, over MREs, the adult flower child said, "I don't understand what it's all about. Today, we have nuclear weapons, bombs that seek out targets, poison gases and all sorts of death-dealing stuff. Why are these Marines out there with rifles and machine guns?"

Lewis leaned back on the wooden footlocker being used as a seat. "There have been places like Tarawa and Iwo Jima that were shelled with high explosives for days, even weeks," he pointed out. "It looked as though every living thing on those islands should be killed in the continuing barrage. But when it came time to go ashore, the Marines found there always was some guy coming out of a hole in the ground, trying to shoot their heads off! Wars are fought in the final effort by those men with rifles and machine guns."

The lady must have agreed, since she quoted her guide verbatim in her newspaper column.

It is our continuing contention that great damage can be done to enemy installations and personnel with aircraft, artillery and even naval gunfire. But again, it is the infantry soldier who must be called upon to make the final assault and do the final cleanup and dirty work!

C. Jack Lewis
Kehena Beach, Pahoa, Hawaii

David E. Steele
Los Angeles, California

ACKOWLEDGMENTS

As has been the case with the previous five editions of The Gun Digest Book of Assault Weapons, this edition could not have been completed without the aid of a number of knowledgeable individuals. It is impossible for anyone anywhere to know all there is to know about today's military weaponry. However, a wise person once said that expertise is not in memorizing information, but in knowing where to find that knowledge and information.

As the military becomes ever more technically oriented, keeping up with even the more simple inventions – good, bad and indifferent – aimed at today's military armament market becomes a mammoth undertaking.

Thankfully, your authors have been lucky enough to know where to find the information needed to complete this latest edition. Thanks must necessarily go to many people foremost among whom are a trio of recognized arms writers, Frank W. James, Jim Thompson and Robert K. Campbell. These three outdid themselves in researching and photographing specific arms and situations for inclusion in this book.

As with past editions, our appreciation also goes to Reed Knight, Jr., who allowed us the run of his full-auto museum in Vero Beach, Fla., where he operates Knight's Armament Co. Of particular help in this segment of research was Dave Lutz, a retired Marine lieutenant colonel, who spent most of his military career testing and evaluating weaponry. He is now vice president of Knight's Armament and devoted many hours in explaining and firing several of the weapons that are mentioned in this tome.

Our thanks also must go to members of various law enforcement agencies and military establishments, including retired Marine Col. Walt Ford, editor of Leatherneck magazine and Maj. Chris Hughes of Marine Corps Base, Hawaii. Officer Isaac Fiesta and Lt. Chad Fukui of the Hawaii Island Police Department have been of great help in testing and evaluating specific weapons listed in the table of contents.

The efforts of Rueselle E. Lewis were of particular value in developing this project. She functioned as chief photographer and proofreader, as well as keeping various word processors and computers operational so deadlines could be met. Without her, there wouldn't be a book!

DEDICATION

This book is gratefully dedicated to the memory of the late Bill Ruger. A design genius as well as a patriot, he believed in protecting the Second Amendment and put his money where is mouth was!

CHAPTER 1

THE BEST LAWMAN'S SUBGUN?

These Days, Lots of Manufacturers Are Making Them, but Here Are Some Definite Ideas on Performance

IN MOST EUROPEAN countries, the sawed-off shotgun is still considered a terror weapon. Historians note that during World War I, German officials protested American soldiers using the venerable Winchester 1897 in trench warfare. As our enemy saw it, there was nothing wrong with ripping a man apart with a saw-tooth bayonet, but to them the shotgun loaded with 00 buckshot was a violation of the Hague Accords.

Europeans fail to accept the fact that Americans have employed the shotgun in wars since colonial times; all too often it was a need rather than a choice based upon a lack of muskets or rifles. Shotguns also were part of the armament on sailing ships and were used by western sheriffs. From blunderbuss to riot gun, the scattergun has been a recognized tool of U.S. close combat.

At the same time in Europe, single-projectile firearms were the rule for the military; police often used the same weaponry. In this century, the standard backup weapon for Continental law enforcement agents has been the submachine gun.

These days European and American police and even soldiers tend to cross-pollinate in terms of weapons and tactics. The police shotgun is available to SO-19, the armed response unit that is part of England's Scotland Yard.

"A friend of mine, a Britisher who is ex-Special Air Service, now carries a Remington Model 870 – sawed off fore and aft – when he runs bodyguard operations

The Heckler & Koch MP-5K personal defense model is meant to provide air crews with a weapon that is particularly suitable to survival, escape and evasion.

David E. Steele tries out the Heckler & Koch MP-5 subgun with a Wilson Arms suppressor. This is the MP-5A3 folding-stock model.

This rare gun-carrying attaché case is rigged for the MP-5K submachine gun. It was designed at the request of German uncover police and SWAT teams.

At the Gunsite Training Center in Arizona, a sheriff's deputy learns proper techniques for shooting the MP-5 submachine gun. Note the .45 ACP Colt backup gun holstered on his thigh.

in the former Soviet bloc," says David E. Steele. "It gets more attention than his Russian AKSU-47, which is familiar to the natives."

However when we pause and take a long, hard look at what has happened in more recent years, it is obvious that most of the modern firearms' changes have come from Europe to America. Faced with the explosion of drugs and associated violent crime, law enforcement agencies in this country have looked to Western Europe and Israel for innovations like high-capacity automatic pistols and submachine guns.

Ironically, America did not invent the submachine gun. That distinction goes to Italy. However, it was a U.S. citizen who invented what probably can be considered the most famous subgun to date—the Thompson.

Gen. John Thompson got his gun into actual production too late for World War I. However, the open-bolt, .45 ACP Model 1921 Thompson – and its subsequent variations – were adopted by the U.S. Federal Bureau of Investigation and some police departments with the express purpose of ventilating thick-bodied automobiles and heavily armed criminal gangs. After Thompson's death, a simplified edition of his subgun – dubbed the M-1A1 – was adopted by both the Army and Marine Corps. The Marines used the Thompson with enthusiasm in the Pacific during World War II after learning of its capabilities during the so-called Banana Wars of Latin American in the 1920s.

"Following World War II, most of the Thompsons were passed to the Chinese Nationalist government. These guns later were captured by the Chinese Communist armies, which used them in Korea against some of the Marines who had once carried them! Among those Marines, recapturing a Thompson subgun was considered a major event and they were sought by everyone I knew," Jack Lewis recalls.

Later in World War II came the Reising gun. First was the Model 50 with a fixed stock, then the Model 55 with a folding stock. Like the Thompson, both were

The Heckler & Koch MP-5A2 submachine gun with its fixed stock is capable of both semi- and full-automatic fire, as well as possessing a three-round burst capability.

The Heckler & Koch MP-5K PDW subgun and the Beretta-made M-9 service pistol are carried by certain U.S. troops. Both guns are chambered for the 9mm cartridge.

This is the HK SP-89 9mm pistol, which has been configured for target shooting. The authors see little future for this particular gun in the U.S. anti-gun climate.

This HK SP-89 9mm pistol does not fire full-auto and may well serve as an entry weapon for SWAT teams and those charged with serving warrants to suspected felons.

chambered for the .45 ACP cartridge. This subgun was adopted in limited numbers by the Marine Corps, but was too delicate for island-jumping combat. In fact, there is a fable that claims Marine Gen. "Howlin' Mad" Smith ordered hundreds of Reisings thrown into the sea off the coast of Saipan after that battle ended. He was not impressed with the gun by that time and neither were his troops. A number of those that remained in Stateside inventories made their way to law enforcement agencies including the Los Angeles County Sheriff's Office and Texas State Police.

In 1949, a gent named Gordon Ingram designed a .45 submachine gun that was similar in external appearance to the once-revered Tommy gun. Ingram produced prototypes with both straight and pistol grip forend variations, calling it his Model 6.

This initial Ingram entry was simpler than the Thompson and, in some quarters, gained the same reputation for reliability. Once in production, Thai police, the Cuban Navy, the Peruvian Army and the U.S. Constabulary in Puerto Rico purchased some of Ingram's guns.

Ingram went on to invent the much better known M-10, which was chambered for the 9mm or .45 ACP, then the .380-caliber M-11. The Military Armament Corp. (MAC), then headquartered in Powder Springs, Ga., produced both models during the 1970s"Famed for its use in movies – not to mention by Miami drug lords – the M-10 and M-11 were promoted by MAC president Mitch WerBell as a police weapon in this country and as a counterinsurgency weapon in Vietnam," according to Steele.

However, neither gun was a serious contender in police circles. It had stamped sights and fired from

an open bolt, making it highly inaccurate in semi-auto fire. When in full-auto mode, for most shooters the minimum burst that could be triggered was four or five rounds. The cyclic rate of fire was too rapid to be considered comfortable.

"The military did take passing notice of the MAC as a possible replacement sidearm for the Colt .45 ACP, but eventually decided to substitute a conventional pistol, the Beretta M-92F. As is usually the case, the Department of Defense gave that pistol a new designation as the M-9," Steele says.

He adds, "With its spindly wire stock and poorly located selector, the Ingram took a back seat in clandestine warfare choices. Suppressed sound guns such as the Sten, Sterling and Swedish K model were more favored. Many considered the Sionics/MAC suppressor to be the best part of the Ingram gun, its only competitive feature."

In the late 1960s, a now-defunct firm known as Interarms imported the Israeli Uzi and the Walther

The HK MP-5/10 is the 10mm version of the submachine gun that was developed to meet a requirement of the Federal Bureau of Investigation. It has a synthetic magazine and a bolt hold-open feature. However currently law enforcement agencies favor the 40 S&W version of this gun.

Noted automatic weapons expert Peter Kokalis, in camouflage gear, poses with members of a SWAT team to which he taught subgun techniques at the Gunsite Training Center. Note that this team is equipped overall with Heckler & Koch MP-5 submachine guns.

After the U.S. Navy gave up the Subic Bay Naval Base in the Philippine Islands, what then became known as the Subic Economic Zone was guarded by local officers trained by U.S. personnel before their departure. Note that all are armed with MP-5 subguns.

MPK for possible police sales. The U.S. Secret Service quickly adopted the Uzi folding-stock paratroop model to carry in special shoulder holsters and even attaché cases.

The Uzi was a more compact backup weapon than a police riot gun," Steele says. "As a specialized federal agency with low possibility of shoot-outs, the Secret Service did not have to justify this decision to local taxpayers as a local police department might well have to do."

Designed in the early 1950s by Uziel Gal, the 9mm Uzi proved itself in both the 1956 Sinai campaign and the 1967 Six-Day War with both woodstock and paratroop versions seeing action.

The original Uzi weighed 8 pounds unloaded, with a 10.2-inch barrel and an overall length of 25.2 inches, which was reduced to 17.3 inches when the metal stock was folded. Firing semi- and full-auto at 600 rounds per minute, the open-bolt Uzi proved to be accurate and controllable enough for military purposes. Its reliability in the desert environment was considered outstanding.

The German Walther MPK, less well known as the Maschinen Pistole Kurz, was the short police version of the MPL (Lang) designed for military service. The MPK fired from the open bolt for a full-auto cyclic rate of 550 rounds per minute. Firing short bursts, it was considered highly controllable. Overall length of this gun was 25.96 inches or 14.75 inches with the stock folded. Unloaded weight was 6.27 pounds.

Steele first tried the MPK, courtesy of Interarms, in 1970 in Tom Nelson's basement range in Virginia. In those days, Nelson was a vice president of Inter-arms. More recently, he is the author of *The World's Submachine Guns.*

"The Walther functioned flawlessly, but it was believed that a gun without a semi-auto capability had little future in U.S. law enforcement. German police, however, were armed with the MPK during

the 1972 Olympic Games' siege by Islamic terrorists," notes Steele.

Also in the 1970s, another German firm, Heckler & Koch, began to export its MP-5 submachine gun to the United States. This was accomplished initially through Virginia-based Security Arms, a company run by Jack Wood. Eventually, Heckler & Koch set up its own U.S. operation in Virginia, but the first guns delivered to Wood were the MP-5A2 fixed-stock model and the MP-5A3, which featured a retracting stock.

"Wood and I took some of these original imported MP-5s to police agencies in the area surrounding the District of Columbia, demonstrating the subgun's capabilities," Steele recalls. "It was a hard sell. So close to the seat of the federal government, local police departments were concerned with the public

Many operators and small arms engineers soon learn that fitting an "A" model MP-5 with a muzzle-mounted suppressor such as this Sionic model creates a long, unwieldy and hard-to-manage weapon.

relations aspects. The expense of the subguns as compared with the price of shotguns was another negative factor.

"We talked to the Secret Service, but they were locked into the Uzi. In addition, they used what they said was a special Canadian hardball load that had a rim too thick for the MP-5 extractor to handle. The cartridge actually had been developed by the CIA, but not more than two months later, Heckler & Koch had changed the extractor for all U.S.-bound production."

For the Secret Service demonstration, Steele and Wood brought along a supply of Finnish-made Lapua ammunition. "It was clear that the MP-5, with its

closed bolt and diopter sights, could easily outshoot the Uzi," Steele notes.

"However," Steele adds, "the Secret Service let it be known that they didn't need a tack-driving carbine, but a compact backup weapon for their issue M-19 pistols that they thought were reliable and more accurate than a shotgun." The Secret Service since has switched to the SIG-Saur P-288 semiauto handgun.

By providing samples to trend-setting agencies such as the Los Angeles County Sheriff's Special Enforcement Bureau, test reports in magazines and a report from the International Association of Chiefs of Police, the German manufacturers began to make headway in reaching the nation's police market, mainly SWAT and narcotics teams. However, the real jump in interest – and sales – appears to have come with a British operation conducted in 1980.

Seven Iranian terrorists took over the Iranian Embassy in fashionable Knightsbridge on London's West End. When the terrorists started killing hostages on May 6, 1980, Scotland Yard immediately

This Chinese Communist Type 64 silenced subgun is chambered for the 7.62x25mm cartridge. The barrel is 8-inches long and features a series of 36 holes to lower muzzle velocity to subsonic levels. It is reasonably effective with lightweight bullets.

turned over operational control to Britain's Special Air Service. Hooded SAS commandos rappelled down the face of the building and swung through the windows. Firing from slings rigged at eye level, they were able to slay all but one of the terrorists with their MP-5A3 subguns. One terrorist was taken alive.

"The action, with the MP-5s in plain view, was telecast worldwide," Steele recalls. "After that, it seemed just about every counterterrorist team in the Western world wanted to be armed with the MP-5."

Less publicized was an operation conducted in Mogadishu in 1977. This effort also involved Britain's Special Air Service and their MP-5s working with Germany's GSG-9.

Two SAS men, Maj. Alastair Morrison and Sgt. Barry Davies, were second to the Western German Border Police's GSG-9 counterterrorist unit. The mission was to rescue passengers from a hijacked Lufthansa passenger jet that had been commandeered in Somalia. The terrorists were attempting to barter for members of the Baader-Meinhold gang being held in German prisons. This particular group was composed of Germany's own homegrown terrorists.

When the German government refused to enter into negotiations, the terrorists killed the pilot, then threatened to murder the rest of the crew and the 80 passengers.

The British SAS troopers had brought a supply of the then-new flash/bang concussion grenades that they thought could be used to distract the suspects prior to a team entry.

After a clandestine flight on October 17, 1977, the GSG-9/SAS hit the plane from both sides, entering through emergency exits above each wing to the accompaniment of the concussion grenades. Reports state that the GSG-9 killed three of the four terrorists, while putting nine bullets into the one female perpetrator.

"The noteworthy event in this assault concerned the effectiveness of the MP-5 for backup," says to Steele. "Hampered by military guidelines, the GSG-9 does not use hollow-point ammunition. When a terrorist appeared holding a grenade, a GSG-9 officer shot him five times with a .38-caliber Smith & Wesson Model 36 revolver. The .38 hardball ammo did not stop him and he was finished off with the 9mm MP-5".

The terrorist's grenade exploded in the aircraft without injuring anyone or doing structural damage. Since that time, pistols carried by GSG-9 agents are either the 9mm or .357 Magnum.

Since 1970, Heckler & Koch has come up with a number of options for the basic MP-5. Frankly, these are aimed at accommodating European and American police agencies as well as civilian shooters.

For SWAT and counterterrorist teams, the MP-5SD suppressed version keeps smoke, flash and noise from

The MP-5SD is part of the entire MP-5 family seen in this factory display of Heckler & Koch's entire range of 9x19mm submachine guns.

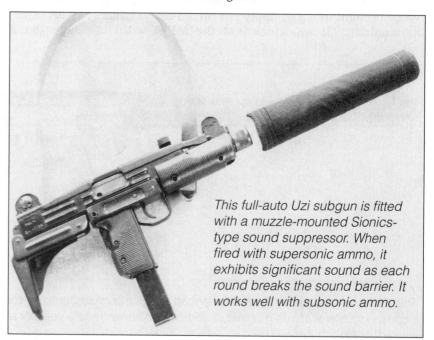

This full-auto Uzi subgun is fitted with a muzzle-mounted Sionics-type sound suppressor. When fired with supersonic ammo, it exhibits significant sound as each round breaks the sound barrier. It works well with subsonic ammo.

This Heckler & Koch MP-5SD has a receiver marking on top of its receiver that indicates its proper nomenclature.

distracting the shooter or giving away his firing position to a suspect. This model also allows teams to take out guard dogs without alerting suspects inside a house or other structure.

A short version of the weapon, the MP-5K is without a shoulder stock but has a vertical foregrip. This model was developed specifically for narcotics and counterterrorist entry teams. "At the usual 5 yards or less distance in a room, this model is considered sufficiently accurate," Steele finds.

The manufacturer also furnishes a special attaché case for concealed carry. More recently, a new MP-5K, the company's new personal defense weapon, has been introduced with a suppressor and a folding stock. This was developed because it is a more accurate model suitable for sidearm carry by NATO support troops.

According to Steele, "The MP-5K also spawned semi-auto SP-89 pistols in plain and target configurations for a civilian market. However, the future of these guns may be like that of the H&K-94 carbine with its 16-inch barrel. Importation was killed off by federal and local legislation in the United States".

The Ingram-designed MAC-11 (top) and MAC-10 (bottom) subguns were often fitted with Sionics suppressers. Note the heat-resistant coverings on both suppressors. In full-auto fire, they become extremely hot.

For a complete look at what is happening with Heckler & Koch, it should be noted that the MP-5A3 has been chambered for the 10mm cartridge now being loaded in the pistols carried by FBI agents. We believe that this may be a dead-end project because U.S. law enforcement agents seem to be leaning toward the .40 S&W cartridge. Meanwhile, the 9mm version is the company's big seller. Even the FBI is issuing a semi-auto-only version, the MP-5SF. The SO-19 firearms response unit of Britain's Scotland Yard has adopted this same gun.

It is common knowledge that the U.S. Navy favors the MP-5 for its SEAL teams, but most people are not aware that this group of violence specialists work with three different models: the MSP-5A3, the MP-5SD and the MP-5K. Special units of the Army, Air Force and Marine Corps have access to MP-5s as needed.

"The number of law enforcement SWAT units using the MP-5 seems to grow daily," says Steele, who believes this choice is "partly due to the trigger groups that are available. The MP-5 always has a safe position on the selector switch. Everything else is optional."

The gun can be ordered semi-auto only, semi-auto plus a two-round burst, semi-auto with a three-round burst, semi-auto plus full-auto, semi-auto plus two- or three-round bursts and full-auto, semi-auto plus full auto with an ambidextrous selector switch. Newer innovations probably are under way as this is written.

"For American law enforcement, the MP-5A2 – especially in its semi-auto configuration – would seem the best bet for special agents, anti-gang units and narcotics teams," Steele contends. "Special weapons units tend more toward the folding-stock MP-5A3, with a muzzle brake, burst capability and mini-flashlights."

There are those who recommend the two round-burst option as ideal, inasmuch as it allows one to provide an automatic double tap on his target.

"For inexperienced shooters, the third shot of a three-round burst tends to pass over the suspects left shoulder," Steele finds. "With a low, groin-level first round, missing is less likely than with the lighter, discontinued VP-70, but two rounds still are more consistent."

The old, heavy, low cyclic-rate guns such as the Thompson could keep a long burst on a man-size target with little problem. However, it has become doctrine that the MP-5, firing 700 rounds per minute, is better used with quick bursts, repeated if necessary.

Military units, of course, retain a full-auto capability for suppressive fire at multiple or area targets. "For police departments, the MP-5 with semi-auto and two-round burst capabilities should be more than adequate, as well as easier to sell to the administration and the public," Steele believes.

U.S. entities such as the Los Angeles County Sheriff's special teams consider precise 9mm fire at close quarters the optimum for indoor combat. They tend to leave the shotguns and long rifles on the action's perimeter, while the entry team carries Beretta M-92F pistols and their MP-5A3s wearing muzzle-brakes and attached mini-lights.

They have taken a lesson from the successes of Britain's Special Air Service and Germany's border guards.

This Sound-Suppressed MP-5 Adds a New Dimension to Subguns

It is not difficult to silence or suppress the muzzle report from any assault rifle, but the supersonic ammunition fired by a modern high-velocity assault rifle cartridge creates some real difficulties when stealth and quiet are the order of the day for a police SWAT team or a military Special Operations tactical team.

Today true select-fire assault rifles are normally found in two flavors when it comes to calibers: 5.56x45mm or 7.62x39mm. Both routinely demonstrate muzzle velocities that are far greater than twice the speed of sound. The really bad news comes, though, when the 5.56x45mm guns are loaded with special subsonic ammo because that same rifle RHWB develops little more muzzle energy than is experienced with a young squirrel hunter's 22 rimfire rifle. Assault rifles are great for the battlefield, but for suppressed Special Operations and SWAT applications, the tactical operator must use ammunition offering greater lethality than that provided with subsonic 5.56x45mm ammo.

So what is a SWAT team going to use? The best answer is probably a suppressed, pistol-caliber submachine gun. Generally acknowledged as probably the most successful today is the Heckler & Koch MP-5SD. This particular version of what is recognized as an extremely popular law enforcement and military tool is the integrally suppressed model chambered for the 9x19mm pistol cartridge. "SD" in this instance stands for the German words, *Schall Daempfer*, which roughly translate to "sound dampened".

"The mass sales of the German-designed and produced Heckler & Koch MP-5 subgun to American law enforcement agencies have forced other designs into the status of second- or third-string players, but that doesn't mean the MP-5SD is the only player on the field. It is simply the biggest player on the field in terms of acceptance by the number of different military and police organizations worldwide. There are certainly other designs, but none offer the success enjoyed by the MP-5SD," says Frank W. James, author of a respected book on the subject, *Heckler & Koch's MP5 Submachine Gun.*

The MP-5SD is able to lower the cartridge's muzzle velocity by some 200 fps. This is accomplished by a series of ports located just forward of the chamber of the barrel as seen in this cutaway sample.

Factory listed as Project 64, development of the Heckler & Koch MP-5 started in the summer of 1964 as engineers at headquarters of the company wanted to utilize the design principles of the German service rifle, the G-3, in a pistol-caliber submachine gun. The first production MP-5 was completed in December 1966 and the German Border Police was the first law enforcement organization to adopt it.

Although the German military forces tested the MP-5 and found it an excellent submachine gun, they were committed to the Uzi at that time.

"The Uzi is a good submachine gun, but many arms-knowledgeable individuals tend to argue it is not as good as the MP-5," James says. "However, due

The MP-5SD has become the tool of the Silent Lions of U.S. law enforcement. No other suppressed submachine gun can challenge its success in popularity and reliability.

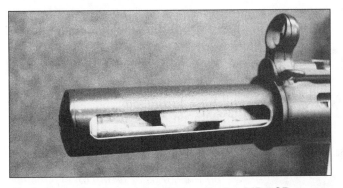

Early German-made suppressors on the MP-5SD employed a series of four V-shaped baffles set at 90 degrees to help reduce the gun's muzzle signature. This cutaway MP-5SD is in the German factory.

to events that took place during World War II, it was perhaps fitting that during the 1950s, when the German Army was being recreated in the form of the *Bundeswehr*, it was the Israeli-origin Uzi that was selected to be the force's issue submachine gun." Interestingly, the Uzi employed by the Bundeswehr was not made in Israel. FN manufactured the Uzi under license in Liege, Belgium, from 1958 to 1971, with proper licensing fees paid to Israel Military Industries, which had developed the gun.

In terms of reduced noise applications, it has been found that the Uzi is not the easiest submachine gun to suppress. The U.S. government expended much effort, energy and money, in attempting to silence the Uzi back in the days before subsonic ammunition was widely available. When the effort ended, the final report came to the conclusion that it was a difficult and certainly not a cost-effective task to silence the Uzi submachine gun.

There was no dedicated suppressed MP-5 in .40 S&W caliber. To suppress this weapon, the maker offered a muzzle-mounted suppressor made by Knight Armament in Florida.

The first successful integrally suppressed pistol-caliber submachine gun was the Great Britain's Sten Mark IIS that was introduced during World War II. There had been earlier attempts to suppress or silence submachine guns, but none of them proved as effective or as successful as the Mark IIS. This gun set the standard for suppressed submachine guns for years if not decades to come, and like the H&K MP-5SD that would be developed three decades later, the Sten Mark IIS employed a ported barrel to lower the muzzle velocity of supersonic ammunition to a subsonic level.

In 1974 when the MP-5SD was being developed, the vast majority of the available 9mm ammunition used projectiles weighing 124 grains, 115 grains or less. Additionally, the suppressor technology at that time often involved heavy, bulky screw-on tube-like devices such as those used with the Ingram-designed MAC-10 and MAC-11 submachine guns.

"While these suppressors work well enough, they were designed for relatively small-bodied subguns like the MAC-10. When mounted to the front of an MP-5, the combination proved unwieldy and hard to balance or even point properly," according to James' findings.

Additionally, there had been almost no work done at the time with heavier bullets in 9x19mm caliber, so Heckler & Koch engineers had to design a quiet submachine gun to fire ammunition that would undoubtedly be supersonic in flight.

"That presented a dilemma, but the eventual solution was to port the barrel and lower the projectile muzzle velocity by 200 fps," James says. He adds, "This would ensure that any supersonic 9x19mm ammunition would fire at subsonic velocities and travel at well below the speed of sound. This design attribute eliminated the ballistic crack, but to maintain balance and ease of handling within the sphere of reason, a lightweight and handy design was essential.

"As an aside, some years ago, I was in northern Spain visiting a manufacturer of both sporting arms and military small arms, when I was offered the opportunity to test their latest submachine gun design. The firm is no longer in business, so it isn't important to identify the manufacturer, but the gun in question was fitted with a muzzle-mounted suppressor of the company's own design.

"Unfortunately, they had only a limited amount of subsonic ammunition on hand, so everyone in the tour group fired a few rounds of subsonic ammo through the piece, which was followed by a magazine or two of supersonic ammo," James recalls.

The firing range was nothing more than a small plastered tunnel that was quite narrow and relatively long. When firing the subsonic ammo in this cramped space, the design worked well. The gun and ammunition proved both accurate and extremely quiet while James and several other arms writers were firing without benefit of hearing protection.

For law enforcement use, these MP-5s have been outfitted with optical sights and quick-release mounts.

"On the other hand, in that tiny space the supersonic ammunition turned out to be so loud it was painful and sounded for all the world like a normal non-suppressed 9mm pistol. My ears rang for hours afterward," James says. There is little value in suppressing any firearm, if the ammunition used is allowed to go supersonic. The ballistic noise can be almost as loud in report as the muzzle blast itself.

The first attempt by Heckler & Koch engineers to port the barrel of the MP-5SD utilized four ports just forward of the chamber. These ports were each 6mm in diameter; testing soon demonstrated something better had to be found.

These large ports shaved bullet jacket material as the jackets passed by and the resulting accuracy was dismal.

The final design that proved most effective in terms of lowering the muzzle velocity of the supersonic ammo—while maintaining the best possible accuracy—was an arrangement of 30 ports surrounding the circumference of the barrel. Each of these ports was 2.5mm in size and was located just forward of the cartridge chamber. When James visited the Heckler & Koch factory in Oberndorf, Germany, several years ago,

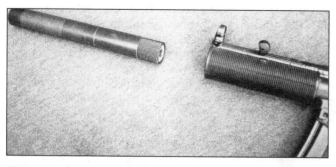

The MP-5SD barrel-cleaning tool resembles an auto-battery terminal circular brush, but is used to clean the exterior of the SD barrel. Here it is installed on the end of the suppresser.

he was given a printed description of the internal suppressor design they were using at that time. Recent information indicates the internal design of the MP-5SD has been changed, but HK engineers are reluctant to release any design data on these new improvements. The original explanation read:

As the MP-5SD fires, the ports forward of the chamber bleed gas off the barrel and into an expansion chamber as the projectile passes by. The bullet travels through a series of inclined baffles. The baffles are straight, but inclined at a 45-degree angle and if it were possible to view them from the side they would represent the letter "V" lying sideways with the projectile entering at the sharp point of the "V". In terms of consecutive arrangement the baffles are turned 90 degrees to each other with a series of four such baffles comprising the entire unit.

This segment of baffles and expansion chamber is a one-piece cast aluminum unit that is sealed inside the outer tube at the factory. The SD suppressor is designed so it can be removed from the gun for routine maintenance by simply turning it off the receiver threads that secure it to the gun. However, the gun will not function properly with the suppressor removed. The suppressor must always be mounted on this model for the gun to work properly.

An O-ring seal surrounds the threads and prevents gas leakage when the suppressor is attached to the receiver. It is important that care be taken to make sure this O-ring is kept in good condition. If this seal isn't routinely inspected or properly maintained, it becomes damaged and the joint between the suppressor and the receiver leaks gas.

Heckler & Koch apparently don't want their end users to take the SD suppressor apart like those offered by so many American suppressor manufacturers. Thus, the end caps of the suppressor are glued on at the factory.

There is a cleaning tool for scrubbing the outside of the SD barrel. This circular brush appears to the uninitiated to be little more than a brush like those used to clean your car's battery terminals and is available at any automotive parts supplier. This tool is screwed onto the receiver end of the suppressor and is used to clean the outside surface of the ported SD barrel. In this application, the suppressor itself becomes a tool handle.

Carbon builds up as a natural consequence of firing the MP-5SD and any significant accumulation around the outside of the barrel makes the report louder due to increased inefficiencies. The circular barrel brush is also important for cleaning individual barrel ports, which will often fill with lead deposits.

As for the carbon deposits inside the MP-5SD suppressor, Heckler & Koch factory personnel advise the operator to repeatedly rap the receiver end of the

These MP-5SD models feature the S-E-F trigger groups and the A2 fixed stock. The S-E-F stands for Safe, Semi-Auto and Full-Auto settings.

For a time, Class II manufacturers in the United States converted Heckler & Koch Model 94 semi-automatic carbines into registered select-fire MP-5 replicas. This is an American-produced replica of the integrally suppressed MP-5SD.

suppressor against a clean wood surface such as a white pine board or plank.

The operator should hit the wood vigorously enough to loosen the carbon deposits, James advises, but not so hard as to cause damage to the suppressor. That's the reason for suggesting a soft wood such as white pine. The manufacturer claims this is all the maintenance the suppressor unit of the MP-5SD requires. Otherwise, the maintenance remains the same for the MP-5SD as it does for the non-suppressed MP-5.

James cautions that "care must be taken in choosing the proper ammunition for the MP-5SD because it does have a ported barrel that will lower the muzzle velocity of any ammunition fired in the gun. Heavy subsonic 9x19mm ammunition is both popular and common in law enforcement circles, but these same loads represent a problem if used in the MP-5SD in a tactical situation."

The MP-5SD was designed for ammunition with bullets weighing 124 grains or less. It reportedly will fire heavier bullets reliably, but it is the terminal ballistics that cause great concern. Heckler & Koch representatives have received reports of substandard terminal performance when MP-5SD gunners in the midst of tactical situations used subsonic ammunition with bullet weights of under 130 grains. The substandard performance cited was not related to malfunctions with the gun, but rather to the failure of multiple hits to stop the bad guy.

The 30 ports in the barrel of the MP-5SD lower the projectile velocity approximately 200 fps for all ammunition fired in the gun – and that includes subsonic ammunition. "The effectiveness of subsonic ammo, in reference to its terminal ballistics, is lowered even further when the projectiles are the lighter bullets," the manufacturer explains.

Since the introduction of the MP-5SD, there have been a number of projects instituted by Heckler & Koch with the aim of building even better suppressed submachine guns. In the mid-1980s, the United States military and the German military cooperated on one such project. Heckler & Koch was the prime contractor; three different prototype submachine guns resulted from the research.

"By this time, however, the heavy bullet 9x19mm ammo was coming on line and was being used more frequently in law enforcement circles," James reports. "In recognition of this trend, H&K designed a valve that was activated by a lever at the bottom front of the receiver on these prototype submachine guns. This device allowed each of these guns to use either supersonic or subsonic ammunition to its own best advantage. The three submachine guns were the SMG I, the SMG II and the SMG 2000."

There is little hard information available on the last of this series, the SMG 2000, but plenty is known on the first two. The key point here is the abandonment of the integral suppressor. Each of these prototypes employed muzzle-mounted "cans", but the overall length of the gun and suppressor when combined was little greater than that seen with the previous MP-5SD.

The big difference was in the provisions made for the ammunition. If supersonic ammunition was in the magazine, the valve at the bottom front of the receiver was turned to open the barrel ports and bleed off sufficient gas to propel the bullets at velocities below the speed of sound. This made the screw-on suppressor extremely effective.

If subsonic ammunition was loaded in the magazine, then the valve was turned to close the barrel ports and no gas would be bled from the barrel at firing. It was also important to note this valve had to be in the closed position before firing when the suppressor was removed from the gun.

Two larger caliber MP-5s were developed for American law enforcement during the 1990s. They were the MP-5/40 and the MP-5/10. The 40 S&W MP-5 was developed to offer greater terminal energy to the tactical officer and to match the surging interest in this caliber by law enforcement agencies all across the United States.

The 10mm version was developed for the FBI, but neither model was offered in an integrally suppressed version. If the police agency wanted either of these two guns suppressed, the manufacturer offered a muzzle-mounted suppressor that mated to the threaded portion forward of the H&K three-lug barrel. A screw-on, knurled thread protector protected these muzzle threads when the suppressor was not mounted. Obviously, only subsonic ammunition could be used with this arrangement. Surprisingly, Reed Knight of Knight Manufacturing in Vero Beach, Fla., manufactured these suppressors because German laws made it extremely difficult to export muzzle-mounted suppressors.

"Currently, interest in the MP-5SD remains strong, if not exactly high," according to James' findings. One of the more practical ways the MP-5SD is used today is in training police officers equipped with the standard MP-5. The MP-5 instructor equipped with an MP-5SD can explain a technique or firing position, then fire a few rounds into the backstop or appropriate target to illustrate his point. The MP-5SD eliminates the need for the line of students having to take the time to don their hearing protection, then take it off again to hear the instructor's follow-up comments.

"Assault rifles are becoming ever more popular in law enforcement Special Operations teams, but the suppressed pistol-caliber submachine gun still offers advantages not found with high velocity and therefore high sound level carbines," James believes. "The

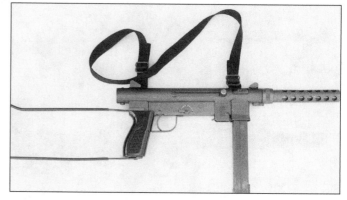

The Smith & Wesson Model 76 9mm subgun was introduced during the Vietnam War. It also served for a time as a tactical weapon for some police departments. It is simple to mount a dedicated suppressed barrel on this model.

Heckler & Koch MP-5SD will most likely remain in military and police inventories for many decades to come for exactly these reasons. It is the proven tool of the silent law enforcement lions."

CHAPTER 2

ISRAEL'S GUNS AGAINST COUNTER-TERRORISM

A Broad Variety of Available Weaponry Is Used to Meet the Continuing Threat to This Nation

"We trained hard ... but it seemed that every time we were beginning to form up into teams we were reorganized. I was to learn later in life that we tend to meet any new situation by reorganizing, and a wonderful method it can be for creating the illusion of progress, while producing confusion, inefficiency and demoralization."

DOES THAT SOUND like some of the grumblings about what is happening within this nation's military forces today? Probably. But this statement was made in 210 BC by one Petronius Arbiter. One's first impression might well be that nothing every really changes when it comes to organizational thinking along military lines.

If there is a modern army, however, that has successfully organized into teams it is the Israeli Defense Force (IDF). They have been at war with their Arab neighbors since 1948, with major campaigns that year and repeats in 1956, 1967, 1973, 1982 and numerous border operations in between. Within this Israeli force, tactics are consistently tested in the crucible of combat. When asked if they planned to eventually incorporate some of the modern American military staffing changes, an IDF colonel said, "No, we have to take war seriously."

Since the 1930s – roughly three-quarters of a century – when Jewish immigrants formed night squads to protect settlements from Muslim raids, there have been special units. Orde Wingate, an eccentric British officer and a distant cousin of D.H. Lawrence – perhaps better knows as Lawrence of Arabia – developed tactics for the night squads. Two of Wingate's proteges in this type of defensive fighting were Yigal Allon and Moshe Dayan. Wingate later went on to fight campaigns in Ethiopia and Burma before dying in a 1944 plane crash.

For obvious reasons, Israel could not use strategies employed by massed armies that were able to absorb huge casualties, like the Red Army fighting the Germans in the 1941-45 period or the Chinese in Korea in 1950. Israel depends instead on comprehensive regional intelligence, material and propaganda support from the United States, a universal draft that includes women to fill support positions, a deep pool of reserves to fight major conflicts and an air force with the world's most proven pilots. There also are specialized infantry units trained specifically to fight the latest Arab terror tactics.

"The Israelis do not believe in what they tend to call 'eye wash,' the expense and time consumed by parade ground smartness," according to Steele, who has worked with these elements firsthand. "A tourist should not waste film on Israeli close-order drill or square bashing, as the British military calls it. On the other hand, if you watch Tsahal (Israeli Defense Force) soldiers double-timing everywhere or running endless stretcher drills, you will know what they are

The most basic weapon of the individual Palestinian terrorist is the knife, usually called a shabriya. As the terrorist attacks, he often shouts "Allahu Akbar!" which means "God is great!"

The Mini-Uzi is the first step up in firepower from the 9mm pistol for Israeli Special Forces.

Recently released from the U.S. Army, David E. Steele lived for a time on an Israeli kibbutz. It was there, in 1969, that he had his first exposure to the standard Uzi submachine gun.

being trained for, which is not close-order drill of the 18th century approach to warfare. Most enlisted soldiers do not even own a dress uniform, unless they are assigned to guard the Knesset (Parliament) building. At the opposite extreme, field gear, particularly for elite units, is modern and efficient."

Steele has high praise for the Israeli fighters, saying, "The Israeli Defense Force is the first army I ever saw that actually lived by the motto, 'Train as you fight.' In contrast, when I was serving in the U.S. Army during the late 1960s, every infantryman spent the first four months in basic training, then advanced infantry training in the European-style tactics that had nothing to do with what was happening in Vietnam, the one hot war at the time. Pentagon planners were still looking toward a conflict with the Soviet Union in Germany, at a time when thousands of Americans and their allies were being killed by Indochinese acting as proxies for Russia and China, the communist countries supplying their weapons."

Shaldag

Sayeret Shaldag (Unit 501) is one of several Israeli Special Forces units that has been created and trained in recent years. This particular unit was formed in 1974 as a result of lessons learned in the so-called Yom Kippur War of 1973. In the 1967 Six-Day War, Arab aircraft were destroyed while sitting on their runways by pilots of the Israeli Air Force, aka Keil Avir, translating as Army of the Air.

By 1973, of course, the military forces of most countries had learned to keep their planes and missiles in hardened sites. Shaldag's primary mission

these days is to "laser paint" enemy installations for air-to-ground smart bombs and missiles. This is essentially the same mission performed by U.S. Special Forces in Iraq in 1991's desert war. The American public as a whole was not aware that so-called smart bombs, though laser guided, required a man on the ground to make them work.

Shaldag's secondary mission concerns counterterrorism and hostage rescue. The standard personal weapon for this organization is the shortened M-4 Carbine version of the U.S. M-l6: the M-4 is currently standard for Israeli Special Forces teams. Israeli personnel often are equipped with this particular carbine with the M-203 40mm grenade launcher. The M-4 fires the SS 109/M-852 NATO 5.56mm cartridge, which has longer range and better penetration characteristics than the Vietnam Era M-l 9 ball cartridge.

The M-4 is backed by the Israeli Military Industries' (IMI) Negev 5.56mm light machinegun, which has replaced the FN MAG 7.62mm and FN M-249 SAW 5.56mm in Special Forces service. The Negev can also be used as a sniper rifle or rigged to launch anti-personnel grenades. For more specialized counterterrorist or hostage rescue missions, Shaldag personnel use the Mauser SR-86 Sniper Weapons System. It replaced the Mauser SP-66 SWS, being phased in between 1996 and 1998. This particular system is designed for short- to medium-range scenarios. Units needing long-range sniping capability have available the Remington-built U.S. M-24 chambered in 7.62mm, the Heckler & Koch PSGI 7.62mm, the American-made 300 Win.Mag., and even the Barrett M-82A1 rifle chambered for the 50 Browning Machine Gun cartridge. Sniper team spotters carry an M-4 Carbine equipped with a laser range-finding device.

Only units who attend the IDF Counter-Terrorists/Hostage Rescue School (Unit 707) are issued handguns.

Steele says, it should be noted that these handguns are carried only on missions, not as an everyday routine. They are generally carried in the tactical vest, not strapped to the leg. Pistols most commonly issued to counterterrorist personnel are the SIG-Sauer P-226 and the FN High Power Mark 3. Israel produces a variety of pistols of exotic calibers for overseas sale, such as the .50-caliber Desert Eagle.

Israeli Defense Force counter-terrorist units use the recently introduced U.S. M-4 Carbine along with this short version of the IMI Galil 5.56mm.

Israeli Duvdevan units prefer the SIG P-226 9mm above all other handguns, but they are scarce when compared with the Jericho model produced by Israeli Military Industries.

However, for domestic use, the 9mm Parabellum – compatible with the ubiquitous Uzi submachine gun – is the universal military and police pistol caliber.

Shaldag operators study closely David Stirling's book on the British Special Air Service's Middle East campaign against the Germans in World War II. Stirling was the founder of the SAS, which has become the original model for this sort of warfare.

Shaldag training, like that of most other IDF Special Forces units, is 20 months long. Training begins with four months of basic infantry, followed by 10 weeks of advanced infantry tactics. Following this is more than a year of specialized training, including a parachute course covering two types of chutes, all-weather terrain navigation, combined service operations, laser designation, counterterrorist/hostage rescue techniques and sniping.

Mistaravim

Mistaravim means "becoming an Arab." Two units were formed around 1987 in response to the Intifada, named for the Arab uprising in Israeli-occupied areas. These were pure counterterrorist units assigned to capture or kill wanted Palestinian terrorists. One of the teams, Shimson – Samson, in translation – was assigned to the Gaza Strip, but was disbanded in 1994 when this territory became Palestinian under the Oslo Accords.

Assigned to the West Bank is the Duvdevan or Cherry Unit 217. As with Shimson, the primary weapons are camouflage, disguise and the ability to speak and understand colloquial Arabic. Training for this unit is 15 months, with four months of basic training, 10 weeks of advanced infantry work, two months of land navigation learning, the three-week counterterrorist/hostage rescue (CT/HRT) course at Unit 707, plus one month CT/HRT unit training. Also required are four months of the Mistaravim course and a final month of specialty training such as sniper or fast driver. In most other Israeli SF teams, the operators stay together until retirement, but Duvdevan specialists form up and train for unique missions. Rappelling

and fast-roping are part of the Duvdevan tactics in this hilly and mountainous region.

Mistaravim units operate like something out of the old *Mission Impossible* television series, with specialists chosen and training conducted for snatching a particular "wanted" person out from the midst of bodyguards and Arab crowds. Sniper teams cover the action while snatch teams get close to the subject wearing Arab disguise; sometimes agents are even dressed as veiled women. Beneath their loose fitting clothes they carry concealed firepower appropriate to the mission.

The standard rifle for Duvdevan is the 10-inch barreled version of the M-16A2. However, missions may require even more compact weapons such as the IMI Micro-Uzi subgun or various 9mm pistols. These handguns include the FN High Power, the SIG-Sauer and the Glock. On occasion, the IMI-made Jericho will be used. This one is known as the Baby Eagle model when marketed in the United States.

"You might question how and why Israelis can use such a variety of pistols. Actually, it doesn't matter which pistol is used, since they are all used in the same way," says Steele. "The Israelis use a variation of the Fairbairn method developed by a British Shanghai policeman of that name in the 1930s. During World War II, Fairbairn was transferred from the police department to the British Special Operations Executive (SOE) and eventually to its American equivalent, the Office of Strategic Services or OSS.

"It was British officers who ran the mandate in pre-war Palestine and Jewish soldiers served in British units during the war, so the training interchange was somewhat natural. The Fairbairn style of point shooting has become popular lately in U.S. police training," Steele notes. "The Israelis have adopted other elements of the method, such as bent knees and empty chamber carry. Israeli doctrine for military, police, and civilians is to not depend on mechanical safeties, to carry the chamber empty, then rack the slide during the draw. This allows all types of autos, and all shooting is done single-action, one or two-handed," he adds.

Israelis carry their personal weapons including pistols chamber-empty. This Browning Hi-Power, once standard for Israeli Defense Forces is brought to eye level where the left hand can retract the slide.

When using the foregrip, David Steele found that the 9mm Micro-Uzi works best when fired full-auto.

Since they have to deal with "wanted" Palestinians at contact distance, Duvdevan commandos train intensively in Krav Maga, a type of empty-hand combat. At close range, a hand strike can be more effective and a lot quieter than a pistol bullet. The idea is to instantly overcome resistance, then get the terrorist into a snatch vehicle and out of the area. The Israelis have been quite successful.

"However, Palestinians do not represent the upper level in either size or strength. To manage powerful individuals, the best tool I have seen is the Kubotai, a modified nunchaku that allows one-hand control of 300-pound miscreants. Also, it must be remembered that Duvdevan are not police, and, if empty hand does not work, they will not be second-guessed if they resort to pistol fire," Steele explains.

As might be expected, approaching Arab villages at night can be tricky, mainly because of the presence of barking dogs. Mistaravim units carry at least one pistol outfitted with a suppressor and laser sight for this purpose. Dead dogs with one or two bullets in the head have become Duvdevan trademarks.

For sniping, Mistavarim use Mauser rifles, the Sirkis Israeli bullpup version of the M-14 and the Galil sniper rifle. Snatch vehicles are civilian models with fake plates. The glass is bulletproof, the engine is turbo-charged, front and rear ends are reinforced. There are hiding places within the vehicle to contain warriors and weapons, particularly sniper rifles.

Weapons Evaluations

You may be asking yourself why Israeli counterterrorist units have chosen American and European small arms, when Israel Military Industries make some of the best weapons in the world. First, the FN High-Power gained a reputation with British forces and particularly with the Special Air Service, which Israeli CT forces respect more than any other foreign unit. The United States has provided M-16A1 and M-16A2 rifles to Israel for a couple decades. The M-16 is reliable and lighter than the standard Israeli Galil used by line units. Counterterrorist units use the Micro-Galil (MAR), which is about 10 inches shorter and half the weight of the original Galilis.

The Tabor AR-21 is a new Israeli bullpup 5.56mm with an 18-inch barrel and a thermoset stock. It has an optical sight attached to the barrel, plus an optional laser sight. An even more compact version is available and will probably see CT use.

"Keep in mind that half of IMI small arms production is slated for foreign markets to obtain hard currency," Steele notes. "Also, keep in mind that import duty is extremely high, so few Israelis can afford a personal SIG, Glock or FN P-35, but as issue weapons, they carry the cachet of the elite. In addition, foreign-made weapons carry a certain machismo for Israeli soldiers even when they are less efficient than those IMI could produce.

"For instance, sometime after the 1967 war, I saw Israeli soldiers carrying captured Egyptian Port Said subguns that were simply the Swedish "K" under license. Others equipped themselves with Kalashnikov assault rifles in preference to Uzis and FN FALS. They also liked foreign headgear. One wore the cap of a Syrian who had expired suddenly. Another traded me out of my GI ball cap."

Still, the Uzi is the combat subgun by which all others are measured. Israeli counterterrorist teams have not gone to the Heckler & Koch MP-5, and there is no reason for them to do so. The Uzi has specialized closed-bolt and suppressed variations.

From 1951 until about 1980, the original Uzi, with its 10-inch barrel and removable wood or collapsible metal stock, was the original Israeli sidearm and personal defense weapon. In major conflicts of the era, paratroops, officers and non-commissioned officers carried the Uzi, while riflemen carried the FN FAL. However, when the IDF went to an assault rifle M-16 or Galil to match the Arab AKM, the submachine gun had to get smaller to fill a niche role for counter-terrorist and executive protection teams.

Around 1980, IMI produced the Mini-Uzi with 7.7-inch barrel and folding wire stock. Then came the Micro-Uzi with an even shorter barrel, wire stock and vertical foregrip option. Usually manufactured with closed-bolt operation, the Micro-Mini Uzi was originally conceived with the pistol role in mind, but it proved to be too bulky.

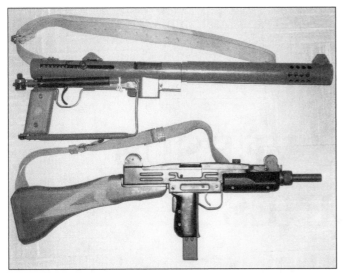

The 1951 Uzi made by Israeli Military Industries is contrasted with the suppressed Swedish K Model used by U.S. Special Forces in Vietnam. During the 1967 Six-Day War, Israel captured numerous Port Said submachine guns. These were an Egyptian copy of the Swedish gun and often were carried thereafter by Israeli combat veterans.

The 9mm Glock 17 is one of the three top pistols for Israeli Duvdevan units, along with the SIG P-226 and the IMI 941. Israeli police and the military do not issue pistols in any caliber larger than 9mm.

In my view, it can't compare to an open-bolt Mini-Uzi for reliability and accuracy, but counterterrorist teams like Duvdevan sometimes need serious firepower that can be easily concealed under Arab robes.

A complete standardization of weapons and equipment is probably not possible in a truly national army, which needs to issue personal firearms to virtually every able-bodied man. Even the Israeli service women train with both the Uzi and the M-16.

Elite units get first pick of the latest weapons, followed by active duty line units, support units, reservists, settlers and government workers in disputed areas in that order. One is likely to find any type of small arm introduced during the last 30 years. They don't have the luxury of storing or destroying obsolescent issue firearms. They have standardized cartridges with the United States and NATO: 9mm, 5.56mm, and 7.62mm, and they have standardized training doctrine for various small arms throughout military and police units.

When American units operate in the Middle East they usually are supported by UH-60 Blackhawk and AH-1 Cobra helicopters. The standard weapon for crewmen is the M-4 Carbine, the same weapon provided to Israel.

CHAPTER 3

SHOTGUNS VERSUS CARBINES

There Are Some Interesting Preferences When it Comes to Patrolling

THE FEDERAL LAW Enforcement Training Center (FLETC) in Glynco, Ga., trains personnel from 63 federal agencies, as well as some local agencies that contract for its services. The U.S. Treasury Department runs the school and treasury instructors teach most of the general courses such as firearms specialties.

Most local departments and many federal agencies issue the 12-gauge pump-action shotgun to their personnel. Instructors teach basic and advanced shotgun uses and techniques, as well as a shotgun assault course. Over the years, two different federal agencies have sent David Steele to the Glynco center, where he went through all training phases of the shotgun course.

"Of course, this was hardly my first experience with police shotguns," Steele quickly points out. "In fact, I had already written several articles on them,

and had tested several shotguns as part of a research project for the International Association of Chiefs of Police. While FLETC training is excellent, I did come to some conclusions as to shotgun practicality. Those beliefs regarding the scattergun and its application in law enforcement were based upon the reactions of the students I was able to observe."

We won't mention the agency to which they were assigned, since it seems the problem is common to most, but in one of Steele's classes, he could see that the females were highly concerned before shotgun training even started. While not talked about publicly, apparently the instructor had also heard this fear from previous classes.

The instructor attempted to reassure everyone that the shotgun's recoil was controllable and certainly would not do the terrible things they had

David Steele uses his custom-rebuilt Remington Model 870 with confidence. It is called the Border Patrol Model and was reworked by Scattergun Technologies for police work.

The Ithaca-made Auto Burglar, a 20-gauge double-barrel was made and sold in the 1920s. It was an attempt to get greater stopping power out of a pistol-size weapon.

heard. The instructor went through the usual lecture followed by weapon familiarization and dummy-round drills. He deftly demonstrated how one could – and should – keep the gunstock seated in the pocket of the shoulder and how to lean into the gun.

In spite of all the lectures and drills, on the first day of shooting, two young women reportedly were bruised and battered by the 12-gauge Remington 870, even with its shortened stock and a thick butt-pad. One of them refused to continue, saying she had been injured.

"The next day, she showed up in class wearing a tube top to show off her bruises, along with a sling, Steele recalls. "Most of us were amused by this elaborate production, which obviously was geared toward avoiding further shotgun shooting. Ultimately, she had to shoot a little more in order to complete the course, but not as much as the rest of us."

Let it be understood that the point here is not to suggest the exclusion of females from law enforcement. The courts have already settled that issue. The question is whether there might be a better backup weapon for modern law enforcement than the shotgun, which was handed down to us from the 19th century lawmen on horseback.

The traditional 12-gauge pump has a number of drawbacks for either male or female officers. Its

recoil has been measured scientifically and matches that of the 375 Holland & Holland African rifle, but without the accuracy, range or power of the dangerous game tool.

The shotgun has a simple bead front sight or a set of rifle-type sights, which may not necessarily be adjusted to the load being used. The patrol shotgun such as the Remington 870 pump-action usually carries only four rounds. Its tubular magazine is slow to load and unload. At less than 20 feet, there is so little spread of shot that the shotgun must be aimed as carefully as a rifle.

"Further," Steele insists, "buckshot – the common patrol round – is a poor choice for crowded areas or a hostage situation, where head shots may be required. Also, buckshot does not penetrate car bodies or for that matter, human bodies with any efficiency."

The riot gun, with its typical 18- to 20-inch barrel, requires two hands to maneuver, and with the pump action, it must be cycled by hand for each round. Additionally, patrol guns are often poorly maintained. In some departments, the guns stay in the cars from shift to shift; they are not assigned to specific individuals who are made responsible for them.

"I've even seen the barrels in patrol guns used as mini-storage receptacles for gum wrappers or extra cigars. The shells loaded in the tube magazine may be deformed from abuse, such as ejecting live rounds onto the pavement, then reloading them. This habit is only setting up the possibility of a jam," Steele says.

In terms of stopping power, it is generally accepted that the best shotgun round is the slug, but in reality, this load is no different than a rifle bullet, except for its shorter range and lack of accuracy. Therefore, the obvious question becomes: Why not simply use the rifle, which has greater accuracy, range and power combined with lower recoil and greater ammunition capacity?

"I cannot claim to be a fan of the 12-gauge scattergun," Steele admits. "Patrol pump guns do not have slings usually for fear that officers will abscond with them, so carrying it ties up both hands. A round cannot be chambered until action is imminent, because accidental discharges are common, even when the trigger is not touched. Studies conducted by the Los Angeles Police Department show about a 50 percent discharge rate, when the stock is struck against a hard object such as a dashboard. Modern semi-automatic rifles do not have this problem.

"The pump gun is thought to be simple to operate and care for properly," Steele states. "However, there are many small parts to break, and pump guns can be jammed in several common ways such as "short-strok-

Entry training for police officers can involve goggles, kneepads and other gear.

David Steele tends to favor his pistol grip Mossberg 500 carried in the over-the-shoulder position by means of a tactical sling.

ing" – moving the pump handle only halfway to the rear. Army recruits rarely have the educational qualifications of modern police recruits, yet they somehow learn to fire and clean modern assault rifles, even with a drill instructor shouting obscenities into one ear."

Also, some officers think that the riot gun tends to become a crutch since it is the one backup weapon available to the patrol officer. He is told war stories of its awesome power to stop or intimidate suspects. Meanwhile, the officer is only given occasional familiarization training with the shotgun – and not with the gun he actually carries in the car.

This lack of familiarization is a recipe for disaster as was shown in an episode of television's *"Top Cops"*, best described as a reality-based show. In this re-creation, a patrol officer caught a robber/hostage-taker by finally locking bumpers with the Corvette the felon was driving.

At this point, the suspect hopped up onto the back of the Corvette and started pumping pistol rounds down through the patrol car windshield. Instead of replying immediately with his service pistol, the officer tried to get the magic shotgun out of the rack and was hit in both the arm and the leg before he could do so. The suspect ran off, but later was cornered by backup officers.

The point is that the handgun is the most maneuverable weapon from inside a car, and the one with which the officer trains the most.

"The shotgun's recoil is felt mostly in the shoulder. Some makers have created or modified shotguns to a pistol grip configuration, removing the shoulder stock altogether," Steele points out. "These can be useful as stakeout guns, but are limited to extremely short range where accuracy is concerned. The recoil is absorbed in the web of the hand, a more flexible body part than the shoulder. The muzzle will rise more, however, so quick repeat shots may be a problem."

The stockless or so-called whipit gun is a descendant of the Ithaca Auto-Burglar 20-gauge double, as well as cut-down pump guns from the 1920s. They are just as impractical now as they were then.

The late P.M. "Mac" Tabor made an excellent kit, including a pistol grip and wrap-around slide to modify police pump guns. Garth Choate has also made a line of conversion grips and accessories.

Remington made a pistol grip and folding stock version of the 870, but the metal stock did not have a good reputation for locking firmly in the folded position. Generally, such guns are better off with no stock at all. From a point of view regarding distribution of recoil, the sloping pistol grip taken from an original stock is easier to hold than the more vertical-styled replacement grip. The sloping grip is less likely to center the recoil in the web of the hand.

"Among the best modifications are those done by Jim Wilson of Brunswick, Ga.," Steele contends. "He

weapon for field agents. This 9mm carbine has better range, accuracy and penetration than buckshot. The closed-bolt operation results in accuracy and the gun is not subject to accidental discharge from jarring.

The Drug Enforcement Agency also uses a 9mm submachine gun, the Colt Commando. For most agents, this gun is blocked to fire semi-auto only. DEA agents and those of the Clandestine Lab Entry Team use a suppressed version to lower the chances of sparks setting off chemical fumes from the labs.

The 9mm carbine or submachine gun also has the advantage of being ammo-compatible with the officers' sidearms, if they happen to be a 9mm S&W, Glock SIG or Beretta. Pistol ammunition also weighs much less than shotgun ammunition, is less prone to be damaged in handling and far more rounds can be carried in detachable box magazines. The hollow-point ammo used in the pistol has even greater velocity and bullet expansion in the carbine. Furthermore, the 9mm carbine is easier and more comfortable to shoot than the pistol, rather than more difficult.

"Unfortunately, in this day of what some of us have come to call assault rifle mania, a police department may not want to have military-style guns such as the Uzi or the Heckler & Koch subguns in marked patrol cars. For this purpose, a cheaper more conventional-appearing, wood-stocked carbine can be an answer. The Marlin 9mm or 45 Camp Carbines are effective in this mode," Steele believes.

One of the most-tested carbines ever in existence has been the original 30-caliber M-1 Carbine developed early in U.S. participation in World War II. This gun has been battle-tested by thousands of soldiers in that war, in Korea and even in Vietnam in the early days of that unpleasantness.

"In spite of its battlefield experience, the M-1 Carbine's appearance is that of a sporting rifle. It also is familiar to most citizens because of the number of war surplus guns in the hands of hunters and plinkers. The 30-caliber carbine bullet has better penetration than the 9mm round and, when used with soft-nose ammo (not military ball), it has a good reputation as a stopper," Steele contends.

Since the 1930s, the submachine gun has been the standard backup weapon for police in continental Europe. The shotgun was considered barbaric and

This agent for the U.S. State Department's Diplomatic Security tries out a 9mm Colt submachine gun at a Navy range in the Philippines.

reworks the Remington 870 into what he calls a Witness Protection version and the ever familiar Mossberg 500 into his Executive Protection firearm. With both shotguns, the barrel is trimmed just in front of the magazine, the stock trimmed to just the pistol grip, then a sling, special choke and hand stop are added. These guns have been carried by those assigned to the U.S. Marshal Service as well as those assigned to other agencies."

Still, the whipit gun is a specialized device, not a long-term answer to the problems of the patrol shotgun. Partly as a response to the 1986 Miami massacre and also as a lesson learned from Hostage Rescue Team experience, the Federal Bureau of Investigation has adopted a semi-auto version of the 9mm H&K MP-5 submachine gun as a standard backup

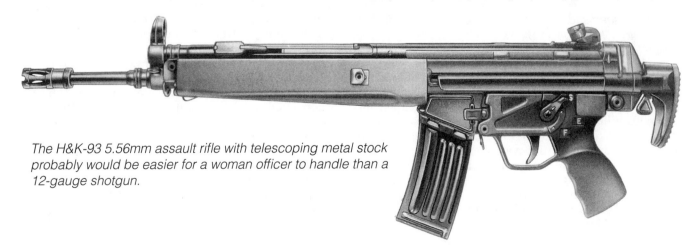

The H&K-93 5.56mm assault rifle with telescoping metal stock probably would be easier for a woman officer to handle than a 12-gauge shotgun.

David Steele also considered the Benelli semi-auto entry gun hard to beat as a modern police shotgun.

The trend seems to be away from shotguns, which are difficult for women to handle. David Steele tries out the Micro-Galil 556mm, which is used by undercover police and army units in Israel.

certainly not aligned with Old World tradition, since they had no pioneer hunters or Old West gunfighters.

The submachine gun was a standard weapon for the paramilitary gendarmerie and citizens were used to seeing it. The MAS 36 and MAT 49 subguns still carried in France are obvious examples. Over the decades, citizens in Europe probably have been less likely to confront the police than Americans. It was comparatively rare that an officer found cause to draw and chamber a round in his service automatic, much less pull a submachine gun.

Of course, this changed in wartime, as did the circumstances involved in responding to the postwar terrorist threat, especially the Red Brigade in Italy. In that country, it is not at all unusual even today to see carabinieri carrying or even standing at the ready with their Beretta Model 12 machine pistols. This is particularly true at vehicle checkpoints.

"American police departments seem to be influenced by European custom as well as by the arming and the experiences of SWAT teams, a post-1967 innovation in U.S. law enforcement. Here in the United States, we also have seen widespread adoption of automatic pistols for patrolmen as well as the move to carbines and submachine guns," Steele points out.

He adds, "The full-automatic weapons will probably remain with special teams, while the semi-auto carbine takes over in patrol vehicles. The biggest single factor in this move will probably prove to be the hiring of more female officers."

It has been found that distaff officers can easily handle carbines up to and including 5.56mm, which is standard for the M-16 rifle used by female members of the nation's armed forces. These light assault rifles have made infantry warfare a reality to even the smallest built person. The M-16 was issued to Vietnamese troops early on as a replacement for the M-2 Carbine.

While the M-16 or AR-15 in the semi-auto version probably will continue as mainstays with SWAT teams or other special units, it is not unlikely that the Ruger Mini-14 5.56mm also will be seen in patrol cars. This is particularly likely in rural areas where the little carbine's extra range, accuracy and penetration over that of the 9mm can be appreciated without presenting extra hazards to homeowners.

"In another 30 years, shotguns probably will be as rare as revolvers in big city patrol units – and for the same reason," Steele contends. "There is a perceived need for greater firepower, with acceptable combat accuracy, for every member of the local police department.

"As in the larger society, where labor-saving machines have opened jobs to those of small physique, modern police equipment has opened law enforcement to females, Asians and Latinos, who do not fit the traditional image of the beefy Irish cop."

CHAPTER 4

ASSAULT WEAPONS & WOMEN

That Infamous Date, 9/11/01, Changed Many Things in Our Lives, Including How We Look at Our Enemies

HAD THIS SIXTH edition of *"The Gun Digest Book of Assault Weapons"* been published prior to September 11, 2001, the day that terrorists struck New York City's World Trade Center, the Pentagon near Washington, D.C., and attempted to destroy the White House, this chapter would not have been written.

However, since that fateful day, the United States and its people have become more realistic and more willing to look at life as it is, instead of through the traditional rose-colored glasses. It is time to look at terrorism, the part that women can play in it and the weapons that any of us may be facing any day in our lives henceforth.

The assault rifle is part of a trend to miniaturization and mechanization applied to warfare. We have read or seen accounts of its use by terrorists. Most of us have not had to deal with the fact that assault weapons have had as much influence on Third World warfare – and more recently terrorism – in the latter part of the 20th century as the heavy machine gun had on World War I. Unlike the traditional battle rifles, the M-16 and AK-47 are light enough to be carried by women and even children in distant climes such as Burma and Vietnam.

A Case History

A former police chief, Al Pickles had retired from chasing domestic, homegrown criminals at the time he accepted a U.S. State Department assignment as a police adviser in South Vietnam. As he puts it, "When my paperwork was done, I took to donning a camouflage, combat police uniform and wandering alone in the jungle. I had Special Forces training and had studied every book, manual and incident report on guerrilla warfare.

"After much experimenting, I traveled ultra-light. I carried an M-16 with its 20-round magazine, plus one spare, and a .45 Colt autoloader with one magazine, a pocket knife, a compass and a small first aid kit.

On one of these sojourns, Pickles was approaching a small clearing roughly half a mile from a Viet Cong-controlled hamlet. For more than two hours, he lay at the edge of the jungle, watching, as an old women moved back and forth carrying water. Eventually, he moved to the edge of the clearing to observe the area from a better vantage point.

In Indochina, against the French, and later in what became Vietnam, assault rifles such as the classic AK-47, were light enough that women and even children could use them in guerrilla operation.

Off to a busy day of planting punji stakes in hidden pits, this Viet Cong peasant girl was armed with a captured U.S. M-1 Carbine.

"I was bracketed immediately by light automatic weapons fire from my right. From a prone position, I fired three bursts into the green jungle," Pickles later reported. "I couldn't see past the grass even inches in front of the muzzle of my M-16, nor could I remember switching the selector to full-auto. Above the fading echo, came a scream and thrashing sounds that seemed to be coming closer rapidly.

"Less than 50 feet away – and coming fast – was a Vietnamese in what we called black pajamas, brandishing a large knife in the left hand. His right hand was bleeding and useless.

"I took deliberate aim and fired two more short bursts – no effect. The knife came chopping down at me, as I sprang backward. My attacker fell with his momentum and we were both up at the same time. Swinging my M-16 by the barrel, I hit him full in the face. He went down and got up again. I repeated this four times and he continued to get up.

"I turned and ran about 20 feet to give myself time to draw my .45," Pickles recalled later. "This Viet Cong was almost on top of me with the knife. I fired my pistol empty before he fell, still carrying through with a swing of the knife. He clawed the dirt and grass, coming toward me, and I beat him again and again with the dangling stock of my broken rifle until he stopped moving," says Peters.

He wondered, "How had I missed with all those bursts? I crawled back to the corpse to examine it. I pulled off his clothes and was amazed. He had been hit no less than eight times with the M-16's 5.56mm round and five times with .45 slugs. The head was mush from the rifle blows. Most amazing of all, this 5-foot, 80-pound Viet Cong teen-ager was a girl!"

The moral of the story is that under certain circumstances female fighters can be formidable. This Vietnamese peasant girl, naive and inured to hardship, was a dangerous adversary on her home ground. The communist cadre had only to supply propaganda and a Kalashnikov.

Traditional Protection

When wars were mostly hand-to-hand combat during an estimated 3 million years of pre-history and 6,000 years of civilization, women were considered the spoils of war, but they still fought in last-ditch home defense. For example in medieval Japan, martial arts training was reserved for men, except for naginatajitsu and tantojitzu. The naginata – actually, a version of the ancient halberd – was wielded by women to defend the castle, if all male defenders had been incapacitated. The tanto, the Japanese dagger, was for the samurai woman to kill herself if the castle fell so the enemy would not dishonor her.

In Western countries, women sometimes went to war with their husbands, serving as camp domestics. For instance during the Napoleonic Wars, the British 34th Regiment fighting in Spain had to retreat under fire from Burgos in 1812. In this retreat, an enlisted man's wife called Biddy Skiddy carried her exhausted husband, Dan, piggyback to safety, while his daughter carried her father's musket. Biddy was quoted at the time as allowing how, "Strong as Samson for the fear I was in, I carried him half a league after the regiment into the bivwack."

Still, the Western ideal of those days, at least for the upper classes, was to keep women as far from the fighting as possible. The Christian and chivalric virtue was to protect the weak. There was no honor for a man or a society that could not protect women.

In this century as war has become total, modern societies – beginning with socialist countries of the Marxist sort – have put women closer to the "sharp end". The modern idea of enforced sexual equality took precedence over family stability, knightly tradition or common sense.

Women Police

"Since the 1970s, various countries have brought women into police work in fields other than the traditional matron and juvenile investigator roles," Steele points out. "As most of police work is talking, it should not be a surprise that their job performance has been adequate in most cases. Because most violent incidents involve what cops term 'batches of blue', a female officer's less-than-spectacular performance is not likely show up in reports."

While the courts may order the hiring of more women police officers, there are those who believe they should be equipped with that which might be termed labor-saving devices that can include improved metal batons such as the Gripton, Handler, ASP and PR-24. They also should be equipped with pepper spray, better handcuffs and modern firearms. According to a Florida State University study, women officers hit their targets with handguns 38 percent of the time, compared to men's 78 percent. This certainly would indicate extra pistol training should be required for women.

"With extra time and a calm approach to training, most women police candidates can be brought along

This Viet Cong woman is armed with an SKS rifle with the bayonet extended. The gun crew in background is armed with a Russian-made machine gun.

were not allowed weapons or handcuffs and could be assigned only to guard duty or traffic direction. In England, distaff Bobbies have just petitioned to have their 9-inch wood truncheons replaced with the 15-inch version carried by male officers.

Women in the Military

Some have pointed to women's comparative success in police work as an indication of their qualification for combat. Politicians usually suggest this along with feminist leaders who have never had any experience in either police work or military service, much less actual combat, according to our research.

Even Time magazine has discovered there are biological differences, not just cultural conditioning, between men and women. Subjected to infantry training at the U.S. Military Academy at West Point (not combat), women cadets developed stress fractures from running in boots, missed menstrual periods and experienced long-term problems involving bone porosity and eating disorders. Besides a switch to tennis shoes, women were allowed to qualify at a physical training standard far below that demanded of male cadets. It should be pointed out, of course, that these women were not brought up in the same social and environmental circumstances as the female Viet Cong who tried to kill Pickles.

Sometime ago the military conducted a media event concerning a female pilot who was being allowed to train for combat The whole idea was highly touted, but no one bothered to ask what would happen when she were forced to bail out of her plane in a combat zone. Aside from the physical rigors of attempting to escape through difficult terrain, possibly having to silently kill enemy sentries en route, she would have to expect rape in the event of capture.

"The first goal of combat is victory, not social engineering to promote a radical agenda unsupported by history or military tradition. United States forces have not experienced heavy ground fighting since Vietnam. Meanwhile, due to staffing shortages and political pressure, women have been integrated into combat support jobs that undoubtedly will result in serious casualties in the next land war," says Steele.

The U.S. military is an expeditionary force, mobile and trained to fight in other countries. It is neither a guerrilla army nor a terrorist brigade. It is in underground units that women have been best employed as fighters. As with the Red Brigades in Italy, female assassins can go places men cannot, including through roadblocks manned by macho policemen.

The favored weapon of Red Brigades' females was the Czech VZ-61 Skorpion .32 caliber machine pistol, the firearm used to kill Italy's premier, Aldo Moro. The Skorpion is lightweight and concealable, with little recoil and significant firepower.

Prior to the widespread availability of assault rifles, the submachine gun was the woman fighter's best

rapidly with a handgun," Steele says. "However, the shotgun is a genuine problem for most of them and the established training sequence is too short time-wise to overcome problems. The usual result of inadequate training is lack of confidence, which leads to failure to employ the weapon when necessary," he concludes.

As mentioned elsewhere in this volume, a better approach may be simply to replace the shotgun with a modern 9mm or 5.56mm carbine. The semi-auto Heckler & Koch MP-5SF 9mm now issued to FBI agents is an excellent but expensive backup weapon. The Ruger Mini-14 5.56mm – advertised as the Ranch Rifle – is widely used by rural agencies, state police and corrections personnel, both male and female. More costly 5.56mm semi-auto rifles include the Colt AR-15 and the Heckler & Koch 53. Those departments that cannot afford up-to-the-minute carbines can still replace the shotgun with rifles such as the Winchester Model 94 lever action and the U.S. M-1 Carbine, both of which have the advantage of long public acceptance.

Thinking back to 9/11/01, there is every reason to believe that sooner or later, our women police officers will be facing armed terrorists, who may also be women.

Other parts of the world are farther behind than the United States in regard to availability of modern equipment for police. Perhaps this is because other nations do not have confiscated drug funds to pay for the equipment.

In Japan, female police officers were just recently issued firearms for the first time. This firearm was the familiar Browning .25 auto. Prior to this change in policy, even after two years of training, women officers friend. In World War II, the French Maquis and Free French females preferred submachine guns like the British Sten model and the German MP-40 rather than the typical infantry rifle with a stock length designed for the average man. The submachine gun also gave greater range and effectiveness than the pistol. In considering the damage these women and their weapons did to the Nazis, we must keep in mind that none of these firearms could be taken to a range for practice in a German-occupied country.

History shows that in Vietnam, the Viet Cong women also used whatever was available, but generally did not go armed with captured M-1 Garand or M-14 rifles. The Russian-made AKM and captured M-16 assault rifles, plus the MAT-49 and M-3 submachine guns along with the ubiquitous M-1 Carbine seemed to be the weapons of choice.

North Vietnamese home defense units often included women armed with such weapons as this Russian-made SKS semi-automatic rifle. It fired the 7.62x39 cartridge and probably was not the woman's choice of arms as it was heavy and long. At the other extreme, it also was deadly.

Learning the lessons of recent history, those women assigned to U.S. conventional forces should become intimately familiar with the dojo, the weight room, and the M-16 range. Support troops may have to fight savagely to avoid capture, as was the situation in the Ardennes circa 1944. At the moment, American women have not developed a reputation as fighters.

Armies fight as teams, not as individuals. Unit cohesiveness is critical, a factor not understood by today's elected congressional leaders, the majority of whom have never served in uniform. The widespread introduction of women, some of whom are highly qualified as individuals, has not increased unit cohesiveness or combat readiness in American forces.

"I have known some formidable women, like renowned kickboxer Graciela Casillas. I also knew a Vietnamese refugee girl who was positively scary when she talked about Communists. She hated them on a personal and visceral level. I've also known a woman who joined the Navy when she was 18. On her first date off-base, she was beaten and raped," Steele reports.

While individual talented women deserve their chance for leadership and government jobs, the nation's survival depends on an Army of expendable men, willing and able to kill and die in a profession extending back to the dawn of time. At the other extreme, if women are to be involved in warfare, it is best that they be trained with the weapons they can handle and handle well.

Note should be made, however, of the fact that the ancient Romans had a few famous and skilled female gladiators, but no one suggested assigning them to the Roman Legions for actual conquest and battle.

This woman member of a World War II French underground unit carried a captured German MP-38/40 9mm submachine gun. On the shoulder of the man behind her is a U.S. M-2 Carbine.

CHAPTER 5

COUNTERINSURGENCY TACTICS & ARMAMENT

Some of the Basics for This Type of Warfare Go Back to Our Indians Wars

WEBSTER'S NEW WORLD Dictionary defines an insurgency as "a revolt or rebellion not well enough organized to be recognized in international law as belligerency."

The same dictionary defines the word counterinsurgency as "military and political action carried on to defeat an insurgency."

"Contrary to popular belief, America did not first engage in counterinsurgency during the Vietnam War," Steele points out. "This is a myth perpetrated by those who wanted to discredit the U.S. Government, and the United States Army and its tactics.

"Like any other strategy, counterinsurgency measures do not work everywhere, every time. In Viet-

North Vietnamese troops were armed with these PPSh-41 7.62 TT submachine guns. Russian troops had switched to the AK-47, and furnished the PPSh-41 7.62 TT submachine guns to other communist forces.

nam, the effort could not overcome a lack of continuity brought on by politics and the one-year tour of duty for those making up our forces. Other faults with the program were corruption in our South Vietnamese ally, insecure borders and the North Vietnamese willingness to accept limitless casualties," Steele explains. (It is now believed that more than 1.1 million Viet Cong and North Vietnamese died in the lengthy war.)

The U.S. strategy was modeled on the successful British experience in Malaya between 1948 and 1960, but Vietnam had nothing in common with Malaya beyond the fact that both countries were in Southeast Asia.

American and British counterinsurgency experience began prior to the American Revolution. The tactics were developed to suppress attacks by American Indians. During the French and Indian War, 1754-1763, Maj. Robert Rogers initiated standing orders for his Rangers, which still are used by our nation's elite forces. His orders originally contained 28 points. The first three of those orders were:

1. *Don't forget nothing.*
2. *Have your musket clean as a whistle, hatchet scoured and be ready to march at a minute's warning.*
3. *When you are on the march, act the way you would if you were sneaking up on a deer. See the enemy first.*

"The positive effect of Ranger training was as clear then as today," Steele contends. "On Sept. 29, 1759, Rogers' Rangers attacked the Abenaki Indians at St. Francis near Montreal, killing several hundred of them. This action destroyed a viable force that had supported the French."

The British spent much of the 18th and 19th centuries suppressing rebellions in their far-flung colonies. While unsuccessful in putting down the

These Philippine police officers undergoing night counterterrorist training are armed with revolvers, Glocks and M-16s.

For example, moving the Indians onto reservations can be seen as a prelude to the "strategic hamlets" of Malaya and Vietnam. In another comparison, killing off the buffalo – the Indian's principle source of protein – is akin to disrupting the enemy's food supply by defoliating the forests and bombing the chief communist supply route, the Ho Chi Min Trail. The U.S. Cavalry's use of "tame" Indians as scouts against other tribes has definite similarities to the U.S. Army's use of ex-Viet Cong as their so-called Kit Carson Scouts during the hostilities of 30-plus years ago in Southeast Asia.

Perhaps the chief differences in the two situations are the fact that the nomadic Indians had no leaders who could match the education and sophistication of communist leaders in Asia and the Indian population could not stand against immigration, better weapons and disease that came with the white man.

At the other extreme, Viet communists used selective assassination, tunneling, night operations, deception – a high art in even the Vietnamese civilian culture – and booby traps. Particularly effective on the part of the communists in Vietnam were demoralization tactics ranging from using children as sappers to supplying our troops with cheap narcotics. They obviously manipulated the American media to counter the U.S. forces' advantages in firepower and communications.

British Examples

The British approach to counterinsurgency varies from our own in terms of unit size and a tendency to disarm the locals in a foreign environment, while imposing strict fire discipline on regular forces.

"The obvious example of this approach is Northern Ireland, where small, professional units such as the Special Air Service seek out terrorists and weapons caches of the Irish Republican Army. At the same time, they are attempting intelligence and even pro-

Americans in 1776 and again in 1812, they had better luck in countries not as well armed nor adamant. The American tactics were based largely upon those learned from the Indians!

Later, the United States fought counter-guerrilla campaigns ranging from the Whiskey Rebellion to Geronimo, then in the Philippines, and with Pancho Villa somewhere in the continuing show of violence. During this time, this nation also fought major wars against Mexico, the Confederacy and Spain. During the 20th century, Americans fought in two world wars, as well as the guerrilla wars engendered by them.

Careful consideration shows that the tactics developed over the centuries of campaigns against the Indians seem to have served as the prototype for those used in modern brushfire wars.

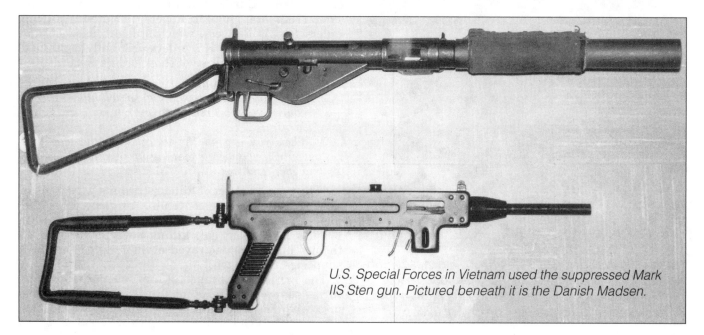

U.S. Special Forces in Vietnam used the suppressed Mark IIS Sten gun. Pictured beneath it is the Danish Madsen.

The Australian Owen and Asten submachine guns were used by Australian troops against Viet Cong insurgents in Vietnam.

paganda operations among the local populace," Steele says.

Between 1958 and 1960, the SAS operated behind the insurgents' lines in Malaya. What began the operation was the fact that a Chinese minority in the country had begun a guerrilla campaign against the British colonial government and the Malay majority.

"The insurgency began," Steele reports, "with a series of murders. British troops and Gurkha battalions were sent in to handle what became known back home in England as 'The Emergency'."

The first British counterterrorist unit to operate in Malaya was called Ferrett Force. It consisted of Iban Dyak trackers from Borneo and former members of Force 136. This force was made up of a wartime group of SOE agents – those who had been attached to an organization with a rather ambiguous title: the British Special Operations Executive.

Each Iban tracker usually carried a .303 SMLE rifle and a native headhunting sword common to Sarawak. Ferret Force was successful in its mission but soon was replaced by the SAS and a new strategy.

Unlike the fray in nearby Vietnam, the Chinese insurgents were ethnically different from the Malay majority and the dissidents could be supplied overland from only one direction. This led the British to fortify and monitor outlying villages, developing defensive hamlets. Long-range patrols of Malayan Scouts – primarily members of the SAS – were airdropped into the jungle to further isolate the terrorists. They had a two-fold mission: kill the enemy and win the hearts and minds of the local aborigines, who were openly puzzled about why all the fighting was going on.

"These patrols were extremely hazardous," Steele notes. "Parachuting into the jungle canopy required that the SAS troopers carry long ropes to allow them to rappel down to the forest floor after their chutes were hung up in the overhead greenery. Tree-jumping, as it was called, was a venture from which many of the British soldiers did not walk away."

Such operations still are based upon the SAS approach, but the chore of deliberately snagging the parachute in a tall tree, then cutting free with a trench knife and lowering oneself on a rope had its limitations. It worked well for these Malayan Scouts, but today's special forces favor fast roping from helicopters rather than the use of parachutes.

The Malayan Scouts, who operated more than 40 years ago, traveled light to conduct their behind-the-lines missions. Light machine guns and mortars constituted the upper limits of their firepower. Most troopers carried the .303 Lee-Enfield jungle carbine, which came to be romanticized as the "Jungle Carbine". Also carried were the Sten gun, a U.S.-made M-1 Carbine or the Browning Model 5 semi-automatic shotgun. The scattergun was stuffed with "Malayan loads" – a combination of buckshot and BBs, which worked well for jungle penetration and suppressive fire. Patrol leaders carried Webley revolvers or Browning P-35 automatics.

According to available records, during the early years of the Malay campaign, the U.S. M-1 Carbine and later the full-auto M-2 model, coupled with the

The French MAS-38 (top) and the MAT-49 submachine guns were used extensively in the Indochina War of 1945-1954. The MAT-49 was associated with French paratroopers and members of the French Foreign Legion.

.303 Bren light machinegun, were responsible for most of the enemy casualties. In later years, Browning semi-automatics and Remington pump shotguns were found to be best suited to close jungle combat due to their multi-hit capability.

Counterinsurgency Weapons

"It has been said that the best counterinsurgency weapon is a leader who understands his enemy and who is willing to spend his entire life trying to kill or convert him," Steele notes.

During our Indian Wars, it was common for U.S. Army officers to spend their entire careers at remote Western outposts continually attempting to suppress Indian uprisings. In contrast – in Vietnam specifically – U.S. officers were careerists doing an actual combat tour of six months or less, thus "getting their tickets punched" for promotion before being moved to the rear for staff jobs.

A situation prevalent at one point in Vietnam involved the Marine Corps' officer cadre. Battalion commanders were being assigned to that duty for periods of only three months before being relieved and moved to staff jobs. The troops hardly had the time to learn the lieutenant colonel's name, let alone his leadership capabilities, before he was gone and replaced by a new, untried officer. Lewis was there with the Marine Amphibious Force in 1970 and saw what was happening. He heard enough grousing from the troops to believe, "It was not a good morale move!"

"What were needed were more officers like Army Lt. Col. John Paul Vann," Steele insists. "He was there from the early 1960s and understood the enemy. He resigned in protest against the high-fire-power, low-intelligence strategy of the Pentagon. He ultimately was brought back to Vietnam as a 'civilian general' with an aid program in II Corps only to die in a helicopter crash in 1972."

These are examples of the famed "grease gun" produced inexpensively during World War II. The M-3A1 is at the top, the suppressed M-3 below. Both were used in ambushes.

Vann told Steele in 1963 that were it up to him, he would arm every South Vietnamese militiaman in the local hamlets with a knife and an M-1 Carbine. Then he would teach these people to defend themselves without depending upon U.S. technology. Ultimately, this self-reliance strategy worked for the Thais in their campaign against communist and Muslim insurgents along the country's three borders. The Thais had learned from the South Vietnamese not to become so dependent on Americans and their firepower.

It is generally acknowledged among military powers that where counterinsurgency weapons are concerned, the most significant development since World War II has been the assault rifle.

Lighter and shorter than the so-called Main Battle Rifles such as the M-1 Garand, the M-14 and the Belgian-made FN FAL, the assault rifle can be used by small-built men, Eritrean women, the Karen boys of the Burmese hill tribes or

Philippine soldiers, battling today's terrorists, practice counterterrorism tactics with M-16A1 rifles with 40mm grenade launchers attached.

Ingram MAC-10 and MAC-11 submachine guns with sound suppressors were used experimentally in Vietnam. A MAC-10 was even used in Israel's 1976 Entebbe hostage rescue raid.

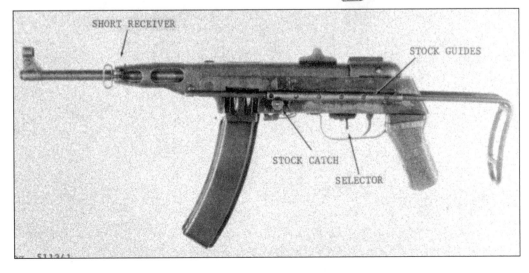

SHORT RECEIVER

STOCK GUIDES

STOCK CATCH

SELECTOR

This North Vietnamese K-50M submachine gun is a modified version of the Chinese Type 50. It fires the 7.62mm Tokarev pistol cartridge that is similar to the 7.63mm Mauser.

37

any other Third World freedom fighter.

The assault rifle, a translation of sturmgewehr, was developed originally in Germany during World War II, as the StG-43/44, firing the 7.92mm Kurz cartridge.

This particular model was designed as a selective-fire weapon to utilize an intermediate cartridge, which would minimize recoil and maximize control during full-automatic fire. The StG-43/44 was roughly the same size as a second generation submachine gun, but boasted a good deal more power, range and potential accuracy.

History has shown that it was a sergeant in the Soviet Tank Corps, Mikhail Kalashnikov, who took the German idea and adapted it to his design for the Avtomat Kalashnikov Model of 1947; today, it is known worldwide simply as the AK-47.

This assault rifle was chambered for the 7.62x39 cartridge designed originally for the Russian's SKS carbine. In one form or another, the AK-47 saw service in all of the so-called proxy wars – with the Soviet Union supplying arms and sometimes even advisers to other communist nations – from the 1950s until 1989.

Versions of the AK-47 have been produced over the years in China, North Korea, Finland, Israel and South Africa. Updated sub-caliber editions of the Kalashnikov design now include the 5.45mm Russian AKS-74 and AKSU-74. The basic design of the rifle also has been used in the Finnish 5.56mm Valmet, Israel's Galil and the R-4 model from South Africa.

For total numbers produced, the Kalashnikov has no peers. More than 50 million – that's 50,000,000 – of the guns have been produced since their introduc-

Fixed stock and folding stock Kalashnikov rifles still are being used today in guerrilla actions around the world.

This is the Colt-produced M-16A2 5.56 selective-fire rifle being issued to U.S. troops today.

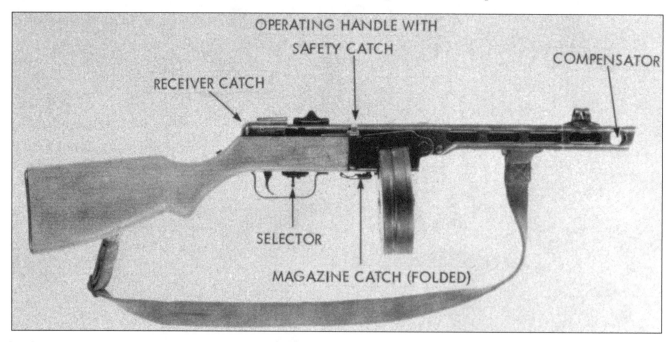

OPERATING HANDLE WITH SAFETY CATCH

COMPENSATOR

RECEIVER CATCH

SELECTOR

MAGAZINE CATCH (FOLDED)

The Soviet PPSh-41 subgun was used extensively in World War II. The drum holds 71 rounds of 7.62mm pistol ammo. It later found its way to North Korea for use against U.S. troops in the 1950s.

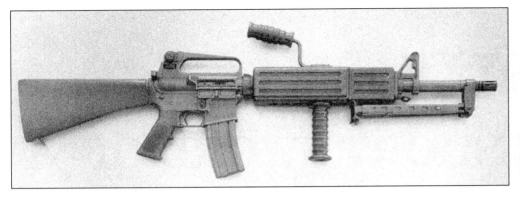

This Colt M-16 is rigged in the light machine gun/squad automatic weapon configuration.

tion in 1947. The closest competitor in terms of numbers has been the U.S. military's M-16 rifle.

The M-16, was developed by Gene Stoner for Armalite as the 7.62mm AR-10 and was aimed at the hope of becoming the U.S. service rifle. The AR-10 was adopted for a time by armed forces of the Netherlands. Stoner and his engineering staff later scaled down the AR-10 design to become the AR-15, firing the 5.56mm cartridge.

The selective-fire AR-15 was adopted initially by the U.S. Air Force for use by base security personnel in Vietnam, thus replacing the M-1 Carbine. During that era, U.S. Army Special Forces advisers to the South Vietnam troops found that the AR-15 was well suited to the small stature of the ARVN soldiers.

The AR-15's 5.56mm cartridge – also known as the civilian Remington .223 – was classified originally as a varmint cartridge, but it was far more powerful and devastating than the .30 carbine cartridge.

Colt bought the rights to the AR-15 from Armalite and eventually the so-called "black rifle" became the M-16A1 and became standard for troops in Vietnam, replacing what had been the Army's standard battle rifle, the 7.62mm M-14.

"There were critics of the move to the smaller cartridge, but most jungle combat was being conducted at under 50 meters, which was overkill for the 7.62x51mm cartridge fired from the M-14," says Steele. "Also, more rounds of the smaller cartridge could be carried by the American soldier on long-range patrols. The normal ammo load for such operations ranged from 600 to 900 rounds.

"The 5.56mm round had considerable – though sometimes erratic – wounding effect at the close ranges common in jungle fighting. A smaller machine gun version of the M-16A1, the XMK-177E1, was issued to squad and platoon leaders in some units fighting in Vietnam. The same weapon also went to border-crossing teams of the Army's Special Operations Group."

Usually called the CAR-15 or Colt Commando, this subgun version had a telescoping stock and muzzle compensator, the latter meant to offset the fireball effect that resulted from gunpowder designed for complete ignition in a longer barrel.

The version of the assault rifle currently in the hands of U.S. troops is designated as the M-16A2. This version has an improved buttstock, an improved forestock and a better selector for choosing mode of fire between full and semi-auto. Current issue for U.S. troops is the NATO SS109 cartridge, which has better range and penetration, though less wounding effect than did the Vietnam-era 5.56mm cartridge.

"While reduced size and improved efficiency have been typical of modern infantry weapons from handguns to pistols to even machine guns, no weapon has given such a boost to personal firepower as the assault rifle," Steele contends.

"If he has the discipline to control it, the assault rifle can make the individual rifleman his own machinegunner. From the Japanese terrorists who assassinated Puerto Rico pilgrims at Israel's Lod Airport to our own Special Operations Group teams breaking contact with North Vietnamese patrols, the assault rifle has provided serious but dispassionate firepower from a compact package," Steele explains.

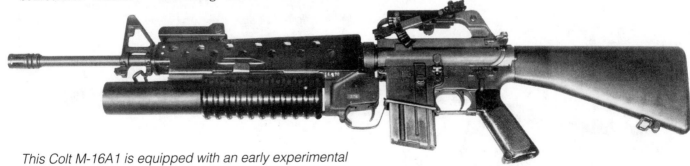

This Colt M-16A1 is equipped with an early experimental XM-203 40mm grenade launcher

CHAPTER 6

THE SHORT SWORD OF MIKHAIL KALASHNIKOV

His Rifle Has Been Compared to the Ancient Weapon Used to Hold Together the Roman Empire!

THE AVTOMAT KALASHNIKOVA assault rifle has several things in common with the ancient Gladius Hisspaniensis short sword of the Romans. Each, in its own era, has been the symbol as well as the instrument of totalitarian imperialism. Both weapons are convenient in size and highly maneuverable. More importantly, perhaps, both were designed for close-quarters battle tactics, with more men and support weapons invariably available in reserve.

The origin of what has come to be called simply the AK is shrouded in typical Soviet obscurantism. As pointed out in the classic book, *The World's Assault Rifles* (Daniel D. Musgrave & Thomas B. Nelson, TBN Enterprises, Alexandria, Va.):

"This (lack of information) results not so much from security aspects as from the Soviet policy of attributing all progress to the Communist Party or to prominent political personalities." In any case, we seem to accept that Mikhail T. Kalashnikov, a senior Soviet Tank Corps sergeant, designed the AK.

The original AK-47 grew out of Russian experience with the German Sturmgewehr MP-43 and MP-44 on the Eastern Front in World War II. This German weapon, chambered for the intermediate 7.92mm Kurz cartridge, is considered the first true assault rifle. It provided more range and penetration than a submachine gun. It also claimed to offer better control on full-automatic fire than a high-power infantry rifle.

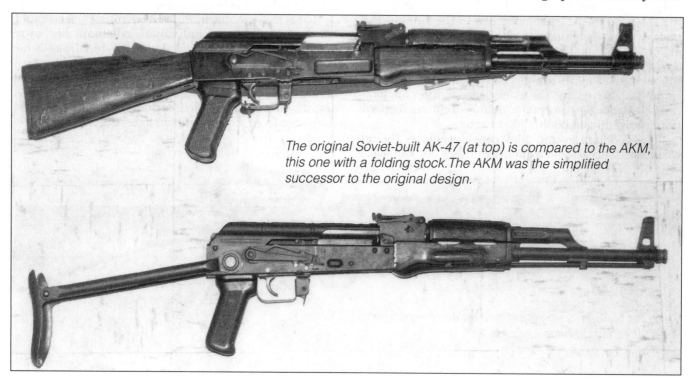

The original Soviet-built AK-47 (at top) is compared to the AKM, this one with a folding stock. The AKM was the simplified successor to the original design.

The MpiK chambered for the 7.62x39mm cartridge was the AK-47 clone that was manufactured in East Germany before the Berlin Wall came down.

The Bulgarians stuck pretty close to the original concept of the AK-47 in building this version for their own forces.

Incidentally, this weapon carried the designation MP (machine pistol) to keep the project secret from Hitler, who favored continuing with the old-fashioned bolt-action rifle "This probably was due to Hitler's World War I experience with the German infantry," Steele surmises. "Of course, this also could be because of the Reich's then-held large stocks of rifles and ammunition; later the designation of the new firearm was changed to StG."

U.S. infantrymen did not come into large-scale contact with enemy soldiers carrying this particular assault rifle until Vietnam. The Russians, on the other hand, learned early. Their tactics emphasized close-range firepower from the time they learned about submachine guns at the hands of the Finns in 1939. This led to the Soviets' adoption of the PPSh-41 submachine gun, a weapon that ultimately became as common as the Mosin-Nagant service rifle on the Russian Front.

Kalashnikov's model of 1947, the AK-47, came into service in 1951. It was eventually supplanted by the Simonov SKS carbine which was the first weapon to use the new M-43 7.62x39mm intermediate cartridge. In 1959, Kalashnikov streamlined his design, simplifying manufacture and gave it a straight-line stock for better full-auto controllability. This was the AKM, which remained standard in the Soviet forces until the more recent introduction of the AKS-74 in 5.45mm.

The AKM is part of a small-arms system that includes RPK light machineguns, PK general- purpose machineguns, PKS medium machineguns and the PKT tank machinegun. Such a small-arms system has not yet been developed in the United States, although the Stoner 63 system came close.

The standards by which the Soviet Army judged small arms in the late 1950s and early 1960s were based upon simplicity, ease of manufacture, reliability and firepower. More recently emphasis has been placed on wounding power as evidenced by development of the 5.45mm cartridge.

When there still was a Soviet Union, weapons were necessarily simple because of the large number of illiterate and foreign (non-Russian speaking) troops in the Soviet Army. (Since the fall of the Soviet Union, there is little to suggest the illiteracy problem has changed.)

"Of course," Steele points out, "some Asiatic troops were not considered politically trustworthy enough by the Soviets to be allowed to carry or even learn how to use weapons; these people were assigned primarily to construction battalions. In campaigns such as their failed effort in Afghanistan, the Reds preferred to use Asian troops since Slavic USSR rulers didn't consider Asian troop significant. Unfortunately, some of the Middle Asian troops sent there turned out to have more in common – language and religion, specifically – with the Afghans than they did with their Russian overlords, making fraternization a problem."

The Soviet approach was that small arms must be easy to manufacture so that plants could be set up in rural areas or Third World countries that did not have access to the highest technology. One of the best examples of the need for simplicity came when arms plants had to be moved to Siberia because of the German invasion in World War II.

"Making guns easy to produce also makes them less expensive and thus allows the government to make more of them," Steele notes. "In any case, the high technology used in American and European assault rifles has not made them more effective than the AK, only more expensive, a fact not lost sight of by Russian designers."

Reliability is of great importance to all military weapons, particularly in the former Soviet Union where the climate is cold and harsh.

The AKM was more reliable than the M-16 in Vietnam, at least until a new cleaning kit, chrome-lined chamber, recoil buffer and bolt-plunger were added to the 16 (the M-16A1). Even now, some authorities tend to insist the AK is still more reliable. Given the early tests of the M-16 in cold weather, chances are that the differences between the two weapons would be even greater in the northern regions where our some of our future wars might be fought.

As mentioned before, firepower has been a major criteria regarding Soviet small arms since 1939. In World War II, the British emphasized aimed fire with the full-power service rifle to make every bullet count. At what might be considered the opposite extreme, the Russians emphasized spray fire with the PPSh-41 submachine gun, following the theory that it was best to "keep their heads down until you're on top of them."

The Rumanian-manufactured AKM stuck close to the concept for the folding–stock gun.

For the most part, American troops were taught a middle approach. Aimed fire was favored with the M-l rifle, with short bursts with the M-3 and Thompson subguns as well as the Browning Automatic Rifle. "The Red Army found also that burst fire had a heartening effect on troops who were poorly trained in marksmanship, something their later counterparts found useful in advising communist guerrillas in Africa," Steele says.

"In the modern day, wounding power has become important, because post-World War II research has shown that at 300 meters – considered the maximum effective range of modern assault rifles – 60 percent of hits are likely to be on the extremities. Combined with the probability that up-to-date armies will soon be issuing their troops lightweight ballistic jackets, the necessity is for a bullet that will incapacitate a soldier consistently with a hit in an arm or a leg.

Traditionalists have widely criticized these so-called "subcaliber" weapons. Based primarily upon experience gleaned from the Spanish-American War to what has been called the Korean Police Action by those who were not there, the individuals contend that .30 caliber is the minimum bullet size that should be issued to fighting men. Perhaps in the back of their minds they don't want to see human targets reduced from big game to varmints species in terms of caliber.

In any case, this does not take into account modern changes in the proliferation of support weapons (which is why assault rifles need be effective only to 300 meters), resupply techniques and cartridge/rifle design. Military traditionalists continue to think of .30 as a proper caliber, just as Revolutionary War soldiers tended to think of anything less than .69 caliber as being too puny.

Small-caliber weapons allow extremely high velocity, a greater probability of bullet upset on impact, flat trajectory (with fewer sight adjustments), easier burst control, softer recoil, faster training and greater ammo capacity both in the gun and in carrying pouches.

"The Russians have been experimenting with small calibers for the AK since at least 1970, which was when Dan Musgrave first showed me an experimental Russian-made.221 cartridge he had somehow obtained," Steele reports.

The cartridge eventually adopted for the AKS-74 is also .221 caliber or 5.45x39.5mm to be precise. Those cartridges brought out of Afghanistan by Galen Geer for Soldier of Fortune magazine have the following characteristics: a lacquered steel cartridge case, bullet weight of 53.5 grains, a boattail bullet measuring .995 inches; and 22.3 grains of ball powder. It was determined that muzzle velocity of this bullet was 2,956 feet per second, with muzzle energy being measured at 1,007 foot-pounds.

"The unique thing about this round is the bullet's construction," Steele believes. "This bullet has a mild steel boattail core with a lead filler and forward air space. The balance is toward the rear, which, along with the long, thin shape, provides good accuracy.

"The air space behind the solid nose should cause both mushrooming and upset upon impact. Few Afghan rebels hit with this bullet survived to reach hospitals in Pakistan; those that did usually required amputation of an arm or leg," Steele notes.

But does this bullet violate the Geneva Accords, which lay out the rules of international behavior? The answer is probably not. The 1905 Accords banned a .303 ball cartridge made by the British at an arsenal in Dum-Dum, India. In this cartridge, and others like it, the bullet jacket, exposed the lead core at the bullet nose. The jacket however, is intact on this Russian 5.45mm round.

Complete data on the AKS-74 is still unavailable in the West. Basically, it is an AKM with a larger, slightly modified magazine, muzzle brake/flash hider, and internal parts modified to the caliber. A folding-stock version, called the AKD-74, has also been seen.

It is likely that these rifles were in the limited-standard category until their value could be demonstrated in Afghanistan, then evaluated. Meanwhile, the AKM was issued to most troops, with the 74s earmarked strictly for elite units.

The basic AKM is a selective-fire weapon, chambered for the M-43 7.62x39mm round. It is 34.25 inches long, with a 16.34-inch barrel. A folding-stock version is available. The weapon weighs 10.24 pounds unloaded, and the magazine holds 30 rounds. Muzzle velocity is 2,330 fps, and the cyclic rate is 600 rounds per minute.

The AK-47 and AKM have spawned similar weapons that have been produced throughout the communist world. Variations such as the Red Chinese Type 56 and the North Korean Types 58 and 68 all are well known to several generations of American servicemen. There are also variations produced in Poland, East Germany, Romania, Hungary and Yugoslavia.

Chris Newport in the May 1979 issue of Soldier of Fortune wrote one of the better articles on these variations. This article, "The AK-47 and Its Variations," covered most of these weapons, and the markings and design changes which distinguish them. None of the listed variations appears to offer substantial improvements over the original AK, but one must keep in mind that the article was written more than 20 years ago. Times and things do tend to change.

The AK design is being produced in at least three Free World countries. Finland's versions are listed as the M-60 and M-62. Basically the same weapon, it is distinguished by a tubular metal stock, a fine utility bayonet and several less conspicuous refinements. It is being produced to handle both the Russian's 7.62x39mm and the American 5.56x45mm cartridges. Obviously, the Finns want to be prepared for windfall

The Hungarians apparently had to show a bit of individuality in their AKM model. Note the distinctive pistol grip forearm that has been added to the design.

This is the M-22, the Chinese communist version of the Soviet AK. It is well known to those who fought in Vietnam.

ammunition from either of the superpowers, not to mention the export potential of such a versatile weapon.

Israel and South Africa are the other Free World countries that produce an AK variant. The Israeli weapon is called the Galil, and the gun has been produced under license in South Africa as the R-4.

The Galil is produced in three basic variations, all chambered for the US M-193 5.56x45inm cartridge. The Galil ARM is an assault rifle/light machine gun, equipped with folding metal stock, bipod and carrying handle. The AR assault rifle is virtually the same, minus bipod and carrying handle. The SAR short assault rifle version has an abbreviated barrel designed to fill the submachine gun role. The Galil fires at a cyclic rate of 650 rounds per minute from 35- and 50-round box magazines.

"Observers will probably notice that Israeli troops also carry M-16A1 rifles provided them by the United States," Steele points out. "Front line troops are seen only rarely these days with the FN 7.62mm rifle, which was standard during the 1967 war. Apparently with good reason. Israeli troops I talked with said the FN was sand-sensitive and hard to strip."

At this point, one might ask what American and European designers are doing about all this. The current M-16A2 and its 55-grain ball cartridge are now 20 years old. Aside from questions about this rifle's reliability, it showed itself generally adequate in wounding power during the Vietnam conflict. It certainly offered substantial advantages over the 7.62mm M-14 in terms of portability of the rifle itself and large amounts of ammo. The 55-grain ball cartridge caused substantial injury at the short ranges normally found in jungle terrain, but it lacked the long-range and penetration capabilities required of sniper rifles and light machineguns. That is why 7.62mm ammo was still used in the Remington-built sniper rifle and the upgraded M-60 machinegun.

"A longer 77-grain bullet has been developed, which has 4.5 times the penetration of the 55-grain slug. Hopefully, this will be the round loaded in belts and boxes for any future SAW (Squad Automatic-Weapon) adopted by U.S. services.

"Incidentally, the SAW itself would have to be designed around this heavier bullet, since a different rifling twist is required to stabilize it although the rifle and rounds could be used interchangeably in an emergency," according to Steele's information.

Eventually, a new rifle and cartridge will have to be adopted to replace the M-16A2/M-193; one that will not merely maintain parity with the Soviet AKS-74 but which will surpass it in firepower and other capabilities. One of the most interesting steps in that direction is the experimental H&K 36 assault rifle chambered for the 4.6mm round. The rifle itself is selective fire with a burst selector for 2, 3, 4 or 5 rounds which makes the high 1,200 rounds per minute cyclic rate controllable and accurate.

The special 4.6mm round for the H&K 36 is called Lofelspitz, which translates as "spoon point". The ogive on this bullet is asymmetrical, and one side is scooped out. This causes the bullet to incline as soon as it impacts. This design accentuates the natural yaw any bullet has in flight. The 4.6mm round has a lead or tungsten core, and it will make wounds in the extremities comparable to or exceeding the Soviet-originated 5.45mm round.

CHAPTER 7

GUNS THAT DIDN'T MAKE IT

Today This Firm Is a Behemoth, but it Had Its Failures in the Field of Military Small Arms

The TRW Episodes

TODAY, WHEN SOMEONE mentions TRW, most of us think of the firm that offers credit reports on most of us, if someone is willing to pay for the information. Actually, that is a miniscule part of the conglomerate's business empire. The corporation is involved in aerospace and defense, government services and support, technology and business systems, plus automotive products and systems. Headquartered in Cleveland, Ohio, the outfit had 93,700 employees at last count, with facilities in North America, South America, Africa, the Pacific Rim countries and Europe.

Founded in Cleveland in 1901, the Thompson Co. developed cap screws and other fasteners. By World War I, the firm was producing engine valves used in Allied fighter aircraft. An experimental hollow sodium-cooled valve helped Charles A. Lindbergh power his Spirit of St. Louis on his historic solo flight across the Atlantic in 1927. Over the years, there were other successes, but it was not until 1958 that Thompson Products entered the electronic and defense markets by merging with the Ramo-Woldridge Corp. in Los Angeles. Since then, the company that became Thompson-Ramo-Woldridge has built nearly 200 spacecraft.

Everyone involved in the defense industry knows that you don't have to have a successful project to collect a lot of money from the U.S. Government in development contracts and that sort of thing. Apparently with this idea in mind, the company became involved in small-arms development at its Los Angeles facility during the Vietnam hostilities.

Thirty Thousand Rounds Per Minute

A branch of the corporation known as TRW Ordnance Systems was established and its personnel began to work on a new High Velocity All Purpose (HIVAP) machinegun. Steele says, "The HIVAP was based on 19th and 20th century design principles that made the machinegun the premier weapon of World War I – and critical in every conflict since."

The 19th century part of the HIVAP was the multiple-barrel Gatling system left over from our Indian Wars, but this one called for an external power source instead of a gunner standing behind the gun and cranking off rounds. Unlike the more conventional 20mm Vulcan and the 7.62 Minigun systems,

The prototype of the HIVAP had these feed trays attached on each side of the gun for demonstration purposes. Fully loaded, the gun had a cyclic rate of fire of some 30,000 rounds per minute.

Photographed from this angle the electric drive gears that powered the feed of firing of the eight-barrel gun area are visible. The Gatling-type barrels were smoothbore.

the HIVAP was designed to use a cluster of eight 26-inch barrels. Each of these barrels would be smooth bore and made of 4150 ordnance steel. The selected bullet size was .31 caliber, with each barrel firing twice per revolution. It had been determined earlier that multiple barrels allow better cooling as well as a higher cyclic rate of fire than a single-barrel system.

According to Steele's investigations, the frame of the HIVAP was of cast steel with heavy end rings and two firing straps. There was a roller-bearing support for the cluster of barrels. "In one prototype, there were two conveyor-type feed trays on either side of the action for the two feed stations. As designed, these were to allow test firing with limited firing duration and recognize the possibility of jams," Steele says.

Steele had an opportunity to see and inspect this gun during its development. "Had the HIVAP gone into actual production, one of its uses would have been placement under the wing weapon pod of an aircraft. In firing, the gun would have been fed via linkless tape from ammunition boxes stored behind the gun. Each feed would have been independent with a pneumatic actuator," he notes.

As designed, the feed mechanism ran at 2.5 times the speed of the barrel. The drive gears for an electric motor were positioned at the rear of the gun, with sprockets and the tapes. In engineering terms, the barrel-cluster rotation was set at 1:1 with the drive motor. This electric-drive motor produced 60 hp. at 1,875 rounds per minute.

"The most innovative 20th century part of the HIVAP was adapted from the little-known 1950 Dardick revolver," Steele notes. "This weapon utilized a triangular plastic shell case that contained the bullet, powder and primer. This system came to be called the Tround. The HIVAP Tround carried a sabot-encased flechette. The HIVAP was tested at 30,000 rounds per minute and was estimated by TRW engineers to be capable of at least twice that rate of fire."

The TRW HIVAP system was the brainchild of a team of Ordnance Systems engineers led by Don Stoehr, who considered the project a refinement of the firearms designs of the past two centuries. According to Steele, Stoehr was quick to credit David Dardick's, who had been an ordnance engineer as far back as the 1930s.

In 1950, Dardick had conceived his radically new open-chamber feeding system, which he incorporated into a unique revolver," according to Steele. "Plastic-cased cartridges of nominally triangular cross-sections – those things called Trounds – were fed laterally into triangular chamber recesses on a rotating cylinder, which supported two of three sides of the cartridge. A fixed-frame firing strap supported the cartridge's third side."

In this unusual handgun, once the cylinder was in alignment with the barrel, the cartridge was fired. When the cycle was repeated, the fired cartridge case was ejected laterally, as the next Tround was fed into the chamber simultaneously. Rotary movement replaced the reciprocating mechanisms of other handgun systems. One of the sales points for the Dardick was that the plastic cases, which did not use brass, provided significant savings in cost, weight and use of critical materials.

The prototype Dardick revolver was chambered for a .32-caliber bullet, but the production model was for the .38 Super bullet. The .38 Series 1500 and a slightly smaller Series 1100 were produced in limited numbers by the Dardick Corp. from 1958 to 1959.

"The revolver was double-action in design, feeding from its fixed, double-stack magazine located in the grip. It was loaded from a left-side trapdoor," Steele says. "There also was a .22 barrel and adapter Trounds so that .22 rimfire cartridges could be fired.

"The Dardick also was available with a long barrel for conversion to a carbine. Management disputes led to the company's early demise," says Steele. Dardick guns are valuable collector items today, he notes.

Maintaining the general design of Dardick's cartridge, the projectile for the HIVAP system was a 35-grain steel flechette housed in a triangular-shaped Lexon case. The case was 3.1 inches in length and incorporated a primer and a charge of 56 grains of IMR 4227 powder. The flechette had a velocity of 4500 fps, while the cartridge had a peak pressure of 47,000 ppsi.

It perhaps should be pointed out that four years earlier than the start-up of the HIVAP project – in 1963 – the old-line New England arms makers Harrington & Richardson had entered into a contract with the U.S. Army to develop a Special Purpose Individual Weapon, which came to be called the SPIW. This was a semi-automatic rifle that utilized a single Dardick-like Tround to fire a salvo of three projectiles through three separate barrels at the same time. Described as a gas-operated, revolving-cylinder weapon, it functioned as designed, but the Army called it overweight and unreliable and canceled the contract.

Unlike the Dardick revolver design, the open chamber and the barrels of the HIVAP from TRW both rotated. As mentioned earlier, this particular weapon had two barrels firing simultaneously. Each of the eight barrels had its own firing pin mounted on the end of the cylinder, rotating with it.

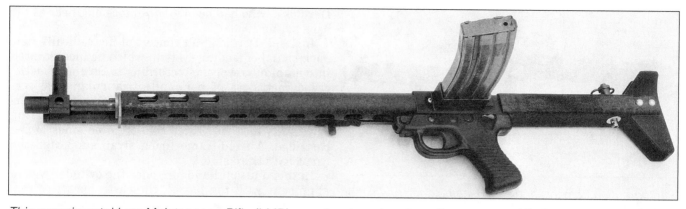

This experimental Low-Maintenance Rifle (LMR) was developed under a Department of Defense contract with TRW Systems. Note that the grip assembly is that of the M-60 machine gun, while the M-16 magazines load from the gun's left side.

In inspecting the HIVAP during its development, Steele noted that, "Two pairs of blades riding in peripheral slots at either end of the cylinder accomplish ejection, scooping fired cases out of the chambers as they emerge from under the firing straps.

"On the prototype, drive was provided by the electric motor, but powder gas also was studied as a power source with some degree of success. Cylinder-rotation pressure produced enough friction to heat the plastic case to its melting point. This self-limits the friction."

With 62 shots per barrel being fired, barrel heating was a problem, as expected by the TRW engineering team. "It appeared to me that barrels made from a composite of columbium or molybdenum for the liner and surrounded by a steel jacket would have been ideal. However, with costs and construction difficulties continually in mind, the development team decided to use steel barrels in their prototype, limiting bursts from 200 to 600 rounds," explains Steele.

Another challenge for the designers was to set up a feed system that could handle 250 cartridges per second. This was complicated by the triangular cartridge, which cannot roll and requires orientation. A link-less feed system was developed, with cartridges being stored in and fed through chutes was developed to solve this problem.

"Feed pressure was provided by a type of fabric tape attached to the gun at one end. This tape was interwoven through the Trounds and pulled at the free end by a drive roller," explains Steele. "Rates of 350 rounds per second per feeder were reached. However, reliability still was not 100 percent. This led the engineers to come up with a pair of simple conveyor feeds carrying 100 rounds each. These were used in demonstration firings."

As indicated, feeding turned out to be the greatest problem in the development phases, but there were other problems, too. One was thermal cracks in the forward main cylinder bearing. Other problems involved the "float" of spring-driven firing pins and complex stresses in the firing cylinder.

"Eventually, all of these problems were solved to one extent or another," Steele says.

Lexon had been chosen for the Trounds cases because of the high pressures involved. This particular plastic is a polycarbonate that combines strength with toughness. The steel flechette – a needle with fins – was mounted in a plastic sabot, which separated after the unit left the barrel.

By late 1969, it was thought that all of the problems were solved. TRW was ready to demonstrate their creation to U.S. and foreign agencies. Such demos were held into 1970, but none of the reviewing agencies were willing to pick up the package for further development. This was in spite of the fact that the HIVAP fired at five times the rate of the then-conventional electric-driven Gatling guns.

"Actually, substitution of electric primers and an advanced ignition system could double the HIVAP experimental rate of 30,000 rounds per minute," according to Steele's findings. "The only mechanical change would be a larger drive. Weight reductions also were available through the use of beryllium and titanium as substitutes for steel."

In this instance, TRW proved the feasibility of the open-chamber principle not just for the HIVAP, but for military rifles, ground machineguns, aircraft cannon and close-range missile defense systems.

But whether this design ever will be developed is an open question.

The Low-Maintenance Rifle

In February 1971, as hostilities in Vietnam appeared to be winding down, the Defense Advanced Research Projects Agency contracted with TRW Systems of Redondo Beach, Calif., for the development of a new infantry rifle.

The chief demand of the contract's small print was that the resultant rifle would require substantially less maintenance than the M-16A1 then in use in the combat zone. The project was to be monitored by the U.S. Army's Small Arms System Agency (USASASA).

The reason behind this project probably is obvious to anyone who knows the history of the 5.56mm M-16, which had been cloned from Armalite's AR-15 that was chambered for the same caliber.

Soon after the M-16 was introduced to the fighting in Vietnam, it became instantly notorious for jamming in less than pleasant circumstances. This problem

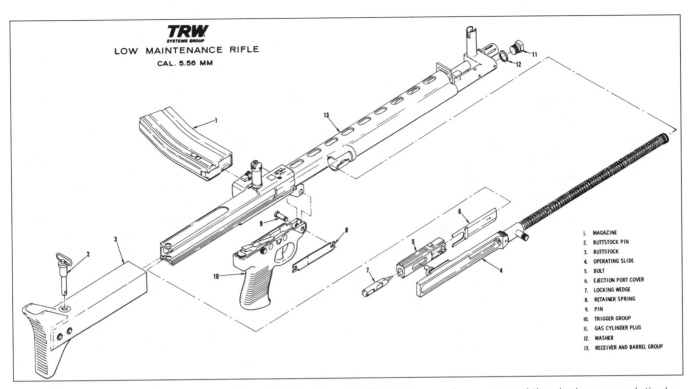

TRW
SYSTEMS GROUP
LOW MAINTENANCE RIFLE
CAL. 5.56 MM

1. MAGAZINE
2. BUTTSTOCK PIN
3. BUTTSTOCK
4. OPERATING SLIDE
5. BOLT
6. EJECTION PORT COVER
7. LOCKING WEDGE
8. RETAINER SPRING
9. PIN
10. TRIGGER GROUP
11. GAS CYLINDER PLUG
12. WASHER
13. RECEIVER AND BARREL GROUP

As evidenced by this exploded view of the TRW-designed LMR, there were few parts and the design was relatively simple when compared to other prototypes being developed during the early 1970s.

eventually led to a congressional investigation. The causes of the jamming problem were powder fouling, internal corrosion and a lack of field maintenance.

The powder fouling resulted from the M-16's cartridge being loaded with the same ball powder used for 7.62 NATO ammunition. The powder did not burn cleanly or fully like the powder designed originally for the 5.56mm cartridge.

During the mid-1960s, Lewis had an opportunity to discuss the matter with ballisticians at Winchester/Olin, which had loaded the ammo. According to the info he received, forces at the ammunition company had advised against the powder chosen, but the Army apparently already had a supply of the 7.62 powder that was bought and paid for. Obviously someone in the hierarchy was more interested in dollars than in efficiency of the round as loaded. That brings to mind the old military adage: "When going into combat, always keep in mind that your armament was produced by the lowest bidder." This would seem to apply to ammo as well as firearms.

The problem with the early M-16s was compounded by the gas tube, which tended to blow residue back onto the bolt and into the chamber, rather than onto a separate operating rod. All of this was made worse by a lack of fire control, with soldiers resorting to full-auto fire at the slightest suggestion of an enemy presence.

Rather than admitting an error in professional judgment and going back to the proper powder, the Army brass decided to line the chamber of each M-16 with chrome and introduce a recoil buffer that would lower the cyclic rate of fire.

The M-16's powder-fouling problem was worsened by the moist Vietnam climate, which would quickly corrode and pit a rifle's chamber without daily care. Somewhere along the way, some soldiers apparently were told the M-16 did not require cleaning. This error probably started with the manufacturer's claims for the AR-10 7.62mm rifle, which had preceded the AR-15. The AR-10 had a chrome-lined barrel as standard. This particular rifle also had a barrel of such diameter that it would not retain water in the bore by capillary

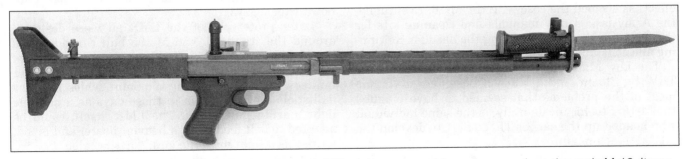

Don Stoehr was the designer of this Low-Maintenance Rifle that was meant to perhaps replace the early M-16. It was built to handle the M-6 bayonet originally designed for the M-14.

These were three variations of the TRW Low-Maintenance Rifle developed between 1971 and 1973. From left, they are the prototype for firing flechette ammunition, the model for handling standard military 5.56mm ball ammo, and the final version of the gun as it appeared before the U.S. Army ended the contract.

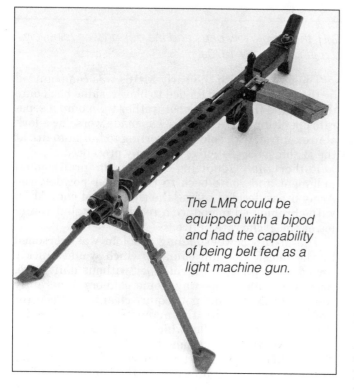

The LMR could be equipped with a bipod and had the capability of being belt fed as a light machine gun.

Rifle was more simple mechanically than the M-16. It had fewer parts and was easier and simpler to assemble and disassemble. The TRW design also required less maintenance due to greater use of corrosion-resistant materials and coatings, solid film lubrication and less powder fouling in the breech mechanism."

The LMR also was easier to operate than the M-16, since it had only one firing mode – full auto. The rifle's ejection port cover operated automatically. Eliminated were such nonessentials as the slide stop and the bolt assist incorporated in the M-16A1 design.

The TRW-prototype rifle was more compact than the M-16A1, being five inches shorter. Eventually, it was shown to be much more effective in full-automatic fire. Field tests showed there was minimal muzzle climb with short bursts, while a lower cyclic rate of fire and the straight-line stock provided ammunition conservation and afforded good control in long bursts.

Actually, when compared in the field, the M-16A1 was shown to be superior to the LMR in only three categories, none of which were in critical areas," Steele reports. "The M-16A1 was a half-pound lighter than the LMR; it was easier to shoot from the left shoulder and it was slightly more accurate in deliberate fire due to a capability to fire in the semi-automatic mode and its closed bolt operation."

In its final configuration, the LMR was 34.3 inches in overall length with a 19.4-inch barrel. It weighed only 8 pounds fully loaded and could handle either 20- or 30-round M-16 rifle magazines. The LMR rifle was fitted for attachment of the M-6 bayonet, which had been designed originally for the phased-out M-14 rifle. The rifle may be gone, but the bayonets still are cluttering up military warehouses. The TRW Low-Maintenance Rifle fired at a cyclic rate of approximately 450 rounds per minute, making use of a simple gas-operated, roller-locked mechanism.

"The original prototype was designed around the 5.6mm XM-216 SPIW flechette, which was at the time considered the military cartridge of the future. However, the SPIW rounds developed problems, which have caused them to be shelved at least for now," Steele says.

"Later prototypes of the LMR all were designed around the standard 5.56 M-195 ball cartridge and the M-196 tracer round. However, future versions of the system could have been designed around other military calibers, including the 6mm, which military ballisticians were eyeing in those days as a possible light machinegun round. The LMR, itself, could be adapted to belt feed, with a heavier barrel and bipod, for use as a light machine gun," says Steele.

According to TRW engineers of the time, a 30-inch carbine version of the LMR also could be produced,

effect, as seemed the case with the M-16. Eventually, the Army issued new manuals and cleaning kits for the troops in Vietnam, stressing the need for continuing and constant field maintenance.

The Low-Maintenance Rifle (LMR) developed for TRW by Stoehr and a team of designers overcame most of the problems that seemed to have plagued the M-16. Stoehr, incidentally, is the same individual who headed up the earlier TRW effort to develop the HIVAP machinegun.

According to Steele, who was acquainted with Stoehr and some of his work, "The Low-Maintenance

Colt's All-American 2000

*If Corporate Lawyers Had Left It Alone,
This Semi-Auto 9mm Could Have Been a
Real Winner*

Seen from the right side, the early Colt version of the All American 2000 has the rampant Colt logo inset in the wood grips, which later were switched to polymer. Compared to the more compact Knight/Stoner prototype, the Colt appears somewhat bunglesome.

Two 9mm handguns rest in an arms vault at Knight Armament in Florida. The guns are very similar. One has a bright finish and bears the Knight Armament markings. The other is blued and is marked with the rampant stallion made famous by the products of Col. Sam Colt.

One of the guns was a failure and became an embarrassment, while the other semi-auto never really got into production. The blued version bearing the Colt identification was introduced at the 1991 Shooting, Hunting & Outdoor Trade Show amid great excitement and promotion. The silver-shaded gun was the prototype for that product. It had been designed by C. Reed Knight, Jr., of Knight Armament and Eugene Stoner, the man who probably was the best-known designer of the past century.

Knight and Stoner were present for the introduction of the pistol that was to be marketed as the Colt All American 2000. Most of those in the show hall were members of the shooting press, with John Nassif acting as master of ceremonies for the event. Knight and Stoner each had things to say about the gun and how it had been developed, but neither of them seemed particularly happy. The prototype, of course, was not in evidence during the introductory celebration.

Knight and Stoner had worked on the gun, designing, prototyping, shooting it and redesigning over a period of several years," according to Lewis, who was present for the ceremonies. "Apparently, they had sold their design to Colt without the right to say much about what happened to it thereafter."

Side by side, it is not quickly apparent that the All American 2000 and the bright gun come from the same design. The Knight Armament prototype is made from aluminum and stainless steel. It is compact and efficient in appearance. The Colt version, Lewis later learned, had been a revision created by the Colt engineers and corporate attorneys of the time.

In 1991, hungry attorneys who had learned that there suddenly were more lawyers than clients were turning the liability factor into lawsuits. Suing a gunmaker for what they called a faulty product was just one more way of making a buck. Thus, it is somewhat understandable that the corporate counsel for Colt got involved in redesigning the gun.

The original Knight/Stoner version had a 6-pound trigger pull," according to Dave Lutz, vice president of Knight Armament, who was on active duty as a Marine Corps ordnance officer at the time of the introduction. "At the attorney's insistence, the trigger pull was increased to 12 pounds. The barrel length also was extended by roughly an inch and the grip was extended as well," he noted.

According to Lewis, who was involved in testing the Colt All American 2000 for Gun World magazine

which would be of benefit to officers, tank crewmen, et al. In fact, the open-bolt operation and low cyclic rate of the LMR was quite similar to that of most submachine guns, but with substantially more power.

Steele found that the "LMR was not impervious to contaminants in the mechanism itself, but was easy to strip and clean. Combined with its corrosion resistance, minimal powder fouling and permanent dry lubrication, the maintenance job of the infantryman would be a minor chore. If the rifle should become clogged with dust, mud or water, the soldier would be well-advised to clean it. Otherwise this rifle would largely take care of itself."

The Army's contract with TRW ended in 1973 and that also marked the end of the Low-Maintenance Rifle project.

"The rifle created by the project was successful, but like many other military projects created by Department of Defense agencies, it is doubtful whether the LMR ever will lead to a new service rifle," Steele says. "Substantial monetary commitments have been made to the M-16 design – including the recent introduction of the M-4 Carbine – and no one likes to admit they have thrown good money after bad. That is especially true of military politicians whose promotions rest all too often on their good – or bad – judgment."

As this volume was being written, Steele once again went to the TRW complex in Redondo Beach, seeking additional information on the two guns. He learned that the individual with the longest term of corporate service had been there only 13 years. No one knew anything about these firearms or even what had become of the prototypes.

The Steyr AUG or Armee Universal Gewehr was adopted by the Austrian Army in 1977 as the Stg77 and production began late that same year. The Austrian Army initially ordered 80,000 AUG rifles.

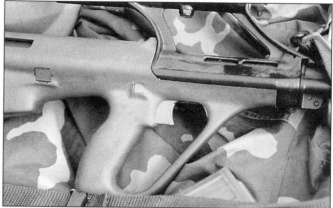

The trigger guard is built for the entire hand of the shooter. The safety is a cross-bolt affair that is located above and slightly behind the trigger. "Safe" is the far-right position on the safety, while "Fire" is the far-left position and indicated by a red dot.

shortly after the 1991 introduction, "The 12-pound trigger pull was impossible. By the time a shooter could muscle his way through the pull, he might be on someone else's target. In short, the weight of the pull had an effect on accuracy."

Lewis believed then – and believes now – that the changes in barrel length and extending the grip tended to interfere with balance – the way the handgun felt in the shooter's hand.

More recently, Lewis had the opportunity to work with one of the original prototypes while visiting Knight's headquarters. "The All American 2000 and the working prototype that now is a museum piece have little in common when it comes to feel, trigger pull, balance and the other things that go into making a handgun acceptable to shooters," Lewis says.

The double-action-only pistol coming out of the Colt works was chambered for the 9mm Parabellum cartridge, had a 15-shot magazine, a 4-1/2-inch barrel and measured 7-1/2 inches in overall length. It was manufactured with either a molded polymer or aluminum frame with a blued steel slide. With the polymer frame, the pistol weighed 29 ounces; with the aluminum frame, weight was 33 ounces. The grips were of checkered polymer. The front sight was the ramped-blade type, while the rear sight was drift- adjustable and featured the three-dot aiming system. The safety was of the internal striker type.

As indicated earlier, the Colt All American model did not strike the fancy of serious handgunners and production lasted only a year. By 1993, it had been dropped from the Colt line.

Oddly, or perhaps, not so oddly, the attorney who demanded the design changes from the original Knight/Stoner prototype later became president of the Colt Manufacturing Co., Inc., a position he held when the organization filed for bankruptcy protection.

The original handgun design is one of which Reed Knight, Jr., is still rather proud. When he looks at the old pistol, there is a definite gleam in his eye. Lewis suggested that it might be a good idea to reintroduce the pistol in its original form with the six-pound trigger pull, et cetera. He also pointed out that all reference to the Colt All American 2000 should be

ignored if the handgun were reintroduced. Knight did not comment, but the gleam was still in his eye.

The Steyr AUG-Silk Purse or Sow's Ear

With the Manufacturer Gone From the Scene, This Is a Question That May Never Be Answered

During the late 1970s and early 1980s European military small arms designers became preoccupied with the bullpup style of rifle. Three prominent military bullpup rifles were accepted into the armed services of Austria followed by France and finally the United Kingdom during that period.

"The best attribute of any bullpup rifle is its compact size and short overall length, while at the same

The bolt carrier can be manually retracted during loading and clearance drills by activation of the cocking handle located on the left side of the receiver. Engaging a small button on top of the cocking handle operates a forward bolt-assist mechanism. Depressing this button and pushing the cocking handle forward allows the operator to silently load the chamber and push the bolt head into battery quietly.

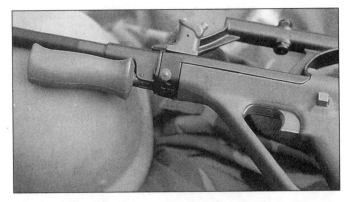

The foregrip assembly is mounted to a sleeve that is sweated around the barrel. It is used to change barrels without the operator touching hot metal when the barrel becomes fouled. The foregrip can be folded forward on all but the shortest barrel because with the shortest barrel that puts the operator's hand in front of the muzzle.

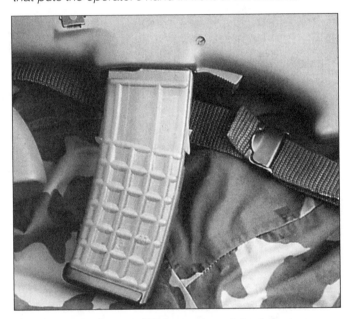

The AUG magazine, with exception of the follower spring, is made entirely of plastic. It is transparent enabling any operator to visually scan the number of rounds remaining in the magazine during an engagement. Two magazines were available for the AUG, one with a 30-round capacity and a second with a 42-round capacity. The magazine latch is located behind the magazine well.

time maintaining a normal length rifle barrel," author Frank W. James contends. We asked him to research this chapter and offer his conclusions. This is in spite of the fact that the Austrian manufacturer, Steyr, is no longer in existence. James found that the building and land once occupied by the old-line arms maker was sold by the bank that operated Steyr while the company was in receivership.

"The Steyr AUG bullpup design with a 16-inch barrel is more than a foot shorter than a comparable M-16 rifle. The same AUG is just one-inch longer than the MP-5 submachine gun with the fixed stock, James notes.

He explains, "This design feat is accomplished because the mechanical action and the magazine are located behind the trigger and inside what would normally be called the stock of the rifle. Additionally, the trigger is located more toward the middle of the overall length of the rifle."

The need for an ejection port on all rifles firing conventional ammunition somewhat complicates this arrangement. That problem is solved simply by declaring that the rifle in question will only be fired by right-handed shooters, or if it is capable of being converted to left-handed operation – solely by left-handed shooters.

All bullpup actions eject the spent case out the side of the stock that is opposite the face of the shooter. Unlike conventional rifles, no bullpup can be considered ambidextrous without specific modifications to the bolt head, the extractor, the ejector and the stock. While this may sound like a simple proposition, it creates its own set of problems, which will be addressed later.

The three bullpup military rifles that were alluded to in the opening paragraph are: the Steyr AUG, manufactured in Austria until the Steyr factory became only a memory; the French FAMAS; and finally the Enfield SA80, which was originally manufactured by Royal Ordnance in the United Kingdom. The Enfield SA80 has now been remanufactured by Heckler & Koch in Germany because of many reported deficiencies in the Royal Ordnance product.

"In terms of commercial sales, both to foreign governments and to law enforcement agencies, the AUG was by far the most successful," James says. "The French FAMAS has not enjoyed the AUG's success, but it is a battle-proven design having endured the rigors of desert battle during Operation Desert Storm. The English SA80 has proven to be an embarrassment to all concerned. In reviewing the numerous reports of its shortcomings in both the field and training exercises, one can only come to the conclusion it is a dismal failure."

In a sense it is unfair to pick on the SA80 because a complete and objective listing of its troubles would probably would take a book larger than this one.

"Suffice it to say, the SA80 experienced an extremely troubled birth. The French FAMAS, by contrast and personal experience, is not a bad design, nor even a poor rifle – except for its ridiculously high rate of fire, but there have been no extremely critical reports on its performance," James reports. "However, in all fairness and objective analysis, it doesn't have a broad track record outside of France or even the regions of French influence."

The Steyr AUG, on the other hand, is fair game. It was sold in quantities to a number of nations like Austria, Oman, Saudi Arabia, Tunisia, Malaysia, Djibouti, Morocco, Australia and the British SAS, as well as various state and federal police agencies in the United States. The most prominent customer in this country was the U.S. Customs branch of the Treasury Department.

To differentiate between the standard AUG and the light machinegun version, the alloy receiver is marked at the factory with the acronym LMG.

To the rear of the cross-bolt safety is the takedown latch that resembles the safety in appearance and operation. It is distinguishable from the safety because it is larger and recessed into the AUG stock.

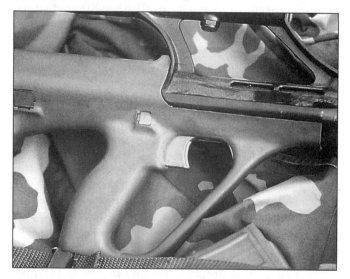

On the select-fire military and law enforcement AUG, there is no selector lever. The two-stage trigger determines whether the gun is fired in semi-auto or full-auto by how far the operator pulls it. The first stage produces semi-auto fire, while a complete pull-through will produce full-auto fire.

The light machinegun version of the AUG is a dedicated weapon firing from an open bolt and featuring the 24-inch heavy barrel with an integral bipod. This squad automatic weapon normally employs a 42-round magazine, but it will work with the 30-round magazine.

Austria was not a sovereign country free to build its own army until 1955. The rifle selected was the FN FAL. It was called the Stg-58, and the first 15,000 to 20,000 were manufactured and purchased direct from FN in Belgium. At the time Steyr was making only Mannlicher sporting rifles, but it received the first contracts to produce small parts for an Austrian-produced Stg-58. Steyr produced 150,000 Stg-58s at the rate of 8000 to 10,000 per year, eventually making in the chief military rifle supplier to the Austrian army.

In 1964 the U.S. Army – then engaged in the Vietnam War – adopted the M-16, making it the first 5.56x45mm rifle to be accepted as a primary army rifle by any major nation.

James' sources tell him that Steyr started research on first a bolt-action rifle to fire the .223 Remington cartridge (the civilian nomenclature for the 5.56x45mm military round). This move was made at the behest of Steyr's American importer, Stoeger. Our sources believe that the high retail price was a major factor for the poor sales of the weapon. However, in 1969 work was begun on another 5.56x45mm caliber rifle that eventually would become known as the Armee Universal Gewehr or AUG.

In 1977 the Austrian Army adopted the new gun as the Stg-77 and production began late that same year. The Austrian army initially ordered 80,000 AUGs, but the cost to the Austrian government was indexed to inflation, which was approximately 3 per-

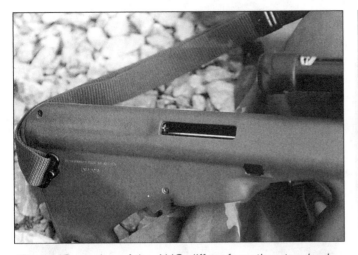

The LMG version of the AUG differs from the standard version in that it fires from an open bolt. The standard AUG fires from a closed bolt. The open-bolt modification was made to lessen concerns over ammunition cook-off and excessive chamber temperatures.

The gun seen in these photos was supposedly one of only two such AUG LMGs allowed into the United States. The stock is marked with the appropriate markings to distinguish it from the standard AUG rifle.

cent at the time of the contract. Later as export sales grew, inflation also grew and cost differences changed. This came back to bite Steyr in the butt, so to speak, when it tried to sell the Austrian government its pistol design.

It seems Steyr was selling the AUG to the Austrian government for approximately 12,000 schillings per gun, while at the same time exporting it to countries like Indonesia for only 7000 schillings. Austrian Army proof inspectors discovered this price difference and raised the factory roof!

The contract was valid, but those in the Austrian Army were angry over Steyr's huge profit. The next Austrian military contract was for a new pistol, and while Steyr wasn't officially frozen out of the bidding for the new handgun, it seemed to many at Steyr that a new contender was heavily favored. "Glock won the pistol contract," James says.

Although the Steyr AUG is now more than 25 years old, it is at first glance one of the most futuristic looking military rifles ever created. It is a modular rifle in that it is made of four main groups of components. They are (1) the barrel group, (2) the receiver group, (3) the stock or butt group, and (4) the magazine.

"One of the key design parameters of the AUG is the ease with which barrels of different lengths can be quickly and easily interchanged," James believes. "With the easily changeable barrels, this 5.56mm rifle can be converted into a submachine gun, a carbine, an assault rifle, a sniper rifle or a light machinegun. The barrels were constructed by cold hammer forging and the bores and chamber were chrome-plated for increased barrel life and endurance. Each AUG barrel features eight machined lugs at the chamber end for engaging the corresponding barrel extension within the receiver."

The barrels that provide this type of utility are of the following lengths: 14 inches, 16 inches, 20 inches, and 24 inches. The last is a bipod-mounted heavy bar-

rel configuration. The barrels feature six land-and-groove rifling, with a twist rate of one turn in 9 inches. An optional barrel with a twist rate of one turn in 7 inches for the SS109 ammunition was also available.

Each barrel featured an external sleeve sweated onto it that contained the gas port, piston, cylinder, gas regulator and vertical foregrip assembly. The foregrip assembly allowed the operator to change barrels without touching hot metal when the barrel became fouled. The foregrip could be folded forward on all but the shortest barrel because that would put the operator's fingers directly in front of the muzzle. "A definite safety hazard," James says.

The aluminum alloy receiver comprised the receiver group; it took 28 machine operations to cut and shape this part. After machining was completed, the alloy receiver was coated with a baked-enamel finish. A carrying handle and optical sight were integral on all AUG models, save the HBAR and the light machinegun variants.

The integral 1.5X scope sight was manufactured by Swarovski and was designed for target engagements from zero to 300 meters. The military reticle also could be used for range estimation, because at 300 meters, a standing soldier would just fit inside the black aiming ring in the center of the reticle. The law enforcement version featured a small black dot in the center of the aiming ring.

The scope sight was adjustable for windage and elevation corrections to 300 meters. In case of fogging, the top of the scope tube featured an emergency – but crude – iron sight system, which had been fitted with tritium luminous dots for use in low-light situations (one dot at the front, two on either side of the rear U-notch).

Austrian military tests demonstrated the 1.5X scope sight provided improved hit potential during low-light engagements when compared to the conventional iron sights found on other combat rifles. The heavy-barreled rifle and light machinegun versions of the AUG lacked the integral 1.5X scope and

All AUG rifles feature an adjustable gas regulator. It is a three-position device with one position (small dot on gas cylinder) for normal operation. A second setting (large dot on the gas cylinder) is for adverse conditions or extreme fouling and a third position is for firing blank cartridges or launching rifle grenades.

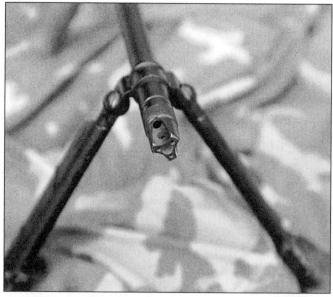

The AUG LMG features a rather complicated looking flash suppressor at the muzzle of the barrel. This piece is machined from solid steel and the outside threads are there for installation of a blank firing device.

instead featured an integral mount accepting any NATO night-vision equipment or telescopic sight.

A steel extension was fitted to the rear of the barrel and it contained the locking recesses for the bolt carrier and barrel. This barrel extension was held in place by two thin-walled steel tubes that also served as bearing points for the bolt carrier's guide rods.

The AUG is a select-fire, gas-operated weapon, but the bolt carrier and bolt head design borrow heavily from the Stoner system as seen in the M-16. Seven locking lugs are positioned on the rotary bolt with an eighth lug found on the extractor. The bolt is rotated by action of the cam-pin in the cam-way positioned atop the bolt carrier.

The bolt carrier can be manually retracted during loading and clearance drills by activation of the cock-

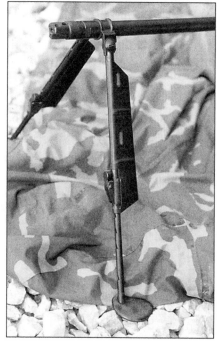

The HBAR and LMG bipod for the AUG is well designed, robust and substantial. It is adjustable for height and can be swung back alongside the barrel to keep it out of the way.

ing handle on the left side of the receiver. A forward bolt-assist mechanism is operated by engaging a small button located on top of the cocking handle.

Depressing this button and pushing the cocking handle forward allowed the operator to stealthily load the chamber and push the bolt head into battery without the noise associated with the M-16 or the AK-47.

The twin rods supporting the bolt carrier serve multiple functions. The right-hand rod works the bolt carrier by channeling the energy driving the gas piston. The left-hand rod serves as the cocking handle; its tip also contains a device for cleaning the gas cylinder.

One of the main advantages of the Steyr AUG was the fact that the stock of the weapon encloses just about everything. The stock was also available in three colors: military green, black for U.S. law enforcement and desert tan for the Saudi armed forces. It is comprised of two plastic halves that are joined through a unique process developed by Steyr that involved pressure, vibration and friction fit.

The trigger guard is actually a full-size handguard so that shooting with a heavy glove in cold weather poses no difficulty. The safety is a cross-bolt affair found above and slightly behind the trigger. Safe is the far-right position, while Fire is the far-left position. The takedown latch that resembles the cross-bolt safety in appearance and operation is located further to the rear of the cross-bolt safety.

The magazine well is positioned at the bottom of the stock, just behind the cross-bolt takedown latch. The magazine release latch is behind the mag well and, while it can be operated with either hand, it can be difficult to reload the gun when it is mounted to the shoulder.

At the rear of the stock is the buttplate, which provides access to the boxed hammer mechanism and a

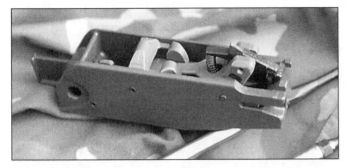

The hammer mechanism for the AUG is contained within a small plastic open-top box. It is accessible after removing the buttplate. It removes and installs easily and without special tools.

small cleaning kit. Removal of the rear sling swivel releases the buttplate from the stock.

The Steyr AUG contains two ejection ports, one on each side of the stock and one ejection port cover," James says. "For reasons that should be plainly evident to anyone attempting to fire this rifle, the ejection port cover must be installed correctly to prevent possible injury to the shooter in the event of a malfunction. Even then it is scant protection when one understands the operating pressures of a typical military 5.56x45mm cartridge."

The hammer mechanism is contained within a small box and most of the components were manufactured from plastic except for the springs, pins, the drop safety and the lock-bolt latch. Even the hammer was plastic, but testing by Steyr indicated the hammer mechanism would withstand more than 100,000 firing cycles before failure.

The magazine – with exception of the follower spring – is also made entirely of polymer compounds. The magazine is transparent so the operator could see the rounds left in the magazine. The body of the magazine tube features a waffle pattern for increased

The AUG rifle is a modular rifle comprised of four main components: the barrel group, the receiver (including the bolt carrier and bolt head as well as the scope mounted atop the receiver), the stock or body group (this includes the hammer mechanism and buttplate seen here) and the magazine.

strength. Two magazines are available for the AUG; one holds 30 rounds while the second was developed for the light machinegun version and holds 42 rounds.

After the last round is fired from the magazine, the bolt locks open. Upon reloading a fresh magazine, the operator has to retract the cocking handle to release the bolt; there is no release tab for the bolt hold-open device.

"In terms of its engineering, there is little question the Austrian produced Steyr AUG was a masterpiece of original thinking and manufacturing excellence, but the important question is how good was this rifle in the field?" James asks.

The AUG stock is plastic and comprised of two halves. It was available in at least three colors: military green, black for law enforcement and desert tan for the armed forces of Saudi Arabia.

The twin rods supporting the bolt carrier serve multiple functions. The right-hand rod works the bolt carrier by channeling the energy that drives the gas piston. The left-hand rod serves the cocking handle and also contains on its top a device for cleaning the gas cylinder.

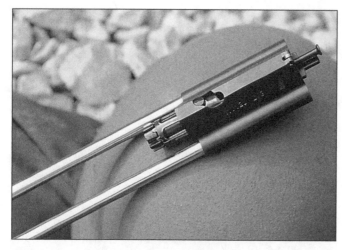

The bolt carrier and bolt head design for the AUG borrows heavily from the Gene Stoner-designed M-16. Seven locking lugs are positioned on the rotary bolt with an eighth lug found on the extractor. The rotary bolt is rotated by action of the cam pin in the cam-way positioned atop the bolt carrier.

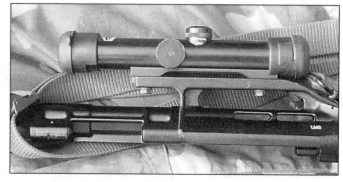

The standard AUG rifle sports an integral 1.5X scope sight, but the HBAR and LMG versions of the AUG lack the integral scope and instead feature an integral mount accepting any NATO standardized night-vision equipment or telescopic sight.

The select-fire AUG does not have a selector lever like the M-16 or the AK-47, as full-auto fire was achieved with a complete pull-through of the trigger. The AUG trigger was a two-stage affair, with the first stage being semi-auto, while the latter half of the trigger movement activated full-auto fire.

"On the semi-auto versions sold to the American civilian sporting arms market before the importation ban was enacted in 1989, the trigger pulls can only be described as lousy," James says. "They are terrible in terms of a precise feel, or exact movement. Although openly acknowledged as an accurate semi-auto military-origin rifle, many shooters will not attribute any of the resulting accuracy of this rifle to a good trigger.

"In terms of quick-reaction drills with the select-fire version, personal observation leaves one to question and criticize the lack of a definite selector lever on the AUG. More often than not, when faced with a pop-up short-range target (less than 35 yards), the average shooter is unable to smoothly engage the trigger for a single shot at the target. Instead, he tends to jerk the trigger hard and pull through to full-auto fire, whereupon the rifle climbs off the target – if it was on the target in the first place! This is because less experienced shooters have trouble locating short-range targets quickly through the scope sight when compared against more traditional rifles employing iron sights."

Steyr did make a concession on the issue of the select-fire activation because there was a later version of the Steyr AUG that had the cross-bolt safety converted to act as both a safety and a selector with positions for both semi-auto-only fire and full-auto fire.

"That said, it should be noted the majority of the AUGs in service feature the two-position selective trigger," James points out.

He adds, "The greatest difficulty, though, with the AUG lies with the tactical use of any bullpup rifle.

The British soon discovered to their chagrin in Northern Ireland that a bullpup is impossible to use tactically from cover when shooting left-barricade."

Because the gun must be shot from the right shoulder due to the ejection of spent cases, the operator cannot switch shoulders while using cover and engage a target with minimal exposure.

"If forced to fire around the left side of a building corner or any type of barricade, the right-handed operator must lean all the way out, exposing his entire body before bringing the gun on target. Conversely, the left-handed shooter with a left-handed AUG has the same difficulty around a right-hand corner," James explains.

"Experienced British troops equipped with right-handed bullpup rifles soon refused to patrol the right side of the street in built-up areas, because they knew if they came under fire, they would have to expose themselves openly to snipers before returning defensive or offensive fire," James notes.

The original thinking on bullpup rifles focused solely on the problem with right- and left-handed operators, not on the tactical development of these weapons. The argument ran that for left-handed shooters, the gun could be converted over to left-handed operation, but that ignored the tactical difficulty when operating in urban areas.

Additionally, it totally ignores the problem of what happens when guns get switched between right- and left-handed operators. If a squad of infantry equipped with these rifles takes a break in darkness, then comes under fire, and a right-handed shooter mistakenly grabs a left-handed rifle to return fire, injury results. The velocity of the ejected case against the face is more than sufficient to remove several teeth as well as create significant facial trauma. This is not conducive to building morale within the fighting unit.

A counter argument is that all shooters using rifles and carbines during hostile engagements should keep the gun on their strong shoulder regardless of which barricade position they use to respond to incoming fire.

The AUG barrels were cold hammer forged and the bores and chambers were chrome-plated for increased barrel life and endurance. Each barrel features eight machined lugs at the chamber end for engagement with the corresponding barrel extension within the receiver.

Under the watchful eye of a Steyr corporate executive, Frank James works with the 9x19mm-caliber submachine gun conversion of the basic AUG rifle. The AUG design allowed not only easy conversion of barrel lengths, but caliber conversions as well.

"During completion of an urban rifle course at Thunder Ranch, instructor Clint Smith revealed it was his experience that only two out of a hundred shooters could transition a rifle or carbine from one shoulder to the other smoothly and without difficulty," James reports.

But could the lack of skill at this task be more an indicator of poor motivation? Incoming fire will motivate most operators to seek cover and make the maximum use of it in a firefight. Any rifle design that forces the operator to expose himself before engagement is working with a serious handicap for any tactical environment.

The AUG has many admirers who loudly tout its accuracy and innovative engineering deπsign; unfortunately few of them are Australian soldiers.

After extensive trials, Australia selected the AUG as the 5.56x45mm rifle to replace its 7.62 NATO FAL rifles. Adopted as the F-88, the Australian AUG has demonstrated a number of problems like cracked and broken magazines, broken cocking handles, and excessive wear from frequent removal of the barrels, according to published reports.

The government of Thailand tested the Australian AUG and quickly eliminated it from the trials when it failed their mud and water testing.

Among the complaints from the individual Australian trooper is the allegation the cross-bolt safety catch is improperly protected and can be accidentally moved to the Fire position. Published reports are unclear if this was the reason that there were 26 accidental discharges of F-88 rifles by Australian troops while stationed in Somalia.

It also is alleged that many of the Aussie AUG magazine springs have had an excessive amount of axial twist, forcing the follower to rub against the magazine wall. This results in rounds falling freely from the magazine. There were so many defects with the Australian AUG rifles that New Zealand refused to accept 8000 of them until a significant number of problems had been corrected.

In the United States, the semi-auto pre-ban Steyr AUG has approached cult status. Prices for guns in good condition (and with spare magazines) range from $3500 to $4000 per gun. American competition shooters have tried a number of tricks to improve the trigger pull. Once a competitor explained how he actually boiled the plastic hammer in order to get it soft enough to bend.

"American shooters often use aerosol automotive brake cleaners to clean particularly dirty firearms, but another report stated some competitors have found certain cleaning solvents will dissolve the synthetic AUG magazine. Now, wouldn't that be fun to have your expensive pre-ban 42-round magazine simply disappear?"

Is the Steyr AUG, a silk purse or a sow's ear? The question has already been answered in one respect, because the Steyr firm is no longer functioning. In James' opinion, bullpup rifles using conventional ammunition are and were a failed idea. Future designs employing unconventional ammunition that don't require an ejection port, however, could prove to be a totally different proposition. Still, for the present, a number of American sport shooters continue to view this sow's ear as a valuable silk purse.

CHAPTER 8

HIRAM MAXIM'S LEGACY

The Machinegun He Designed Changed the World and Is Still in Battle Use!

FEW WEAPONS TRULY changed the whole world, but Hiram Maxim's great designs rearranged the whole shape and nature of battlefields and of warfare. His was the very first really successful machinegun, using kinetic energy rather than muscle power to accelerate rate of fire. If there were any doubts when the British subdued colonials with the invention in the 1880s, the soldiers of 1914 quickly came to know how foolish it was to attempt a Napoleonic advance against these water-cooled demons.

In December 2001, author Jim Thompson was grinding away on a new book series. Concerning the first truly successful machineguns, he had just written: "Alas, Maxim's brainchild is no longer seen on the modern battlefield." He looked up to see a CNN tape byte of an Afghani Northern Alliance fighter pumping rounds out of what was unmistakably an old Soviet/Russian Maxim, complete with its wheeled Sokolov mount.

A product of the 19th century, it appears that this eldest of old soldiers has not yet belched its last.

Maxim Principles

Maxim was an American born in Maine, but his gun was developed primarily in and for the European market. As late as the first decade and a half of the 20th century, American authorities were convinced there was no need for fast-firing automatic guns, and took great pains to belittle Maxim and his guns.

"Navies saw this differently," Thompson's research shows. Their expensive, elaborate new warships were

In early fighting in the winter of 1914, Maxims were highly effective. This German unit is preparing for an advance under the cover of a well-concealed MG.8.

Early commercial Maxims sported wood rollers on their feed groups and beautifully fitted bronze water jackets. This M.1887 Maxim was Russian-produced and had been rebuilt several times.

under threat from fast, steam-powered torpedo boats and they wanted to spew out projectiles to stop them. As a result, guns in calibers from half-inch to four-inch poured from factories all over the world.

Thompson says, "Later, they would be turned skyward to deal with another threat, this one in a vertical dimension. The airplanes might fire back with their own Maxims, trying to kill the crews of the heavy 'pom-pom' guns. Maxim's guns were an eventual success and still are considered marvelous studies in engineering."

Maxim saw the pressure and recoil of a fired cartridge as a source of energy being wasted. Based upon this thinking, he devised a rotating cam and breaking toggle, the function of which was similar to that of the human knee – to absorb and spread shock, control the recoil mechanism and provide a sure, steady path, as the action reciprocated.

In the Luger (P.O8 Parabellum) pistol, this action can be seen right out in the open, but in the Maxim machinegun, it is all contained in the huge, deep receiver. Based upon the inventor's 1885 design, all later Maxim variations utilized ignition to lock together the cartridge, breech and barrel. These move rearward a short distance, moderated and reciprocated by a sturdy fusee spring which normally is housed on the receiver's left.

With the bolt fully back and the mechanism opened, the extended fusee reverses the thrust, thus re-initiating the cycle. The robust feed group and the cam-controlled lock control cartridge timing and feed.

In various Maxims and the later Vickers guns, shortening the recoil stroke and polishing parts were used to speed up the guns. Feed and bolt control were handled by the robust activator or charging handle. Positioned on the right rear of the receiver, this handle moved with considerable thrust as the gun operated.

According to Thompson, "Novices unfamiliar with the Maxim –regardless of where made or used – are often bewildered by the long list of stoppage causes listed in the manuals. However, what these really reflect is the excellent engineering and research

behind the guns. If maintenance is done properly, especially with modern pan-thermic greases, a Maxim almost never stops firing, unless ammunition becomes the problem."

The Maxim machinegun entered military consciousness about the same time that the use of black powder was being phased out. Several families of so-called smokeless powders were in use by 1890. One of these was the cordite family of British powders.

"This is a nitrocellulose product formed in strips or strands that resemble miniature pieces of chewing gum or bits of string in varying thickness and lengths," Thompson explains. "Almost no one but the British used cordite for very long and even they had abandoned the erosive stuff for most uses by the late 1940s, so those mentions of cordite fumes in most of today's junk novels are hogwash."

Nonetheless, these new low-smoke propellants meant the new automatic weapons would not generate as much smoke or accumulate the ugly tars of powder fouling which would have made the machinegun a ridiculous field item just a few years earlier.

"Stop and consider for a moment," Thompson suggests. "At almost exactly the same time the Earps and the Clantons were engaging in their shenanigans half a world away in Tombstone, Ariz., another American was demonstrating a firearm that fired at a reliable 350-450 rounds per minute. This was the demonstration that would change the shape of the battlefield and, ultimately, the whole 20th century."

For some time, though, Maxim's mechanized concoction was viewed as a silly novelty item. The prophets of European warfare were convinced that only lesser colonial types – that is, the "barbarians" – would be much impressed by all the rounds popping off. Quality Euro-

By 1918, twin Maxim LMG.08/15 guns featuring ventilated jackets were being installed on the Kaiser's D.XII fighter planes. The setup offered 700 rounds per minute from each gun.

This is the left side-plate of a standard German GM.08 of 1916 vintage. Visible are the grips, feed, fuse cover and optics.

In 1904, the U.S. ordered Vickers-Maxim .30 caliber machineguns that were produced in England and by Colt in the United States. About 1475 were produced by both makers.

pean cavalry and infantry, the pundits insisted, would simply ignore such ridiculous noisemakers. Besides, such a gun would surely suck up an entire army's ammunition supply very quickly. European officers of rank were certain the machinegun was just another silly fad. American officers were not even that kind.

"Actually, had some of the original tactical designs stayed as static as they were, the higher-ups might have been close to correct," Thompson concedes. "But the gun's original huge high mounts were trimmed so that by 1912, most combat Maxims could be deployed just inches above the surrounding turf, and moved by quick-carry techniques or simply by dragging. The mounts almost all weighed at least 30 pounds and virtually all the guns more than 40 pounds without water. The bronze water jackets, fancy furniture and hardwood rollers disappeared. By the turn of the 19th century and into the 20th century, the guns began to look more subdued. The modern term is stealthy!"

Rejected in his own country, Maxim eventually acquired British citizenship. Vickers, Nordenfeldt

Even before World War I, navies were using the 37mm Maxim-Nordenfeldt pom-pom gun produced in England around 1890. On a revised mount, it was used against enemy aircraft during World War II. Rate of fire was 250 to 300 rounds per minute.

and others gunmakers produced his guns in great quantities and the orders poured in. "By 1910 or so, every nation on this planet owned Maxim guns and they had become standard in most countries," according to Thompson's research. The guns were manufactured in England, Turkey, Finland, Russia, China, Austria and even the United States, among many other places. Czarist Russia tested the guns almost as soon as prototypes were available.

One sometimes reads that Russia began producing Maxim guns around 1900. However, a Tula-made machine that was produced about 1889 existed in the National Firearms Museum near Phoenix, founded by oil heir Doug Champlin. The former property of an Arizona-based soldier of fortune, Col. Russell Burnham, the gun had been rebuilt many times and upgraded. Near the end of its service life, it apparently had been chambered for some large rimless cartridge. Conjecture is that it probably was rechambered for the early 8x64 Brenneke Schwere. This was an early high-velocity round in today's magnum ballistics category.

This ancient machine originally sported a bronze fusee cover and jacket, with a very tight fit to the receiver. Disassembled, it was amazing to note the quality of parts and fit. Most of the major assemblies hold concentricity and parallelism to tolerances of less than one-thousandth of an inch.

"Highly polished parts were like glass," says Thompson, who had an opportunity to inspect the aged Maxim. "At the time of its production, such weapons cost easily $1,000 with accessories. In that era, a Colt Single Action revolver could be purchased for around $22!"

The concepts of redundant strength – more than necessary – and spreading stress made the Maxim what it was and is. How brilliant Maxim was can be experienced first-hand by simply tearing down a Maxim, remembering that this is the fountainhead of all modern firearms design. There had been nothing like it before and everything afterwards has copied principles Maxim pioneered. He held well over a hundred patents, only a third of which were related to firearms.

The Maxim Goes to War

The Maxim had been used by colonial powers to cut up local insurrectionists for at least 20 years before the Russo-Japanese war of 1904-1905 saw both sides deploy the Maxim. By then, the Japanese were equipping most infantry units with air-cooled guns, but still used their ample supplies of Maxims on both land and sea.

In World War I that the Maxim came into its own as a serious weapon of war. Dug in and sighted for overlapping, deep crossfire patterns, the Germans used the Maxim to its greatest effect to change the terminology and tactics of warfare forever. By 1914, the Russians were on their second generation of issue Maxims. While their gun was every bit the equal of the German MG.08, their tactics, planning and leadership were extremely poor.

While the greatest killer of men in World War I was artillery fire, it was the machinegun – mainly the Maxim and its spin-off, the Vickers – that confined soldiers to static positions where they could be mauled by heavy shells.

"The whole language of warfare changed," Thompson points out. Terms like "no man's land" and "over the top", with all the dread and horror they inferred, entered the language.

"Water-cooling of machineguns was always controversial," Thompson reports. "Like the radiator in a car, steam is generated. If a water supply is not convenient, then the light barrels are restricted to short bursts. But if the barrels can be kept cool, a murderous rate of fire can be sustained, many times in excess of what is possible with air-cooled weapons. Barrel changes are more cumbersome, but are less frequent, especially if the water can be kept cold," he adds.

Air-cooling, incidentally, is actually merely the reduction of temperature by time, patience and fire discipline.

A huge water port was added to the Russian version of the Maxim in 1910. Ice and snow could be packed into the jacket, greatly reducing barrel temperature and thus prolonging barrel life. Water-cooling systems and the attendant jackets also increase barrel rigidity.

"With good ammunition all Maxims – and this includes Swiss, Argentine, American, British, German and even Russian guns – are capable of bewildering accuracy and most fire slowly enough that shots can be individually aimed," notes Thompson.

"The huge jacket and the clearance between the thrust line of sights and barrel assure that muzzle blast virtually never interferes with the sight picture," he adds.

As might be expected, Maxims require quality ammunition for best function – and the ammunition must be powerful. Loads of 20 percent or so below published maximum levels often cause jams; oil in the chamber can cause hydraulic seizures and case separations.

"Because our troops faced them in combat, the most famous Maxim to Americans has been the big German MG.08 on its hefty sled mount and its lightweight spin-off, the MG.08/15. The latter was developed at Spandau as a light machinegun and later adapted to specialized aircraft use," explains Thompson.

At 39 pounds without water, the MG.08/15 was never really light. However, it was produced at many factories. Eventually the receiver was trimmed and the Germans discovered – as Maxim had long ago

This much-tortured Maxim SPS M.1910 was captured from the Japanese in Manila in 1944 after being subjected to numerous bullets and even a flamethrower. Sights had been blown off the gun during the action.

This is the right side view of an MG.8/15 light machinegun, with the condensation can and optics. Possibly the most complete example in the world, this gun is in a private collection.

surmised – that muzzle boosting by gas recapture and careful polishing of the breech mechanism and lock could greatly accelerate rate of fire.

World War II Maxims

"The Maxim was too cumbersome and heavy for World War II, the Germans decided, and they were specifically forbidden to produce the guns under the terms of the Versailles Treaty," according to Thompson's findings. "The Soviets, Finns, Chinese and many others, however, had committed to the gun long since and had well-developed logistics behind the system."

Finnish guns were manufactured in many countries and were comprised of what they called the Models 09, 21 and 32. Also in their inventory, frequently remarked "SA" (Suomi Armee), were many captured Russian Maxims as well as surplus purchased from all

The defector-plate muzzle device was designed to seal off the gun's accelerator and offer some protection from the "dazzle effect" of night firing.

This is a typical German MG.08/15 light machinegun with the ammunition drum mounted. Note the sling for carrying. In the box are two additional loaded drums.

over the world. All of the Finnish guns were in the Soviet loading, 7.62x54R. This round is often called the 7.62x53, also correct, depending upon how one measures the rim and crimp.

Many Czarist-produced – and even export and "contract" – Maxims from the English and Austrian manufacturers were used in World War II and much later. In fact, in the Korean War, the SPM Maxim was still the standard light machinegun of the Chinese and North Korean forces. They also were a fairly common capture in Vietnam.

The Chinese had produced Maxims of many patterns, but the Model 24 was a standardized gun, based upon a combination of features and fittings from Swiss and German prototypes. Virtually all were in the German 7.92x57 loading, including a wide variety of imported guns. Their standard tripod was the British type, rather than the Soviet Sokolov or German Sled style.

It should perhaps be noted that given a good supply of parts, most any rifle-calibered Maxim can be converted to just about any other standard rifle caliber without a great deal of work. With the various Mauser calibers, only the barrel need be changed. With the heavily rimmed Soviet, French and British cartridges, the extractor, lock and feed groups must be altered or changed out.

The aforementioned is why so many used Maxims were sold all over the world in a variety of incarnations and calibers. However, the Model of 1910 Soviet Maxim was designed for Russian conditions and Russian soldiers. The guns straddled the most turbulent times in world history, including the Russian Revolution, yet changed very little in their 50 or so years of first-line service.

The Sokolov wheeled carriage was the most common mounting in Soviet service, but at least four other carriages were produced, including the lightweight Goryunov-style assembly found on a gun captured from the Japanese in Manila during World War II. This carriage apparently had been repaired and reconfigured by welding with parts from an old Sokolov apparatus.

Invariably, westerners tend to criticize the wheeled mounts. However, as is clearly shown in World War II photographs taken on the Soviet Front, the skids or locked wheels allowed the gun to be hauled around like a child's wagon, rather than lugged on the back or shoulder. This was particularly convenient in mud or snow, common in the eight- or nine-month winters of the Russian north. The Finns liked the Soviet mounts, too, and improvised their own or used what they captured.

The ultimate deployment of the SPM or Sokolov Pulemyot Mazima OBR 1910 GODA (its full Soviet designation) was in 1943, at the greatest armored battle in history. The Soviets knew what was coming at Kursk and they set up firetraps. These efforts were fully the equal of anything the Germans had contrived in World War I, perhaps better, and surely deeper, up to 4000 meters, with artillery and anti-tank guns pre-registered over every meter. The death toll was horrendous and many of the finest German units were simply written off, having been completely wiped out.

During this engagement, the Soviet Maxim said to be deadly at two miles, made the claim a proven fact. The German secret weapons and their vaunted blitzkrieg tactics simply brought them death in wholesale lots. German infantry casualties may have been as much as 10 times higher than those of the defenders.

"Parenthetically, it is worth noting that almost every European army involved in World War II used the light Maxim," Thompson points out. "In modified form, it became an antiaircraft gun and the Soviets at Kursk used thousands of them, in multiple mounts of four, for low-flying aircraft defense.

"By then, the Maxim was already old, some even said senile, but it was literally match accurate and supremely reliable. The Goryunov M-43 series, designed specifically to replace the Maxims, never really did until some 20 years after World War II.

"Based upon current conditions, perhaps the Maxim's job is not quite yet done," Thompson concludes.

CHAPTER 9

OF ARMOR AND VESTS

Such Protective Means Are Almost as Old as Warfare Itself, but They Are Getting Better

YEARS AGO, IN the heyday of the pulp fiction magazines, such folk heroes as The Shadow were reputed to wear bulletproof vests that saved them from all sorts of destructive efforts up to and including artillery barrages.

"As youngsters, we heard talk of Melvyn Purvis and his G-men capturing or slaying such outlaws as John Dillinger, Pretty Boy Floyd and Baby Face Nelson," Lewis recalls. "Some of those lawless types were reputed to wear what were called bulletproof

The scene is a combat area called Bunker Hill on the Korean front. The time was the early 1950s. During a lull in the battle, none of the U.S. Marines involved removed the armored vests that were being issued in those days. They had saved countless lives.

vests, but the fact that most of them died in a hail of lead pretty well proves there was no such animal in those days." Supposedly the FBI agents involved were wearing similar body protection – and some of them died, too.

For what it's worth, there is no such animal these days either. There is protective armor that can be worn to help stop a bullet, but just the shock of being hit by a projectile traveling at 1,000 feet per second or so is enough to kill some people. Even with a vest, if one is struck in the chest area by a .45 ACP bullet, he probably is going to be sent buttocks over the proverbial teakettle. It is going to take time for this individual to decide he isn't dead, just hurting a lot. He may even have some broken ribs. It has happened.

Body armor is thought of as being a more or less modern creation. However, virtually from the time ancient men began to battle each other, there have been efforts to dull the blows from an enemy's weapon. For centuries, the Japanese Samurai protected themselves with wooden armor; later came the Knights of the Crusades and similar actions with their metal armor that was so heavy it often required a crude crane to raise the knight into his saddle. It was the English longbowmen, who created bows and arrows that could puncture this type of protection.

"Armor has been used sporadically by lawmen for more than 100 years," points out Robert K. Campbell, who has made a study of such protective gear. "There are those who claim that Wyatt Earp's tightly woven silk vest was a type of body armor, but little proof exists to support this theory. The premise, however, is not far removed from the construction of the modern Kevlar vest. Against typical black powder cartridges of Earp's day, a tightly woven vest might work reasonably well, but not against the full-power .45 ACP cartridge or Plus-P rounds of this day and age."

The assassinations of President Garfield, then President McKinley spurred efforts to create some type of protection for the torso. An attack on President Theodore Roosevelt failed because a thick pad of papers in a pocket stopped the small-caliber bullet fired at him. Handguns of that era were mostly pocket pistols that fired low-velocity lead bullets. It didn't take much resistance to stop them. However, the prohibitive cost of such vests – more than $1,000 by today's standards – tended to stifle development.

It is a reality that mobsters used bulletproof vests during the 1920s and 1930s," Campbell states, "but little is known of their construction. Several patent applications for body armor are on record as having been filed in the period between our two world wars. The flak jacket worn by some troops during World War II was large, bulky and suited best to stopping shell fragments. Army Air Corps gunners invariably were outfitted with such jackets. This vest, however, was not effective in stopping bullets from rifles and machineguns."

Despite those shortcomings, an earnest effort was made during World War II to develop lightweight, wearable body armor. A shortage of metal resulted in the development of high-grade non-metallic materials. One such effort was a combination of nylon and fiberglass that came to be known as Doron. The name of this material came from the surname of Army Brig. Gen. Georges F. Doriot, then chief of the U.S Army's Military Planning Division.

The Air Corps and the Navy both were working on light armor for aircraft application. Early contributors to the ongoing research were Dow Chemical, Hercules Powder, American Cyanamid, Monsanto, Bakelite, Firestone, Westinghouse, Formica, Continental Diamond and United States Rubber.

The result was an armored jacket that utilized Doron. Among the first demonstrations was one involving a pair of U.S. Navy lieutenant commanders. One of them, Andrew Paul Webster, fired a .45 caliber bullet at Lyman Corey. The vest stopped the bullet and impressed onlookers. Development proceeded quickly enough that Doron armor was used in the closing months of the war in the Pacific.

As is usually the case with warlike projects, experimentation faded with the Japanese surrender. However, one important change was made when construction of the Doran plates was switched from flat to a curved surface. The Korean War saw more than 90,000 vests being used in the combat zone, saving many lives.

"Front line troops probably gave the Doron vest more credit than it deserved at the time," Lewis suggests. "It so highly regarded that Marines I saw were cutting up vests that had been discarded because they had suffered bullet damage. These men were attempting to make sets of shorts out of the old vests, thus protecting the family jewels in a minefield and in similar combat situations."

There also is an old Marine Corps legend that has been handed down over the past half century concerning early experiments by the Leatherneck service. It seems that the brass had accepted an armored vest for Marines and wanted to show it off to the press. They arranged for a demonstration at the Marine Corps Base at Quantico, Va., just south of the nation's capital.

A Marine volunteer stood up in front of the crowd, while a top Corps marksman shot his vest with a Colt .45 ACP pistol. The round knocked the man down, but a couple of photographers didn't get what they wanted. They asked for a repeat performance.

The volunteer dutifully took his place once more and the marksman took aim. The problem was that he aimed at the same exact spot where his first bullet had gone. The second bullet pierced the material and killed the volunteer. Apparently, the first bullet had fractured the life-saving material in the vest and the second bullet had passed through the weakened area.

"I cannot vouch for the truth of this incident," Lewis says. "I've heard the story repeated for at least half a century. The man who was reported to be the officer in charge of the demonstration – now a retired colonel – is an acquaintance of mine and he swears it never happened. Others swear it did."

Following the Korean hostilities, development of advanced protective vests was more or less stalled until the 1970s, when more than $3 million was scheduled for research by the National Institute for

Justice, with both the Edgewood Arsenal and the Aberdeen Proving Ground being involved.

"Originally, the police-oriented vests were designed to stop .32- and .38-caliber bullets," Campbell says. "Those calibers were the most common threat in those days. Today, vests are rated to stop .38-caliber bullets with 90 percent certainty and a less than 10 percent chance of surgery being needed. Vests offering an even greater degree of resistance are quickly becoming popular."

Vests currently being marketed are proofed against the 9mm Luger bullet, the .45 ACP and even the more powerful .357 Magnum handgun cartridge. There also are several types that will stop rifle bullets, but such vests are heavy and a working police officer is not likely to feel comfortable wearing one under his uniform.

"Ammunition testing has shown that modern vests do indeed work as designed," Campbell claims. "Depending upon the angle of bullet travel, some will stop a more powerful round that we would expect.'"

With the development of light, wearable body armor, military ammunition has been developed to pierce such protective cover. Some of this ammunition also has been developed for the express purpose of penetrating vehicle bodies and light cover. Still, it is accepted that body armor is a consideration that should not be ignored. It has been found in actual combat that even a soldier's web gear and weapons sometimes provide a considerable obstacle to enemy bullets and flak.

"Such bullets are manufactured with a steel core and are known as penetrator bullets," Campbell explains. "These seldom reach the hands of common criminals, but many of the terrorist groups operating around the globe have access to the weapons of what once was the Soviet Union. During the Cold War, the Russians sponsored many terrorist organizations including Germany's Baader Meinhof Gang, the Palestinian Liberty Organization and others.

"The Soviets also used the slaying talents of the infamous Moscow-trained assassin, Carlos the Jackal. When Carlos killed two Surete agents in Paris, the penetration of his CZ 52 pistol was such that the bullets that killed each officer continued on to penetrate several walls in the apartment building where the slaying took place. Soviet-bloc weapons still remain the most common of the terrorists' arms."

Armor-piercing or even standard steel-core ammunition runs a poor second these days to much of the modern steel-core bullets, most of them coming from Russia.

"One of the most fearsome cartridges – one with which I've had no personal experience – is said to be the 9.3x64mm Russian round. A bonus for most steel-core ammunition is that it often is very accurate," Campbell states. "Made to exacting standards for consistency, such a cartridge often exhibits more accuracy than standard match-grade ammo. Thus what we have is a race between vest development and bullet technology."

What we commonly refer to as bulletproof vests took a quantum leap under the direction of one Rich Davis, who developed the Second Chance vests. At the other extreme, it is not just the good guys who wear such equipment.

"Not long ago, one of our officers arrested a mule – a drug courier – who told us that some runners such

Today, Marines and Army personnel wear body armor as a matter of course. As one Marine put it, "It's like putting on your socks every morning."

Modern raid vests such as this style from Beverly Hills Body Armor are worn over the uniform and often carry a placard on the back identifying the wearer as a police officer.

A good example of a modern vest, this one is lightweight and can easily be worn beneath a uniform shirt. As noted in the text, the opening between the back and front panels can be dangerous, but this matter is being rectified.

as himself were wearing vests. As a result, my officers felt we should be loading armor-piercing rounds in our 9mm handguns," Campbell relates. "Considering the fact that some motorcycle outlaws and other bad guys have been found to wear such protection, we should be giving such a course serious consideration."

Statistics show that bulletproof vests have saved the lives of perhaps 3000 officers during the past 20 years, but it appears to be true that police officers and the baddies are in an equipment race. As an example, some street gangs have managed to make up crude but effective vests from radial automobile tires.

"There's no doubt this gear is effective," Campbell says. "Shoot into the sidewall of such a tire and the bullet will puncture it, but few will penetrate fully.

"But the well-heeled criminal can find vests elsewhere. Quite a few companies restrict sales to law enforcement personnel, while others will sell to anyone who has a clean record. That is as it should be, with numerous jurisdictions already adding penalties to those wearing a vest during a criminal action."

There are two basic types of vests in common use these days. One is what many call a flak vest. Similar to that issued to the military, this vest is worn in the open over other clothing. Special operators, SWAT teams and other special units most often wear this type of protective apparel. Some, but not all, of these vests will even halt a bullet from a high-power rifle.

The other type of vest can be worn under the uniform or even a shirt, offering some protection from handgun bullets.

There are many levels of vests and most are as light or as heavy as the wearer can handle. A Level IV armored vest that will stop a .30/06 bullet is heavy and hot. Level I is more comfortable and will stop most – but not all – pistol bullets. In between are the comfort and weight levels available to choice.

To clarify, the National Institute of Justice has divided bulletproof vests into several categories. Type I is listed as one that will stop edged weapons; Type IIA is soft and concealable; Type II is a heavier armor that can be concealed beneath a shirt, while Type III is a still heavier concealed armor. The Type IV vest is the type that uses ceramic and/or steel plates. Wearable body armor weighs from 7.8 to 11.2 ounces per square foot, with an obvious trade-off between protection and comfort. Level II can weigh as much as 15 ounces per square foot, for example.

"Davis is widely credited with developing wearable body armor," Campbell says, adding, "but such protection has been around for some time. I have always understood that the .357 Magnum and the .38 Super handgun cartridges were developed to combat motorized felons. However, a look at police museum displays and old photographs show quite a few heavy bulletproof vests. They look as though they could stop a .38 caliber bullet.

"Those early-day gangsters vests tend to resemble the quilted vests worn by the Chinese communist soldiers in the war in Korea. Not all of the Chinese had them and they certainly would not stop a .30/06 bullet, but they were issued in numbers. For the most part, these vests were from outdated technology using metal inserts for protection."

A number of companies ultimately began offering protective vests fashioned from tightly woven materi-

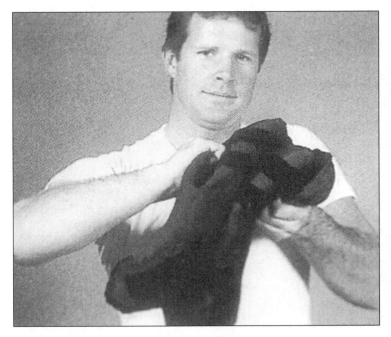

Bob Campbell has found that good body armor should be lightweight and made from a compressible material.

als related to the nylon family. Experience shows that such materials often would turn a bullet away or grip it, stopping its rotation and robbing it of velocity.

Davis' Second Chance vest is known as soft body armor. This was one of the first vests made of what now is called ballistic nylon. Davis used it to build a vest that can be concealed under street clothing or even a uniform.

"Davis has faith in his product," Campbell says. "Over the years, he has become famous in law enforcement circles for putting on one of his vests, then shooting himself. Other than a few bruises, he has survived. So have several hundred cops who have bought his vests."

Today, most vests are made of Kevlar, which is credited thus far with saving some 3000 officers from death or serious injury.

In attempting to handcuff a suspect, Campbell once suffered a rabbit punch to the kidneys that caused him to pass blood for two days. "It was painful and sickening," he recalls.

"When struck, I fell but took the subject to the ground with me. My vision was going gray as I drew my Combat Magnum. I knew if I lost consciousness I could not expect the subject to sing me a lullaby. I grasped the gun by the barrel and slammed the felon hard in the mouth. That did the business, but I was in pain for several days," Campbell says.

Later as a patrol lieutenant, Campbell became involved in a fight outside a local bar. "A two-by-four came swinging out of the darkness and I was struck in exactly the same place, but with much more force," he recalls.

"The piece of timber took the hammer and front sight off of my .44 Magnum revolver and made a deep impression in my vest. It was one of Rich Davis' circa

An undercover officer wears this jacket from Beverly Hills Body Armor. It is the jacket that is bulletproof in this case.

1978 models. The result could have been at least four times worse than the earlier naked blow had been. You don't have to be shot to appreciate body armor. In this case, the blow only made me angry!" Campbell says.

Recently, Campbell was given the opportunity to test Second Chance vests against some of the more powerful handgun ammunition available. In this test, he shot an actual vest, as well as samples that Davis sends those who are interested in his product. Campbell also fired on a large ceramic vest that had been declared surplus by a nearby nuclear facility. This was the type of vest worn by the Hollywood bandits several years ago, when they outgunned police officers.

On duty, Campbell found that the Second Chance vest is "friendly, comfortable, supple and works. I wore mine with a Kramer Confidant T-shirt/holster with a .40 S&W caliber Kahr backup. After a lot of use, the vest still is in fine condition."

Testing a vest identical to his own increased his confidence. "While rated to stop pistol bullets, I found that some rifle bullets would be stopped, if fired at a glancing angle.

"The big ceramic vest was impressive, too. I fired .223, .308 and even 7.62x19 Soviet rounds into it without any penetration. The ceramic plates were chipped a bit, but held up."

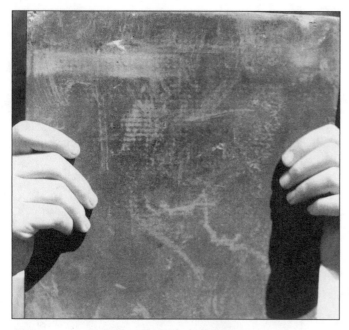

This is a ceramic insert that was utilized in the armored vest worn by a federal officer. Although it was marked up by gunfire, none of the bullets penetrated.

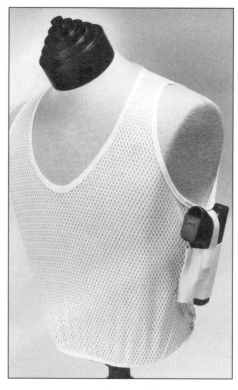

This lightweight shirt is surprisingly protective against pistol bullets. It also features an attached holster. It is the Confidant model and is favored by Officer Bob Campbell.

Directing parking during a change-of-command ceremony at an Army base, this military police officer is clad in combat-type body armor beneath the armored vest.

Although dressed in informal fashion, these officers are equipped with duty belts and firearms as well as the lightweight armored vests hidden beneath their polo shirts.

There have been incidents in which officers have been killed when a bullet penetrated the body through the small open section in each side of some types of vests. Modern law enforcement teams are adopting vests or fillers that cover such vulnerable areas.

"When choosing a vest, be certain it is comfortable in action," Campbell advises. "More than one user has worn a vest for a time, then discovered he could not hit or punch with his fist while wearing it. Others found they could not hold a firearm in the normal Weaver stance. Being certain the vest fits properly can be a life and death situation."

In his tests of the Second Chance vest and the samples provided, Campbell found that the material stopped bullets in calibers such as the .38 Special, 9mm Luger, .40 Smith & Wesson, .357 Magnum, .41 Magnum, .44 Magnum and the venerable .45 ACP.

In the majority of cases, the bullets penetrated no more than four layers of Kevlar before being stopped. Hollow-point bullets fired were mushroomed in the material.

More recently, Campbell had the opportunity to test a light, wearable vest manufactured by Point Blank. The panels of this vest stopped such bullets as the .22 Magnum, .38 Super, 9mm Luger, .357 Magnum, .44 Magnum and .45 ACP. Several bullet weights were fired in each caliber.

One must keep in mind, however, the frequent complaint from working police officers: All too often, the bad guys have high-tech equipment ranging from bullets and guns to protective armor before they can be acquired by law enforcement personnel.

CHAPTER 10

REED KNIGHT'S CAVE-BUSTIN' SR-47

Here Is the Rifle Used to Clean Out Enemy Caves in Continuing Actions Against Mid-Eastern Terrorists

"THIS IS UNDOUBTEDLY the last of the SR series rifles," Lutz announced, as he handed Lewis a rifle that had a somewhat odd look. As first glance, it appeared much like the other SR rifles created in the mind and on the drawing board of the late Gene Stoner, but this rifle carried a curved magazine of the type used on the AK-47 and its various clones.

The inspection was taking place in the headquarters of Knight Armament Co. where C. Reed Knight, Jr., president of the company, has continued to introduce weapons designs thought up by Stoner, his late friend and occasional business partner. The company produces hordes of other accessories for military and police weaponry including rail systems, night sights and sound suppressors.

"This is the SR-47," said Lutz, now a retired Marine lieutenant colonel. These days Lutz is vice president of the company in charge of military sales and services "It's chambered for the 7.62x39mm cartridge." That cartridge, of course, is of Russian origin and is fired in most of the world's AK-47 assault rifles. Lutz pointed to the curved magazine. "This rifle uses the AK-47 magazine."

"Why the AK magazine?" asked Lewis.

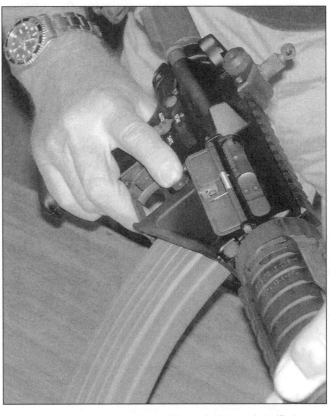

The magazine release is positioned above the rifle's trigger guard. It is spring-loaded to cause the magazine to literally jump out of the magazine well.

Jack Lewis (left) listens closely as Dave Lutz, a retired Marine Corps lieutenant colonel, explains how the new rifle differs from others manufactured previously by Knight Armament. Lutz is a vice president of Knight Armament.

The right side of the SR-47 assault rifle resembles a stretched-out M-16 until one notes the curved AK-47 cartridge magazine extending from the angled magazine well.

"Only days after the World Trade Center attack on 9/11, the Special Operations Command issued a call for a rifle that would handle the 7.62x39 cartridge," Lutz explained. "There were two other bidders for development of the weapon and our approach won the competition."

"How many are you making?" Lewis asked.

"That's still up in the air," Lutz said, "but so far, we have furnished only six to the U.S. Government. They were ordered by the U.S. Special Operations Command shortly after the effort to assassinate the president of Afghanistan. That was when the State Department was made responsible for the Afghan president's welfare. The chore was passed to the department's Diplomatic Security Service, which ordered two of our SR-l5 rifles chambered for the 5.56mm NATO cartridge. It may be that the SR-47s went to the same service.

"On the other hand, I suspect the six SR-47s went to Special Operations units that are fighting in the network of enemy caves, picking up dropped or captured AK-47 magazines for additional ammunition. The truth is, we don't know where the rifles ended up."

All of the other SR models – the letters standing for Stoner Rifle – have been built around the original AR-15/M16 design. For the SR-47, however, the basic

dimensions had to be enlarged a trifle. The upper and lower receiver have each been increased a quarter of an inch in length in order to handle the Russian-designed cartridge. The exterior controls, however, remain the same. The magazine release for the new rifle is equipped with a spring-loaded plunger that causes the empty magazine to literally leap out of the well, making reloading faster.

A major departure from previous Stoner-designed combat weapons lies in the fact that each of the earlier variations has been built around a somewhat complicated gas system. Utilizing Stoner's gas tube used in all of the arms inventor's designs, the AR-47 is operated by means of the blowback system that has been used in automatic weapons for almost a century.

A special sound suppressor also was designed for the rifle. Its identity is stamped on the end of the unit in red designating the caliber of the rifle. According to Lutz, a pin has been introduced in the

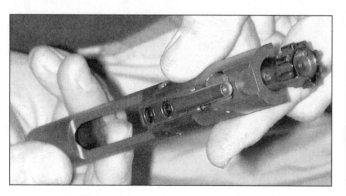

The bolt of the SR-47 is little different from other rifles in the Knight line, although strength of the lugs has been improved through redesign.

Firing controls are found in virtually the same positions as those on other rifles in the Knight-manufactured SR rifle series.

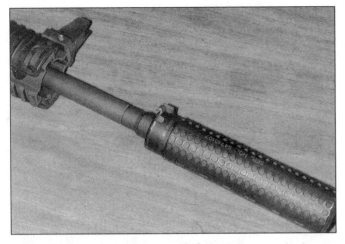

The length of the suppressor adds less than two inches to overall length of the rifle. The suppressor weighs only a few ounces. Jack Lewis believes that the addition of the suppressor improves the balance of the rifle.

SR-47 design that keeps the 5.56mm suppressor from being mistakenly installed. Each rifle is equipped with a custom-made barrel from Obermeyer Barrels, a firm headquartered in Wisconsin. Before shipment to the government's receiving agency, each rifle was fired to be certain it produced minute-of-angle groups.

"The usual reason for chambering any firearm to handle an enemy's cartridge is so that ammo captured or even picked up on the battlefield can be used," Lutz points out. However, the reasons for choice of the caliber by the Special Operations Command are classified at this point.

In testing the SR-47, Knight called on his staff to fire every available type and brand of 762x39mm ammo they could find and acquire.

"Most of the ammunition was dirty," Lutz recalls, "but we shot it just the way it came out of the manufacturer's packaging. The Egyptian ammo was particularly dirty and we found that some of the Chinese cartridges would not fire at all. This was in spite of the fact that there was a definite firing pin indentation in the cartridge primer."

This intrigued Knight and other members of his staff. With great care, they dismantled a number of the Chinese-made cartridges and discovered that the primers carried no propellant. There was nothing there to ignite the centerfire cartridge's powder load.

"It sounds like a case of China's prison labor trying to get even," one individual commented.

The tests showed that the SR-47 is more accurate than any AK-47 the Knight organization could lay hands on for the sake of comparison. Testing ammo in the SR-47 was done with the Knight quick-detachable suppressor attached. Although length of the rifle's barrel is 14-1/2 inches, the suppressor brought the length to 16-1/4 inches.

Firing Federal's 7.62/39mm ammo, velocity was recorded at 2266 fps; with Remington ammo, the muzzle velocity was 2248 fps; and with Cheetah ammunition manufactured in Africa, velocity was recorded at 2379 fps.

Records were kept on three other brands as well. The Norinco cartridge manufactured in China showed a muzzle velocity of 2332 fps; Sellier & Bellot, a Czech-made round, scored 2293 fps and the Wolf brand manufactured in Russia for export to the United States and other countries registered 2380 feet per second. Although velocity figures were not available for Winchester's 7.62x39mm cartridge at the time Lewis was checking out the new rifle, Lutz reported that it was the most consistently accurate of the thousands of rounds tested.

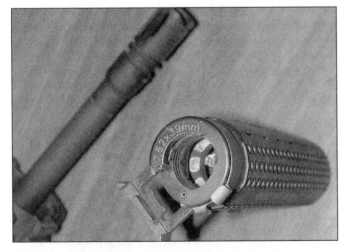

The specially designed Knight-created sound suppressor for the SR-47 is plainly marked to identify it as being made to be fired with the 7.62x39mm cartridge used in the original AK models. The device extending from the suppressor is utilized to attach the unit to the rifle barrel.

The SR-47, like others in the line, is simple and easy to assemble and disassemble by means of the pushpin technology utilized in manufacturing.

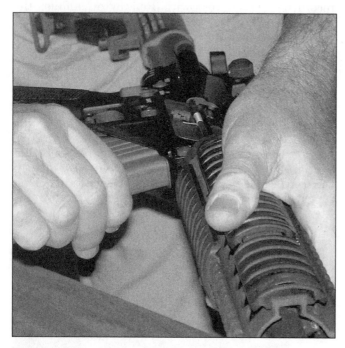

The magazine well for the SR-47 was somewhat redesigned to handle the curved magazine that has to be rocked into position and secured by the magazine latch.

The sliding butt stock of the SR-47 can be locked in any of four positions. With the stock fully extended overall length of the rifle is 34-1/8 inches. With the stock at its first closed detent, length is reduced to 33-1/4 inches; closed at the second detent, length is

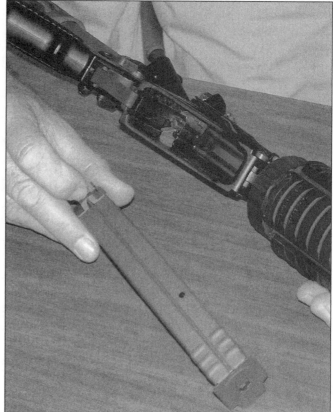

The unloaded 7.62x39mm magazine weighs only 12.7 ounces. Without any of the available accessories and with iron sights, the SR-47 weighs 7 pounds, 12.8 ounces.

32-1/2 inches and with the stock closed and detented, length is reduced to 30-7/8 inches.

Carrying an unloaded 30-round magazine, the weight of the rifle is 7 pounds, 12 ounces. Sturdy though it is, the sliding buttstock weighs only 6.7 ounces! Carrying a 30-round magazine, maximum height of the rifle is 10-3/4 inches, a definite disadvantage when one is attempting to fire from the prone position on truly flat ground.

"At this point in history, there is no telling what may be the future of this particular rifle," Lewis concluded. "Counting the prototype being held by Knight's Armament, there are only seven of the rifles currently in existence, even though made individually to fill the immediate needs of the U.S. Special Operations Command, parts are interchangeable."

Lutz noted that for now the rifle is meeting the special needs for which it was created: possibly protecting the Afghan president against assassins or being used by the Tunnel Rats searching for terrorists in the vast cave network in Afghanistan.

CHAPTER 11

THE SHOOTING SCHOOLS

This Outfit Teaches *When* to Shoot as Well as How...Such Knowledge Can Be Important in Criminal Court

Lethal Force Institute

THE SHORT LIST of well-respected combat shooting schools has included Chuck Taylor's American Small Arms Academy, Clint Smith's Thunder Ranch, Ray Chapman's Academy, Defense Training International and Jeff Cooper's American Pistol Institute. The latter is now known as the Gunsite Training Center in Arizona and has new owners and operators.

However, the one shooting school that undoubtedly spends more time teaching students when – and when not – to shoot as well as how to shoot is the Lethal Force Institute operated by a gent with the unlikely name of Massad Ayoob.

Although based in Concord, N.H., this is a traveling school with Ayoob conducting courses at selected firing ranges around the nation as well as overseas. His basic course is called simply LFI-I; the subtitle on his promotional material says more, describing his approach as Judicious Use of Deadly Force.

"As presented by Ayoob and his chosen assistants, this is a 40-hour course. Taught over four or sometimes five days, this is immersion training that goes beyond standard police academy or law enforcement classes in lethal decision making," according to Steele, a graduate of the course.

About 40 percent of the course is devoted to combat shooting with the student providing his own sidearm and ammunition. The rest of the time is devoted to weapons selection, tactical training, taking suspects at gunpoint and particularly, the aftermath interaction with police, investigators, attorneys,

Standing beside a target on which he has just illustrated various techniques, LFI training assistant Mike Izumi explains that he wants students to emulate his target.

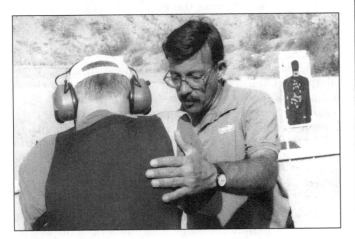

Massad Ayoob adjusts a student's shooting stance during one of his courses.

During live-fire shooting drills, Massad Ayoob demonstrates safe reholstering with the thumb on the back of the hammer and finger outside the trigger guard and holster.

In competition shooting, Massad Ayoob uses an unusual ready position that puts his left hand at the same distance as his sights will be so that he will not have to refocus.

prosecutors and possibly juries if one should shoot another person even in self-defense.

"This is a thorough course, which has been found to be attractive even to attorneys who realize their school training relating to criminal law and torts was brief at best," Steele explains.

Background

Ayoob is well-known to most gun buffs due primarily to the books and the more than 1000 magazine articles he has written since 1971. His law enforcement experience began in 1972 and he still is working as a part-time police officer in New Hampshire, his home state. He is a captain in charge of training for a local police force. His full-time career is that of director of Lethal Force Institute, P.O. Box 122, Concord, N.H. 03302.

Ayoob teaches between 800 and 1000 police officers and civilians interested in protecting their lives, families and property each year. These courses are taught in several countries. Ayoob also is a nationally ranked competitive shooter and law enforcement instructor in a variety of less lethal weapons as well as firearms.

He is a third-generation American, whose grandfather came from Damascus to start his own business in New England. The family view always has been that the men work for themselves, not as "wage slaves for someone else." In years past, Ayoob's father and grandfather had to defend themselves against armed robbers. Ayoob apparently inherited this tradition of entrepreneurism and self-reliance.

"His Lethal Force Institute has been an outgrowth of Ayoob's experiences as a working police officer, as well as the other police and shooting schools he attended since the 1970s," Steele explains. "While there were other shooting schools, there were none with an emphasis on legal tactics, particularly for civilians."

As Ayoob put it not long ago, "The late Bill Jordan was an optimist in titling his classic book *No Second Place Winner*. There is no second-place winner in a gunfight, but there also is no first-place winner when the usual residue involves thousands of dollars in legal bills and months of family stress. Unlike the military, civilian society looks at even justifiable homicide as the death of a citizen."

Thus, among other things, LFI teaches students what to do and say should they be involved in a defensive-shooting incident. Purpose of the Ayoob-led training is to minimize the possibility of jail time or a successful lawsuit against the home defender.

Weapons

"While Ayoob's repellent tactics against legal sharks probably need to be experienced in the classroom, his views on weapons are comparatively easy to report," according to Steele.

When the student is accepted for enrollment in LFI-I, he is sent a copy of Ayoob's book, *In The Gravest Extreme* with instructions that it be read before attending the formal classes. The student is told to bring a good handgun, three spare magazines or speed loaders, a concealment holster, a flashlight – and 500 rounds of ammunition!

"Once in the classroom, the student soon learns that Ayoob's recommendations as to weapons and backup gear are detailed without being excessively

During an instruction period, Massad Ayoob uses a Beretta auto to illustrate the head-down isosceles shooting position, which he teaches to students.

Massad Ayoob illustrates the kneeling position using the isosceles grip.

doctrinaire," Steele reports. "As a primary self-defense gun, Ayoob believes in no caliber smaller than 38 Special in a revolver and 9mmP in a semi-auto. Beyond that, he believes the gun should be reliable and safe, but since emphasis in the course is on threat management – holding a suspect at gun-point – the venerable Colt .45 1911 and its immediate clones are not given the stature accorded them in some shooting schools," says Steele.

According to Ayoob's teachings, when fighting a false charge of accidental shooting, it is easier to defend a gun with a double-action trigger, be it a revolver or an auto such as the Glock.

Ayoob also insists that defense ammo must be factory-produced and not a student's favorite reload. He says the round should carry bullets of hollow-point construction and of a velocity that causes the bullet to expand and not pass through the body.

"Ball ammo and other over-penetrating bullets should be avoided," Ayoob insists. "Such loads have

For overseas police training, Massad Ayoob finds the Browning P-35 the most common pistol. Countless Third World armies and police officers use this model.

been the subject of adverse media campaigns that could influence potential jurors."

He also points out that all other things being equal, guns with just model numbers or socially acceptable names are more easily defended before a jury. Thus a Colt Agent certainly would seem to have a symbolic and perhaps psychological advantage over the Colt Cobra, although both are identical when it comes to function.

Often, when conducting his course overseas, Ayoob finds himself teaching police officers whose Browning Hi-Powers are loaded with ball ammunition, but in our own country, shooters have a greater choice of defensive firearms and ammo. This, according to Ayoob, allows not only a better tactical response but a better legal answer as well.

"For reasons of speed, accuracy and convenience, not many LFI students bring revolvers to the school these days, but I have no doubt a good student could max the qualification course with a high-quality wheelgun even with a two-inch barrel," Steele contends.

"Ayoob carried a Kahr 9mm when I took the course and scored a 299/300 with this mini-nine, but he is shown in many of the videos included in the training sessions using a Smith & Wesson M-629 revolver chambered for the .44 Magnum cartridge. That's a formidable piece to any man!" says Steele.

Ayoob prefers a holster that rides inside the waistband, including a style that is of his own design, but he is quick to admit that at one time or another he has used virtually every style made.

"Had I shown up at the course with my favorite Horseshoe Leather shoulder holster or cross-draw, I would have been allowed to use either, but probably would have been placed on the left side of the line so as not to frighten the other students," Steele says. "As it was, I used the Galco Yanqui Slide and Hellweg paddle holsters for the three days of shooting, so I would not distract anyone with an unconventional technique."

Behind the line of fire, Massad Ayoob supervises an LFI-I class at Southern California's San Gabriel Valley Gun Club.

This Benelli semi-auto shotgun with a 14-inch barrel, a powerful and maneuverable 12-gauge, is in common use at the LFI-II course.

Massad Ayoob illustrates a one-handed shooting position. His feet are spread more than shoulder width apart and a bent finger off the trigger manages the threat and is ready to fire.

Steele adds, "I used my SIG-Sauer P-226 9mm, with four magazines. This is the gun I take to 'unknown risk' shooting courses. I like shooting two-inch detective-type revolvers for the handicap factor, but not in front of strangers. On the LFI course, I had no great difficulty in shooting a 300/300 with what I consider to be a superb service auto."

Ayoob runs what is termed a "cold range," which no doubt has to be a major factor in his school's perfect safety record. Students shoot in strings of six rounds, then reholster an empty gun. Each student is taught to holster the gun with his – or her – thumb on the hammer to prevent the slide from retracting. The trigger finger is well outside of the trigger guard.

For holding suspects at gunpoint, Ayoob recommends positioning the index finger along the frame in a slightly bent position. Most police academies teach trainees to hold the finger straight along the frame, but Ayoob contends this style provides less strength in case a suspect or felon tries for a gun takeaway.

For maximum stopping power in a handgun, Ayoob believes the choice, based upon street experience, lands behind the .357 Magnum with its 125-grain jacketed hollowpoint bullet. The .45 auto, firing a 230-grain JHP, has plenty of mass and power to put down a felon even if the hollowpoint does not expand in going through heavy winter clothing.

However, the instructor believes in maximizing the potential of whatever weapon is available by skill at arms. "No pistol cartridge can make up for inadequate shot placement," he says.

In one of the more shocking videos Ayoob uses in his instruction, the footage shows a state trooper who hit his heavyset opponent five times with .38 Special 110-grain +P+ bullets, but was himself killed by a .22 Long Rifle bullet from a mini-revolver. The bullet entered his side – an area not covered by body armor.

Backup Gear

Ayoob offers opinions on everything. He believes the best hearing protection is the Wolf Ears product; the best flashlight is the Sure-Fire. He also believes in utility knives, particularly those produced by Spiderco. For police officers, he thinks knives should be marked with a badge or ID number so that a patrolman cannot be accused of carrying an untraceable "throw-down" weapon to cover up a bad shooting.

In addition, Ayoob vocally favors redundancy in the field as an aid to handling emergencies: two guns, two knives, two flashlights, ad infinitum.

Ayoob recommends high-quality body armor such as that produced by Second Chance, along with less-lethal backup weapons such as the Kubotan or the similar Dejammer tool, which can clear a gun barrel as well as apply pain-oriented compliance techniques. He offers advice on home alarm systems, cell phones and backup shotguns.

Fighting Techniques

Ayoob favors a bag of tricks beyond firearms' capabilities, noting that guns fit only a narrow niche of the possibilities relating to defense. Several of his assistant instructors, for example, are experts in the martial arts. One of the best known is Graciela Casillas, who was the undefeated bantamweight women's boxing champion in the 1980s.

Today, this feisty lady teaches various martial arts at the Boggs-Casillas Institute in Nitro, W.Va. At certain times each year, she teaches the LFI-I all-women course, which adds an extra day of hand-to-hand combat techniques for women.

All of the LFI instructors are qualified to teach the basic LFI-I weapons course. Given attention here is what is termed the Ayoob Wedge, with the offhand index finger pinched in under the trigger guard in a two-hand hold. Students are exposed to the Weaver shooting stance, the Chapman stance and the isosceles stance. They also learn to handle what is called the McMillan cant, which means turning the sights 45 degrees inboard for greater control. Other techniques have such names as the one-hand Kempo punch, the speed crouch, high kneeling, low kneeling and the star.

Since Ayoob teaches in various corners of the world, his assistants usually reside close to the class location. It would be financially unfeasible to haul the same instructional crew all over the country.

The LFI-I class Steele attended was at the San Gabriel Valley Gun Club near Duarte, Calif. In this instance, Ayoob's instructing assistants were Larry Hickman and Mike Izumi.

During the course, Izumi demonstrated street and Filipino knife-fighting techniques that students might have to defend against. Students were called upon to perform the Tueller Knife Assault Drill. This consists simply of running 21 feet against a stop-watch, so that each can truthfully testify one day that an attacker armed with a contact weapon can cover that distance in two seconds – or less.

"During this particular course, my class benefited from the presence of John Mathews, president of Laser Products. He offered an excellent lecture on the tactical use of his Sure-Fire flashlights," Steel reports.

Classroom Training

Steele found that the majority of the LFI-I training course was conducted in the classroom with a variety of lectures and specially produced training tapes.

"Some of the tapes are of Ayoob himself lecturing to previous classes. This is not meant to save wear and tear on his baritone voice, but to make the lecture completely reproducible in court should that ever become necessary," Steele notes.

During this particular training session, Ayoob had to make a court appearance in San Francisco one day, so the tapes allowed his assistants to conduct all of the necessary sessions.

"Of course, Massad is present as much as possible during the course," Steele points out. "After all, this is a cult of personality as is the case with most famous martial arts schools."

Each student is given a compendium of Ayoob articles, which is distributed as "LIF-I Supplementary Study Material". This is combined with handgun dry-fire practice for homework. The supplement, of course, is added to the student's notes for future reference. No tape recorders are allowed in any of the classes.

Students are given a 30-question written examination on the final day of the training sequence. Steele was somewhat proud of the fact that he had a perfect score.

David Steele used his tuned SIG P-226 on both the LFI-I and LFI-II courses, and his custom-rebuilt Remington 870 12-gauge on the second course.

"These tests are discoverable in a potential future trial," he explains, "and give evidence of the student's prior training on a certain subject, which may be at issue in a questioned shooting incident."

Steele has been through advanced infantry training, three police academies, innumerable shooting, officer survival and martial arts courses, as well as having known and read Ayoob for years. "However," he admits, "I still learned a great deal from LFI-I. I learned shooting techniques, teaching methods and some new legal use-of-force perspectives. The course is designed primarily for civilians, who it is known use guns on criminals every year far more than do the police, but who do not have access to police survival courses.

"Even so," Steele says, "it can be an important and useful school for sworn law enforcement officers and probably will exceed officer-involved shooting investigation training provided by any police department."

The LFI-II course covers the use of long arms including rifles and shotguns, as well as their tactical use in law enforcement or home defense situations.

Submachine Guns & Front Sight Training

This One-Day Course in Subgun Basics Is Aimed at Building Business; the Technique Is Working

A lot of you may have seen the advertisements in the firearms press concerning a free $500 submachine gun course that is offered by an organization known as the Front Sight Firearms Training Institute. Like us, you may have wondered, "What's the catch here?"

In spite of our initial doubts, we decided that Steele should attend the one-day training session. The training institute's "campus" is located in a desert area about 38 miles from Las Vegas. The closest community is the quiet desert town of Pahrump, Nev. While the school is in Nevada, the contact address is Front Sight Firearms Training Institute, P.O. Box 2619, Aptos, Calif. 95001.

Ignatius Piazza holds one of the suppressed Ingram Cobray M-11 submachine guns with which he and his staff teach. Piazza heads the Front Sight Firearms Training Institute.

Massad Ayoob demonstrates the left-handed Kempo punch technique using the Kahr-9 pistol.

As is usually the case in this geographic area, the weather was clear and warm – and the course was indeed free as advertised.

"So far as the training session being worth $500, one must keep in mind that the school pays for ammo, furnishes properly registered submachine guns and provides the services of a half dozen first-class uniformed instructors," Steele notes.

"The catch – if there is one in such a promotional offer – is somewhat obvious. Along with hands-on training, you will be introduced to the school's philosophy regarding such training, you will be fully briefed as to the institute's plans for the future, and you will have an opportunity to sign up for future courses. However, there certainly is none of the arm-twisting associated with weekend real estate agents or get-rich-quick promotions," Steele says.

The founder and director of Front Sight is Ignatius Piazza, who holds a degree as a doctor of chiropractic. He also has a Four-Weapon Master ticket from Chuck Taylor, who has been involved in similar training programs in the years since his service in Vietnam and knows his subject well.

Piazza's desert-bound school teaches handgun, rifle, shotgun and martial arts courses, so why is the submachine gun used for the promotional course?

"If I were to guess, I would say that the submachine gun has several advantages, says Steele. "First, civilians, who make up the major portion of the firearms market in America, rarely have an opportunity to shoot anything as exotic as the subgun. In fact, if one is not with a police SWAT team or perhaps a military reserve counterterrorist unit, the chances are that the average civilian will never have the opportunity to fire one," says Steele.

He adds, "Looking at it historically as well as what may be from a practical standpoint, submachine guns were pretty much phased out of our nation's conven-

tional Armed Forces in favor of assault rifles starting in the late 1950s. In the past year, even the Marine Corps, which has an admitted love for full-auto armament, has begun replacing its Heckler & Koch MP-5 9mm subguns with the Colt-built M-4 5.56mm carbine, which also is a selective-fire tool.

"Another reason I think that Piazza and his staff teach this free submachine gun course lies in the fact that such an armament is fun to shoot, with lots of firepower and little recoil," Steele theorizes. "Also, such an unconventional weapon is an excellent way to show off the exotic firearms skills of the training staff. Too, it is obvious that subguns are common in today's action movies and television shows, giving the course some free advertising from that direction.

"Another thought to be considered is that knowledge gained from this particular course is unlikely to be misused; in the less likely event a student were to later misuse a firearm, it would not be a submachine gun. I suspect the submachine gun course also is designed so that instructors can evaluate each student and determine whether they really want him as a trainee on more available types of firearms."

The Guns

The primary gun used in the Front Sight submachine gun course is the 9mm Cobray M-11. This is one of several incarnations that succeeded Gordon Ingram's models made during the late 1960s and 1970s for the now defunct Military Armament Corp. The MAC-10, in 9mm and .45 ACP, as well as the later MAC-11, in .380 ACP, were designed as a sort of Volks Pistole. (This term translates to People's Pistol, a term that dates from the cheap firearms made for the final defense of Berlin in 1945). The Ingram designs are similar in concept to the German H&K VP-70 and the Czech VZ-61, which were used by South Vietnam defense forces, guerrillas and hunter-killer teams organized by Special Warfare units and the CIA. The most notable features of the

One of the instructors at the school tries out a folding-stock Uzi that was brought to the course by a dealer with the proper Federal licensing.

MAC-1O and -11 were their compact size and efficient Sionics sound suppressor.

In 1970, Steele was 26 years old and supervisor of the Police Weapons Center project for the International Association of Chiefs of Police (IACP) in Washington, D.C. The purpose of this particular project was to research various firearms under the financial auspices of the Department of Justice during the Nixon Administration.

"This was the era of large-scale urban riots, minority rights demonstrations and anti-war protests, not to mention the everyday terrorism being carried out in Indochina and Korea," Steele says. "The technical manuals we wrote on various firearms were distributed to some 3000 police departments. One of my projects was Report Series 3-70, *Submachine Guns in Police Work*. Most likely, this was the world's first book on the subject and definitely the first published in North America, where the submachine gun was not then a common tool in law enforcement efforts."

To research this book, Steele personally tested every submachine gun he was able to obtain from

The Ingram MAC-11 .380 submachine gun was produced first in the 1970s as a weapon for ambush operations in Vietnam. It also was made in 9mm chambering and called the MAC-10.

manufacturers, importers, the Marine Corps' Museum at Quantico, the State Department's Diplomatic Security arm, the Secret Service, Army FST elements and a variety of other sources.

"When it came to compiling my final evaluations of the guns tested, I rated the H&K MP-5 as number one," Steele says. "That was the first year that particular subgun was imported into the United States and decades before it became the standard for SWAT teams and counterterrorist organizations.

"My judgment at that time placed the Smith & Wesson M-76 dead last. In my view, it was a poor copy of the Swedish M-45. I didn't think the MAC-10 and -11 were up to police requirements for either accuracy or burst control, although both variations worked fairly well. Minus the suppressor and with its standard wobbly wire stock, I thought both of the MAC models were fit only for combat in a phone booth."

Much more recently, the MAC-11 .380 has been scaled up to accommodate the 9mm cartridge in what now is called the Cobray model. This offering still operates from an open bolt and suffers a stiff trigger, making short bursts difficult. Front Sight has wisely welded the Cobray's wire stocks in their open, extended position and the mandated suppressors stay in place, so the firearms the one-day subgun students are issued offer as much accuracy as the M-11 is capable of providing.

At one point in Steele's training session, Piazza demonstrated the impossibility of using the Cobray as a full-auto pistol. Minus its wire stock and the suppressor, the first shot is the only one that hit the target in his demonstration.

The MAC variations, with their stampings and fixed sights, were designed for ease of manufacture as were the British-made Sten and what came to be called the "grease gun," the U.S. M-3. Some Ingram-designed guns were used on a few well-known missions, such the 1976 Entebbe raid, but these guns never really found a significant military contract. As the Thompson submachine gun, with its rotary magazine, came to be best known for its use by beer barons in 1920s Chicago, the MAC became best known for use by the so-called cocaine cowboys in Miami in the 1980s.

"Interestingly, what was designed as a 'plumber's delight' for Ruff-Puff's – more officially designated as Regional Popular Forces – in South Vietnam had escalated to a unit cost of $2,000 by the time Front Sight located the pre-1986 models that qualified for non-government issue," Steele says. "At that cost, one can rest assured that Front Sight's M-11s are inspected and maintained with great regularity. In addition, students on the firing line are required to tighten the suppressor as part of the instruction routine.

"While the Cobray M-11 is adequate for instructional purposes, I was lucky that on the day I was taking the course, a Class III dealer also had reported for training. Properly licensed to own and

In 1970, David Steele tested one of the first two Heckler & Koch MP-5 subguns imported into this country from Germany.

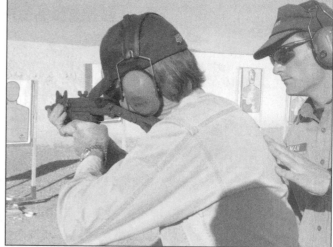

Lead instructor at Front Sight coaches a student with Uzi at the one-day promotional SMG class.

handle selective-fire or full auto-only firearms, he had brought with him three 9mm Uzis.

"The first time I used the Uzi subgun was in Israel in the 1960s. Issued to the Israeli Defense Forces, that particular Uzi model was issued with a wood stock. I've since had the opportunity to use every Uzi model since made. I'm familiar with the model carrying the paratroop stock, as well as the Mini-Uzi and Micro-Uzi, firing from both open and closed bolts of the trademarked lineup."

For the Front Sight course, Steele was able to borrow a paratrooper folding stock Uzi, a gun with half the cyclic rate of the Cobray – 600 versus 1200 rounds per minute – but with an unparalleled reputation for reliability.

"I have used a number of other submachine gun models in other schools," Steele points out. "Somewhat earlier, I employed a Colt Model 633 for Gunsite's one-week subgun course in Arizona. A team led by Peter Kokalis, former arms editor for *Soldier of Fortune* magazine, taught that one. I was able to borrow a Heckler & Koch MP-5A3 for the Global Studies Group entry-level course taught in Huntington Beach, Calif., by former SEALs Harry Humphries and Dennis Chalker." Humphries, incidentally, was technical director on the movie, *Blackhawk Down*.

In testing submachine guns, Steele has had opportunities to fire everything from the ill-fated World War II Reising and the British Sten gun to the Beretta M-12 and the Heckler & Koch VP-70. Speaking objectively, he continues to believe that the H&K MP-5 is unsurpassed for police work, even superior to the Walther MPK, while the Uzi has an unexcelled reputation in military field conditions.

Subjectively," he contends, " the most fun gun to shoot was the Czech-made VZ-61 Skorpion .32 machine pistol, which is surprisingly accurate and controllable, featuring a superb trigger."

The Course, The School, The Plan

The Front Sight one-day subgun course is all fired in the offhand position at distances ranging from 3 to 25 yards. Most of the live firework, however, is conducted at less than 10 yards. All drills are practiced first with dry fire, giving the student the opportunity to learn about the gun. Each student eventually shoots about 300 rounds in the gun's live-fire, full-auto mode.

However, there is plenty of instruction on trigger control for doubletaps and head shots. There is a five-step clearance drill: lock back the bolt, strip out the magazine, engage the safety, then both visually and manually check the chamber and magazine well. The student that fired each M-11 is required to inspect the gun and tighten the suppressor. A ratio of four students to each instructor ensures both safety and progress in the day's training effort.

The submachine gun stance taught at the Front Sight operation is similar to that of the handgunner's Weaver stance with the elbows tucked down to prevent torque and thus dampening recoil dispersion (as well as providing a more narrow profile for SWAT entry tactics).

Failure drills are emphasized, with a two-round burst followed by an assessment and, if indicated, a head shot. The full assessment involves a quick look over the left, then the right shoulder (tunnel vision may block out enemies or friends) before doing the Gunsite-style follow-through, bringing the gun down, then swinging it to the left, then to the right.

Front Sight students start with schooling on the subgun combined with a safety lecture. Each stance is demonstrated by a specialist, followed by dry fire, then live fire. Range coaches correct each student on the line, as well as ensure safety at all times. In this submachine gun course, at the end of the day each student fires two magazines in the full-auto mode into the silhouette target. Aside from being fun, this exercise stresses the sight alignment and strong torque-control

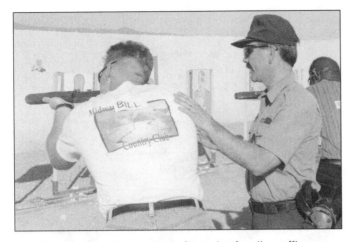

Piazza oversees instruction of a pair of police officer students at the Front Sight submachine gun course.

The low ready position is approximately 45 degrees down from the line of sight. The main point is rotating the gun up to the line of sight and not bending the head down to the gun.

positioning learned previously. The trick, of course, is to control the gun while keeping the sights aligned.

The one-day course does not include learning to fire a submachine gun in the sitting, squatting, kneeling or prone positions. In short, the few hours involved are simply devoted to an introduction to the basic nature of the submachine gun.

"However, in spite of its brevity, it is probably more complete than the subgun course given to some agents of the Office of Strategic Services, our World War II spy organization, before those individuals parachuted into France," Steele is quick to point out. "Also, 300 rounds is not insignificant compared to the four practice rounds typically given Viet Cong guerrillas before they were sent into combat in the late Southeast Asian unpleasantries."

At this writing, most of the activity at Front Sight is conducted in tents and outdoor ranges. However, Piazza's plan for his 550 Nevada acres includes a 1000-yard rifle range, plus various other ranges to include private ones for VIP training. He foresees an airstrip and hangar, armory, pro-shop, rental storage lockers and a martial arts gym. He also envisions commercial buildings, a community center, a private school, and residences on 177 one-acre lots.

Memberships are available for nonresidents. The private ranges and airstrip are for Piazza's vision of a celebrity shooting resort, like a golf or tennis resort, except his approach will be providing useful defensive skills for the executive or film star. In addition to learning home defense weaponry, the actor may need to project competent firearms handling on screen.

Steele believes that Piazza and his staff present a polished image attractive to the Hollywood elite, who might not relate to the blue-collar style of some shooting sports. Piazza has even been able to get positive press out of network television and the ultra-liberal *Los Angeles Times*!

The Man, The Reasons

As founder of this school Piazza is quick to point out that he has no military or law enforcement background. As he puts it, most serious shooters "have never heard of me. Prior to 1988, I was just your average gun enthusiast.

"Then, one evening a group of anti-socials drove through my quiet neighborhood and blasted away everything that represented the fruits of a decent work ethic. During this random, drive-by shooting spree, I was struck by a sudden and frightening realization. Although I owned firearms and shot them regularly at the range, I never had been taught the skills required to use a gun when it is needed most – to defend one's life!"

That revelation began the doctor's search for training. He initially ended up under the tutelage of Cooper, the self-deemed Father of Modern Pistolcraft. Cooper also was the founder of Gunsite, which came to be known as the American Pistol Institute.

"After 13 week-long courses and thousands of hours of practice over a three-year period, I finally had Cooper's signature on certificates authenticating my standing as an expert with pistol, shotgun, carbine and rifle courses," Piazza says. "Cooper's teachings inspired me to reach others and I conceived the Front Sight Firearms Training Institute."

Piazza examined many teaching techniques and course formats. Among them were Ayoob's Lethal Force Institute and Clint Smith's Thunder Ranch. As he continued to evolve his plans for what he hoped would be the ultimate firearms training institute, he looked for machinegun training. His search took him to Chuck Taylor, who was then the only Four Weapons Combat Master in existence.(It perhaps should be noted that Taylor developed the test criteria himself in 1981.)

"I began a 6-month daily regimen to prevail in this test," the chiropractor says. "I finally was rated as a master with handguns, shotguns, rifles and submachine guns."

Frank W. James works with his eight-shot Remington Model 870 12-gauge shotgun under the watchful eye of Louis Awerbuck. Although critical of fighting shotguns, James found the course well worthwhile.

Louis Awerbuck has been teaching combat shotgun techniques for more than 30 years. He is recognized as one of the world's leading authorities on the combat shotgun.

Piazza's favorite business aphorism is "exchange in abundance." This is a shorthand way of saying that if you give the consumer more than he expects, he will trust you and return as a repeat customer. The student has already experienced getting less than his money's worth on a daily basis; now he is getting a free course from world-class instructors. This is an excellent way to build loyalty. Hundreds of students return to the desert site for pistol, rifle, shotgun and subgun courses every year, as well as for specialized martial arts and police training.

Piazza, his operations manager, Brad Ackman, and the staff of half a dozen carefully uniformed instructors are doing their best to make the Nevada Front Sight facility world class. Selected police officers and military personnel already use the facilities for submachine gun training. It is one of the few places that civilians can shoot submachine guns, much less gain expertise with them!

Yavapai Combat Shotgun Training

This Firearms Academy Specializes in Scattergun Tactics That Can Help You Stay Alive

"I don't like shotguns, at least not for fighting."

That declaration comes from Frank James, who adds, "To some this will sound like heresy, but the biggest problem with the fighting scattergun, in my opinion, is it more often than not has the wrong ammunition loaded in it for what the situation absolutely demands."

Many argue that one of the fighting shotgun's greatest virtues is the versatility offered by the wide variety of ammunition the average police shotgun is able to use and fire reliably. Police and military shotguns can be loaded with slugs, buckshot, birdshot, gas rounds, lock-breaker rounds (frequently referred to as 'Avon' rounds), specialty rounds like those featuring large buckshot tied together with a wire, or even the alleged non-lethal beanbag rounds. All of these rounds are task specific and provide the shotgun-equipped officer with the ability to perform assignments that are virtually impossible for the sidearm-equipped police officer. In spite of all this, James still has his reservations.

It was because of his reluctance concerning the scattergun that James enrolled in a basic shotgun class taught by Louis Awerbuck, who operates the Yavapai Combat Shotgun Academy, Ltd., with headquarters in Prescott Valley, Ariz.

A native of South Africa and now a citizen of the United States, Awerbuck has been teaching combat shotgun techniques for more than 30 years. He is easily recognized as one of the foremost authorities in the world today on the combat shotgun. The class was coordinated and sponsored by Capt. Ken Campbell of the Boone County Sheriff's Department in Lebanon, Ind. The training, itself, took place at the Boone County Sheriff's Department range.

Probably, the most popular combat or law enforcement shotgun used today can be classified as some sort of pump-action model. "This was certainly true in our class, as eight of the 10 guns used were manually operated pump-action models," James notes. "One was a Mossberg and the remaining seven were all Remington Model 870s. The other two shotguns in the class were semi-auto Benelli shotguns."

Awerbuck demonstrates the indoor ready position with the 12-gauge pump-action shotgun. The operator is taught to keep the gun as close to the body as possible while making sure the muzzle does not sweep his feet. Awerbuck used a plastic inert shotgun model to teach specific teaching points and operational techniques.

Capt. Ken Campbell of the Boone County Sheriff's Department, Lebanon, Ind., tightens the side-mounted spare ammunition carrier on a student's gun. Awerbuck emphasizes the routine and regular checking of equipment. His experience has taught him that when things are allowed to loosen, systems fail.

Awerbuck believes that the self-defense handgun is part of the shotgun system just as the holster is part of the handgun. It is one big family or system. Naturally, this instructor thinks that one should always have a backup to the primary weapon and that is the main purpose of the handgun.

The main purpose of the shotgun, however, is to deliver its payload on target. With a shotgun and slugs you are dealing with a big game bullet (we're talking African big game here) without big game rifle recoil. In terms of buckshot, every shotgun barrel out there will print uniquely. That's why each shotgun should be patterned with the duty load at specific and known distances. The results should then be recorded on a paper template, which is then taped to the side of the shotgun stock. This provides a quick reference about the gun and ammunition combination's capability for anyone picking the weapon up for the first time.

The biggest deficiency with all combat shotguns, whether they are pump-action or semi-auto, in Awerbuck's view, is the fact the stocks are too long.

Sporting shotgun shooters use the old rule of positioning the butt of the stock inside the bend of the elbow, then determining where the trigger finger is in relation to the trigger on the gun. If the stock length is correct for the sporting shotgun shooter, the trigger finger should be at the same location or just a little forward of the trigger, Awerbuck tells his student class. For the combat shotgun operator the trigger finger should be well forward simply because there is a greater need for a shorter stock. The shorter stock allows a quicker mount and becomes mission essential when used in combination with current technology tactical soft body armor or tactical vests.

An absolute must for the combat shotgun is the installation of a sling of some description. Currently cross-body tactical slings are all the rage among tactical operators and while they have their good points they also have some bad points. According to Awerbuck, for most users tactical slings are simply not necessary. Any carry sling will suffice if it is mounted securely to the weapon. A big concern with the sling is not the sling itself, but rather the sling studs and swivels, which through time and the course of most drills will work themselves loose unknowingly. Therefore, as part of any check procedure with the combat shotgun, one must be sure to check the security of all sling swivels, studs and attachments continuously and regularly.

Because the sling is such an essential piece of equipment on the combat shotgun and is, in essence, the holster of the gun, there is also a corresponding need for a relatively short forearm on any pump-action shotgun. If the forearm is too long or covers the front of the receiver when it is in its most rearward position, it is a natural act for the sling to become caught between the over-length forearm and the receiver during quick, multiple shot drills.

"The only way to free the forearm when this happens is through the application of brute force," the long-time instructor told the class. "If this can't be accomplished quickly, then a transition to the sidearm is in order." That declaration explains why Awerbuck emphasizes the so-called family approach to weapons systems.

The Remington Model 870 pump-action shotgun is an extremely popular shotgun for police duty use. Many Emergency Response Entry Teams use the 14-inch barrel Model 870.

Each student is taught to shoulder the shotgun in the American Carry, which is on the strong side shoulder with the muzzle of the shotgun up or African Carry with the shotgun slung on the offside shoulder, muzzle down as demonstrated by Awerbuck as he talks to a student about the assigned drill.

Sighting systems on combat shotguns run the gamut from a simple steel bead atop the muzzle to ghost ring rifle sights. While ghost ring sights are wonderful, they are not critically necessary. Awerbuck believes there is a need for something more than a plain bead simply because of the need to match point of aim with point of impact.

When firing slugs through a gun with a plain bead sight, the impact point will usually vary by as much as 5 to 6 inches high at 25 yards and more than 14 inches high at 50 yards. If the gun is shooting right or left windage on top of this error, then the operator has a real problem when engaging moving targets that shoot back.

Remington Arms has recognized this problem and corrected it to some extent on their newer model police guns by putting a ramp under their plain bead police shotgun barrels to eliminate or reduce the excess impact height problem.

A better solution is the installation of some sort of rifle sights. Even the factory sights used on common deer slug barrels are better than simple bead sights when properly adjusted and after the adjustment screws have been correctly secured and tightened.

In addition to the sling, James learned that Awerbuck also believes the combat shotgun should have a tactical lamp system on the gun for low-light environments simply because in North America the legal situation demands the operator identify the threat target before engagement. As to the specific light system, he voiced no preferences.

Awerbuck endorses those spare ammunition carriers that are mounted on the left side of the receiver because the average police Remington Model 870 fea-

tures a four-round magazine tube and the need for more than four rounds. The trick here is to make sure all the screws are tight and well secured. "An initial check of the five ammo carriers used in our class found three of them needed tightening. Pure and simple when the screws come loose, systems fail," James reports.

Awerbuck didn't go into it at great length, but it was plain to everyone that all these additional systems – the sling, the light and the side-mounted ammo carrier – add considerable weight to what already is a heavy weapons system. "When push comes to shove and the operator has to hold this weapon against a felonious subject in a covering mode for any length of time, it will soon become obvious all these extras come at great cost," James points out. Muscle fatigue often is made worse as the adrenaline dump wears off. It is vital that the operator does not add more weight than his ability to sustain the gun and all attachments up and on target for any length of time.

Awerbuck detailed at great length the various buckshot loads that are now available. Two that he recommended were the 12-gauge mil-spec 00 buckshot load from Estate Cartridge, Inc., a firm located in Willis, Texas, and the buckshot load from Hornady Manufacturing Co., in Grand Island, Neb. Both products shoot extremely tight buckshot patterns.

Awerbuck pointedly lectured all to avoid the low-recoil or so-called tactical loads that many departments purchase for those personnel who are unable to cope with the heavier recoil of more traditional loads. The problem with low-recoil slug loads is the veering off target of the slug after traveling no more than 25 yards. The low-recoil buckshot loads are often characterized by inconsistent patterns and reduced penetra-

The author (first row, second from the left) with the fellow students and Awerbuck of the Yavapai Firearms Academy Ltd. at the completion of combat shotgun training.

tion. Both are necessary and essential characteristics needed for effective buckshot loads.

Awerbuck also discouraged the use of sabot (a French word for shoe) slugs for a number of reasons, the main one being its reduced diameter, which makes it less effective. Another reason they should be avoided is that the sabot will often become a secondary projectile that is quite capable of serious injury and/or death and is, for all practical purposes, unguided.

A systems check for the Remington Model 870 pump gun requires the lock ring that secures the forearm to the action bar be checked for tightness. "All seven of the seven Model 870 shotguns in our class, including my own, were loose," James admits.

If allowed to remain loose, this lock ring can loosen to the point the forearm will be all the way forward and the bolt will still not lock into battery. If the bolt is out of battery, the Model 870 shotgun will not fire. If you have a Remington 870, tighten the lock ring holding the forearm to the action bars. The bolt carrier can be used temporarily to tighten this ring, but it is better to order the specific tool for this task from Brownell's Inc., Montezuma, Iowa.

James learned that for those who work with shotguns using screw-in chokes, it is important to know that whenever the choke is removed, changed or replaced the shotgun should be re-zeroed with the duty issue slug load. The point of aim will change with each change of the screw-in choke tube, so the gun requires a new sighting-in process after each change.

Because of the relatively small receiver opening on the bottom of the Remington Model 870 receiver, Awerbuck recommends the operator reload by first finding the trigger guard, then running the shell forward along the outside of the trigger guard into the receiver opening. This allows the operator to maintain visual contact with his adversary, at the same time reloading the weapon until full.

"It was a technique I found easy to master," James said. "Others in our class continually wanted to fill the tube before loading the chamber, but Awerbuck would remind them to …LOAD THE GUN! He wanted them to load the chamber first before filling the magazine tube.

"The trigger guard technique wasn't required by our lone Mossberg shooter simply because the Mossberg has such a large opening on the bottom of its receiver. The Benelli-equipped shooters had to first load the chamber by reaching over the top of the receiver, hit the action tab, then load the tube until full."

As for malfunction drills, Awerbuck pointed out there isn't a lot one can do to clear a shotgun. This was emphasized throughout the three-day class during which there were more than five instances wherein shells were loaded backwards into the tube during the stress of drills. In each case the gun be taken down into individual components before it could be cleared and returned to service.

About the only quick fix taught was to wipe out a smokestack malfunction. For the Model 870 operators, a 45-degree butt stroke hard on the ground while also pulling on the pump action forearm should release a double feed on the shell carrier, if both shells are facing forward. Otherwise, the user better be able to transition to his handgun quickly.

"The drills Awerbuck put the class through were simple, yet demanding and I soon learned Dutch loading of any combat shotgun was impractical under stress," James says. Dutch loading is alternating slugs with buckshot loads. Many departments use this technique as standard operating procedure. The problem is that one may lose count and not have a clue about what exactly is in the chamber. The problem becomes extremely serious when the required shot demands the use of slugs because of the proximity of hostages or other innocent targets.

"I still don't like shotguns for fighting, but at least now I know a whole lot more about their capabilities and what a combat shotgun should have on it: as little as possible. I now understand what I can do and cannot do with this weapons system," James says.

The Teachings At Thunder Ranch

This Texas Combat School Offers a Broad Range of Courses to Help One Stay Alive and Well

In recent years, we have heard a great deal about an outfit called Thunder Ranch, located near Mountain Home, Texas. The owner and chief instructor is Clint Smith. His wife, Heidi, handles the administrative details.

Firearms writer James has made several visits to the ranch to improve his own skills, so we asked him to brief us and readers about the ranch's educational benefits.

"A long wooden plaque at one of the many Thunder Ranch ranges probably best describes the philosophy and goal of the training at this facility," James says. The sign states:

You Have The Rest Of Your Life To Solve Your Problems. How Long Your Life Lasts Depends On How Well You Do It!

This privately owned training academy is approximately 48 miles west of Kerrville, Texas. "It is one of the most impressive facilities ever built for shooting and tactical small arms training – anywhere!" James is quick to declare.

He adds, "The property, itself, consists of 2400 acres in the rolling hill country of southwest Texas. Clint and Heidi Smith have a long-term lease on the land, where they have built a firearms training range that rivals anything owned by the federal government – or anyone else for that matter. Bluntly stated, Thunder Ranch is the state-of-the-art facility for gunfight survival."

For many years, Smith traveled back and forth across the United States training both civilians and

Using the Main Street setting at Thunder Ranch, students learn to take advantage of cover and still complete their mission.

law enforcement professionals to fight with small arms. (He still travels to the students under the umbrella of his mobile training academy, International Training Consultants, Inc.)

Smith is a combat veteran of the Vietnam War – two tours – and he didn't spend his time in the rear. He was in the field and has the scars and a Purple Heart Medal to prove it. His experiences during that war obviously colored his thinking and it is still evident in his logic and the school's course of study.

One of the courses taught at Thunder Ranch is how to survive in a confrontation that involves motor vehicles.

The training facility is configured so that hundreds of different scenarios can be used in training personnel. This particular problem includes a kitchen, complete with a cooking range.

Wearing night-vision goggles, trainees at Thunder Ranch learn techniques for armed entry against a suspected felon who may be armed.

Exercises involving situations that may evolve in a manhunt include approaching a felon by means of a ladder or stairway. Smith's training is realistic and based upon his own experiences.

After he came home from the war, he worked as a deputy sheriff in a large metropolitan area of the Midwest for seven years. He worked all phases of law enforcement and served as head of the department's firearms training unit, SWAT team member and senior counter-sniper.

James says, "Smith left law enforcement, because he is – for lack of a better description – a zealot when it comes to small arms training and he chose as his profession the life of an itinerant small arms instructor.

His zeal translates into a teacher who employs humor, laughter, smiles, an easy-going manner and an extremely strict and demanding course of study to get his message and methods of dealing with small arms confrontation across to his students. It is a subject he knows intimately and one he refuses to dilute or detract from with personal war stories. His opinion of war stories is: No One Cares."

Smith will tell you how many hours it is by automobile from Los Angeles to his former home near Fort Wayne, Ind., – 40. And he laughs when he recalls "those weren't the good old days, they were just the old days," when he spent most of them in getting from one instruction assignment to the next.

Smith always dreamed of his own facility, James learned during a session titled Home and Vehicle Defense. "He probably dreamed of it most often while working as senior instructor and operations officer at Jeff Cooper's American Pistol Institute in Arizona. Later, he left Gunsite to serve as director of training for Heckler & Koch's International Training Division."

Smith admits that on the day Thunder Ranch opened for business, it was everything he had ever dreamed of in a small arms training facility. He had big dreams, but then he had 20-plus years to visualize the concept.

"Smith has always earned accolades for his rifle training. He teaches a course entitled simply Urban Rifle and every expert who has taken it raves about it. When it comes to rifles, Clint and his staff really come into their own element," says James.

Smith always wanted a facility that represented the real world and one that would provide the best physical plant available. He also wanted the best available instructors for handgun and shotgun classes, as well as both his short-range and long-range precision rifle courses.

"Thunder Ranch is not the private enterprise equivalent to a Marine Corps boot camp," James discovered on his first trip to the facility. "There is no yelling, nor are there any negative or demeaning expressions used to describe incorrect student techniques."

The staff members suggest corrections. They don't tell the student to perform a particular drill in a certain manner just because they said so. The instructors will often ask the student why he carried out a drill in a specific manner. The important point is not that the student did the drill wrong, but that the student has a reason for his or her actions. If the student doesn't have a reason, then the instructors will probably suggest that the student try the designated drill in a manner which they then illustrate.

You could do it this way and this is the reason why," is the official teaching procedure.

Mandated rules of expected student behavior are stated early on the first day in the classroom – and the gun savvy students would have been uneasy during the ensuing week had those rules not been clearly expressed and defined. The absence of such statements would have represented a lack of resolve, which James believes is a serious deficiency in any school teaching self-defense with firearms.

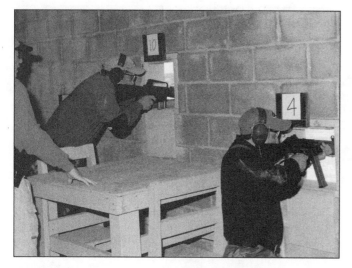

Several of the training installations are built of cement block with firing ports. Seasoned instructors oversee the efforts of trainees, correcting any mistakes.

Smith and his staff train policewomen and female members of the Armed Forces in use of the various types of weaponry they may encounter in their professional lives.

Thunder Ranch offers a wide choice of training courses ranging from classes designed for the beginning handgun shooters to classes for the most experienced counter-sniper veteran out there. The U.S. military sends some of its highly trained people to Thunder Ranch for instruction, and as expected, identities are not revealed.

The first four primary ranges are named after the color-code system adopted by the U.S. Marine Corps during the stages of island invasions in the Pacific Theater of World War II.

The White Range is a general-purpose range that is 50 yards wide by 100 yards long. It is an all-weather range featuring stationary, wobbler and high-speed turning targets.

The Yellow Range is another general-purpose 50-by 100-yard range used for preliminary work in shotgun, submachine gun and some pistol courses. "This range was used during one phase of our training with vehicles," James recalls. "The target options are steel, paper, hostage, stationary, wobbler and movers."

The Orange Range is 50 yards by 50 yards and it has a unique "charger" program to represent a threat advancing on the student. This range was used on the last day of school and the experience was applauded by even the most cynical of the students. It was amazing how slow students recognized and reacted to a threat charging toward them while seated in a vehicle.

The Red Range is used primarily for all handgun work. It is 50 yards by 50 yards and offers turning, stationary and wobbler targets. It is the range used for most of the basic handgun training drills.

The Terminator is one of the most modern structures available for training in defensive tactics. Like a motion picture or television set, the interior of this building can be dressed to represent a home, a motel or an office environment. Tactical drills are conducted with handguns, shotguns and rifles. A number of different reactive targets are employed in this structure built of concrete, steel, reinforced concrete block and covered

For specialized training, Smith hires a helicopter piloted by an experienced combat pilot. Smith says his setup is the culmination of a dream.

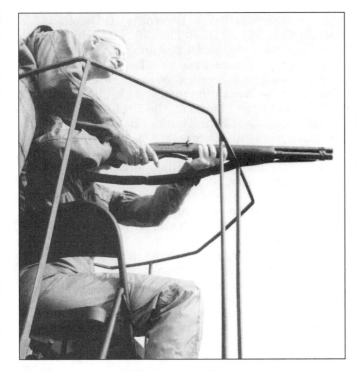

Combat shotgun work is among the course taught at Thunder Ranch. Students practice shooting from unlikely locations such as this tower.

An entire street of storefronts resembling a motion picture set has been built at Thunder Ranch. There is no glass in the windows for obvious reasons.

by a 70- by 140-foot free-span roof. Training won't be interrupted by bad weather or poor lighting conditions.

The Terminator features movable walls that have the potential to make 400 different floor plans. "It is an extremely impressive structure and one of the greatest teaching tools for tactics ever seen," says James.

But, that isn't all there is to Thunder Ranch. A building known simply as The Tower is a monolithic four-story reinforced-concrete block structure. Each of the floors is reached by a flight of stairs deliberately designed to be completely different in terms of rate of ascent, number of steps and even stairwell width. The Tower is a live-fire tactical simulator and live fire can be employed in all the rooms and stairwells. Additionally, problems can be addressed from either internal entry or external rooftop entry. The four stairwells leading to the top floor make this building one of the most realistic training ranges currently available.

Thunderville is 200 feet long, an in-depth facade that represents a conventional street setting. It was purposely built for rifle training and to represent realistic rifle applications and doctrine. There are more than 60 target options including movers, hostages, runners, wobblers and computer-controlled targets. The range computer also controls such things as lights, doors, movement, timing, hit documentation and tactical applications. Thunderville is used in both day and night applications.

Additionally, there are a 300-yard rifle range and a 1200-yard rifle range for long-distance shooting. Another range called Thunder Valley is a field reaction course.

Smith points out that most individuals spend the majority of their time at one of three locations: their place of work, their home or within the confines of their vehicle. The average American spends 17 percent of his or her time in a motor vehicle or on foot commuting to work, to shop, to visit friends and so forth.

"Smith starts the instruction for the Home and Vehicle Defense Course in a classroom environment," James says.

He has learned the basics for holding the students' attention as he drives home the points essential to surviving a gunfight. He breaks home defense into three elements: warning, shelter and pre-established fields of fire.

The big thing with warning is to become aware "they" are coming before "they" arrive. "A friend who was formerly a hunter of felony fugitives told how easy it was to catch the fugitive asleep in bed. You just broke the door down and rushed quickly to the bedroom. If the subject was deep in slumber, he might possibly recognize the sound of the crashing door, but most didn't. The only ones he didn't catch were the ones who escaped out the bedroom window while still naked!" Smith says. Think about that illustration for a minute – that's how little time there was for the fugitive to react.

Smith teaches that the shelter element deals with what he terms the defensive core in the home. What is the strongest part of the home? For most, it is the bedroom.

The "pre-established fields of fire" element deals with considerations, funnels and backlighting. Smith points out that the first thing the individual has to consider is what firearms or other weapons are legal for home defense where he or she lives. Important considerations for firearms are caliber and penetration. A powerful centerfire African hunting rifle would be a poor choice for protection if a residence is in an area of tightly packed housing such as a mobile home park.

It isn't too likely that one will need to slide down a fireman's pole in pursuit of a felon, but it's part of the training in some courses at the Texas training center.

pair of Model 3913s), a Browning Hi-Power and a custom Colt 1911 pistol. The .40 S&W chambering was found in a Sig Model 229 and a Glock 23. There was a pair of custom-made Colt Delta Elite in 10mm Auto, as well as a Smith & Wesson revolver in .357 Magnum. The remaining pistols were universally .45 ACP in caliber and based on the 1911 format.

Every day during the Thunder Ranch course was a learning moment. There were so many neat little tricks to put into everyone's personal bag of goodies that each student left feeling fortunate at having attended this class," James says. "Unlike some facilities there is no end–of-session shoot-off or comparison competition among members of the student body. Smith truly wants to teach and leave a positive slant on the week's work."

"I'm not bringing the students here for five days to judge 'em. I'm bringing them here for five days to teach 'em!" Smith says, as he explains his outlook on the management of this shooting school.

Probably more meaningful for Americans than anyone else, but just as true regardless of where you live, was his simple statement early in the week when he said, "When you shoot a threat, your trouble doesn't end. It's just beginning," James notes.

This is just one example of the reality taught at Thunder Ranch. The courses are reality-oriented. Physical structures and class material are directed toward the real world. Nothing is artificial. The instructors intentionally teach that you may learn to survive the lethal force assault, but you may also suffer years of court action afterward. Life is hard. It isn't the way a Hollywood film ends where everyone lives happily ever after.

However, the most important point Smith stresses is for one to live afterward," notes James.

Throughout the week Smith emphasized two tactical rules to a gunfight: (1) Always Win! and (2) Always Cheat! As James points out, "There are no rules in a gunfight. The objective is to stay alive!"

Other considerations include the number of family members in the home and where they are. How quickly can they be moved into one location such as the master bedroom?

"There is so much material presented in the Thunder Ranch class for the student to absorb that there is no way a synopsis of the course material can be fully presented in these scant few pages," James contends

Firearms used during the class James attended included pistols chambered in 9mm, .40 S&W, 10mm Auto, .357 Magnum and, of course, .45 Auto. The 9mm pistols were represented by Smith & Wesson (a

CHAPTER 12

FN'S SPACE-AGE P-90

This Personal Defense Weapon May Look Like Something Out of Action Comics, but it Works Well

IN THE SUMMER of 1998 two American embassies in Africa were bombed by Al Qaeda, the same Muslim terrorist group that later destroyed the World Trade Center in New York. At the time of the 1998 attacks, Steele's daughter, Minnie, was working as an intern at the U.S. Embassy in the Philippines.

"I was visiting her there after the African attacks, when the State Department received a bomb threat," Steele recalls. "The local Filipino employees did not show up to work, but I told Minnie that Americans had to set an example, even those such as herself who were not paid. She took my advice and reported for work. The Manila embassy remained secure, although a high-powered, plainclothes Army Special Forces team was sent in just in case."

While Steele was visiting his daughter, she arranged for him to go on a shoot with her friends from the State Department Diplomatic Security Service. One of the DSS agents took father and daughter to a Philippine Navy range where the trio hooked up with other DSS and Drug Enforcement Agency (DEA) agents as well as Philippine Marines and a few other security-connected civilians.

"One of the DSS agents loaned me a Beretta M-92 and Minnie a Glock 19. He then ran the two of us as well as the other agents through a morning of Gunsite-style pistol exercises. Rolling around in the grass in Philippine heat and humidity is quite a training experience," Steele says.

The DSS provides security for foreign dignitaries overseas and sometimes in the United States. Over recent years, their protectees have included the Greek Orthodox patriarch, chairman of the Palestinian Liberation Organization Yasser Arafat, England's Prince Charles and more recently, Afghan President Hamid Karzai. They also protect the U.S. Ambassador and his embassy staff. An assigned DSS agent also acts as "Regional Security Officer," to advise employees of local security risks. Steele learned that their training and expertise are somewhat similar to that of U.S. Secret Service agents.

"After the pistol run, we tried out some of the shoulder arms that had been brought along. They included the 9mm Colt Commando submachine used by DEA personnel as well as the Heckler & Koch MP-5 subgun issued to the DSS agents," Steele recalls.

"A Filipino Marine major had brought along an FN P-90 Personal Defense Weapon and let us try it out. Unusual, high-tech guns like this often turn up in the Third World. Some are so-called orphan guns that a manufacturer hopes will catch on and result in a significant purchase. This approach, of course, is something of an uphill battle in a country that is supplied with free M-16A1s, courtesy of the U.S. Government.

"Minnie and I each tried the Belgian-made FN P-90, as did the DSS and DEA agents. There were no failures or stoppages and all of us were impressed by the gun's capabilities. One of the testers was Daniel 'Snooky' Cruz, a Filipino investigator for the DEA, as well as a SWAT instructor for the Philippine National Police, Steele says. The PNP is the successor to the paramilitary Philippine Constabulary.

Prior to becoming a nation independent of the United States in 1946, the constabulary was equipped

A member of the Drug Enforcement Agency works with the FN-made P-90 submachine gun at a Navy range in the Philippine Islands.

with .50-caliber machineguns, rifle grenade launchers, Thompson submachine guns, U.S. M-2 Carbines and the venerable Garand M-1 rifles. As a civil police agency, the PNP has M-16 rifles as the top of its firepower continuum, along with Remington Model 870 shotguns and Heckler & Koch MP-5 submachine guns. Also in the array of duty weapons are .38-caliber revolvers from Smith & Wesson, Taurus and Squires-Bingham, as well as 9mm autos from Glock, SIG-Sauer and Smith & Wesson.

In designing the P-90, Belgium's Fabrique Nationale – more commonly known simply as FN – calculated that at least 60 percent of a modern army is made up of soldiers designated as something other than infantry. Such other categories include tankers, artillerymen, helicopter and fixed wing crews, medical and communications specialists, headquarters staff and all sorts of support troops. Armed with a variety of pistols, carbines and submachine guns, there is only one constant: A full-size infantry rifle is too bulky for efficient performance of the primary duties of these individuals.

Technically, the P-90 is not a submachine gun because it does not use a conventional pistol cartridge. Instead, it fires a special 5.7mm bottleneck round that moves at 2400 fps. This would seem to move the little gun into the assault rifle category or perhaps that of the .221 Fireball used in the experimental IMP survival weapon.

The P-90 is usually called a Personal Defense Weapon (PDW) after its designated role. However, other manufacturers such as Steyr-Mannlicher, GIRT and Heckler & Koch have made PDWs, sometimes in 9mm Parabellum, which is the standard NATO cartridge for pistols and submachine guns. The 5.7x28mm FN centerfire cartridge can penetrate soft body armor with the same efficiency as the 5.56mm NATO round, but with the minimal blast and flash of a pistol-caliber carbine.

The P-90 is made by FN in Herstal, Belgium; the ammo is made there and by Winchester in the United States. It is produced in SS90 ball, saboted high velocity, tracer, subsonic, dummy and blank rounds for different tactical and training situations. Assuming that future armies will employ body armor as well as improved helmets, the SS90 round was designed to penetrate 24 layers of Kevlar, the U.S. M-1 steel helmet, the currently issued composite helmet and a car windshield at 100 meters. None of these things can be accomplished with the 9mm Parabellum rounds.

"The SS90 will penetrate a NATO 3.5mm soft-steel plate at 30 meters, while the high-velocity round will do the same at 250 meters. That is assault rifle performance by any standards," Steele declares.

According to ammunition technicians at Winchester, the 5.7x28mm ball round destabilizes as it hits tissue, but it can still defeat body armor up to level IIIA. This is due to the bullet's two-part core. The forward third of the core is steel, while the rear section is of aluminum, all covered by a copper-plated steel jacket. The 31-grain slug reportedly travels at 2300 fps, with the terminal stability provided by a forward shift of the center of gravity.

Equipped with its standard optical sight, the P-90 is a handy piece of equipment for close-quarters work. It was designed originally for troops other than those equipped with standard infantry weapons.

The P-90 looks pretty much the same on one side as on the other, making it ambidextrous and easy for a left-handed shooter to handle. The expended cases are ejected straight down through the bottom of the gun.

As for specifications, the P-90 subgun is best described as a polymer-framed bullpup. In standard form, the P-90 has an overall length of only 19.7 inches, substantially shorter than either the MP-5 subgun or the M-4/M-16 Carbine. Barrel length for the P-90 is a mere 9.8 inches. The little gun currently is available in four versions: the STD is a select fire bullpup. Then there is a semi-auto carbine version. Third is the LV (laser visible), which has a red dot laser built into the frame of the forward handguard. The fourth is the TR (Triple Rail), which has a Picatinny rail instead of an optical sight. A number of accessories can be attached to this rail. With a loaded 50-round magazine, the P-90 weighs 6.6 pounds.

The personal defense weapon requirement around which the P-90 was designed was specified in the 1980s, first by the U.S. Army as a part of its Small Arms Master Plan, then by NATO in its document AC225. However, the little FN creation first proved itself in an actual combat situation in 1997 when Peruvian commandoes rescued diplomats held hostage by Tupac Amaru revolutionaries at the Japanese ambassador's residence in Lima. It was found then that the P-90 and its cartridge easily defeated the body armor worn by the terrorists.

"There are several unique features to the P-90 besides its 5.7mm cartridge," Steele discovered. "As a select-fire, bullpup weapon, it has its 50-round plastic magazine mounted flush above the receiver. The magazine locks in place between the charging handles and the optical sight."

One version of the P-90 is equipped with a Picatinny rail, which allows a scope or other sighting devices to be installed.

The method by which the loaded magazine rides parallel to the receiver and the gun's barrel is visible in this photo.

Steele also found that loading the individual cartridge in the magazine forces the rounds under it to rotate 90 degrees into a double stack. The rotation allows the compact magazine to ride parallel to the receiver. The magazine features a follower with rollers and a constant force spring, making loading easy.

The cartridges go through a four-step process to become fully aligned in a double stack. The first round enters the magazine at 0 degrees, the second causes the one under it to rotate to 82 degrees from bore angle, the third round makes the first rotate to 87 degrees, and the fourth make the first move to the 90-degree position, according to specifications furnished by FN engineers.

The P-90 strips into six basic components: barrel and reflex optical sight assembly, bolt and dual main operating spring assembly, hammer group assembly, frame and stock assembly, magazine assembly and buttplate.

A sound suppressor from Gemtech is available for it. FN Herstal asked Gemtech of Boise, Idaho, to develop a suppressor meeting military specifications, which would be compact, could snap on and would tolerate full-automatic fire. The final result is a suppressor that is 7.25 inches long and snaps onto the barrel via a patented Bi-Lock quick mount.

Steele said, "The rotary selector is located at the base of the trigger, with positions for safe, semi- and full-auto fire. There are two thumb-holes moulded into the stock for right and left hands, plus a moulded projection in front of the forward handhold to prevent the hand from slipping accidentally in front of the muzzle."

When FN launched its "Project 9.0" in 1989, they were using the NATO projection of the soldiers of most future armies being equipped with body armor. With this view, the typical NATO 9mm Parabellum pistol cartridge was projected to be obsolete. It had been determined that what NATO needed was a vest-punching round superior to the 5.45x18mm PMT.

Soviet designer Aleksandr Bochkin had developed this particular cartridge in 1979 for the PSM (Pistolet Samozaryadniy Malogabaritniy) sub-compact pistol.

According to Steele's findings, "The steel core projectile for the PSM will penetrate 55 layers of Kevlar at service pistol distances. Muzzle velocity is reported to be 1033 fps. The PSM was issued to the KGB and other special units, but it would probably have seen wider service if there were not so many Makarovs available – not to mention the breakup of the USSR around 1991. That spelled the end of many upgrade projects for the Russian army."

The P-90 has a companion pistol, marketed as the FN Five-Seven, for the same cartridge; its magazine carries 20 rounds of the same ammo as the P-90 and fires double-action only. It makes use of modern polymer technology and fieldstrips down to three main parts. Because of its body armor-penetrating qualities, it is sold only to police in the United States.

"This is an absurd restriction, considering the fact that virtually any centerfire rifle cartridge, including the .22 caliber centerfires, will penetrate standard police body armor, as will a $1.50 icepick," Steele contends.

"I believe that the FN Five-Seven was originally designed with the high capacity 9mm service pistol role in mind. It would be more commercial in a compact pistol, however. The Five-Seven has a 4.82-inch barrel, with an 8.2-inch overall length. It is 5.65 inches in height and it fires with a gas-delayed blowback operation. It weighs only 1.64 pounds with the 20-round magazine fully loaded," Steele adds.

The P-90 comes equipped with a positional nylon tactical sling. Military truck drivers can easily sling it in front, while motorcyclists can sling it in back. Gunsite instructors often refer to the sling as a "holster for a long gun." This certainly applies in the case of the P-90, a small, convenient package indeed.

The P-90 optical sight is made from a solid piece of glass, with no risk of nitrogen leakage or subsequent fogging in the field. It has two reticle patterns for differing light conditions:

— A day reticle, projected into the sight from the front, has a circular reticle for fast target acquisition, a large reticle for close range and a smaller one for 100 meters, with a tiny dot for precision.

— A night reticle, for low-light situations, has a replaceable tritium cell, which projects into the optical sight from the rear. It is invisible in bright light. When in use, a horizontal reticle runs across the center of the field, with a vertical reticle running from the bottom to a small circle.

The P-90 trigger is a two-stage type with a short pull resulting in single shots and a longer pull resulting in full-auto fire. Controlled bursts typically run three or four rounds, with a cyclic rate of 900 rounds per minute. Empty cases are ejected straight down. The P-90 is a straight blowback design, with a bolt that rides on a pair of steel rods.

Fourteen countries have adopted the P-90, according to FN. Several other nations, including the United States, have purchased samples. U.S. Army military police have evaluated the weapon for use by Special Reaction Teams. Special Operations troops also have this particular weapon under consideration at this writing.

CHAPTER 13

TODAY'S DESIGNATED MARKSMAN RIFLE

Like Dracula, the Venerable M-14 Rifle Refuses to Die

THE SUPPLY OF surplus U.S. small arms from World War II and the Korean War has pretty much dried up. There are plenty of M-1 Garands and .30 M-1 Carbines around, of course, but the majority of them are in the hands of collectors or avid weekend competitors.

This situation, however, is not all bad. The distribution of these firearms by a joint effort of the National Rifle Association and the Civilian Marksmanship program has introduced a great number people to the shooting sports over the years.

The M-1 Garand was replaced among United States armed forces by the M-14 in the early 1960s. Even at that time it was termed an interim weapon and it lasted as the principle infantry rifle only until the Department of Defense could settle on a smaller cartridge and the M-16 to handle it.

Gunnery Sgt. Tom Gilbert favors using the DMR without its leather sling. He points out that in most instances, he – and other designated marksmen – would be utilizing the Harris bipod.

Inasmuch as the M-14 was designed with a selective-fire capability, none of these rifles ever have been released on the surplus market for civilian purchase. The closest anyone has come to reproducing the original M-14 is a civilian organization named Springfield Armory, which operates out of Illinois. The company's chief product is its M-1A1, a nearly exact copy of the M-14, but sans the full-auto capability. Springfield Armory's price for its M-1A1 starts at around $1600 for a standard model with a black fiberglass stock. The price peaks at somewhere in the neighborhood of $3000 for the M-21 Tactical model, which boasts an adjustable cheekpiece. It is suspected that a lot, but not all, of the original military rifles were stripped of their stocks and stuffed into blast furnaces along the way.

During 2002, the Marine Corps issued what it calls the Designated Marksman Rifle to special units. This creation is an M-14 that is sufficiently different in outward appearance that it is barely recognizable to the unpracticed eye.

When the Corps decided it needed a rifle as a backup for snipers, explosive ordnance destruction and other specialized purposes, they looked to the Naval Surface Warfare Center in Craine, Ind. It was there that some 10,000 M-14 rifles chambered for the 7.62mm NATO cartridge were stored since they were gathered up and replaced by the smaller caliber M-16.

A Marine Corps inspection team was sent to the Indiana installation, where team members spent several months closely inspecting all 10,000 of the aged, but well preserved, M-14s. What were considered to be the best 1000 were chosen and shipped off to the Marine Corps' Marksmanship Training Unit at Quantico. Following established practices of the Government Accounting Office, the Marine Corps paid only $1 for each of the rifles!

I don't know what the price is today," Lewis admits, in viewing the federal accounting system,

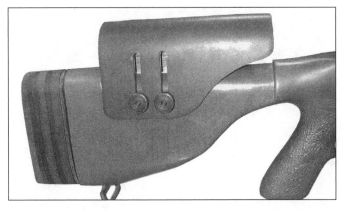

The stock has an adjustable cheekpiece fashioned from steel, then covered with rubber for marksman's comfort.

"but there was a time when the GAO charged only $1 for a B-25 bomber, if you would haul it away."

Not all of the chosen 1,000 rifles have been reworked, because the signals have changed once more. As this is being written, approximately 300 of the supposedly obsolete rifles have been refurbished and sent to Corps' Explosive Ordnance Disposal detachments stationed around the world. As for the true sniper rifle, sources at Quantico say it will be introduced soon. It will be a bolt-action manufactured by Remington and called the Model 24-B in the Marines' tables of organization. This one has been upgraded from the current sniper model to meet current Leatherneck standards for shooting the enemy at extended desert ranges.

As indicated earlier, the M-14 was a selective-fire rifle, but the selector switch allowing full-automatic fire has been removed from the DMR reworks. The Marine and Civil Service armorers at the Marksmanship Training Unit have done away with the original walnut wood and installed a new stock made by McMillan Fiberglass Stocks of Phoenix. The stock of the rifle Lewis had the opportunity to inspect was a grayish green in color, which contrasted somewhat with the brown-shaded upper handguard, which had been retained from the original M-14.

Of particular interest to Lewis was a quarter-inch rubber recoil pad that was marked Old English in raised letters. Positioned between the pad and the plastic of the stock proper were roughly two inches of fiberglass spacers that could be removed or added to, giving the marksman an opportunity to either lengthen or shorten the stock to his or her personal preference.

"This approach could mean that in modern warfare, there may no longer exist the tradition that one-size-fits-all when it comes to rifle stocks," Lewis commented after eyeing the number of spacers. Atop the stock was a steel cheekpiece covered with soft rubber. This device can be adjusted to the preferred height of the shooter.

At Quantico, gunsmiths reinforced the rifles' recoil shields and reworked the operating rod spring before installing a new medium-heavy custom barrel made in Germantown, Wis., by Krieger Barrels, Inc., in each rifle These barrels measure 22 inches without the flash suppressor. A Harris bipod also has been added as standard equipment. Overall length of the DMR is

44 inches, half an inch shorter than the original M-14. The 20-round magazine for the rifle is the same as those issued with the M-14 more than 35 years ago.

The sighting system is unchanged, but standard on each rifle is a Leupold Mark 4 M-3 10-power scope. This sighting unit measures 13.125 inches in length and weighs 21 ounces. It has the usual adjustments for windage and elevation and an 11.1-foot field of view at a hundred yards. The 30mm scope tube is mounted to the action by means of rings and mounts manufactured by G.G. & G, a custom outfit headquartered in Tucson, Ariz.

Equipped with the scope, a full 20-round magazine, the bipod and the Old Corps leather sling rather than the more modern nylon carrying strap, the DMR weighs in the neighborhood of 18 pounds.

A spokesperson for the Marine Corps Systems Command, one Maj. Tom Varmette, has said, "This is going to provide designated marksmen with the ability to rapidly engage targets from longer ranges than the M-16. Since the 7.62mm round has good penetration, it can be used by Explosive Ordnance Disposal people to detonate mines and similar explosives."

According to the major, the rifle can handle targets accurately out to 800 meters. Equipped with the 10-power scope, he says this combination allows a qualified shooter to fire 15 well-aimed rounds per minute. That calls for a round every four seconds, with well-aimed as the key phrase in the exercise!

Having carried the nine-pound Garand M-1 semi-auto for a few years in his youth, the idea of having to lug a rifle rig that weighs twice that for very far causes Lewis to shudder. The saving grace lies in the fact that, in most instances, a designated marksman is not going to have to hump his gear too far to get into an adequate firing position.

The story persists that it cost the U.S. military's now-closed Springfield Arsenal in Massachusetts $7 million to rework the M-1 Garand to become the M-14. Lewis views this expenditure with a bit of taxpayer-inspired jaundice, since he first saw a full-auto firing Garand equipped with a Browning Automatic Rifle magazine on a range at Marine Corps Schools in Quantico in early 1945.

The 10-power Leupold scope is held in place by a sturdy mounting system. Note that the original M-14 sights remain in place.

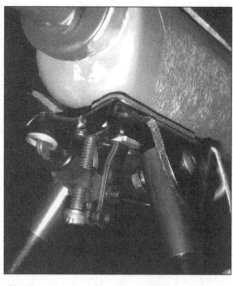

The Harris bipod is quickly and easily installed or detached from the fiberglass stock of the DMR.

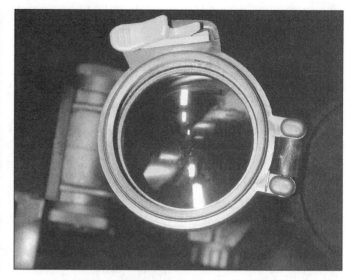

The Leupold scope operates electronically for brightness and clarity, the coated lenses adding to its utility in long-range shooting.

"It worked well," Lewis recalls, "and it did not cost $7 million. It had been created by a Marine gunnery sergeant with a set of basic gunsmithing tools."

It also should be pointed out for the sake of context if nothing else that the first batch of M-14s to come off the production line was turned down by the military powers. Manufactured by Harrington & Richardson under what has been described as "a hurry-up contract," it turned out that the receivers of that particular shipment were poorly tempered and were considered too soft to be safe.

So much for ancient history!

Lewis' familiarization with the semi-new DMR rifle came at Marine Corps Base Hawaii, a complex situated on Kaneohe Bay on the island of Oahu. Some 50 years ago, he was stationed on the same site with the 1st Provisional Marine Air-Ground Task Force, so he was not on strange ground; just surrounded by different – and younger – people.

Mentoring Lewis in the familiarization program regarding the new/old rifle were Warrant Officer 5 Walter D. Romine and Gunnery Sgt. Thomas B. Gilbert. It was the latter who explained that the folks at Quantico recommended the DMR be fired with Match ammunition for best possible performance in EOD work. However, such ammo had not yet arrived at the mid-Pacific base at the time Lewis reviewed the rifle and its capabilities. All training to that time was being conducted with standard issue 7.62mm NATO cartridges, according to the gunnery sergeant.

The Quantico-based force that had put together this DMR insists the piece has accuracy out to 800 yards. However, the warrant officer at the Kaneohe base told Lewis that most of their demands at present are at ranges of no more than 300 yards. At that distance and the ranges between, they had found that the DMR functions well and delivers accuracy as advertised. At the length of almost three football fields, they have used the 10-power scope to knock out cluster bombs that are approximately the size of a golf ball.

As Romine explained, "After our aircraft or those of friendlies have used cluster bombs to clear an airfield, taking out personnel and damaging aircraft,

there is a big chance that we may want to occupy the same ground. Experience shows that invariably some of the cluster bombs still will be on the runway or close enough to it to be dangerous. It becomes our mission to destroy each of the little bombs. For personal safety, we prefer to do that at 300 yards."

The staff at the EOD headquarters in Hawaii has been called upon to disarm a wide array of explosive devices. Also present is a collection of weapons taken during Desert Storm. "Some of these were captured, but no one knew how to unload them," the warrant officer explained. "They came to us. Many of them have odd mechanisms and require a bit of study to determine how best to make them safe."

By Romine's own admission, the 7.62mm bullets fired by the DMR would not be effective in attempting to destroy some of the explosive devices we had the opportunity to look over at close range. For some, a .50-caliber weapon fired at safe ranges would be a better bet.

Romine is an 18-year veteran, 16 of which have been in EOD. Prior to that, he was assigned to communications.

The noncommissioned officer in charge of the Hawaii EOD detachment is Gunnery Sgt. Gilbert. He has 15 years service, with a decade devoted to EOD work. Over the years, he has been assigned temporarily to the Marine Corps marksmanship team a number of times. He competed as a member of the Marine Corps rifle team in 1984-85, 1987 through 1989 and again from 1995 through 1997. It was he who demonstrated for Lewis the capabilities of the reworked M-14.

Gilbert was quite frank in his evaluation of the DMR that had been issued to the Hawaii EOD detachment. He called it "a high-maintenance shooting tool."

In short, this 7.62mm NATO-firing rifle is not a firearm that one can toss around the terrain. Experience has shown that if dropped in the heat of an exercise, banged against a hard surface such as a rock or a tree, it becomes necessary to re-zero it.

The rings and mounts holding the Leupold scope are manufactured by G.G.&G, Inc., a firm headquartered in Arizona.

The DMR rifle is used to explode cluster bombs, such as those shown, to clearrunways and other areas to make them safe for landing aircraft or advancing troops. In training, the Hawaii Marines take out these deactivated golf ball-size bombs at 300 yards.

The gas system requires frequent cleaning and can be somewhat temperamental – sometimes at inopportune moments.

Quite often, says the gunnery sergeant, "Something goes wrong that requires a qualified armorer to fix – and there's not always an armorer available. These are problems we find in actual use and learn to circumvent as much as possible."

Viewing the whole concept from afar, Lewis still was left with an impression he has tended to live with since sometime during World War II: The more complicated a piece of combat equipment, the more time necessarily will be devoted to maintenance and repair.

For EOD work, where actual firefights are seldom likely, the DMR seems to be more than adequate and reuse of the old M-14s has saved the Marine Corps – and ultimately, the taxpayers – a batch of money.

CHAPTER 14

DRAGON FIRE

Assault Troops Need Support to Make the Enemy Keep Their Heads Down; Here is a New Approach

Rick Lindsay activates the Dragon Fire mortar. The mortar shell is visible at the top of the photo just above the explosive fireball.

COMBAT ASSAULTS ARE conducted by troops with rifles and other small arms in hand, but every man involved in such an assault is depending upon supporting weapons to help make the effort easier as well as successful. Down through the ages, big-bore machineguns, mortars, artillery and even naval bombardment have been used to advantage in this type of warfare. And that need is the reason for the development of a new weapon the Marine Corps is developing as a mobile support system called the Dragon Fire.

Development of what has been designated as the Dragon Fire 120mm Automated Mortar began in the Marine Corps' Warfighting Laboratory at Quantico. According to retired Marine Corps Lt. Col. Forrest R. Lindsay, the project officer for the new mortar, the laboratory's purpose is "to improve current and future expeditionary warfare capabilities across the spectrum of conflict for current and future operating forces."

Lindsay adds, "The lab provides the opportunity for the operating forces to experiment and assess the value of promising technology. The lab also recommends changes to required documents; proposes block technology insertions into programs of record and provides alternative ideas to meet acquisition objectives as a result of experimentation."

"That," Lewis insists, "is a high-priced way of stating the Quantico-based Warfighting Lab is devoted to finding better ways to fight and win by keeping up with the trends of modern-day science and using that knowledge to achieve that particular goal."

Lindsay spent most of his active-duty career in artillery units. He is quick to explain that the new mortar system—still in the experimental and development stages—receives the actual fire mission,

This mockup displays how the Dragon Fire 120mm mortar is packed up for movement behind a vehicle or for loading into an aircraft. The original version weighed 7000 pounds and was considered too heavy. The newest version of the Dragon Fire has been reduced to 3000 pounds.

loads its 120nnm projectile and fires without any help from humans.

Broken down, this means that this rifled mortar can receive fire mission data from a forward observer via radio. Automatically, the gun tube is swiveled to line up with the target and fire with accuracy on a target as far away as 8 miles.

Lindsay states that the system is "functionally perfect. It is a hundred times more accurate than a human being!"

In the beginning, it required four or five Marines to operate the Dragon Fire. However, that workload has been reduced to simply emplacing the mortar, supplying it with ammunition and protecting it from enemy attack.

"It is the gun itself that sends messages back to the forward observers, supplying the same data that a human would, except that this is in alpha-numerical script," Lindsay explains, adding, "We've actually had complaints from forward observers because they didn't have a chance to adjust fire. The Dragon Fire is surprisingly accurate on even the first round of a fire mission."

The project began in 1997 as a Marine Corps initiative to automate indirect fire. The project initially was known simply as the "Box Mortar". The first step was to convince the French firm of Thomson Daimler Armaments (TDA) to sell the Corps an experimental armored vehicle mortar, which that company had developed. The Army's Armament, Development and Engineering

Command at the Picatinny Arsenal was called upon to develop the carriage and system integration. A firm known as Allied Signal then came up with the aiming and fire control systems for the new weapon. Because of this cooperative effort, Lindsay and his staff at the Warfighting Lab had the experimental weapon complete and ready to fire by September 1998.

Most mortars in use today have a fixed firing pin in the bottom of the tube. When the mortar shell is dropped down the mouth of the weapon, the shell falls until the primer comes in contact with the firing pin and the shell is launched. That is definitely not the case with the Dragon Fire, according to Lindsay. It is the unit's computer that makes the determination as to when the mortar shell will be fired.

"If the mechanism doesn't sense recoil from the shell being fired, it will refire immediately," Lindsey explains. "The mortar also realigns itself after each use, thus compensating for any movement that might have occurred due to recoil. Even with the resetting after each round, the Dragon Fire can launch up to 10 rounds per minute."

The original prototype of the Dragon Fire, which has been utilized for further experimentation and development, spurred the Marine Corps to push the Department of Defense for a new Expeditionary Fire Support System requirement. Lindsay admits that a major problem seen immediately in the original prototype lay in the fact that the weapon weighed 7,000 pounds. However, this prototype was used to prove that the concept—if not the immediately available hardware—was practical.

The next generation of the Dragon Fire has been developed and weighs only 3000 pounds. It is small enough and sufficiently lightweight that it can be transported internally in the NW-22 Osprey aircraft, although further efforts are being pursued to reduce the weight and size even more.

The Dragon Fire has its own built-in radio fire-control computer and Global Positioning System. According to Lindsay, this arrangement makes it virtually impossible for the troops out there on the line to be subjected to "friendly fire". He insists that it will not fire, should the device somehow be aimed at a known friendly troop concentration or even a small patrol.

The original system operated off of batteries, but it was found that it was draining the power source too rapidly. A generator became a requirement. This problem has since been solved, according to Lindsay. "The range for the Dragon Fire is 8,200 meters, but this can be increased to 13,000 meters with what he calls rocket-assisted projectiles. A broad array of mortar shells also has been developed for the Dragon Fire. Included are high explosive, white phosphorus and illumination as well as several types of special-purpose shells.

"The circle of probable error is 50 meters at all ranges," the project manager states, "but it usually is held to 25 meters." The mortar utilizes a NATO Ballistic Kernel for all ballistic computations. Aiming is accomplished with what is known as a ring laser gyro system for each shot, the fire-control computer aim-

As retired Marine Lt. Col. Rick Lindsay (left) watches, a crew of enlisted Marines from the Marine Corpsí Warfighting Laboratory prepares the Dragon Fire mortar for action.

Marines involved in a demonstration of the Dragon Fire mortar stick their fingers in their ears as protection against the explosion when the weapon is fired.

ing the weapon through what is called a power traverse and elevation system.

"Response time is almost unbelievable, when comparing the system with the mortars the Marine Corps has been using for the better part of a century," Lindsay points out. "The Dragon Fire can be aimed and ready to fire only 20 seconds after receiving the fire mission."

Lewis thought back to the times in the Korean War when he saw racks of rockets airlifted by helicopter into reverse slope positions for firing at the enemy. As several dozen rockets were launched almost simultaneously, there would be mammoth clouds of dust kicked up by the multiple back blasts, marking the area. It would be only minutes before the North Korean's retaliatory fire would plaster the area. For that reason, the moment the rockets were launched, the crew, the launcher—and their helicopter—were on their way to safer climes before the rockets ever landed.

"There is no doubt that an enemy will know where the mortar shells are coming from in short order," Lindsay acknowledges, "but that has been taken into consideration, too."

To get the mortar out of danger's path or simply transport it to where it is needed, the weapon can be towed behind the familiar Humvee or other vehicles. With the MV-22 slated to replace aging Marine Corps helicopters, work on using this means of aerial delivery and extraction are being pursued. The currently available Dragon Fire model also can be emplaced for firing within a modified light-armored vehicle within five minutes.

CHAPTER 15

THE FRENCH HAVE A GUN FOR IT!

From Indochina to Yugoslavia There Has Been a Pattern in Guns the French Favor for Violence

IN THE DAYS before World War II, a popular play was titled "The French Have a Word for It". The war pretty well proved that the French also had a

Two French partisans prepare to use their air-dropped M-3 submachine guns against the Nazis during World War II. Subguns and grenades were common weapons supplied by OSS and SOE operatives during that period.

gun for whatever problem they faced, making do most of the time.

The Maquisards, the local guerrilla units battling the Nazis on French soil during World War II, used whatever weapons were available, sometimes including farm tools such as scythes and pitchforks. As for firearms, the Spanish-made Ruby .32, the LeFrancais .25 and the old M-1892 revolver were among the first arms obtained by these clandestine operators. These firearms were easy to conceal for defense purposes – and for assassinations. Prior to the Allied Forces landing in 1944, pistols and grenades were the chief weapons involved in the countless small-scale operations conducted by these French patriots.

Eventually, the British Special Operations Executive (SOE) and the American Office of Strategic Services (OSS) air-dropped heavier weapons to the Maquis. Included in these drops were Enfield and Smith & Wesson .38-200 revolvers, as well as Colt .45 1911A1 pistols. Some weapons drops included full auto-firing Sten guns, the U.S.-made M-3 .45 APC Grease Gun the UM D-42, Thompson submachine guns and M-1 Carbines. Other items of personnel destruction included Gammon grenades with impact fuses and even light mortars with appropriate shells.

U.S. advisers were also parachuted into France. One of these agents, Gen. Jack Singlaub, was later famous in the military for his border crossing teams in Vietnam, which were organized under the lofty title of Studies and Observation Group (SOG). Singlaub, however, started his career of enemy disruption during World War II. He served as an OSS Jedburgh team leader in occupied France. His team's watchwords were Surprise, Mitraillage, Eveanouissement, which translates to: Surprise, Machinegun, Disappear!

As the war progressed, the most prominent French weapons during this period were the LeFrancais (Manufrance) 6.35mm, the MAB Model D 7.65mm, the Model 2 1892 9mm revolver and the MAS 1935A 7.65 Long, which later was developed into the Swiss SIG P-210 9mm. Other guns used with some frequency were the MAS 1938 submachine gun chambered for the 7.65mm Long cartridge, which was noted for its lack of power and reliability. Also in frequent use was the MAS 1936 bolt-action rifle chambered for a 7.5mm round. The Maquis generally preferred the .32 ACP cartridge to the .380, because these guns usually carried more ammo in their magazines and gave away little in the way of power.

Foreign weapons included the British and U.S. models already listed, plus British SMLE rifles, Bren guns and Commando knives. Captured German small arms used to arm the guerrillas included P-38 pistols, 9mm MP-40 submachine guns and 7.92 KAR-98 rifles. One point of interest lies in the fact that so many of the German-manufactured P-38s were captured that it became the closest thing the French Gendarmerie had as a standard pistol in the years immediately following the war. During the war years, France had been stripped for the most part of its overseas possessions. Notable among these was Indochina. This land mass then covered what now are the sovereign states of Vietnam, Laos and Cambodia. The Vietnam area encompassed a district in the north known as Tonkin, while the center was known as Annam and in the south was Cochin China.

These territories had been seized by the French during a gradual 19th century expansion of colonies, and then had been consolidated in 1893. When France fell to the blitzkrieg tactics of the Germans in 1940, the Japanese immediately claimed Indochina and occupied it.

According to Steele, "History, of course, shows that during this occupation, the communist movement headed by Ho Chi Minh and Vo Nguyen Giap used the subsequent nationalist and obvious anti-Japanese sentiment to organize the Viet Nam Doc Lap Dong Minh Hoi."

The term translates to League for the Independence of Vietnam. The term later was shortened to Viet Minh, the name kept by communist guerrillas into the war with the United States. It was President Diem, then the leader in South Vietnam, who coined the name Viet Cong to point out the communist rather than nationalist agenda of these people.

Utilizing guerrilla tactics that were adapted from Soviet as well as Chinese models, the Viet Minh battled the Japanese occupation forces from 1941 until 1945. In fact, it has been established that Ho Chi Minh actually met with American OSS agents during the war. Little is known of what took place during the meeting.

After the Japanese surrendered, their occupation troops were withdrawn and the British and U.S. governments chose to assist France in regaining her colonial hold. This decision apparently was because the independence movement under way was communist controlled. It would seem that the so-called Cold War already had started.

Efforts were made to negotiate, but when these failed, Ho Chi Minh began to use the tactics employed so successfully against the Japanese. This time, the tactics were aimed at the returning French.

The French arms industry had been wrecked by the Nazis, but their military had been equipped with Brit-

French and Vietnamese troops operated in the Indochina war in 1953. Note the 9mm MAT-49 French submachine gun carried by the soldier with the machinegun tripod.

This French soldier fighting in Indochina in 1953 carried the MAS 49 7.5mm. Note the rifle grenade mounted at the muzzle.

ish and American small arms, which meant that the French forces still had far greater firepower available than did the Viet Minh with its rustic weapons.

"However, the French tended to use this firepower with conventional tactics," says Steele. "This proved less than sufficient against the Viet Minh's sophisticated subversion, hit-and-run attacks and clever use of the terrain they knew so well."

As time passed, the Viet Minh cadres scattered throughout the country were able to obtain better weapons by attacks on small French outposts, and were supplied by communist allies. According to available records, in 1950 alone the French lost 6,000 men, 13 artillery pieces, 125 mortars, 450 trucks, 940 machine guns, 8,000 rifles and 1,200 submachine guns.

Lewis was in Wonsan, North Korea, in the early winter of 1950. At that time, China Air Transport, an airline operating out of Taiwan, was flying occasional contract supply flights into that area. One of the soldier of fortune pilots was a former Marine known as "Earthquake" Magoon. He also had been flying resupply missions into what then still was considered Indochina, since the French were fighting to hold it.

Magoon told Lewis every flight into the tiny airstrip at Dien Bien Phu was "a rehearsal for suicide." The pilot died in a crash not long after.

"Eventually, the French depended on U.S. assistance for heavy weapons ranging from .50-caliber machine guns to aircraft. However, in the matter of small arms, the country set out to become independent," explains Lewis.

The Petter MAS 1935S was developed into the 9mm MAS 1950. Manufactured at St. Etienne, it still is used by Gendarmerie riot police. The MAS 1950 is a conventional single-action service auto with fixed sights and a nine-round magazine. It weighs 1.8 pounds, has a 4.4-inch barrel and measures 7.6 inches overall.

"The abysmal MAS 38 7.65mm Long submachine gun was replaced by the MAT 49 firing the 9mm cartridge," Steele says. "The MAS 38 fired full-auto from a blowback action, ammo being fed from a 32-round magazine.

"Many of these guns were captured in Indochina by the Viet Minh and some were rebarreled to fire the Soviet 7.62mm pistol round. Some captured MAT 49s were rebarreled to handle the same cartridge," Steele explains.

The MAT 49, manufactured in France's Tulle Arsenal, grew out of a 1946 project initiated by the Section Technique de L'Arme. "After war-long experience with various home-grown and Allied weapons, it was decided that the 7.65mm Long cartridge was too long, while the .45 ACP round required a heavy weapon. The answer was to adopt the European standard 9mm Parabellum," Steele reports.

"While the MAT 49 has what is described as a 'wrap-around' open bolt, this firearm still is second-generation in its overall size and the use of stampings in its manufacture," he adds.

The MAT 49 has a sliding wire stock that is less than stable, a rear grip safety and a dust cover. The front sight is a hooded blade, while the rear sight is an L-type, flip-up style with apertures for 100 and 200 meters.

The gun weighs 9.41 pounds unloaded and fires full auto at a cyclic rate of 600 rounds per minute from a staggered box magazine. Barrel length is 9.05 inches, with an overall length of 28 inches; this length is reduced to 18.3 inches when the stock is retracted. Steele's belief is that "the most unique feature of the MAT 49 is a forward hand grip that can be stowed parallel to the barrel, then pulled vertical for insertion of a loaded magazine.

Whatever else it might be, the MAT 49 is probably the most distinctive and stylish of 20th century French small arms. It was even chosen by artist Frank Frazetta for his famous 1965 poster Number 62, "Combat". During the war in Indochina, this weapon was issued primarily to paratroopers and tankers, although some could be found in virtually every French unit.

Going into the Indochina campaign, the Foreign Legion and other French units were often saddled with the uninspired MAS 36 bolt-action rifle, which still can be found among older Gendarmes.

A folding-stock CR-39 version sometimes was issued. The MAS 36 fired 7.5mm M-29 ammunition from a five-round magazine. The rifle also was equipped with an epee-style bayonet.

During this war in Southeast Asia, the semi-automatic MAS 49 7.5mm rifle entered French service. It

This French gendarme, packing a MAS 50 9mm pistol, is on duty at a government building in Paris.

Dress uniforms of Paris police are worn for formal occasions and state visits of foreign dignitaries. The female officer is armed with the Manurhin .38 revolver.

used a 10-round magazine and also could be used to fire rifle grenades.

These rifles, pistols and submachine guns were supplemented by a variety of support weapons ranging from the automatic weapons to artillery, all of it supplied by the United States and Britain.

However, France had – and still has – Europe's largest communist party. Conventional firepower was simply not enough in the face of dissension at home and the sophisticated guerrilla tactics of the enemy.

"Eventually, Vo Nguyen Giap was able to lure the French forces into setting up a major base in a valley called Dien Bien Phu. The decision was based on the fact that French commanders did not believe the Viet Minh could bring artillery pieces to the surrounding hillsides. Coolie labor, however, did just that. Despite heroic reinforcement, in 1954, Dien Bien Phu fell to the communists and Paris politicians negotiated an end to the war," Steel explains.

The United States soon picked up the anti-communist baton and supplied advisers and regular assistance to the South Vietnamese regime, which was set up after the 1954 treaty. This was part of the U.S. government's policy of "containment" that began after the communists overran China and took over that nation in 1949. Part of the resulting U.S. program was to aid any Asian government fighting Red subversion. The Korean War was another result of that policy.

"At one point, early in our Vietnam involvement, the United States dispatched what was called an advisory platoon," Lewis relates. "The average size of a platoon at that time was in the neighborhood of 40 bodies traditionally led by a second lieutenant. The so-called advisory platoon had more than 900 personnel and the platoon leader was a colonel!"

In 1965, when Special Forces advisers proved insufficient, U.S. regular forces were committed to the effort and managed to prevent a communist takeover that year. Again in 1968 when the communists launched their so-called Tet offensive during a Vietnamese holy season, U.S. forces prevented a communist victory and virtually destroyed the Viet Cong as a viable military force.

In 1972, Giap again attempted a conventional invasion of South Vietnam, but U.S. bombing missions halted it at the border.

"However, as had been the case with the French, the United States had not covered its own rear base," Steele charges. "Leftists and draft resistors on the home front forced withdrawal of U.S. forces in 1973 and Congress halted military aid to South Vietnam. The demoralized South Vietnamese army became an easy target for a conventional invasion in 1975. Fortunately, the 12 years of U.S. involvement had shored up regimes in several neighboring countries."

Modern French Weapons

Indochina was not the last colonial disaster for France. They next lost Algeria, which had long been the headquarters of the French Foreign Legion. Reports are that following Algerian independence, even then-President Charles De Gaulle had to be careful in choosing his bodyguards for their personal loyalty to him.

Among these bodyguards was Raymond Sasia, who was well-known in that era as a judo and self-defense expert. Steele's investigations show that it was Sasia who set out to reorganize French handgun training based upon what he had seen at the FBI Academy in Quantico in 1961.

For the national police, the bodyguard-turned-instructor instituted the combat crouch, two-handed pistol shooting, silhouette targets, the Hogan's Alley realistic combat range – and the three-inch Smith & Wesson .357 revolver.

Sasia also created the Centre National de Tir, a police shooting school devoted to training instructors in his methods. The Manurhin MR 73 revolver chambered for the .357 Magnum cartridge was produced at France's Muhouse factory specifically for police and the Sasia method of shooting. The MR 73 is a high-quality weapon with a 7.7-pound double-action trigger pull. In single action, the pull is approximately 4.2 pounds. Barrel lengths ranged from 3 to 7 inches."

As late as 1981, handguns manufactured by Colt, Smith & Wesson and even Llama were being used by French police officers. That was the year that Manurhin began manufacturing a cheaper version of the MR 73 for general police service. Designated as the F-1 model, this handgun uses the Ruger Speed-Six-style frame and action. Not as finely made as the MR 73, the F-1 had a double-action trigger pull of 11.5 pounds; the single-action pull was 5.5 pounds. Barrel lengths ran from 2.5 to 4 inches.

Today, towns with populations of under 10,000 residents, as well as border areas and government centers, are patrolled by the Gendarmerie, which is part of the French army. Formed in 1791, this outfit's Gendarmes – translated as "men at arms" – have served in most of the nation's wars as military police, infantry and even cavalry. Distinguished by a distinctive blue dress cap, the gendarme today is equipped with either a MAS 50 or the newer MAS G-1.

The counterterrorist elite within the Gendarmerie is the Groupe d'Intervention de la Gendarmerie Nationale. More commonly known even in its own country as the GIGN, this element gained fame in December1994 for retrieval of Air France Flight 8969 at the Algiers airport. In that engagement, the GIGN killed four Islamic hijackers with no friendly fatalities. Those assigned to this elite unit are allowed to carry any weapon considered necessary for the job, although they are best known for their use of the MR 73 revolver, the Heckler & Koch MP-5 subgun and the FAMAS assault rifle.

A French army patrol forms a security perimeter in Bosnia. The soldier in front has an FRF-1 sniper rifle.

The FAMAS is the standard 5.56 assault rifle of the French army. A bullpup design like the British SA-80, the FAMAS has been nicknamed "the bugle" for its shape, which involves an AR-10-type carrying handle. This handle serves as a sight rail and offers protection to the cocking handle. This particular weapon offers selective fire, featuring semi-automatic, full-auto and three-round-burst fire. It can be used to launch grenades, a bipod can be attached without problem and bayonets are affixed for parades.

GIGN and French army patrols on United Nations duty in Bosnia also have available the FRF1 7.5mm sniper rifle. Refined from the MAS 36 rifle, this one is a bolt- action with pistol grip, bipod and a Model 53 sight.

An overall look at French small arms production leaves us with the impression that while hardly a development center, France has produced some interesting weapons for that nation's military and national police. The experience of citizens as guerrillas during World War II, then as counterinsurgents in Indochina and Algeria, have served as lessons in national survival.

CHAPTER 16

BARRETT'S BIG BLASTERS

In These Big-Bore Rifles, the .50 BMG Cartridge Is Enjoying a Whole New Life and Reputation

WHILE OTHER MILITARY cartridges come and go, eventually being declared obsolete, there is one that just won't go away. That is the 50-caliber Browning Machine Gun round, perhaps more familiarly known as the .50 BMG.

Back in the 1970s, the cartridge was considered to have seen its day along with the Browning-designed gun that fired it. The gun was at the point of being retired, when Saco Industries came up with an improvement for the M-2 pintle-mounted machinegun. Originally, changing a barrel on the gun was a major project, but the new barrel replacement system proved to be simple and user-friendly, as they say on Madison Avenue. That move helped keep the cartridge alive.

The Browning .50 Machine Gun was in the development stages during World War I, but did not get into actual production until that war had ended. At that time the gun – and its cartridge – were being produced primarily for use against armored vehicles and aircraft. As thicker and better armor was developed, the .50 machine gun seemed to become less important to military planners and suppliers.

In spite of this bureaucratic negativism, late in the last century a group of civilian shooters began to experiment with shoulder-fired rifles built specifically to handle the pressures of the .50 BMG cartridge. Today, that group is known as the Fifty Caliber Shooters Association, Inc., with headquarters in Monroe, Utah. Members of this group did virtually all of the development and experimental work involved in developing the various rifles now being built and marketed to handle the .50 BMG round as a long-range military sniper cartridge. Jim Schmidt, who heads up Arizona Ammunition, Inc., in Phoenix, has been a leader in developing specific loads for hunting, practice and competition.

The Marine Corps chose the Barrett M-82A1 semi-automatic as its extended-range sniper rifle. It fires standard .50-caliber Browning Machine Gun ammunition to 2,000 yards with accuracy.

In the beginning, all of the rifles built to handle the big .50 were of the single-shot, bolt-action design. Most still are. However, Ron Barrett eventually developed a semi-automatic rifle to handle the .50 BMG cartridge. That was the semi-automatic rifle ultimately chosen by the Marine Corps for use as a long-range sniper rifle against vehicles, supply dumps and other large targets. There have been recorded human kills at as far as 1,800 yards, but those have been the exception, according to available documents.

Today, Barrett's M-82A1 is in service with the Marine Corps, the Navy SEALs and the U.S. Army's combat engineers, as well as explosive ordnance disposal (EOD) units throughout the Armed Forces. According to Barrett, this particular model has also been sold to Australia, France, England, Greece, Turkey and Norway.

In November 1991, Marine Capt. Jeffrey E. Dearolph spoke to members of the American Defense Preparedness Association at a conference in Atlanta. At that time, he was the officer-in-charge of the Scout/Sniper Instructor School at the Marine Corps'

Combat Development Command at Quantico. He talked about the use of the rifle firing the .50 BMG during Desert Storm.

"In September of 1990, the Marine forces in Southwest Asia identified a requirement for a long-range, multi-shot weapon with good penetration characteristics to destroy or disable equipment-type targets at 2,000 yards," the captain explained to his audience. "Due to time constraints, an off-the-shelf, currently produced .50-caliber rifle would have to be considered for procurement."

The weapon selected was the Barrett Light Fifty rifle being produced by Barrett Manufacturing Corp. in Murfreesboro, Tenn. Designated by the Marines as a Special Application Scoped Rifle, this one was selected for its reliability and lethality to a range of 2,000 yards.

During the Gulf War, the Barrett was equipped with the same Unertl scope used on the M-40A1 .30-caliber sniper rifle," according to Dearolph. (During that same time period, Unertl began designing a scope specifically for the .50-caliber rifle at its headquarters in Mars, Pa.)

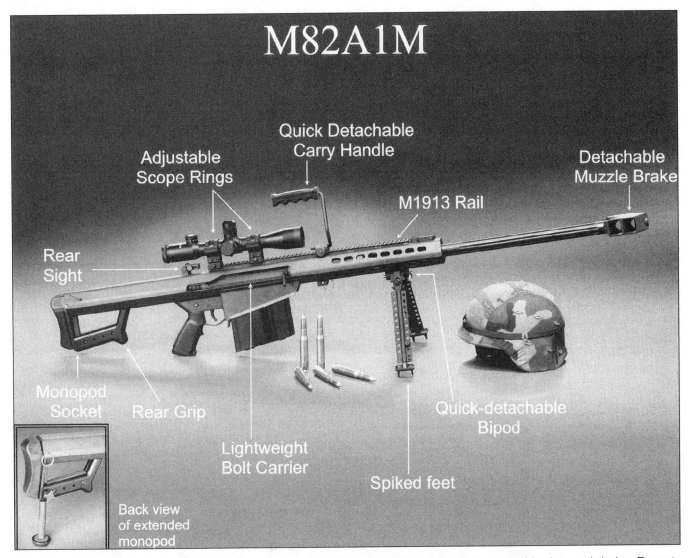

This marked photo identifies the various features of the Barrett M-82A1 that made it a tool in demand during Desert Storm. In Afghanistan, it has been used by the Canadian army as well as the U.S. forces.

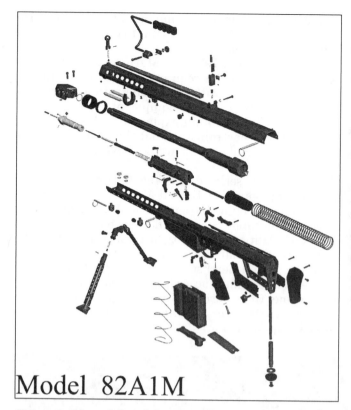

Model 82A1M

This artist's rendition of the disassembled M-82A1 offers some idea of the complications that were involved in the design of this recoil-operated rifle.

The primary round used in the rifle during Desert Storm was the .50 Raufus cartridge developed by the Raufus Co. of Norway. It consists of a high-explosive tip combined with a tungsten carbide penetrator," Dearolph told the gathering. "The Barrett also can fire the standard Browning .50-caliber ammunition.

The weapon was designed to be fired from the prone position using a bipod. However, the bipod may be folded either forward or backward for firing with optical support. There also are vehicle-type mounts available. The Barrett may be disassembled for carrying in a backpack specifically designed for the purpose.

The Picatinny rail atop the upper receiver of the Barrett .50 rifle allows all sorts of sighting devices to be attached. The rail is a military standard item.

Although the Marine Corps snipers traditionally work in pairs, a three-man team was developed for the Barrett gun because of the weight of the weapon and its ammunition and for team security measures.

An element called the Tiger Brigade was organized prior to the start of the ground war in Desert Storm. Ninety Marine Corps scout/snipers and 40 U.S. Army snipers were trained with the 53 Barrett guns then available in the Southwest Asia war zone, according to Dearolph. He added, "In less than 7 months, the Marine Corps procured and fielded a new weapons system and trained a large number of scout/snipers on how to use it."

An example of what was accomplished by this group is reflected in wording of the citation accompanying the Secretary of the Navy's Commendation Medal awarded to Marine Cpl.Greg A. Gradwohl, the

Actor Tom Berringer, who portrayed a Marine gunnery sergeant in the film, "Sniper", had an opportunity to become acquainted with the Barrett M-82A1 rifle during a session on the rifle range at the Marine Corps' Camp Pendleton in California.

enlisted team leader for what was – and still is – called a Surveillance Targeting Acquisition Platoon.

Between Feb. 23 and Feb. 28, 1991, "Corporal Gradwohl led his team through numerous engagements against enemy mechanized forces while protecting sniper support by utilizing the M-821A1 .50-caliber sniper rifle."

During an engagement with an enemy mechanized unit on Feb. 24, in the vicinity of the Al Burqan oil fields, the corporal's team "encountered a mechanized enemy brigade. Traveling in a vehicle with no armored protection, he again provided accurate long-range fire on enemy troops and tanks."

Now the chief firearms instructor for a police sniper program, Gradwohl recalls that his team "had multiple kills out to 1,600 yards with this weapons system." During most of the conflict, he points out, "our usual .30-caliber M-40 (sniper rifle) was next to worthless due to the extreme range and a lack of cover available. Without the M-821A, my sniper team would not have been nearly as effective as we were during that conflict."

The manufacturer describes the Barrett M-82A1 as a short-recoil, semi-automatic rifle with a 10-round detachable box magazine. It has an overall length of 54.7 inches and weighs 30 pounds without a scope and ammo. The rifle is constructed of steel stampings, castings and machined parts. The barrel is fashioned from 4140 chrome moly steel, weighs 8 pounds and is 28 inches long. Fluted to reduce weight, the barrel carries eight grooves with one right-hand twist in 15 inches.

The telescoping bipod can be used in five different positions and is detachable. According to Barrett engineers, the patented muzzle brake reduces recoil by 69 percent. The trigger pull is set at the factory at 7 to 9 pounds, while flip-up iron sights – front and rear – are part of the package. Adjustable for both windage and elevation, the sight scale is calibrated for the .50 BMG cartridge. However, most important to the military sniper is the Picatinny rail that measures 19.125 inches. A scope or a wide range of other accessories can be attached to the rail.

Safety features of the M-82A1 include a manual external safety as well as a firing pin block to keep the gun from firing out of battery. Removal of the receiver lock pins facilitates separation of the upper and lower receiver sections for further field-stripping for cleaning, adjustment or repair.

Marine Corps Gunnery Sgt. Capps prepares to fire the .50 Barrett rifle as part of a surveillance target acquisition platoon in Kosovo. The Corps calls it their Special Application Sniper Rifle.

Using elevation-adjustable scope rings is recommended with the M-82A1," says Dennis Carp, a Barrett Co. spokesman. "With the adjustable scope rings, the user is able to elevate the rear of the scope. This allows the scope to be zeroed at a hundred meters, yet have enough elevation adjustment to reach out to 2000 meters and beyond."

In addition to the elevation-adjustable aluminum rings, the Tennessee manufacturer also offers a number of options, including a mil-dot scope, a reticle scope, a soft mount, a soft carrying case and a combination transport case and shooting mat. Not all of these accessories have been ordered by the military, however.

In firing the Barrett .50 semi-automatic, the barrel, bolt and bolt carrier travel rearward as a unit for a distance of 2.9 inches. At this point, motion of the rifle barrel is halted by the barrel stop. The cam pin immediately engages a helical groove in the bolt body. This causes the bolt body to turn, thus unlocking from the barrel extension.

According to Carp, the bolt and bolt carrier then continue to the rear, ejecting the spent cartridge case and compressing the recoil spring at the same moment. As the bolt turns, the new round is stripped out of the magazine and chambered. The striker is held in place by the sear during this action, the bolt entering the bolt extension and rotating for its three-lug lockup.

Apparently operating on the theory that the day a business loses forward momentum and tends to rest on his laurels, it is going backward, Barrett and his staff haven't settled for the company's success with the semi-automatic .50-caliber. Meeting the needs of sportsmen interested in long-range target work, the company is producing several bolt-action repeaters. Police departments that believe their snipers don't need all of the bells and whistles have shown interest in these rifles, which are less expensive than the military's choice.

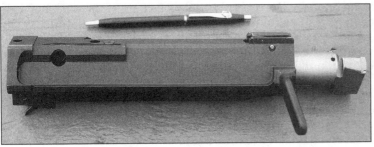
Some idea of the size of the bolt and bolt carrier of the Barrett-made .50-caliber rifle is seen in the comparison with an ordinary ballpoint pen. These parts are carefully machined.

The Barrett Model 95 bullpup configuration is a bolt-action repeater with a magazine that holds five rounds. Note that the magazine is positioned well behind the trigger group.

The Barrett Model 99 single-shot is aimed at big-bore shooters interested in competing in long-range contests. It has many of the features of the M-82A1 as evidenced in this photo.

Currently in production in Murfreesboro is the Model 95M, a bolt-action repeater that is of the bullpup design. It has an overall length of 45 inches and weighs 22.5 pounds unloaded. Like the M-82A1, it features the M-1913 military-spec scope rail as well as flip-up iron sights. The magazine carries five rounds of .50 BMT ammo.

The folks at Barrett are calling their Model 99 the Big Shot. This is a single-shot bolt-action design that measures 50.4 inches in overall length. Barrel length is 33 inches, with a barrel weight of 14 pounds. Total weight of the unloaded rifle is 25 pounds.

Described by Barrett as a lightweight tactical rifle designed for law enforcement, the Model 99-1 is another single-shot bolt-action type. This one measures 46.4 inches overall and has a 29-inch fluted barrel. Without ammo, total weight is 21.25 pounds. There are no sights, but the Picatinny rail for scope mounting is part of the package. According to Carp, the company is listing the Model 99-1 as being good for penetration of barricades, for disabling vehicles and for explosive ordnance disposal.

In the past, Barrett has cooperated with Swarovski in recommending a pair of the scopemakers' models that now are marked with the Barrett name. Both of these scopes are 10-power items that are built to withstand the heavy recoil of the .50-caliber rifles. One scope is equipped with the mil-dot, which the other is a ranging reticle scope.

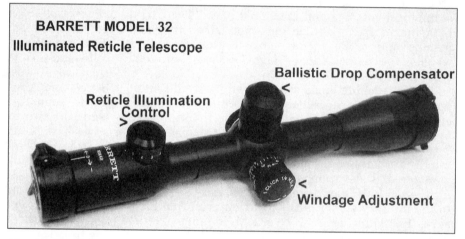

BARRETT MODEL 32
Illuminated Reticle Telescope

Ballistic Drop Compensator

Reticle Illumination Control

Windage Adjustment

The Barrett Co. now is marketing its own scope, the Model 32, which is built to withstand the recoil of .50-caliber rifles. As indicated, it carries an illuminated reticle.

More recently, however, the folks in Murfreesboro have come up with a scope of their own that they are calling the Model 32. It is being furnished with some of the Barrett rifle models as part of the package. It is a 10x42mm model with an illuminated reticle. The Model 32 has a coated-glass reticle, matte black finish and 32mm tube diameter. We don't know who did the underwater testing, but the Barrett sales staff insists their scope is waterproof to 10 meters, meeting all military standards for reliability and durability.

Barrett has come a long way from a professional photographer who had enough interest in firearms to ultimately realize a dream!

CHAPTER 17

THE WHAT AND WHY OF CARBINES

The Short Rifle Has a Long History and Is Still With Us in One Form or Another

IN THE PAGES of *Memoires pour l'Artillerie*, a volume published in 1548, a passage suggests that the term carbine came from the Spanish cavalry units of that historic era called Carabins. No matter what the origin, this short rifle has been with us since shortly after the birth of firearms and still is in use in one form or another.

Generally, any rifle with a barrel of 22 inches or less is classified as a carbine. Historically, it was a cavalry weapon, a shoulder arm that could be maneuvered from the saddle. With the exception of the shorter barrel and possible modifications to the stock and forearm, the carbine was – and is – the same as the standard rifle, using the same lock work and the same cartridge.

Steele holds a commercial version of the M-1 Carbine made after World War II by Universal Arms. This carbine was the U.S. Army's initial effort to replace the Model 1911A1 automatic pistol with a more effective two-handed sidearm.

"A good modern example of this is the so-called Jungle Carbine," says Steele. "This is a version of the British Lee-Enfield rifle, which was used in the South Pacific during World War II. Earlier it had been carried by British cavalrymen, but with the demise of the horse as a tool of warfare, the Jungle Carbine came to be used by support troops and marauders who needed the maneuverability of a short weapon around vehicles and when fighting in dense jungle undergrowth."

In 1940 that the U.S. Army's Department of Ordnance approved specifications for a new type of carbine. This was to be a weapon that would not use the .30/06 Springfield of the standard army rifle. Instead, it was to have its own cartridge. At that time, the 1903 Springfield and the Garand M-1 – just coming into its own – fired the high-powered .30/06 rifle cartridge. The new carbine was not to be used as a replacement for either of these long guns. Instead, it was meant to be a substitute for the .45 1911A1 service pistol then in common use by company grade officers, some non-commissioned officers and special troops.

As later became evident, the Colt .45 auto never was replaced, except by another handgun. First came the Smith & Wesson Model 15 revolver, which the Air Force adopted, then came the Beretta Model 42 9mm, which was adopted for all U.S. armed services as the M-9. The requirement for a sidearm – particularly for military police, vehicle and gun crews, officers, special forces and pilots could not be met by a carbine or a submachine gun.

Steele says, "After some thought by the military powers, the carbine and the shotgun were considered too cumbersome, too threatening or too unsafe to fill the role of a sidearm. The MAC M-10 and M-11 submachine guns that were designed as potential replacements for the .45 auto were considered, then largely ignored.

"It was recognized that the officer, the medic, the military policeman and the tank crewman needed a

Before it was put on California's banned assault weapons' list because of its unconventional appearance, Steele had the opportunity to work with the J&R M-68 9mm Carbine.

weapon that could be carried constantly and safely for emergency self-defense. Members of a SEAL team or even a clandestine operator with the OSS – later the CIA – needed and still needs – a short-range, semi-automatic weapon that can be concealed and silenced easily for terminating enemy soldiers and guard dogs. The pilot needs a compact weapon he can carry on his vest as a part of his survival gear."

In spite of these special needs, there were more M-1 Carbines produced during World War II and the Korean War than any other weapon. About 5 million of them came off production lines.

"The reason the M-1 Carbine became popular appears to be the fact that it was more accurate than the .45 pistol and easier to carry than the M-1 Garand," Steele says. "Given the large number of support troops in modern armies, the advantages just mentioned would provide a large market for the little carbine. There is no doubt that combat leaders were better off armed with it than with just an issue pistol. Small-sized indigenous troops such as the Vietnamese could use the carbine better than any shoulder-mounted weapon, until the development of the M-16."

The U.S. carbine was manufactured in four versions: First was the semi-automatic M-1, then came the folding stocked M-1A1, the selective-fire M-2 and ultimately the infra-red scoped M-3, also with a selective-fire capability.

Weight of the basic weapon was 5.5 pounds. Barrel length was 18 inches and overall length was 36.6 inches with the fixed wood stock. The cartridge was a .30-caliber intermediate round, with power somewhat greater than that of the later .357 Magnum cartridge. Cyclic rate of fire with the selective-fire M-2 version was 750 rounds per minute.

Nine companies in the United States manufactured the carbine during World War II. Most notable was the Inland Manufacturing Division of General Motors. Lewis recalls carrying one in Korea that was stamped as having been made by Wurlitzer, which was better known for production of jukeboxes.

Plainfield, Universal and others produced commercial versions of the M-1 Carbine following the

war. These two companies, which based their future on continuing demand for the little carbine, have been out of business for years. In Italy, however, Beretta produced its own version, which it called the Model 1957. Gunmakers in Morocco almost immediately copied the Beretta clone. Closer to home, the Dominican Republic produced its own reproduction which they called the Cristobal M-2 Carbine.

"This carbine is highly favored by some police departments because of its convenient size and relatively low power, making it safer for use in urban areas where large crowds and thin walls are common," Steele points out.

Usually, the M-1 semi-automatic version is favored in police work. Such weapons are in service with the Royal Ulster Constabulary as well as many other foreign departments.

"I have seen them carried in the war wagons – weapons and communications trucks – used by special weapons teams of the Chicago Police Department," Steele reports. "The New York City Police Department used the M-1A1 folding stock model with a shortened barrel and soft-nosed ammunition for its controversial stake-out unit that operated between 1967 and 1971. Members of this outfit generally believed the M-1A1 Carbine was more likely to drop a suspect with a single round than either their service .38-caliber handguns or the Ithaca 12-gauge shotgun."

Military forces still using the M-1 Carbine include Chile, Ethiopia, Honduras, Japan, South Korea, Norway, the Philippines, Taiwan and Tunisia. It also was used extensively in Laos, Cambodia and Vietnam during the communist insurgency years, 1945-75.

"I will always recall a pair of carbines kept by the check-in desk of the Majestic Hotel in Saigon," Steele says. "They were used by security guards against the so-called Honda Cowboys that loved to ride by, the driver traveling at top speed, while his rider loosed a fusillade of rounds in the direction of the hotel."

The M-1 Carbine has been used extensively by both the national police and communist guerrillas in Thailand, although the nation's military forces and Border Patrol officers now are equipped with the M-16. British Special Air Service troops – the vaunted SAS – used the U.S.-made carbine in the Malayan Emergency between 1948 and 1960, although they also used the British-made Lee-Enfield carbine.

"The so-called intermediate cartridge usually is developed by either shortening a standard rifle cartridge or upgrading a pistol cartridge," Steele notes. "The U.S. M-1 Carbine made use of its own special cartridge, but it actually was based on the commercially marketed 1905 .32 Winchester round for autoloading rifles. In shape and power, however, the .30 Carbine round is closer to a pistol cartridge than to those intermediate rifle rounds such as the German 7.92mm Kurz and the Soviet 7.62x39mm. In fact, the carbine round produces less than half the muzzle energy of the Soviet 7.62x39mm cartridge, which was developed originally for the SKS carbine, then used later in the AK-47 assault rifle.

"It was the issue of stopping power that served as the death knell for the U.S. carbine. That was coupled with the development of assault rifles of comparable size that offered the infantryman far greater power," Steele explains.

The one-shot kills experienced by New York City police officers with the M-1 .30 Carbine were made with 110-grain soft-point ammunition, a far cry from the use of the weapon when loaded with hardball military ammo.

The Geneva Convention and the finicky ammunition demands of automatic weapons under combat conditions both require hardball bullets. Unfortunately, the hardball bullet tends to over-penetrate, and when combined with the comparatively low 1,970 fps velocity of the carbine round, there is extremely little hydrostatic shock.

This poor stopping power, along with a lack of mechanical reliability at low temperatures or when firing full automatic were the major complaints against this carbine model during the Korean War.

In one of his books, Gen. S.L.A. Marshall quoted Marine Lt. Joseph Fisher after the defense of Hagaru-ri in the winter of 1950: "About 30 percent of our carbines gave us trouble," Fisher said. "Some wouldn't fire at all, others responded sluggishly. But the main reason my men lost confidence in the carbine was because they would put a bullet right in a Chink's chest at 25 yards and he wouldn't stop.

"That happened to me. The bullet struck home; the man simply winced and kept coming. About half a dozen of my men made this same complaint; some of them swore they had fired three or four times, hit the man each time and still not stopped him."

It has been reported that sometimes troops in Korea would not even bother to pick up discarded M-1 Carbines after a battle. They apparently figured that they would be of no use to the enemy.

"Investigation has shown that part of the problem was the select-fire M-2 version," Steele says. "The weapon apparently was not adequately redesigned for full-auto fire. It did not have a straight-line stock, a recoil buffer, a chrome-lined barrel, a burst-control device or any other aid to effective full-auto shooting.

"At that point, the M-2 was the equivalent of a first generation submachine gun like the Reising, but with a somewhat more powerful cartridge. Although cold-weather lubricants were not as effective in those days as now, the design of the carbine was considered to be at least as much to blame for winter weather malfunctions."

Lewis recalls that in the winter of 1950 and again in 1951 while in Korea, some of the immediate action treatments for several weapons were rather crude by military standards. When a rifle or carbine was gummed up with lubricant that was hardened by cold weather, Marines tended to urinate on the bolt and other innards to remove the grease. After the grease was removed, some would use the graphite from an ordinary lead pencil to coat the parts.

"Some official sources have said this didn't happen," Lewis notes, "but they weren't there. I was and saw what worked."

History has shown that full-automatic fire with the M-2 Carbine also led to quick expenditures of ammunition. In Korea, those armed with the M-2 usually fired most of their ammunition at the beginning of an enemy attack. This was particularly true of night attacks. These shooters generally were out of ammunition long before those armed with the M-1 Garand. Generally the expended full-auto rounds accounted for little or nothing in the way of enemy body counts.

Those facts led General Marshall to conclude, "The carbine, made full automatic, has provided no additional power to the infantry line in virtue of the change, but to the contrary, in the hard terms of tactical practice has served but to weaken the infantry fire base."

There were reports, of course, of effective action with the carbine in Korea, but it is generally thought that these shows of accuracy and effectiveness usually were performed by someone's "pet piece," a weapon that had been reworked and especially cared for. In one action, an Army lieutenant used his carbine on full automatic to kill two onrushing Chinese at a distance of 5 yards with a single burst. He then held off other charging enemies long enough for his men to evacuate their position.

"Such examples were the exception to the rule," Steele declares.

The M-1 Carbine was phased out of front-line service in 1957 in favor of the M-14. This 7.62mm NATO weapon had a selective-fire capability, too, but knowing commanders removed the full-auto switch from all rifles that were not meant to fire full-auto in a battle situation. By the mid-1960s, when the M-16 and its 5.56mm cartridge began to replace the M-14, the .30-caliber carbine was more a memory than anything else, even among the old-timers.

Even in its current full dress M-16A2 configuration, this service rifle is only two pounds heavier and three inches longer than the M-1 Carbine. The M-16A2 also boasts substantially greater velocity, energy and accuracy.

"The current M-16 is much better designed for full-automatic fire, with its straight-line stock, chromed chamber and three-round burst control," Steele insists. Collapsible stock versions such as the Model 733 Commando and the Model 323 Carbine provided even greater portability, while still using the standard

This out-of-production Bushmaster carbine utilized 5.56mm magazines from the M-16. The receiver is held against the right forearm with the left thumb for firing.

In this World War II photo taken in 1944 the soldier on the right carries the carbine version of the Mauser K-98 rifle that was used in World War I.

5.56mm cartridge, which has far greater stopping and wounding power than the .30-carbine round."

It would appear at first glance that the modern assault rifle has co-opted the carbine role. Many of the world's currently in-use assault rifles are as compact as the M-1 Carbine – or more so – while using a cartridge that is strong enough to serve as a main battle rifle. Among these short rifles with folding stocks are the Israeli Galil and the Russian AKR-74, the Belgian FNC and the U.S.-made AR-18. Even shorter in bullpup configuration are the Austrian AUG and the French FAMAS.

The one thing most Korean War soldiers liked about the M-1 Carbine, other than its diminutive size, was its well-designed bayonet. Unlike the bayonet of the Garand M-1 of that era, the M-4 knife/bayonet has a usable edge and length. The latter was only 6 inches compared to the 10-inch length of the Garand stabber. The M-4 could be used as a utility and fighting knife, as well as decorating the end of a rifle as an improvised pike.

Our research shows that the M-4 bayonet used the blade and handle designs of the World War II M-3 trench knife that was issued to airborne units.

"In modern combat, a bayonet is far more likely to be used off the rifle than attached to it," says Steele. For that reason, the M-3 blade has been used not only on the carbine, but also on the last edition – called the M-5 – for the Garand. Then it became the M-6, as the bayonet for the M-14. When the M-16 was adopted as the U.S. service rifle, the same bayonet – now called the M-7 – was issued with the weapon.

"Attached to the end of a rifle, a knife-type bayonet is not particularly efficient, since it can become stuck in bone or cartilage quite easily. However, our soldiers seem to prefer a bayonet that can be used as a tool rather than as a more effective pike. It should be noted that the triangular and spike-type bayonets have been shown to be the best for repeat thrusts into an opponent's carcass, but they are useless outside of the narrow arena of close combat," Steele explains.

It should be pointed out, too, that a clone of the M-16, the M-4 Carbine, now is being issued to special units throughout the U.S. Armed Forces. It also is replacing handguns in some units. Some Army artillery officers and gun crews are being issued the M-4. In the Marine Corps, the MK-4 Carbine is replacing the Heckler & Koch MP-5 9mm submachine gun in reconnaissance units as well as others. Like the M-16, this one fires the familiar 5.56mm cartridge.

"The M-1 and M-1A1 carbines still maintain a role in police work in some localities and they still are produced commercially for hunting and even home-defense. Used within the limitations of range, accuracy and power, the carbine still can serve a role," Steele contends.

"As an example, in Hawaii where handguns are forbidden without a lot of investigation and paperwork, my local guide carried a carbine for backup when I was hunting wild boar with only a Randall knife," he says.

In a northern California hunt Steele used a Universal M-1 Carbine chambered for the .256 Winchester Magnum to take a 200-pound Russian boar. The cartridge is a necked-down .357 pistol round designed originally for a Smith & Wesson revolver. The 60-grain hollow-point bullet struck the boar in the neck just behind the ear.

"I have seen carbines still in service all over the world," Steele admits, "but if I ever had to carry one in jungle combat, I would make certain I had a box of unauthorized soft-point ammo with me."

Lewis agrees. He recalls a bitter cold night during the winter of 1951 when he was attached to an element of the 7th Marine Regiment. There was a moonless attack by the Chinese, who were coming through the wire just ahead of his foxhole. Lewis, as best he recalls, fired six rounds into the man before the gun jammed. Those .30-caliber bullets didn't even slow him down. Someone then used a Thompson submachine gun on the invader, virtually cutting him in half.

The next day, Lewis learned that the subgun had been picked off a dead Chinese soldier some weeks earlier by its new owner, a Marine corporal. After a bit of haggling, Lewis managed to obtain the gun for two quarts of whiskey and the corporal went back to using his Garand.

The carbine that had jammed during the night's excitement had the barrel jammed into the crotch of a tree down the mountain from the front lines. A bit of weight on the rear of the gun gave the barrel a near-perfect 45-degree turn and broke the stock. Lewis considered the useless weapon war surplus and tossed in unceremoniously into a creek..

Later, when checking out of his parent organization, he told the supply officer about the incident and what had happened to the carbine he was supposed to be turning in. The supply officer was sympathetic, but Lewis ended up paying for the missing weapon, adding insult to what was almost serious injury.

CHAPTER 18

A GOOD SCOUT

That Title Is Straight Out of 1930s Slang, but It Fits Our Feelings Regarding Springfield's M-1A1 Scout

"I DON'T KNOW the reasoning behind the decision at Springfield, Inc., to call this rifle the M-1A instead of the M-14. Maybe it's because a lot more people carried the M-1 Garand. Name recognition is certainly a marketing tool," Lewis said as he sat in a jungle canyon in the Hawaiian rain forest, pontificating on the vagaries of the advertising business as related to firearms.

At hand was Springfield's recently introduced Scout version of the rifle listed as the M-1A. As described in our sister publication, the Gun Digest, this product is the "commercial equivalent of the U.S. M-14 service rifle with no provision for automatic fire."

For those old enough to remember it, the M-14, chambered for the then-new NATO caliber, 7.62mm, was developed and issued to military forces as "an interim weapon" to fill the gap between the M-1 Garand .30-06 and what came to be the M-16 with its

Chad Fukui thought that the Springfield 7.62mm Scout was a bit heavy but made up for the weight with excellent balance.

smaller 5.56mm bullet. The M-14 was introduced in the early 1960s and had been relegated for the most part to military warehouses before the end of that decade.

Lewis made himself somewhat unpopular with then-commandant of the Marine Corps, Paul X. Kelley, a number of years ago during a face-to-face meeting. Lewis blamed the M-14 and the M-16 for turning American service men – including the Marines – "into a nation of sprayers, instead of the nation of riflemen we once were."

Lewis, of course, was referring to the full-auto capability of both weapons. At least with the M-14, troop leaders were able to take the control switch away from their soldiers so that they were forced to resort to aimed fire in the semi-auto mode.

"No such option existed with the M-16 and the improved versions that followed. With the ability to empty a magazine with a single extended pull of the trigger, the hail of bullets going downrange did help the economy. The continuing demand for re-supply made the ammunition manufacturers wealthy!" says Lewis.

The observation has been made that military armament does not become obsolete. As one expert, the late lawman and shooting champion, Bill Jordan, put it, "Most military arms designs get improved, upgraded or the guns are used for some other purpose." As an example of that, choice, hand-picked M-14s have been upgraded to what the Marine Corps terms its new DMR that is being issued to selected units. (That improved version is discussed elsewhere in this book.)

Brothers Tom and Dennis Reese head Springfield, Inc., which is headquartered in Geneseo, Ill. – population, 5,990. Their arms factory stands on land once farmed by their father.

Following the end of World War II, the senior Reese began filling his barn with war surplus weaponry instead of hay. It wasn't long before the surplus weapons business outstripped the product of the

Recoil of the 7.62mm Winchester cartridge didn't seem to bother Fukui, who weighs about 160 pounds.

The model number, name of the manufacturer and the rifle's serial number all are stamped on the rear of the receiver.

cornfields. Later, when the surplus supply ran out, the father and sons entered the arms manufacturing business, using tried and true military designs such as the Model 1911Al semi-auto, the reworked M-14 and others. Most recently, they have introduced a replica of the M-1 Garand rifle that is difficult to tell from an original except for the name of the manufacturer stamped into the metal.

Among the rifle variations being marketed by the Reese brothers and staff is the Springfield M-1A Scout, which boasts an 18-inch barrel. The barebones M-1A1 comes with a walnut stock and hand guard. The Scout version can be had with this woodwork, but the style Lewis and his crew had the opportunity to check out featured black fiberglass. However, the same checkering pattern that is cut into the walnut-stocked version is impressed on both the pistol grip and the forward handguard. Both Lewis and his shooting pard Ace Kaminski like the Scout's positive two-stage trigger.

Lewis had weighed the gun before the gathering in the jungle clearing. It weighed an ounce or so over 9 pounds while wearing an empty 10-round magazine. Using his RCBS Premium trigger pull scale, he found that the trigger pull was a crisp 4.5 pounds. It should be noted that a recoil reducer had been added to the 18-inch barrel that brings overall length of the Scout rifle to 40.75 inches. The front sight is the familiar square-blade military style with curved protective wings that date back to the original M-1 Garand. The rear sight is the click adjustable type that Lewis first worked with on a range at Parris Island, S.C., some 60 years ago.

"This sight system works the same as the original," Lewis notes, "but it's smoother and more eye-pleasing than the one on the rifle I was issued."

Depending on what the laws and rules are in your locality, the M-1A Scout is available with 5, 10 and 20-round magazines, which tilt easily into the magazine well. "You know it's seated when you hear a solid snapping sound. It's there to stay, until one puts proper pressure on the magazine latch located just ahead of the trigger guard," explains Lewis.

The trigger, trigger guard and safety are virtually the same as those on the original Garands. The safety is a flat piece of drilled metal that extends through a slot in the trigger guard. A padlock can be passed through the hole in the safety, thus making the rifle inoperable. Lewis also recalls passing a steel rod or cable through the holed safeties of all of the rifles in a gun rack, then locking the rod or cable. That kept any and all of the rifles from being removed from the rack until the device was unlocked and removed.

When the safety is pushed inside the trigger guard, the gun is on safe. When it is pushed forward – assuming the gun is loaded with a round in the chamber – the Scout rifle is ready to fire.

There on the edge of the rain forest, Lewis hefted the rifle. "This is a great jungle gun," he declared. He put the shorty to his shoulder and sighted through the BSA Red Dot sight that had been installed by Kaminski. In working with the sighting device, he quickly found that a red button on the left side of the unit controlled the intensity of the scarlet dot. Kaminski had used the BSA device earlier in sighting in the Scout.

Lewis hefted the rifle, again, nodding approval. "I like it better than the standard model," he said. "On this one, the balance is great!"

Chad Fukui, who has three decades of law enforcement work behind him, was also called upon to offer his views on the Springfield M-1A Scout. Now a lieutenant in the County of Hawaii Police Department, his duty time is devoted to drug enforcement on the island.

The area of the island of Hawaii where we were operating averages about 140 inches of rain a year. That helps create the jungle and it also helps create the marijuana crop that is a continuing headache for law enforcement types.

Working with the Hawaii National Guard and the Federal Drug Enforcement Agency, Fukui spends a good deal of time in the local jungles, where many of the

The red button on the left side of the BSA unit is the battery control and also handles intensity of the red dot in the sight.

The impressed checkering in the Scout model's pistol grip and forend is meant to be functional. It meets that need.

pot farms are hidden. We figured he would be a natural for testing the scouting capabilities of the M-1A Scout.

Kaminski is also a law enforcement type, an investigator for an agency of the State of Hawaii. Eventually it became possible to find a Saturday morning when neither of the officers was on duty and we decided to meet in the jungle clearing. Lewis and Kaminski reached there an hour early in order to set up the course of fire.

Kaminski had obtained a trio of three-dimensional target dummies from Law Enforcement Targets of Minneapolis. These had been dressed in old, faded camouflage clothing that had been purchased at a Hilo thrift shop.

The path into the jungle once had been a route used by marijuana growers. Members of Pig Hunters of Hawaii, Inc. are the primary users of the vague trail today. The group is devoted to reducing the population of feral hogs that are devouring the flora native to the Hawaiian Islands. Many of the plants that suffer or are being destroyed are on a lengthy endangered list.

Kaminski and Lewis didn't have to carry the dummies and target-planting equipment far up the overgrown trail – no more than 50 yards – to find spots where the camouflaged figures could be well hidden in the greenery.

Each of the plastic dummies was erected on a steel stake that Kaminski pounded into the ground. Walking back to the far edge of the clearing where they had parked their trucks, Kaminski and Lewis paused to look down the vague trail. Neither could see any of the targets.

"We may have made this a little too difficult," Lewis commented, somewhat disturbed at seeing nothing although he knew it was there.

"Let's wait and see how it goes," Kaminski suggested confidently. Kaminski and Fukui had been partners when the former first entered the law enforcement field.

Fukui had never fired an M-14 or any of its copies that have made their way to the market place. Lewis briefed him on the Scout rifle, then watched as the shooter tilted the magazine into the well, swung it into place until he heard the expected click, then bolted a round into the chamber.

While Fukui was accomplishing this and setting the safety, Lewis explained that he and Kaminski were interested in how long it would take him to spot the three figures hidden out there in the greenery, then take them out.

When he spotted his first target, Fukui was to fire three rounds on it. He was to repeat the performance on the other two miscreants. The last round of the ten in the magazine could be used on any of the targets he was not totally certain he had hit.

On a signal from Lewis, who started the stopwatch at the same instant, Fukui crossed the clearing in the direction of the ambush setup. Holding the Scout rifle at port arms, he had stalked no more than 15 yards, when he halted, jerked the rifle to his shoulder and triggered off three closely spaced rounds.

Switching sides of the trail, Fukui moved forward only a few steps before he repeated his initial performance, sending three fast-triggered rounds in the

The rings supplied with the BSA Red Dot sight were installed on the Weaver-type mount that came attached to the rifle. It was a good combination.

117

direction of the second target. From the same position, he dropped to one knee to take out the third of the plastic bad guys. He didn't bother to fire the tenth round. Instead, he elevated the muzzle of the Scout and pulled back on the operating handle to remove the round. Then he turned to grin at Kaminski and myself. Talk about self-confidence!

"What was my time?" he asked.

The entire exercise had taken only 65 seconds...not nearly as long as it had taken to set up the course of fire!

"You did well," Lewis told him.

Fukui shrugged and said, "It's easy enough when no one's shooting back at you."

"Neither Ace nor I could spot those targets from where we were standing," Lewis told him, then asked, "How did you manage to see them so fast?"

"The colors," Fukui answered.

Lewis was plainly puzzled. "Colors? The green?"

"When you've searched through enough grass and brush out there, in time, you get to know what's real and what's not," Fukui explained. "You eventually come to know what kind of stuff grows in each area and what color it should be.

"Marijuana, for example, has a different shade of green from most of the jungle that surrounds it. That's the method we use to spot the hidden pot plantations."

Fukui's explanation made sense. Twice he took a leisurely walk down the lava ash road, while Kaminski and Lewis changed the positions of the targets and attempted to camouflage them better. Their efforts probably could have been considered a waste of time and ammunition. On the next run, Fukui's time to spot and take out the three plastic dummies was a little less than a second better than his initial

The operating rod handle, which is used to activate the bolt, is virtually the same as that used on the original M-1 and later the M-14.

65-second run. On the third run, Kaminski and Lewis must have done a better job of hiding the baddies; it took Fukui 72 seconds to end the exercise.

To this point, neither Kaminski – who owned the Scout – nor Lewis had fired the piece on these targets. Kaminski loaded the magazine with a full 10 rounds, then stood in the offhand position to trigger them off in rapid succession on one target. Lewis did the same on another of the plastic felons. The targets were approximately 50 yards away and Lewis and Kaminski had the advantage of knowing where they had planted them.

Inspection of each of the targets revealed that all 10 rounds each shooter had squeezed off rapid-fire style turned out to leave a hole that would have been a fatal or near-fatal wound in a real-life situation.

Police Lt. Chad Fukui, who had never had fired the M-14 rifle or any of its clones, checks out on the Springfield Scout variation prior to beginning of the jungle-based exercise.

The rear sight of the Springfield Scout is the same type as used on the M-14 and the earlier M-1 Garand. The knurled knobs on each side handle elevation and windage changes.

The 147-grain 7.62mm cartridges from Winchester did their jobs. In some cases, they trimmed foliage from in front of the targets, but that didn't seem to affect accuracy.

The plastic figures from Law Enforcement Targets were moulded from polymer and had been used in half a dozen previous firearms' tests. The earlier bullet holes had been covered with flesh-colored tape to make it easier to keep track of new hits.

Inspecting the targets after the Springfield Scout test, Lewis shook his head. "It's time we gave these guys some kind of burial," he suggested. "I think they've had it."

Kaminski agreed. "I'll drop them in the county dump on the way home."

"I'll order three more," I promised. "That should give us a fresh start on the next gun test."

This test wouldn't have been complete without a critique of the Scout by our duty expert. As we were packing up, I asked Fukui what he thought of the gun.

"To me, it seems a little heavy," he said, "but the balance makes up for that. I think there's a place for it in drug work in this kind of jungle. I normally carry a custom-built .223, but in dense undergrowth, the bullet doesn't always make it through the heavy cover. The 7.62mm bullet would solve that problem."

Something more should be said about the optical sight. The BZ30SB Red Dot sight comes from BSA Optics of Fort Lauderdale, Fla. It is of machined aluminum and accepts Weaver-style scope rings without a problem. In fact, the BSA came equipped with the Weaver rings. The sight has a matte rubberized finish and weighs only seven ounces, so it adds little to the overall weight of the weapon.

The rubber recoil pad of the Scout is not the same as those on earlier military rifles from which it was cloned. Those rifles had steel buttplates.

When shooting, Fukui used the BSA unit, which is battery-powered and is turned on by pressure on the red button on the side of the unit. This is the same button used in changing intensity of the internal red dot. The maker recommends that the batteries be removed and stored when the sight is not in use.

When Kaminski and Lewis went for their rapid-fire exercises on the rapidly disintegrating plastic targets, they removed the scope. Both used the Scout's iron sights and Lewis claimed he found them just as good as he remembered them from what he tends to refer to as the Late Great Hate – World War II.

CHAPTER 19

THE CENTURY INTERNATIONAL ARMS SAR-2

Its Number of American-Made Parts Gives This Semi-Auto AK-47 Legality in Most of the Nation

THE CENTURY ARMS International SAR-2 is a Kalashnikov design, but specifically it is a semi-auto version of the AK-74 in 5.45x39mm caliber. It is a legal firearm under current United States federal law even if it lacks many of the more obtuse, but mandated, features now required for importation of any semi-automatic military-style rifle.

Essentially, there are two major types of military small arms in the world today: the AR-15/M-16 style of rifle and those derived from the Kalashnikov design. There are many others in existence like the Steyr AUG, the French FAMAS and the miserable British SA-80. But on a worldwide basis, you are more likely to encounter either an M-16 or an AK of some sort, with the latter being by far the more numerous of the two. Some published estimates run as high as 100 million Kalashnikovs and its variants produced around the world since the design's introduction.

Some years ago, author and experienced shooter Frank James embarked upon a campaign to test a variety of Kalashnikov rifles, which originated in Russia. Included in his test lineup were examples from North Vietnam (most of these were Southeast Asian war trophies), Egypt, Finland, Yugoslavia and China. The rifles included both military select-fire examples and the more commonly available semi-auto variants, which were imported for the civilian sporting arms market in the United States.

"The differences between the various examples were relatively minor, even if they were distinct, and the process took more than three years to complete before opinions were formed about the basic gun and design," James explains.

Without exception, combat veterans from the American involvement in Vietnam all praised the Kalashnikov for its reliability at a time when the newly introduced M-16 was horribly unreliable. Many shooters believe that one probably could wrap a log chain around the AK-47, hitch the chain to the rear of a four wheel-drive vehicle and drag it across the back 40, jump out, clear the barrel and muzzle and the gun still would function.

Kalashnikovs are unbelievable for the amount of foreign matter they will ingest and still operate. James says many military veterans want this kind of rifle in their hands when they are living in a mud hole and people are shooting at them.

However, after lengthy personal research and a number of interviews with combat veterans, James believes the weapons have a down side. He says it is readily apparent that

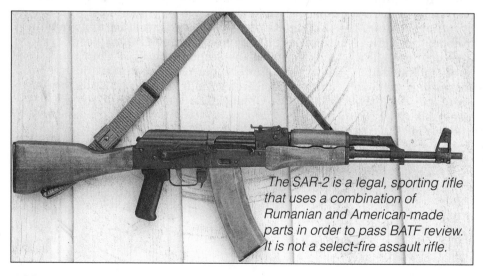

The SAR-2 is a legal, sporting rifle that uses a combination of Rumanian and American-made parts in order to pass BATF review. It is not a select-fire assault rifle.

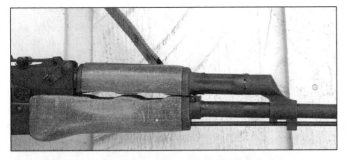

Nothing is more characteristic of any Kalashnikov design than the gas system used to operate the rifle. This is the Kalashnikov-style gas system found on the SAR-2.

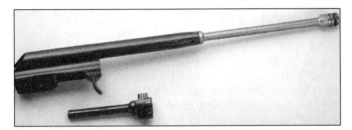

The SAR-2 features the same style bolt carrier and bolt head found on any semi-auto Kalashnikov rifle. This system is one of the most reliable and rugged operating systems ever created for a semi-auto rifle.

no matter how reliable these guns are generally, they also have earned a solid reputation for poor accuracy. One of the AK-47s he tested – a side-folding stock, semi-auto AK from China – refused to keep five rounds inside 13 inches at 100 yards while being fired from a sandbag position on a concrete shooting bench.

"It was an astonishing display of poorer than poor small arms accuracy," James says. "One could easily conclude the rounds were lucky to even hit the target and frame, let alone the impact berm standing several feet above the target.

"Never in my personal experience, prior to testing the SAR-2, has any AK performed close to the typical AR-15/M-16 in terms of target range accuracy. An example would be the select-fire M-16 I once owned that would routinely put five rounds from a prone firing position inside an inch and a half at 100 yards even while the gun rattled like a cigar box full of marbles. Against performance like that the luster of the AK dims by comparison," he explains.

Many experts believe that the military source 7.62x39mm ammunition is a major part or cause of much of the AK's infamous inaccuracy problems, but after working with different SKS rifles using the same ammo, James finds that particular theory is more than somewhat suspect. "The typical SKS is certainly no tack-driver, but when compared to the typical AK, it is a virtual target rifle," he claims.

The problem, according to several knowledgeable sources in the match rifle community, has more to do with the Kalashnikov receiver than anything else. However, they are also quick to point out that East

One of the American-made parts on the SAR-2 is the pistol grip assembly. As long as 20 or more parts on the rifle are made in America, this product can have a pistol grip stock.

European or Chinese standard military 7.62x39mm ball ammo is not known for its match grade characteristics and downrange accuracy.

According to Edward Ezell, author of *The AK-47 Story*, the original Kalashnikov receiver was of stamped steel, before it was changed to a milled steel receiver, a change made because of manufacturing difficulties. However, this production cycle was followed by the AKM series, which re-introduced the stamped steel receiver. Experts now believe the stamped steel receiver of any Kalashnikov rifle will twist ("torque" is the term they specifically use) when the rifle fires. In comparison, the Stoner-designed AR-15/M-16 alloy receiver with its two halves is far more stiff and stronger. Many believe this so-called torque factor is the major reason for the Kalashnikov's fabled inaccuracy problems and the reason behind the greater accuracy experienced with the AR-15/M-16 series.

The success of the 5.56x45mm round was established in Vietnam. It proved the concept for a centerfire .22-caliber military rifle and has since gone on to greater fame by being adopted by every major army in the Western world, including Switzerland, the land renowned for high-mountains and long-range riflemen.

For whatever reason, the Soviet Union in 1974 introduced a new round displaying many of the characteristics of the now NATO-standard 5.56x45mm, plus one or two distinctive characteristics of its own. To make things even more interesting, the Russians got to test their own caliber in a war of their own making in Afghanistan.

"As for the actual diameter of the 5.45x39mm Russian projectile, while a true 5.45mm calculates to a 21.9 caliber, my Vernier caliper measured the diameter of a pulled projectile at .2255 inch. It is safe to say the Russian 5.45 bullet is little more than a .22-caliber projectile," James reports.

At the time of introduction, the small arms chambering this new round and the ammunition itself were virtually unobtainable in the United States, but within the past several years, the situation has

The safety is positioned on the right side of the sheet metal receiver of the SAR-2. The UP position is SAFE, while the DOWN position is FIRE.

The SAR-2 uses a semi-automatic receiver made in Romania, but the internal parts were made in the United States.

The magazine latch shown here with the politically correct 10- round magazine is a flapper-style that must be depressed to release the magazine from the receiver. When inserting the magazine into the receiver the magazine must be inserted at the front and then rocked back into position.

changed dramatically. Due to a clause in the United States federal law – specifically, Chapter 18, Section 922, subparagraph (e):

> *imported rifles featuring 20 or more parts that are made in the United States may legally use large-capacity magazines and feature pistol grip stocks.*

Hence, the appearance and form of the subject SAR-2 from Century International Arms, Inc., head-quartered in Boca Raton, Fla.

By its inherent design, the Kalashnikov rifle has many attributes beyond its reputation for reliability that tend to attract it to those going into harm's way. The rifle is extremely well balanced and the SAR-2 tested by James was no exception.

"Relatively light in weight, the SAR-2 tested weighed 7.6 pounds unloaded, so it is an easy rifle to carry and shoulder if hiking. It has an overall length of 34.5 inches, which may help explain its comfortable balance and the ease with which it can be handled," James says.

He found that many shooters of northern European heritage complain that the length of the stock on the average AK is too short. "If one always shot in

warm weather while wearing nothing more than a light shirt, then it would be natural to concur with that viewpoint, but most don't," James warns.

The test SAR-2 featured a solid wood stock, not one of the folding stocks that Kalashnikov once copied. That particular design first was seen on the WWII German MP-40 and comes with an inherent wobble and infirmity. Experience has shown that the folding stocks on Kalashnikov rifles add little to their effectiveness and even less to their stability. "The solid wood stock is far better, even if a little short in overall length," James says.

Because of cold weather outer clothing and the fact that many police and military personnel have to contend with ballistic vests, harnesses and web gear – all of which add to body thickness – a subsequent need for a short pull stock is easily established for a rifle like this. On the test SAR-2, the distance from the trigger to the end of the buttstock was 13 inches; the distance from the butt to the front of the pistol grip only 11.5 inches.

"I found the short overall length and the short pull of the stock to be a great asset," James notes. "In many ways, the gun reminds me of an extremely well-made, well-balanced carbine, which is essentially what it is."

The SAR-2 is a Kalashnikov rifle through and through, from the gas system to the bolt carrier and right down to the trigger system, which incorporates completely American-made parts. The entire trigger group, parts and springs, together with items like the pistol grip add up to the required number of Made-In-America parts to allow the sale of this firearm to civilians in certain areas of the United States.

"The rest of the rifle is made in Rumania and while the gun is reliable, little effort was spent on its metal finish. After several test sessions during the humid summer months the gun would literally rust before my eyes," James says. "The remedy was to develop the habit of coating the metal surfaces with a liberal dose of a good quality lubricant after each range or inspection session."

Like all Kalashnikov rifles, the magazine on the SAR-2 must be rocked into the bottom of the receiver in order for it to latch properly. The sample SAR-2 came with three magazines – two synthetic 30-round magazines and a 10-rounder formed from metal. Additional synthetic 30-round magazines are available from Century International Arms for a modest cost.

The safety lever is the same as the one used on the select-fire military rifles, only here the two positions are UP for safe, and DOWN for fire. As is characteristic for all rifles in the Kalashnikov line, the safety lever makes a distinct and audible clicking sound when moved from one position to the other.

Charging the chamber is accomplished by pulling the bolt group to the rear by means of a cocking handle that extends from the right side of the receiver. Experienced right-handed Kalashnikov shooters learn to rotate the gun to the left 90 degrees and pull the cocking handle back with the edge of their left hand while holding the pistol grip in their right hand.

Everything up to firing the first round was pretty much what was experienced with all the previous Kalashnikovs James had tested in years past, but the 5.45x39mm round was a surprise. Wolf Performance Ammunition of Anaheim, Calif., provided a quantity of their Russian origin 5.45x39mm for testing. This round features a 60-grain bullet in a lacquered steel case that is smaller than the corresponding 7.62x39mm case in terms of both width and case-head diameter. "Additionally, the recoil for those used to the 7.62x39mm round is far less and much more pleasant. Although the SAR-2 lacks any form of muzzle compensator or flash suppressor (muzzle threads are still illegal under U.S. federal law), the recoil, report and overall sensation is much subdued from its larger bore predecessor," James says.

In shooting the SAR-2 at 25 yards, James experienced no problem in keeping five rounds inside an inch, but moving to 100 yards, he soon found the sights lack the definition necessary to maintain good tight groups. Being able to get three rounds inside the black bullseye of a 25-yard slow-fire pistol target at 100 yards was a completely new experience in accuracy with a Kalashnikov rifle. But James found that the indistinctness of the round, shiny front sight inside the narrow U-notch of the mid-position rear sight made it difficult, if not impossible, to keep all the rounds inside the black.

"Flyers were experienced," James admits. "Yet, the experience was encouraging, because this gun is without question one of the best-shooting Kalashnikovs I have ever seen.

"Also, there is a solution to the iron sight problem with the SAR-2, because the gun comes with a Russian-designed scope mount base already riveted to the left side of the stamped steel receiver. All one has to do is install one of the Russian-designed removable scope mounts for installation of either a red dot scope or a conventional cross-hair scope for an improvement in sight acquisition and resultant accuracy."

He added, "As for the ballistics of the 5.45x39mm cartridge, seven rounds were chronographed with an average velocity of 2929 fps. Due to the overall shape and ballistic coefficient of this Russian designed

The Russian-developed 5.45x39mm round makes the SAR-2 a light recoiling as well as one of the more accurate Kalashnikov-type rifles ever fired by author and an Indiana Deputy Sheriff Jim Martin.

Martin found the SAR-2 accurate enough that he would easily consider it for use as a patrol rifle. It is easy to handle and operate.

Until recently, the 5.45x39mm round has been difficult for many in the West to work with, but range sessions with the SAR-2 demonstrated it is an accurate and light recoiling cartridge.

The rear sight on the SAR-2 is typical Kalashnikov in design. It features a sliding bar that changes elevation and a small u-notch rear blade.

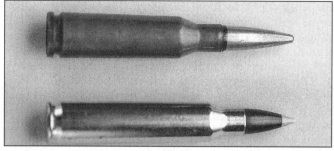

The 5.45x39mm cartridge is not a reduced-bore version of the well-known 7.62x39mm Chicom round. Shown with a commercial Winchester 50-grain Silvertip .223 Rem. cartridge for comparison, the 5.45x39mm round is as small in case diameter as the 5.56x45mm or .223 Rem. The 60-grain projectile of the 5.45x39mm cartridge, however, offers good down-range ballistics.

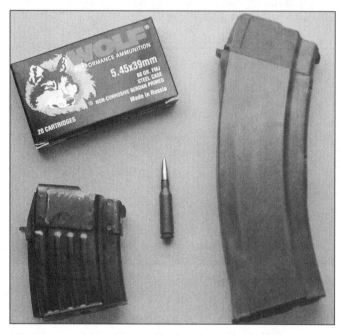

Wolf Ammunition, located in Southern California, imports the 5.45x39mm lacquered steel case ammo from Russia. The steel 10-round magazine is shown here next to a synthetic 30-round magazine. Because of an exemption in the United States federal law the 30-round magazine is legal to use with the SAR-2.

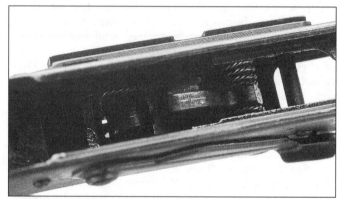

These internal parts are made in the United States and not an Eastern Bloc country. The addition or substitution of 20 or more American-made parts has allowed the importation of the SAR-2 rifles into the United States.

round, if the sighting equipment is up to it, it should prove to be no problem to engage targets up to 300 meters with an expectation of reasonable accuracy."

As for the furnished iron sights, there definitely is a way of improving accuracy with the SAR-2 or any virtually other Kalashnikov model. "Red dot reflex sights are the way to go if you want to increase your target acquisition time and speed," James insists. "The action-oriented target shooters have proved this simple fact over and over again. However, there is a small problem with this great leap in technology – most of the better examples seen today all depend upon a battery to power the red dot.

"When it comes to batteries in any combat weapon or vehicle, Murphy's Law dictates that whenever the situation is the worst and the battery is absolutely, positively, without question needed most desperately, that's when it's going to go dead! In this application, a battery-powered sighting system could leave you without a sight reference of any kind with some weaponry."

This is the major reason many knowledgeable shooters and firearms trainers have resisted and even discouraged red-dot reflex sights on combat weapons. The consequences when the batteries fail are too serious for the law enforcement or military professional to be without a redundant sighting system that can be employed immediately and accurately.

"The basis of a redundant sighting system is simple," James explains. "Two sighting systems – the reflex sight and the factory iron sights – are combined to yield a redundant system that offers the best from both types of sights. From the reflex sight, you get fast sight acquisition time and with the iron sights you maintain the reliability necessary for any combat weapon."

In comparison to many other rifle systems, it is rather easy to develop a redundant sighting system

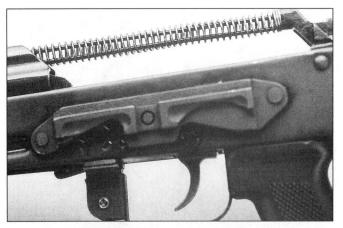

The recoil spring assembly on any Kalashnikov rifle is one of the simplest and easiest to maintain of any semi-auto rifle in current production.

The 5.45x39mm round demonstrated sufficient accuracy potential, but the author believes the standard sights on the SAR-2 are inadequate for the best performance from this rifle. This small round front sight post was indistinct and hard to contrast when shooting for really tight groups.

for the AR-15/M-16 series of rifles because the iron sights are high in relation to the boreline. But what about the Kalashnikov series?

One answer to establishing a redundant sighting system for any Kalashnikov rifle is the UltiMak Optics Mount from Keeney Bros. Distributing in Moscow, Idaho. The big problem with establishing a redundant sighting system on any AK is the low sight position on a typical Kalashnikov rifle in relation to the boreline and the shooter's cheek position on the stock.

The UltiMak Optics Mount replaces the original gas tube on the Kalashnikov rifle with one made from a solid piece of 6061 T-6 aluminum that has been extruded before being machined to its final shape.

"The top surface of the UltiMak Optics Mount approximates the Picatinny rail, but UltiMak's representatives admitted they have never worked with the Picatinny device," James reports. The designers of the UltiMak Optics Mount employed the dimensions they received from the U.S. military and found they corresponded closely to those found on a typical Weaver-style rail. The crosscuts made in the top surface of the rail carry military specifications in dimension, but they are set on one-half-inch centers for spacing.

To install the UltiMak Optics Mount on a Kalashnikov rifle, the gas tube forward of the rear sight must be removed from the gun. The UltiMak mount is available in two versions: one with side gas ports and one without. The mount James received was the version with the side gas portholes. The printed directions for installation of this mount are well written and explain clearly how to disassemble the gas tube and forearm assembly on any Kalashnikov rifle.

A problem for the manufacturers in designing a replacement gas tube involved the wide variation in dimensions one is liable to encounter among Kalash-

A scope base-mounting rail is riveted to the left side of the sheet metal receiver on the SAR-2. James believes it is needed to wring the maximum out of this rifle and cartridge. Unfortunately, he didn't have access to a scope mount to see just how accurately this rifle could really shoot.

nikov rifles produced in a host of different countries around the world. To this end, your first impression upon attempting to install the UltiMak gas tube/optics mount will be that they made it too short.

The UltiMak gas tube mounts to the rifle by means of two u-shaped clamps that encircle the barrel and hold the mount firmly in position. Each clamp is secured with two hex-head screws; a pair of aluminum shims is provided for the 5.45x39mm caliber rifles because of the smaller outside diameter of the barrel.

Positioning the UltiMak mount midway between the gas block at the front and the receiver at the rear is best for reliable functioning. The clamping system, while simple, works well and holds the mount securely to the rifle barrel.

"Even though there was a gap between the UltiMak gas tube and both the receiver and the gas block, the test SAR-2 functioned perfectly," James says.

This group was shot from a distance of 25 yards. The best group at 100 yards put three rounds inside three inches, while the remaining two rounds of the best five increased the group size to five inches.

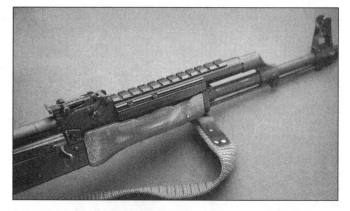

The UltiMak Optics mount for Kalashnikov style rifles replaces the original gas tube with one made from a solid piece of 6061 T-6 aluminum that has been extruded before machining to its final shape. The crosscuts made in the top surface of the rail are mil-spec in dimension, but they are set on half-inch centers for spacing.

The basis for a redundant sighting system is simple. Two sighting systems, the reflex sight and the factory iron sights are combined, yielding a redundant sighting system that offers the best from both systems. From the reflex sight you get fast sight acquisition and with the iron sights you maintain the reliability necessary for any combat weapon.

The big problem with establishing a redundant sighting system on any AK is the low sight position in relation to the boreline and the shooter's cheek position on the stock. For this reason, a Tasco PDP4 red-dot reflex sight with a 42mm tube was mounted on the rifle. This large tube red-dot reflex sight worked well although it was a sporting arms piece

On the test rifle, clearance had to be made in the lower forearm for the mounting clamps. This was easily accomplished through careful use of a high-speed rotary tool and a wood-shaping bit.

Lyle Keeney of Keeney Bros. Distributing reports that they have used a number of different red-dot reflex sights that allow dual-sight redundancy with good results. What is needed in any rifle application is a red-dot reflex sight with little or no parallax. Unfortunately, the mil-spec Aimpoint Comp ML-XD James had on hand was set up for the AR-15 series of rifles and had a base that was too high for this application. (The Aimpoint Comp ML-XD can be used with this mount,

but it requires the use of a shorter height base that is available from Aimpoint, Inc., in Falls Church, Va.)

In its place, a Tasco PDP4 red-dot reflex sight with a 42mm, marketed by Tasco in Lenexa, Kan., was substituted. "This large tube red-dot reflex sight works well even if it is a sporting-type sighting device lacking the mil-spec ruggedness demanded by most law enforcement and military professionals," James insisted.

"Until you have worked with a dual redundancy sighting system you just can't imagine how much faster you can acquire the target at any reasonable distance, shoot and move to the next target in comparison to iron sight applications. The advantage with dual sight redundancy is if Murphy does strike, you just keep aligning the sights, acquire a good cheek weld, and continue to deal with the problem – even when the dot disappears."

CHAPTER 20

TODAY'S MINI-14/5

This Sturm, Ruger Has Been Around for Several Decades, But the Company – and Others – Keep Improving It

IN LOOKING AT tactical problems in law enforcement, we have to ask when is a handgun the best answer? The answer: Almost never! The handgun is handy; it is always hanging on our belt, but a long gun is more likely to settle an issue of violence.

When a police officer needs a long gun, he may reach for a precision-sighted rifle, a shotgun or even a submachine gun. "Most of the time, a handy, short-barreled rifle is the best choice," law enforcement veteran Campbell insists. With the high cost and ever-increasing price of military-type variants, Sturm, Ruger offers a semi-automatic rifle that is affordable, rugged, reliable and accurate at moderate ranges. It also is politically acceptable in most geographic areas.

"During 22 years as a law enforcement type, some type of rifle was nearly always in the trunk of my cruiser," Campbell says. "Sometimes, years ago, it was a lever-action .30-30, later the SKS and occasionally an AR-15. I always considered the rifle a solid companion.

"I have seen police officers paralyzed and helpless in the face of rifle fire from a felon," the South Carolinian explains. "I resolved long ago it would not happen to me.

Law enforcement veteran Bob Campbell takes a braced position off his police cruiser. He has found the Ruger Mini-14 excellent for this type of shooting.

"My reason for choosing a rifle as a duty companion has been its versatility and long-range performance capabilities. The shotgun is an awesome short-range weapon and the submachine gun acceptable in highly trained hands, but my personal experience favors full-power rifles or carbines. And when I need a rifle, I need a real rifle, not a carbine chambered for an under-powered pistol cartridge," Campbell explains.

"A study of barricaded felon and sniper incidents shows a need for accuracy and penetration. The patrol rifle is a need that fits between the shotgun and the police marksman's precision rifle. If it is a stopgap, it is a very good one," Campbell adds.

The Ruger Mini-14 bears a strong but size-reduced resemblance to the Army's semi-obsolete M-14. The military M-14 was basically a modified M-1 Garand, the rifle credited with winning World War II. The M-14 chambers the 7.62mm NATO (.308 Winchester) cartridge. It is a reliable, accurate weapon, worthy of respect and is still in use for some military purposes requiring both range and accuracy.

The Mini-14 obviously played upon the M-14's reputation; the late Bill Ruger admitted that was a planned marketing move. However, the Mini-14 also reflects some reasons for the popularity of the U.S. M-1 Carbine. That light, handy piece of armament was less powerful than an M-1 Garand, but undeniably easy and simple to use and to maintain.

Still a controversial little gun in some respects, the .30 carbine, as it came to be called, acquainted Americans with a light centerfire firearm with plenty of firepower. Initially issued as a semi-automatic, by the time it was introduced for combat in Korea it had taken on a selective-fire configuration and had been designated as the M-2 Carbine.

"Today," says Campbell, "the .30 M-1 Carbine is a popular plinker, but it certainly is not considered a top-flight defense or police-issue firearm. The Ruger Mini-14 in 5.56mm –also known as the .223 Remington – not only stepped into the gap created by a dwin-

The Ruger rifle is handy, reliable and well suited to law enforcement use.

The receiver of the Ruger Mini-14 is robust, heavy and handles the pressures of the 5.56mm/.223 Remington cartridge well.

dling supply of M-1 Carbines, but it also offered an alternative to the AR-15/M-16 series assault rifles and their proliferating clones."

As currently manufactured, the basic Mini-14 features traditional styling, which includes a steel-reinforced stock cut from American hardwood. Offered from the factory with a five-round magazine, it is not classed as an assault weapon and has not been tested to the same extent as the AR-15 series, but Campbell believes that it offers a valuable alternative.

The Mini-14 is manufactured in several configurations, though all are marketed as the Ranch Rifle, perhaps a marketing move to eliminate the original relationship to the military M-14 design origins. All of the versions are marketed with the five-round detachable box magazine.

Overall length of the Mini-14 is 37.25 inches. Its barrel measures 18.5 inches and has a rifling twist of one turn in 9 inches. As for sights, the front is a ramp type, while the rear is fully adjustable. The little auto-loader is gas-operated by means of a fixed piston and features positive primary extraction. In recent times, the ejector system has been redesigned and a new buffer system is being used.

The Mini-14/5R Ranch Rifle has a blued finish and is sold with Ruger scope rings. The K-Mini-14/5R is the same rifle, but is constructed primarily of stainless steel. Both also are marketed without scope rings. The K-Mini-14/5P is of stainless steel, but carries a synthetic stock; the K-Mini-14/5RP is the same as the 14/5P, but is marketed with the same Ruger S100RH scope rings as some of the other variations.

During his lifetime, Ruger was violently opposed to others attempting to improve upon the firearms he designed and produced. In spite of this, whole industries have developed by providing the aftermarket accessories and would-be improvements for most of today's popular firearms.

As an example, Cabela's, the mail order outdoor supply operation operating out of Sidney, Neb., has come up with an entire line of add-ons or substitutions for the Mini-14. Included are moulded stocks that feature recoil pads and quick disconnect swivel studs. There also is a skeletonized folding-type stock that doesn't fold. Due to federal regulations, this particular stock has been welded in the extended position. Other add-ons include a camouflaged synthetic stock, Mini-14 scopes and scope mounts, barrel shrouds, flash-hiders, an FN-style ventilated handguard and high-capacity magazines that will hold as many as 40 rounds. Other manufacturers offer similar items, some of them good and others that are poor and obviously meant to separate the shooting enthusiast from his money.

As a police patrol carbine, Campbell considers either the blued or stainless Mini-14s as "just about ideal. I like them much better than either the Ruger 9mm or the .40 Smith & Wesson caliber carbines by the same maker. Both of these are good guns of the type and seem to sell well, but if I need a 9mm, I want it holstered on my hip. If I have to handle a gun with both hands, I want it to be one that fires a long bottlenecked case."

Campbell believes that the Ruger Mini-14 is popular among the law enforcement community for a number of reasons. One is the fact that "the Ruger looks right. For those who revere the M-1 Garand, M-1 Carbine, and the M-14, this is a friendly gun. For those more used to handing shotguns and sporting weapons, the Mini-14 is friendlier still. There is no pistol grip – at least not in the standard configuration. It handles in a manner similar to a Ruger 10/22 or some other light hunting rifles," says Campbell.

He adds, "Police gunfights with felons usually occur at close range. Handling, getting the sights quickly and being able to move the gun in action are paramount. The Mini-14 is well balanced to meet those requirements."

The Mini-14 is considerably larger and heavier than the M-1 Carbine, but it chambers a more powerful cartridge. The stopping power of the M-1 Carbine has always been somewhat debatable; those who have seen a great deal of combat are divided as to the weapon's effectiveness.

"I would hesitate to take a .30-caliber carbine deer hunting," Campbell says, adding, "but I have taken deer-size game in numerous instances with .223 bullets of the proper weight. The thousand feet per second difference in velocity between the two calibers means a great deal. Like most longtime peace officers, I have seen a few hits made on felons with rifle cartridges. The results are memorable, when discussing hydrostatic shock and high-velocity fragmentation."

Campbell says, "The 5.56mm has power in spades when it comes to personal defense use. Not at its best in

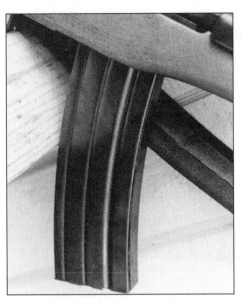

Campbell says that aftermarket magazines work only sometimes; only those from Ruger can be counted upon without a thorough test.

Black Hills ammunition offers bullet weights in several categories. These range from 52 to 68 grains.

ripping light cover and vehicles apart, the 5.56mm is decisively effective against animate targets.

"The 5.56mm often creates a void in tissue, something unheard of with handgun cartridges. The 5.56mm is not prone to ricochet, and seldom exits the body. Standard loads have been shown to penetrate less deeply than the average 9mm JHP loading. In my experience, guns that fire the 5.56mm are usually very reliable, even after long storage in a vehicle and with little maintenance."

A problem with using the Mini-14 for personal defense lies in the availability of suitable extended capacity magazines, but Ruger will sell high-capacity magazines to law enforcement agencies. Most law enforcement types consider the added cartridge capacity cheap life insurance.

"A question often comes up regarding accuracy of the Mini-14," Campbell notes. "Some officers contend that the gun is not in the same class as some of the competition-rigged assault rifles. They say the Ruger needs a heavy barrel. This is a strange comment. I for one can remember when all we had as long guns were the Garand and the M-1 Carbine, and no one criticized the carbine on that basis. It was criticized on its own merits to be sure, but we understood these guns were designed originally for different uses than local law enforcement. The Mini-14 will not be going to Afghanistan.

"Most police battles take place inside 100 yards, a big majority a lot closer. A patrol rifle that can perform a headshot at 25 yards and hit a man-sized target at 100 yards is adequate. The need is to arm the law enforcement folks with a weapon that will allow them to maintain distance and extend their reach well past conversational range. The pistol cannot do that. A carbine will."

Over the years, Campbell has used two Ruger Mini-14s extensively. One is the stainless steel model, the other the blued steel version. He reports that neither has failed to feed, chamber, fire or eject in firing an estimated 6000 rounds of factory-loaded ammunition. About 5000 of those cartridges were fired in the blue steel gun.

"Accuracy has been decent. I have tested several loadings in these guns with good results. Hornady's V Max cartridge with its polymer tip, would seem a candidate for being rammed and jammed by the slam-bang Ruger action, but this is not so. The V Max rounds feed perfectly.

"Many of the loads fired have been from Black Hills. The 52-grain Match load is wasted in this gun, being little more accurate than the 55-grain JSP. The 60-grain JSP is my choice for personal defense, offering slightly better penetration, excellent expansion and it functions well. The heavier bullet loads seem to afford good accuracy but probably are best reserved for a match-grade rifle. In my findings and tests, 40-grain bullets of all types offer sluggish feed and function. They are fine for varmints, but lack several necessary ingredients for anti-personnel work. I think they may lack penetration to the point of being dangerous to the shooter," Campbell explains.

"I stick to proven loadings in my gun," Campbell says. "I have used several hundred rounds of military surplus purchased from Century International in Boca Raton with fine results. Surplus ammo, of course, is one resource for feeding the voracious appetite of a semi-auto rifle. I have handloaded for the Ruger, but not on the scale I do for pistols. I have found that Accurate powder works well in reloads for the Mini-14, keeping the gas ports clean. Maintenance is minimal with the Ruger, but dirty powder can ruin a semi-auto shooter's day. This powder and the Sierra 55-grain jacketed soft-point make a good combination."

Campbell contends that if the Ruger Mini-14 were going to misfeed or jam, it would have done so by now. "I tend to be somewhat lax on maintenance," he admits, "but the Ruger has never failed me. I keep it oiled with Birchwood Casey gun oil and occasionally smear a little gun grease on the long bearing surfaces."

The Ruger Mini-14 obviously was designed to be simple to manipulate. Load the magazine, rack the bolt and it is ready to fire. A simple Garand-type safety in the front of the trigger guard is positive and quick into action. The sights are well made, offering a good flash sight picture for quick work, but if needed, an accurate shot can be taken. The magazine can be released and another loaded smartly even in a stressful situation if you manage to miss with the first 20-rounder.

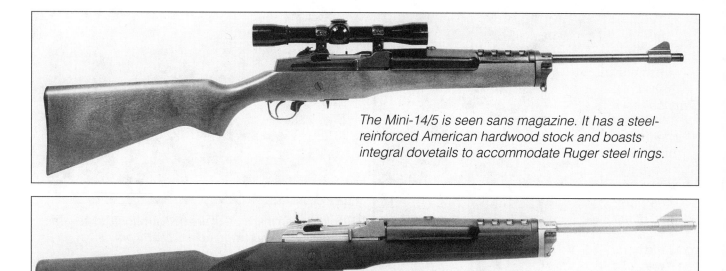

The Mini-14/5 is seen sans magazine. It has a steel-reinforced American hardwood stock and boasts integral dovetails to accommodate Ruger steel rings.

The Ruger K-Mini-14/5P is of stainless steel with a stock of man-made materials. It is designed to defeat inclement weather. Like all of the Mini-14s, it is chambered for the 5.56mm/223 cartridge.

"I am not sure mediocre accuracy is a factor in law enforcement suppression of a civilian sniper," Campbell said. "In most instances, the crazed shooter is in clear sight. We simply do not have the right tools on hand with which to reach him. The worst nightmares have occurred when cops, who never fired their pistols past 25-yard paper qualification targets, have had to confront armed felons at much longer distances. He is usually just out of pistol reach. The Mini-14 can handle that type of shooting. And while my old Winchester .30-30 was more accurate and hit harder at long ranges, the Mini-14 offers an instant second shot."

(The Los Angeles Police Department had .30-30 lever action rifles on hand for many years and issued them as recently as the early 1970s. So did the Washington State Patrol. These simple rifles could solve a lot of problems.)

What is the accuracy potential of a stock Mini-14? The accompanying tables tell the tale on that score. Generally, the individual who can fire a five-inch group off-hand at 100 yards will find the Mini-14 a handy tool. The bench-rest shooter will bemoan its poor accuracy.

On patrol, Campbell normally carries the Mini-14 with 18 rounds in Ruger's law enforcement-issue 20-round magazines. He has the rear sight folded on the blued gun. The stainless gun has the more modern sight with covering ears, which makes it far more rugged. Occasionally, the carbine rides in the front seat. "Few of us practice scrambling out of the cruiser with a long gun in hand. When I've done so, I have found the Ruger has fewer protuberances such as a forward handgrip to snag in the car. My left arm pulls the stock, the right guides the pistol grip. It takes a second or less to charge the handle when I clear the cruiser," Campbell says.

"Some officers have the mistaken belief that the handgun is more useful at short range than the carbine. This is nonsense! The rifle has more power, more penetration and is easier to get on target quickly. The rifle is seen as a drawback on searches, but this is not true either. Hold your pistol at full extension in the Weaver stance. Now hold a rifle in the firing stance. Both are about the same in extension. If care is taken not to lead with the rifle's muzzle when clearing corners, the rifle is no drawback. On the contrary, the rifle is easier for retaining good leverage against a gun-grab attempt," he explains.

In accuracy tests, Campbell fired from a bench at 100-yard targets. All groups were of five shots and were measured from the inside of the bullet hole to the inside of the bullet hole of the most widely spaced holes. Measurements shown are in inches. The groupings from the two Ruger M-14 carbines are listed separately.

Of the handloads fired, all were loaded with Accurate powder. Only one handload was fired in the stainless steel version.

Factory Ammo	Blued Mini-14	Stainless Mini-14
Hornady 75 grain TAP	2.2	2.25
Hornady 60 grain TAP	2.4	2.35
Black Hills 52 grain MATCH	2.5	----
Black Hills 52 grain JSP	2.6	2.45
Black Hills 60 grain JSP	2.4	2.6
Black Hills 68 grain JSP	2.2	2.6
Indonesian Surplus	3.0	3.45
Handloads		
Hornady 40-grain V MAX	3.9	4.25
Hornady 55 grain JSP	2.0	
Hornady 60 grain JSP	2.5	
Sierra 55 grain JSP	2.6	

CHAPTER 21

STONER'S MARK 11 MODEL 0 SNIPER

That Is the Designation Given This Rifle by the U.S. Navy, But It's the Redesigned SR –25

THE U.S. NAVY spent a good deal of time in choosing a new rifle for its SEALs and for other missions such as destroying enemy mines at sea. At first glance, Lewis announced, "I've seen this rifle before." The fact is that he was involved in publishing one of other first magazine articles on the piece. That was printed back in 1995 and the rifle was called the Stoner SR-25.

According to the honcho of Knight's Armament, which introduced the rifle, "That particular version was viewed by gun buyers as more an accurate tool for serious target work than a rifle built for combat purposes. That was where a lot of the early rifles went: to target shooters."

Lewis learned even back in those days that a lot of police departments were interested in the rifle as a sniper tool, but purchase invariably was voided by the bureaucratic bean counters who seemed to assume that adequate sniper work could be accomplished with a BB gun.

The Marine Corps had tested the original SR-25 with the idea of issuing it as a backup rifle to be handled by the spotter teamed with the sniper.

"Apparently politics of some kind got in the way, as it was told to me," Lewis, says. "The story I got was that the Marines in charge of the program discovered that Stoner's 7.62mm semi-auto SR-25 was as accurate as the reworked Remington Model 700 bolt-action that was the basis of the USMC sniper tool. Obviously, it was not likely that any service would blithely abandon a program that was

David Lutz, vice president of Knight's Armament, leans into the Navy-issue Stoner Mark 11 Model 0, which he helped perfect from the earlier introduced SR-25 precision target rifle.

Davie Lutz and author Jack Lewis (left) discuss the attributes of the Stoner Mark 11 Model 0 sniper rifle that now is being issued to SEAL units and those involved in destroying enemy mines at sea.

approved, funded and well under way to make way for an even better replacement."

Several other nations showed an interest in this new rifle that had been designed by Stoner and produced in Knight's Florida compound. Eventually, it came to the attention of Navy procurement people and a lengthy, involved relationship resulted. This led to the reworked SR-25, which is so different from the original that the Navy has given the rifle its own designation. Hence, the Mark 11 Model 0 identification.

"For all practical purposes, it is a new rifle," says to David Lutz, a vice-president for military sales for the Knight's operation. Changes to meet the Navy's needs include a new firing pin, ejector, extractor, extractor spring, feed ramp, barrel extension and a new bolt. There is also a new one-piece gas ring and a redesigned spring for the magazine that handles 20 rounds.

Each rifle is tested at the Florida installation using Remington Express .308 ammo with a 168-grain boat-tail bullet that appears to be a hollowpoint. Actually, the hollowpoint on this particular bullet is an open tip, since the bullet is manufactured from the front. Unlike actual hollowpoint ammo, this bullet does not expand and meets the international rules – such as they are – of modern warfare. For use in the field, Knight recommends either the military's M852 match ammo, or for combat, the M118 LR round. Firing the latter cartridge, muzzle velocity averages 2571 fps.

An accessory rail developed and manufactured by the Knight's organization tops the rifle. To this is attached a Leupold Tactical 3.5x to 10X scope.

Markings on the magazine well of the rifle leave no doubt as to the model, caliber and manufacturer. Knight's Armament is a subsidiary of Knight's Manufacturing Co.

In checking out the Mark 11 at the Knight's factory, Lewis found that the scope operated as advertised, including a control knob that makes adjustments for parallax at various ranges.

An available accessory is the Knight Scope. This high-resolution, night-vision sighting tool offers universal night-scope capability for day scopes and was created by Knight's Armament Co. and Optical Systems Technology. In simple terms, the KAC Model 007 is a large one-power pocket scope that is intended primarily to augment currently mounted and zeroed day scopes as well as other optical scopes that can be mounted on a variety of weapons. In addition to rifles, it has been tested on the M-249 light machinegun. The compact night aid measures only 7.25 inches in length and weighs less than 2 pounds. Test show that it remains fully operational after being submerged up to 67 feet in salt water.

A patented accessory rail attached to the top of the Mark 11 Model originally was manufactured for the earlier SR-25 rifle, but also fits the newer model.

Perhaps equally important for sniper work is the sound suppressor that is mounted on the business end of the barrel. This suppressor is another Knight's product that has been developed specifically for this rifle. It is known as the SR-25 Model QD – meaning quick detachable. At this point, it is produced specifically for this Stoner rifle and has a novel installation system. After being slipped onto the barrel, a pair of what are best described as over-size pushpins is shoved down to match groves in the rifle's gas block, thus holding the suppresser firmly in position.

This baffle-type suppressor brings about a 28- to 32-decibel drop in sound intensity. It measures 12.25 inches, weighs 1.87 pounds and is made of stainless steel.

"This suppressor is good for a minimum of 10,000 rounds," Lutz said. "In fact it will outlast the rifle's barrel." Tests have shown that it does not affect accuracy of the rifle. The purpose of a sound suppressor on a sniper rifle, of course, is also to totally suppress muzzle flash, making it more difficult for an enemy to pin down the position of the hidden rifleman.

Maximum effective range of the Stoner-designed rifle is 1000 meters. Overall length is 39.5 inches, with a 20-inch barrel. The barrel carries five grooves and has one right-hand twist in each 11 inches of length, according to Lutz.

"Particular importance is attached to the barrel of each rifle," Lutz says. "Each rifle is tested for minute of angle accuracy before it leaves our factory. If the Navy thinks that accuracy is lacking, the rifle comes back to us for a barrel change. That is something we don't like getting involved in, so every precaution is taken to see that each barrel is perfect. To date, none have ever been returned." Each of the barrels is made individually by Obermeyer Rifled Barrels of Bristol, Wis. There are currently more than 400 Mark 11 rifles in service.

Unloaded and not equipped with sights, adapters or mounts, the rifle weighs 10.44 pounds. A loaded magazine carrying the standard 20 rounds of 118 LR ammo weighs 1.62 pounds.

While the rifle usually will be deployed with a mounted scope, the Mark 11 Model 0 also has backup sights that are novel in the fact that both front and

The sniper rifle has backup iron sights that lie horizontal to the scope but can be flipped up for use at a moment's notice. Note the body of the rear sight beneath the scope.

rear fold so that they do not interfere with mounting or operation of the scope. The front sight is a post type with protective wings, while the rear sight can be adjusted to correct for both elevation and windage. The front sight is spring-loaded and can be raised into sighting position by pushing a metal button. The rear sight is raised and locked into position by hand.

The Knight's organization also has issued a rifle operator's manual that has interesting information about which most shooters give little thought. One section concerns rates of fire for the rifle.

It points out that in training or peacetime, the rifle should never be fired with unnecessary rapidity or past the point where the barrel/sound suppressor become so hot that they cannot be held comfortably in the bare hand. "The mechanism is capable of an extremely high rate of fire," Lutz says, "but abuse of this capability will lead to premature barrel wear and loss of match-grade accuracy."

As for the maximum sustained rate of fire, Reed Knight recommends firing no more than five rounds per minute for four minutes, then a two-minute cooling period with the bolt open.

"After 100 rounds, allow the rifle to cool completely before repeating," Knight says. "The bore should be cleaned during cooling periods to completely de-foul copper from the bore. This will increase barrel life and provide the best accuracy. In combat, one may be

The front sight of the rifle also lies flat and parallel to the barrel until needed. Pushing the button seen here activates it, causing it to swing upward and lock in position for instant use.

The Leupold Tactical variable scope is seated firmly on the accessory rail that is a standard part of the Stoner-designed rifle. It has adjustments for windage, elevation and parallax correction.

required to exceed the maximum sustained rate to accomplish the mission. In training one should rarely – if ever – approach the maximum sustained rate of fire."

There also are some rules – most of them basic common sense – for operating the rifle under adverse weather conditions. For example, one is cautioned to be careful not to accidentally fire the rifle when inserting a gloved finger into the trigger guard area. If gloves or mittens are worn, depress the trigger-guard plunger and open the trigger guard for ease of trigger access with the gloved fingers. "In fact," Knight says, "for extended operations in extreme cold, we recommend that the operator have an armorer remove the trigger guard."

It also is suggested that ammunition and the inside of the magazines be kept dry to avoid malfunctions in cold weather operations. Do not lubricate ammunition. There is more, but an important suggestion is to unload and hand function the rifle every 30 minutes to keep the parts from freezing.

There are different rules if one is armed with the Mark 11 in a hot, wet jungle climate or if fording a stream. The first rule is to perform maintenance more frequently to prevent corrosion. Keep a light coat of lubricant on all metal surfaces and wipe away moisture left by finger and handprints.

Knight says one should unload and check magazines, magazine springs and ammo daily, wiping cartridges dry with a clean cloth before reloading. Again, ammunition should never be lubricated.

"If rain or water gets into the bore, field strip the rifle and clean the bore from the chamber end," Knight says. "Always check that the bore is clear if you fall or drop the rifle at night or in the mud. The same should be done after fording water obstacles. One must clean, dry and lubricate the rifle if it has been submerged."

After fording a stream or having to swim with the rifle, the tactical situation may not allow time to clean the bore properly. The procedure then is to keep the muzzle pointed down and remove the muzzle cap if there is one. Shake the rifle vigorously, then pull the charging handle only two or three inches to the rear, thus partially extracting the round in the chamber. Allow water to drain out of the muzzle. Next release the charging handle to reload the chamber, and then close the dust cover. When time and the situation permit, unload and hand-operate the rifle, then clean the drain hole in the buttstock with a pipe cleaner and a drain buffer tube.

Desert climates come in several varieties. Some are hot, some are cold, some are both; most are dry, sandy and dusty. In such climes, the exterior of the rifle should not be lubricated unless corrosion becomes a problem, but the internal moving parts should be lubricated properly.

Lutz, who has been there and done that, suggests using a muzzle cap to keep sand out of the bore, especially during a stalk or in maneuvering through a trench line. Use the drag bag or the overall rifle protective bag if the tactical situation permits. Use magazine bags to protect magazines and ammunition.

"In order to seal airborne dust and blowing sand from the receiver's interior while in an administrative area, keep the bolt closed on an empty chamber, the dust cover closed and an empty magazine in the magazine well," Lutz suggested.

In a hot desert environment it also is important to keep the magazines and ammunition, as well as the optical scope, out of the direct rays of the sun. Ammo

In this photo, the Knight night sight has been attached directly ahead of the Leupold scope. The two work compatibly and there is no reason to remove the variable unit.

The muzzle of the Stoner Mark 11 Model 0 is shrouded by the special sound suppressor created by Knight's Armament. The quick-detachable suppressor adds 1.92 pounds to the weight of the rifle.

that has been warmed by a hot sun may not shoot to the rifle's zero.

Magazines should be unloaded and wiped and ammo cleaned on a daily basis. Again, the ammo should not be lubed but the magazine spring should be lightly lubricated in desert environs.

It is a good idea for the shooter to know how his rifle works. The Knight's organization has produced an operator's manual that makes it simple to understand the Mark 11's operation by following an eight-step explanation of the functioning cycle:

FIRING – With a round in the chamber, bolt locked and the hammer cocked, the safety is rotated to the fire position and the trigger is pulled releasing the hammer. The hammer drives forward under tension of the hammer spring. The hammer strikes the firing pin and the firing pin strikes the cartridge primer. The primer is detonated and ignites the gunpowder inside the cartridge case. Pressure of some 50,000 ppsi is generated inside the case as the powder burns. The bullet is pushed from the case by this pressure and travels down the barrel and out the muzzle at some 2600 fps.

UNLOCKING – Expanding gas pressures enter the gas tube through a port in the forward area of the barrel. This pressure travels through the gas tube into the gas key. Via the gas key, high-pressure gas enters the carrier interior, but is trapped by the bolt rings at the front. Consequently, expanding gas pressure begins pushing the carrier to the rear – away from the bolt. The bullet already has left the barrel, but as this gas continues to expand, the bolt carrier continues moving rearward overcoming the tension of the action (recoil) spring. The cam groove of the bolt carrier acts on the bolt cam pin. This, in turn, causes the bolt to rotate and the bolt lugs to disengage from the barrel extension locking lugs.

EXTRACTION – As the bolt now begins movement to the rear, the lip of the extractor – hooked to the rim of the cartridge case – pulls the case out of the chamber. The lip maintains its grip on the case's rim through tension of the extractor spring as the bolt passes the ejection port.

EJECTION – As the case clears the barrel extension, stored energy of the ejector spring is applied to the case's rim by the ejector plunger. The plunger completes its action as the case clears the ejection port and is rotated free of the extractor lip and the bolt. This sequence throws the case through the ejection port and clear of the rifle.

COCKING – The thrust of the carrier assembly continues to move the carrier and bolt assembly fully back into the receiver extension. As these parts move to the rear, the bottom surface of the carrier passes over the face of the hammer, forcing it back and down against the tension of the hammer spring. The hook of the disconnector engages the rear hook of the hammer, holding the hammer to the rear and down until the trigger is released. The hammer then is held back by the sear as the trigger is released. The recoil spring is now compressed fully and is prepared to thrust the recoiling carrier and bolt assembly forward.

FEEDING – As the bolt and carrier move forward under tension of the recoil spring, the lower feed lug of the bolt strikes the base of the top cartridge in the magazine. The force of the bolt strips a round from the magazine feed lips. As the round begins to move forward, the tip of the bullet hits one of the two feed ramps of the barrel extension. The angle of the feed ramp helps force the round up and into the chamber, as the bolt continues to move it forward in the feeding cycle.

CHAMBERING – Chambering occurs when the cartridge is fully forward in the chamber. If there is

The trigger guard of the Stoner Mark 11 is large enough that it can be used with a gloved hand. However, it also is constructed so that an armorer can remove it in cold weather.

an obstruction in the chamber, the cartridge case will not fit the chamber properly and the bolt will be prevented from locking.

LOCKING – With a cartridge fully in the chamber, the bolt has entered the barrel extension and has stopped moving forward. The extractor lip has snapped over the rim and into the extractor groove of the cartridge case; the ejector and its spring are fully compressed. The carrier, however, continues forward under continued force of the action (recoil) spring and through the action of its cam pin groove on the cam pin, causes the bolt to rotate. Rotation of the bolt moves its locking lugs into alignment with the barrel extension locking lugs. When this rotation of the bolt is complete the bolt is locked. The shooter can release the trigger for the next shot.

Reviewing this sequence, it becomes relatively obvious that the sniper rifle designed by Stoner and perfected by Knight and his crew is a piece of precision equipment and some may tend to question how it fares on a battlefield. The obvious point is that this is not a rough-and-tough assault rifle like the AK-47 or Stoner's original AR-10, which were designed with the capability of getting full of sand, grinding it up and spitting it out, as the operator went about the business of warfare.

"The Stoner Mark 11 Model 0 is a rifle designed for a special mission: sniper work. As such, it will see

This knob, which sits atop the Leupold Tactical scope, is devoted to making corrections for parallax, working in conjunction with the windage and elevation correction knobs on the unit.

special care by its operator and the armorers who support it," Lewis pointed out. "It is not supposed to be used to lay down a base of fire and consume endless rounds of ammo. It is meant to fire one carefully aimed round at a time, with the mission of killing a specific enemy. That may be a cold-blooded appraisal in the minds of some readers; actually, it is simply a fact of life as we know it today."

CHAPTER 22

THE SPECIAL WEAPONS-5

Here's a U.S.-made Civilian-legal Version of a Banned Carbine from Heckler & Koch

SOME PEOPLE FEEL the Hawaii Visitors and Convention Bureau would have the rest of the world believe these islands are devoted chiefly to the cultivation of orchids and pineapple, with flower leis, pristine beaches and surfing waves for everyone, while life there is just one big cocktail party. That's not quite the way it is.

Hawaii's main vacation attraction is Waikiki on the island of Oahu. The entire state's population is roughly 1.5 million permanent residents. Of those, more than 1 million live and work on Oahu. At the other extreme, Lewis lives 200 miles away on the island of Hawaii, complete with its active volcanoes. All of the other islands in the chain could be dropped down on Hawaii, known to locals as the Big Island, and there still would be room for Tahiti and probably American Samoa. The big island has a population of about 150,000.

For more than a century, the Big Island was devoted primarily to the sugar industry, but when that agricultural industry closed down, the economy went into recession and crime seemed to rise.

"Don't get me wrong," Lewis says, "there still are pineapple, leis, beaches, surf and cocktail parties. We also have the nation's oldest and largest cattle ranch with working cowboys tending the herds. There also is a degree of crime that has to be controlled."

Thus, on the island of Hawaii, the police department has been organizing what they term a Rapid Reaction Force. The slowly increasing population has contributed to new problems. As one of the involved officers put it, "RRF really translates to SWAT." The less-violent sounding, more politically correct title is meant to be less frightening to those in the tourist industry.

"As an unofficial favor to one of the officers involved in selecting proper armament and other equipment, I made some initial recommendations and agreed to do some additional research. That is what brought me to Magnum Firearms, Art Ong – and the Special Weapons-5 rifle," Lewis says.

"This called for a flight to Honolulu, but what I knew of this particular shooting machine made a trip via our monopoly-driven inter-island airline seem mandatory," Lewis recalls.

Ong owns Magnum Firearms, the largest retailer of arms and shooting supplies in the state. In addition, he has established his own highly protected indoor range on the premises of his establishment in

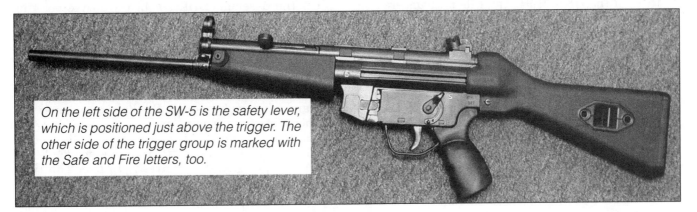

On the left side of the SW-5 is the safety lever, which is positioned just above the trigger. The other side of the trigger group is marked with the Safe and Fire letters, too.

The shooting stalls on Ong's range are padded with carpet for comfort in shooting and to hold down the noise level.

downtown Honolulu. There he handles rifles, shotguns and handguns within the bounds of Hawaii's all-encompassing and confining anti-gun laws, supplies ammo to shooters and rents firearms for on-site target practice. He and his staff also offer instruction in proper and safe gun-handling to those who want to get involved in competition shooting or simply want to have a home-protection tool close at hand.

A large part of Ong's business comes from the state's law enforcement agencies on the various islands.

During a telephone conversation concerning availability of .50 BMG ammo to be used in chapters for this book, Ong told Lewis about the semi-auto SW-5. He described it as "resembling the Heckler & Koch M-94 rifle, which had been banned for importation in 1998 by the anti-gunners of Bill Clinton's BATF."

In Ong's shop a few days later, Lewis had the opportunity to inspect the firearm. "At first glance, I noted that it bears a striking resemblance to the H&K MP-5 9mm submachine gun. The first thing I noted was that the cocking systems are identical," Lewis says.

"But this one is made in Arizona by this company called Special Weapons," the gunshop owner said.

Lewis found this bit of info further intriguing. The exterior specifications of the SW-5 are almost identical to those of the H&K M-94. The rifle is chambered for the 9mm Parabellum cartridge and measures 34.59 inches overall. Length of the barrel is 16.54 inches and there is a sighting radius of 13.39 inches. Without the 9mm magazine, the rifle weighs 6.5 pounds.

Special Weapons can furnish magazines with capacities of 10 rounds for civilians and those packing 30 rounds for law enforcement agencies. Weight of the empty 10-rounder is 4.2 ounces; the 30-round magazine weighs an even 6 ounces.

Disassembled, we found that the rifle has many parts that are the same as those used in the M-94 rifle, the MP-5 subgun and several other Heckler & Koch products.

I later learned that the individual who heads up Special Weapons, Todd Bailey, had been looking ahead when the ban on importation of the M-94 went into effect on April 6, 1998. Less than three months later, on June 29, 1998, he wrote to the District of Columbia headquarters of the Treasury Department's Bureau of Alcohol, Tobacco and Firearms, asking for information "regarding a proposed U.S.-made parts kit for imported semi-automatic SLG-95, SR-9 and other Heckler & Koch type sporter rifles."

Lewis came up with a copy of the letter that was routed to the BATF. It leaves little doubt that Bailey had contacted H&K about purchasing parts meant for the rifles that had been banned. The law states that in assembling such rifles, only 10 parts of foreign manufacture can be used. Some 20 parts are on the list, providing quite a choice spread.

The BATF letter to Bailey stated, "Based on the information that you provided, it appears that installation of a U.S.-made buttstock, pistol grip, trigger, sear, floorplate and follower would result in an assembly of a rifle with only 10 of the listed parts and would not constitute a violation. However, installation of any additional imported parts such as a foreign muzzle–mounted device or a complete magazine of foreign manufacture would be a violation."

Edward M. Owen, Jr., then chief of the Firearms Technology Branch, also warned that "a semi-automatic rifle having an ability to accept a detachable magazine and at least two of the following features would be a 'semi-automatic assault weapon'." The banned items listed by Owen were:

1. folding or telescoping stock
2. pistol grip that protrudes conspicuously beneath the action of the weapon
3. bayonet mount
4. flash suppressor or a threaded barrel designed to accommodate a flash suppressor
5. grenade launcher.

As produced in Arizona, the SW-5 fires from a closed bolt, which most shooters agree is a boon to accuracy. This is a recoil-operated rifle with a stationary barrel and a delayed roller-locked bolt system. The SW-5 is made up of six assemblies: the barrel and receiver that includes the cocking tube and sights, the bolt assembly, the grip assembly and trigger mechanism, a back plate attached to the stock, the hand guard and, the magazine.

On the assembled rifle, a heavy-duty steel ring protects the front sight, while the rear sight is the familiar rotary type that has three diopter holes. These allow the sight to be adjusted selectively for firing at ranges of 50, 75 and 100 yards. There also is an open V-type sight, which to Lewis suggests overkill. The rotary rear sight can be adjusted for elevation and windage by using a Phillips screwdriver.

The safety lever is positioned on the left side of the rifle's grip assembly. When the lever is directed to the letter S, the rifle is in the safe mode. When moved to the letter F, it is ready to fire. The right side of the grip assembly also is marked with S and F. This degree of overkill tends to suggest that the

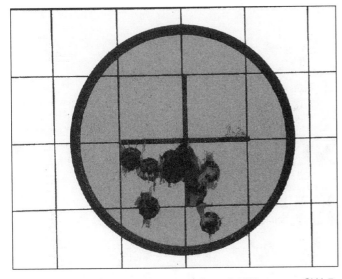

The target shot by Ong with the Special Weapons SW-5 9mm rifle was tight, but he was disappointed by the two holes that were not touching the others.

Back in Ong's gunshop after firing the SW-5, the shooter and Jack Lewis inspect the target punched by the 9mm Winchester ammo.

designer started to incorporate an ambidextrous safety, then changed his mind.

Functioning of the rifle is pretty much within the parameters seen in other H&K designs of the past. With the loaded rifle's safety set in the firing mode, when the trigger is pulled, the hammer is released and strikes the firing pin. In turn, this ignites the cartridge, the fast-burning powder producing the gases that drive the bullet out of the barrel.

These gases also exert simultaneous pressure on the cartridge case, which is still in the chamber. This force is divided to act on the face of the bolt head, the receiver and the bolt head carrier. The balanced ratio of the locking piece and the barrel extension cause delayed recoil movement of the bolt head. Thus, the bolt keeps the barrel locked until the bullet has left the muzzle.

Once the locking rollers have been cammed into the bolt head, the bolt continues its recoil movement. The result is that the empty cartridge case is ejected and the hammer recocked. In this milisecond, the recoil spring is compressed, returning the bolt to its forward position. A fresh cartridge is drawn from the magazine and chambered.

At this point in the continuing sequence, the extractor engages the extracting grooves milled in the cartridge case. The locking rollers are cammed against the supporting surfaces in the barrel extension and the rifle is ready to fire, again.

Art Ong was familiar with the SW-5 and he fired it first. After loading a 10-round magazine with Winchester 9mm NATO ammo carrying 124-grain full metal jacket bullets, he led the way into his shooting range, where he used the electronic target system to run a target out to 50 feet. As I watched, he stepped into the booth and took up his position, using the built-in bench as a rest, while pressing his right elbow against the padded wall. It looked like a stable position.

With only seconds between rounds, he fired off all 10 rounds. Obviously, he had played with this shooting tool before. Eight of the rounds formed one ragged group, while the two flyers were a quarter of an inch removed to the left.

Inspecting the target moments later, Ong was quick to indicate the pair of flyers, muttering, "I must be getting lazy!"

Ong describes himself as "an American-Chinese, not a Chinese-American," and there are no doubts as to where his loyalties lie. He got his start in business by supplying equipment needs to racecar drivers and those wanting to soup up their personal vehicles.

"I wasn't particularly interested in firearms," he explains, "until I saw that gun owners were being threatened by the horde of anti-gun laws that were being introduced both here at home and on the Mainland. As a protest, I went out and took the test and trained for a hunting license, then bought my first firearm.

"After that, I was hooked," he admits. "I had found a field of competition where the result was pretty much up to the individual no matter how much he paid for his gun."

Ong soon opened Magnum Firearms and the rest of it is history. Like Topsy of *Uncle Tom's Cabin*, his business just "growed!"

Lewis had an opportunity to try his shooting talents with the SW-5, but didn't do nearly as well as Ong. The group he fired had all of the bullet holes within the 3-inch red circle, but as he put it, "If I said any of the bullets were touching, I'd be lying."

Whatever the pedigree of the parts of the SW-5, Lewis believes it is a well-made and assembled tool that could find a place in law enforcement circles.

"It is rugged in construction and, as a result of my close inspection of the innards, I believe the rifle could take the punishment such weapons often suffer in the field," Lewis says.

CHAPTER 23

WRINGING OUT BUSHMASTER'S M-17S

This Bullpup .223 Offers a Frightening Appearance That Could Lead to a Felon's Instant Surrender

SOME CONTEND THE menacing appearance of a firearm or other tools of military use or law enforcement often is enough to make a miscreant drop his firearm and raise his hands in surrender. Steele points to the sawed-off, short-stocked slide-action shotgun he often carries on official missions. Lewis' choice is the Bushmaster M-17S bullpup rifle, which is chambered for the 5.56mm NATO cartridge. Incidentally, this particular model is the only non-banned, American-made bullpup on the market today.

When it comes to size and weight in armament, Lewis favors anything smaller that works as though it is larger. It must be remembered that when he joined the Marine Corps some six decades ago, he stood 6-feet tall, weighed 147 pounds and seemed destined to spend the balance of World War II lugging the weighty base plate for his outfit's 81mm mortar. As he puts it today, "I've always been allergic to weight."

The M-17S – manufactured in the factory of Bushmaster Firearms in Windham, Maine – is the culmination of a long program of producing firearms that have as their basis the now public domain AR-15/M-16 military rifles. In designing the M-17S, the folks in Windham went to great lengths to give it a barrel measuring 21.5 inches, with the overall bullpup ending up less than 10 inches longer. From butt to muzzle, it is only 30 inches. The barrel is hard-chrome lined, as is the chamber and features a right-hand twist with a ratio of one turn in every 9 inches of length. Even better, in Lewis' time-tempered opinion, is the fact that it weighs only 8.2 pounds.

As a gas-operated semi-automatic weapon, it is marketed with a 10-round steel magazine, but the makers insist their product will handle virtually any known AR-type magazine. Other specifications state that this is a short-stroke piston, self-compensating, air-cooled weapon. They're quick to tell you right up

The Bushmaster M-17S is a tidy little package that should find a place in law enforcement and perhaps clandestine operations. It measures only 30 inches in overall length.

Ammunition used in the field test was Winchester's .223 Remington Power Point Plus. This high-velocity round carries a 55-grain jacketed bullet.

front that it comes with an extended, two-year parts and labor warranty.

The M-17S has 25-meter open sights that are built into the see-through channel under the scope rail, but actually it is designed to be used with a scope, a red-dot sight or a night-vision device. The Picatinny-type rail will accept any of these sighting aids.

One of the first things Lewis noted once he had the little rifle in hand was its simple maintenance. A hinged pushpin system allows the upper and lower receivers to be separated in a matter of seconds. This allows quick access to the innards and the moving parts. The bullpup is marketed in a foam-lined hard-sided carrying case.

Other features that brought a plus grade in Lewis' opinion were the lower receiver including the pistol grip that is made from 43 percent glass-filled nylon. This helps in the weight department, as well as being impact-resistant. The carrying/charging handle is fashioned from the same material, while the upper receiver is of hard-anodized aircraft-quality aluminum that meets military specifications.

All of the gun's exterior metal surfaces are coated with military-grade magnesium phosphate. The ambidextrous magazine release is positioned on the lower receiver and a last-round bolt catch is on the left side of the gun's lower receiver.

In checking out such weaponry, Lewis likes to get input from working law enforcement personnel and those in the military who have a day-to-day, hands-on association with the tools of warfare. The principle question for any weapon of this type is: Will it work for them?

Lewis contacted three members of the Island of Hawaii Police Department. Leading off was Fukui, a 48-year-old with a life-long history in law enforcement. Patrolman Isaac Fiesta has 10 years in law enforcement and another 10 years of military experience, both active-duty and reserve. Patrolman Wendell Carter has been a uniformed police officer for four years, with prior background as a youth corrections officer.

In this type of test, Lewis goes somewhat beyond the standard paper-punching routine involved in most requalification shoots. The three officers arrived in civilian clothes. Fukui and Fiesta had worked with Lewis on various testing projects in the past and wore heavy, full-length trousers. When Carter arrived, Lewis realized he had neglected to brief the young man fully – he was wearing walking shorts.

The three officers gathered about the folding table on which the Bushmaster and a supply of Winchester's PowerPoint Plus ammo had been laid out. The box listed the .223 Remington cartridges as producing high velocity. Lewis briefed the trio on the operation and capabilities of the shortie rifle, then each of the officers took the opportunity to try the bullpup for shoulder fit, aiming downrange and dry-firing to check out the trigger pull.

Each man seemed intrigued by a 3000 red-dot aiming device that had been attached to the rail. Earlier, Lewis had loaded the batteries into the Aimpoint device and zeroed it in on a white rock protruding from the face of the lava quarry where the shoot was to take place. The Aimpoint worked well enough at an estimated range of 75 yards.

The standard Bushmaster 10-round magazine had been sent with the gun, but Fukui had brought along a 20-round M-16 magazine he wanted to try. It worked as well as the shorter mag.

For all practical purposes, the M-17S has no stock as such. The gun's action and the magazine are positioned well behind the trigger guard and the ejection port is only a few inches from the shooter's face when this weapon is positioned properly against the shoulder.

"The bullpup is held in position primarily by the right hand, which is clutching the pistol grip, the index finger extended to the trigger for firing," Lewis explains.

A fast survey showed that all three of the law enforcement agents had no previous knowledge of the weapon. Even before this, Lewis had decided that the conformation and the claimed capabilities of the little shooter called for a special type of testing.

"The folks back in Maine where the M-17S is made say that it has a maximum range of about 3850 yards, with an effective range of 600 yards," Lewis told the trio.

That brought some mutterings. The attitude seemed to be that if appearance had anything to do with efficiency, the bullpup might be better suited to such short-range missions as forced entries.

Prior to the arrival of his test team, Lewis had set up standard silhouette targets at what he paced off to be approximately 60 yards. Each shooter was to start the exercise from a sitting position at the folding table on which the gun and ammo had been placed. Each was to fire five rounds with no particular time limit. In this segment, Lewis was interested in group size for each of the shooters.

Lewis assigned the shooters on the bases of seniority – age, in this case, rather than rank. Fukui fired his five. Checking showed that all were in the X-ring in the center of the silhouette's chest area, the group measuring roughly four inches in diameter.

As a Marine Corps-trained sniper, Fiesta chose to try for head shots with his five rounds. While lining up and squeezing them off, he complained that as such short range, the red dot in the Aimpoint tended to cover up the black image of the silhouette's head. In spite of his complaints, he managed a three-inch group in the forehead area of the target.

Least experienced and youngest of the trio, Carter appeared somewhat nervous as he slid onto edge of the plastic chair. He pressed the bullpup's butt into his shoulder in approved fashion, then took his time

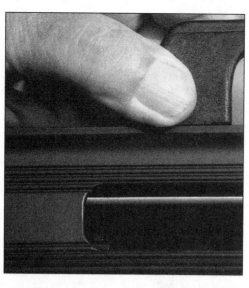

The action is controlled by what is part of the carrying handle. It is drawn to the rear to cock the little rifle.

The Aimpoint 3000 red-dot sighting device comes with its own rings that mount on the gun's Picatinny-type rail. The unit took some getting used to by the test shooters.

in triggering off his five rounds. Inspection showed that his shots formed an eight-inch pattern in the paunch area of the target.

"Relax, Wen," Fiesta, advised as he and Carter walked away from the target. "You're not being graded on any of this."

In the second segment of the exercise, each shooter would start at the edge of the table and walk toward the second target, which was fresh and unmarred. (Lewis had not explained the various phases of the exercise in advance because he wanted to present some sort of in-the-field problem for the shooters.)

During the walk, the little M-17S was to be held against the shoulder, muzzle angled toward the ground and trigger finger extended beside the trigger guard. Roughly seven yards from the target, Lewis had upended a plastic coffee cup on the lava gravel. When the shooter reached this point, he was to drop to his knees, find the target beyond the red dot in the sighting device, but not loose his five rounds in rapid-fire mode until the order, "Fire!"

"It wasn't until then that I noticed that Carter was casting a worried look at the rough lava flanking the coffee cup. If you've never dropped to your bare knees in that razor-edge material, you've never known real pain!" Lewis says.

Fukui called a time out and made for his truck. He returned with a yellow raincoat, folded it to form a pad and spread it beside the upturned coffee cup, and then stepped back.

"Fiesta had played similar shooting games with me in past exercises," says Lewis. "He volunteered to go first."

Lewis observed, stopwatch in hand, as Fiesta strode forward, dropped to his knees beside the white plastic marker and brought the barrel of the bullpup up to center on the target. "It was obvious that this time, he was not trying for head shots," Lewis recalls.

At the command, Fiesta squeezed off his five rounds in relatively rapid succession, taking a fraction of a second between each round to get the sight back on target. His clocked time for the five shots was slightly less than four seconds.

Inspection of his target showed an interesting group — or what might be interpreted as groups," notes Lewis. Holes from two of the rounds were

almost touching in the chest area near the heart. The holes from the other three rounds were similarly spaced two inches lower.

Fukui strode toward the target, gun muzzle lowered, his eyes on the target the whole route. He dropped to his knees on the folded raincoat, raised the muzzle quickly to squint through the Aimpoint 3000 sighting device. At Lewis' command, he started firing.

Chad's time was about three-tenths of a second longer than that recorded for Fiesta," Lewis says. "A fraction over four seconds."

Inspection of Fukui's bullet holes showed four of them almost overlapping with the fifth round's puncture four inches away.

"I got sloppy on that last shot," Fukui admits. "It looked so easy that I sloughed it off."

Carter shoved the magazine reloaded with five fresh rounds into the well. He checked that the ambidextrous safety was on before he began to march resolutely toward the target. When he reached the coffee cup, he dropped one bare knee on the folded yellow raincoat and used the other knee as a brace for the arm holding the bullpup.

He seemed to struggle for a moment with the safety," Lewis recalls, "as I shouted the order for him to fire. It became obvious he wasn't interested in setting time records."

The junior member of the team fired slowly and with concentration. He was interested in building a respectable group. "He wanted to show the old hands he did know what it was all about," Lewis said later.

It required a fraction over eight seconds for Carter to trigger off his five rounds. When his group was inspected, it was smaller that those fired by either of the others. It measured a trifle under 2-1/2 inches center-to-center. When Lewis announced the measurement, Carter grinned broadly.

This exercise had been conducted early on a Saturday morning because the three police officers had to report for duty before noon. Soon no one was in the lava quarry except for Lewis and his wife, Rueselle, who had handled the photo chores.

"I policed up the Winchester brass, taking time to inspect each of the expended cartridge cases. All were

Police Lt. Chad Fukui stepped off smartly toward the target, muzzle of the M-17S lowered and his finger extended beyond the trigger.

Fukui gazes toward to target after squeezing off his five rounds from the kneeling position. He liked the little bullpup model.

The M-17S has a waffle-patterned butt that is cast into the stock. With the light recoil experienced with the .223 cartridge, it works well for the shooter.

excellent candidates for reloading. There was no evidence of dings or dents in any of the brass," Lewis says.

"I have found that this particular Winchester round with its 55-grain bullet enclosed in a full metal jacket is pretty much foolproof when fired in either a semi- or full-auto weapon. The cartridge is built to feed," he says.

According to the maker, the rate of fire for the Bushmaster M-17S is listed at 450 rounds per minute, offering a muzzle velocity of 3,100 fps. Considering this and other info regarding the little rifle, Lewis loaded up the 10-round factory-furnished magazine and propped himself and the firearm up on the folding table that had been used as a firing bench.

"I chose a different part of the silhouette target for each shot," he notes. "Using the 3000 Aimpoint, I took my time and squeezed off each round. When the magazine was empty, I sauntered down to the target. My wife joined me and noted that each of my rounds was in the black. I didn't tell her that at least three were about 2 inches from the point where I was aiming. If she wants to think I'm a crack shot, I won't disillusion her."

That is a round about way for Lewis to admit he was impressed with the rifle. As for the Aimpoint 3000, it comes with rings that fit on the rifle's rail. It is powered by a three-volt lithium battery housed in its own compartment that is air and moisture-tight. Brightness settings range from low to high, but it is wise to turn off the unit when not in use, preserving the power source.

Springfield Armory out of Illinois markets the Aimpoint 3000. Thinking back to his days of lugging the base plate for that 81mm mortar, Lewis made particular note of the fact that the Aimpoint weighs only a few ounces!

The five-shot group fired by Carter measured approximately 2-1/2 inches center-to-center.

CHAPTER 24

CARBINE MARKSMANSHIP

In Some Combat Situations, Accuracy May Be More Important Than Velocity or Weight of the Bullet

DURING WORLD WAR I, our troops were handicapped in trench warfare and in house-clearing operations by the long, heavy 1903 Springfield rifle. Foreign troops of the allied nations were no better armed. However, the rifle was ideal in such long-range shooting affairs as that glorified by Sgt. Alvin York's heroic action in slaying and capturing German soldiers.

During World War II, the short carbine came to be recognized by some as a desirable weapon. "It seems strange to me that the .30-caliber M-1 Carbine was criticized on the basis of a lack of power compared to the Garand battle rifle, while the Soviet's short Degtyarev PPD-40 – popularly known as the 'burp gun'

At extremely short ranges, a covering position can be used that is well suited to immediate fire. This is a shotgun-type position with the stock under the arm. It's good for 3 to 7 yards, but works best if the sight is raised to the eye.

and firing a pistol cartridge – is praised," says veteran police officer Robert Campbell.

"The M-1 Carbine – and later the M-2 selective-fire version – are more powerful, reliable and accurate than any World War II submachine gun," he admits, "but much less powerful than a true battle rifle. History shows that house-to-house fighting in Europe as well as the jungle warfare of the Pacific put an emphasis on quickly directed firepower. Long-range, pinpoint accuracy was not as desirable as quickly delivered hits and practical accuracy. Even those who lamented the passing of the bolt-action Springfield 1903 eventually came to realize the Garand was far more efficient in getting a quick hit in combat conditions," Campbell says.

The rest of the story is familiar to gun enthusiasts. The M-16 program began in the 1950s and has resulted in giving us the longest-lived service rifle in American history. Now considered prolific, effective and simple in spite of a rocky beginning in Vietnam combat, the M-16 is among the most formidable weapons systems of all time. The rifle fires an intermediate-range cartridge that can be effective to 300 yards, but is at its best at less than 200 yards, Campbell points out.

"The AR-15 rifle – the semi-automatic civilian-legal equivalent of the M-16 – has gained wide acceptance not only in civilian competition but also by numerous police agencies," Campbell adds.

He also believes that "It also is a formidable home defense weapon with many good qualities. The cartridge is less offensive in terms of penetration and ricochet than are most handgun cartridges, but offers considerable improvement in wound potential over any handgun. In civil settings, the range is often short. It is true that the potential for a Texas Tower-type sniper-provoked tragedy always exists, and the more powerful battle-type rifle can serve well in such an incident."

As a former training officer, Campbell sometimes is asked what constitutes a good marksman and how

It is Campbell's contention that aperture-type sights are the best for rapid, sure shooting.

The veteran officer believes the kneeling position is okay for light-recoil weapons, but he has never used it in the field. In this instance, he is using a .45 caliber Uzi carbine.

an individual could rate his or her talents. "A qualified combat marksman is good not only at trigger and sight work, but also in deployment and manipulation," Campbell says. "A good shot should be able to stand erect in a solid shooting position and hit a paper plate target at 100 yards with four out of five shots. He should be able to do the same from a sitting position at 150 yards and from prone at 200 yards, with the 5.56mm rifle or carbine. He should have a good understanding of the requirements for hitting moving targets, as well. Offhand shooting is far more difficult to master than bench or barricade shooting, but is a far more useful skill. If you can shoot offhand, you can shoot even better from the bench."

The first perquisite for such training is to find a range that allows offhand shooting. All do not. This may mean a longer drive to a cooperating range, but Campbell insists the extra effort will be worthwhile. In the meantime, dry-fire practice with a triple-checked unloaded firearm is valuable.

"If you cannot stop muscle tremble and your sights shifting during dry-fire exercises, then live fire will really whip you! Get with the program and master the basics. Trigger compression, sight picture and sight alignment will carry the day," Campbell says.

The basics could also include developing the ability to quickly get into proper firing position. This means getting the stock to the shoulder and the cheek welded to the stock quickly. Bring the carbine's stock hard into the shoulder and support the forend. If you have a sling, learn to wrap the sling around the support elbow and brace the gun. "Incredibly precise shooting can be done in this manner," Campbell insists.

"The three primary shooting positions are standing, sitting and prone," says Campbell. "I find that the prone position affords an excellent braced position. Precise shooting can be accomplished while offering a low profile. A disadvantage is that the prone position is difficult to break out of quickly, but its advantages are many."

When getting into a sitting position, Campbell says to "melt into the position all around the rifle, seeming to surround it, and hold it solidly. Good shooting can be done from the sitting position." Campbell points out that the military also teaches the kneeling position, adding, "I do not care for kneeling very much, but it may have its moments."

One must remember, too, that textbook solutions don't always work when the brass is flying. "The real world is more interesting and more demanding," Campbell philosophizes. "Consider the lessons of the dojo. If you spar with the same partner for months, you think you know the moves he'll make. Then you start to work with a new partner, who breaks out from another, entirely different section of the 12 angles of attack and you are confused. In a situation such as this, we use basic, traditional skills to allow the implementation of flexible tactics.

"The same approach can be applied to gunfights. In the United States, most police shoot-outs occur at short to medium range. Normally, we must identify a threat and recognize the fact that we are in danger in order to respond with deadly force. This will happen at long range only rarely, so a quick response is needed.

"In such situations, the carbine is the tool of choice for many professionals. It offers much more power than a handgun and more range when needed over the shotgun. The average gunfight ends before one needs to reload, but should that need arise, the carbine is faster to reload than either the shotgun or pistol. It also carries more cartridges than either of the other two weapons."

145

This posed photo is all wrong for actual combat. The officer is in a target-shooting stance, with a poor grip on the forend. In actual combat, one holds the forend tightly as a control factor.

As with any weapon, the carbine is no better than its operator. To effectively deploy and quickly use the carbine requires more skill than bench-rest shooting. In training, Campbell sometimes will stand squared to the target, but then will move at various angles to face the threat. The tactical shooter will use a more squared stance than the precision shooter, who more often is involved with a target that is not going to shoot back. Campbell teaches less-experienced officers to stand with the knees flexed and the weak-side foot ahead of the strong-side foot. Weight bias is slightly forward to aid in controlling the flip of the carbine's muzzle.

"This is a comfortable stance that may be assumed quickly and with little effort. It can be held for much longer than the bladed stance favored by target shooters. The individuals also can break out of this stance quickly and move laterally or even make a turn to the rear with a long side step," Campbell explains.

After working with a number of shooters who have varying skill levels, Campbell learned that the most common deficit in shooting styles is a failure to achieve cheek-to-stock weld.

"Moving the butt of the carbine to the shoulder and getting the sights on target quickly without proper cheek weld results in poor shot placement," Campbell says. "In real life, in-the-field situations, we cannot be content with just a hit on the target and happy with area aiming. We are looking for good shot placement. We may even be forced to take a hostage rescue shot. After all, this is the forte of the long gun.

"An ever-changing cheek weld results in an inconsistent sight picture and poor results. A ready position with the rifle pointed slightly downward, but with the cheek well into the stock should be practiced."

One will be carrying the carbine more than using it, and there are few occasions when even a peace officer can cover a person with the muzzle of a gun without it becoming a life-threatening situation. Campbell insists that police officers or even military types armed with the carbine should practice their ready positions.

When the moment comes to fire, the weak arm moves the forend upward and into position. The strong-side hand grips the gun. The sights should be lined up on the target at this point and trigger compression started.

"A rifleman can jerk the trigger precipitously and miss at a ridiculously close range," Campbell has found. "A smooth straight-to-the-rear trigger compression is demanded.

"There are three ways of acquiring the sights quickly, each depending upon the sight system. The peep, ghost ring or aperture sight is the most common and preferred combat sight. To use this rear sight quickly, bring the gun to the cheek weld, look through the sight and bring the post front sight into it. With leaf sights such as that found on the AK, one must find the front post first and bring it into the rear sight.

"When using the increasingly popular optical sight, I take a quick sighting over the top adjustment knob before checking out the target with the reticule.

Campbell favors the prone position over others since it offers the most stability and gives an opponent a low-image target.

Campbell gets the measure of the Colt 5.56mm with a Bushnell HoloSight II installed. He found it a fast, hard-hitting combination for moderate ranges.

Campbell's soldier son places his grip on the hand guard just forward of the magazine, which he believes affords better control. It also is the technique taught in the Armed Forces.

While Campbell offers definite rules for carbine marksmanship, he also believes in doing whatever works. Here, his left arm is extended to the extreme front of the hand guard, a technique that is not recommended by most firearms instructors.

This helps align the scope on the target and saves time in centering the crosshairs. I have used this technique many times in the hunting field. For me, at least, it works well, with scopes of both high and low magnification," he says.

Campbell firmly believes that if a shooter tends to think too hard – and too long –about the shot, he will have a problem. With the basics of sight alignment, sight picture and trigger compression learned, one should simply bring the gun to the shoulder and stop the gun at the middle of the target, compressing the trigger.

"The speed and accuracy of such simple movement will surprise most shooters," Campbell says. "I also attempt to come on target in the centerline instead of across the subject's body, increasing the chances of a telling hit. Bringing the muzzle up and down allows a natural pause, while winging across the target makes for jerky motion," he explains.

When using the carbine at short range, one should be extra aware of the point of aim. At short range, the rifle will shoot low. Most AR-15s and variants reflect a 2- to 3-inch deviation of the point of aim versus point of impact at 10 yards.

"This means that your shot on the brow of the perpetrator holding your wife by the throat probably will strike the victim in the forehead, if this drop is not taken into account; a sobering thought," says the veteran lawman.

"With a handgun, I have always practiced double taps – two rapid shots – into the target at close range," says Campbell. "I do exactly the same with the carbine. It is cheap insurance, but as distance increases the need for speed decreases, while the need for precision increases inversely proportionally to the distance.

"There is one shooting technique I have adopted that works. Called Stressfire, it was developed by Ayoob and is adopted from a time-honored handgun technique. Using only the front sight has been practiced by such legendary gunfighters as the Old West's Wild Bill Hickock and is used often by soldiers and modern day peace officers."

At short range – 10 yards or less – the front sight is superimposed over the target and the shot fired without respect to the rear sight. This makes for extremely fast shooting. Campbell says, "The gun must actually be fired for one to understand the relationship between the front sight's position and point of impact of the bullet. That point invariably will be several inches above the front sight's placement on the target, but this technique can be a lifesaver in low-light situations in which one cannot see the rear sight. Normally, I prefer using the sights – both of them – but sometimes we have to go with what we know will work.

"To make life more simple, I have fitted my personal Delta HBAR with self-luminous iron sights from Innovative Weaponry. In dim light, the sight seems to simply hang there, visible when nothing else is."

Campbell contends that carbines not only are more powerful than handguns, but are more accurate and more effective, but notes that "their successful implementation is limited if the operator does not have a base of skill on which to build. Training, practice and, most of all, sufficient thought are necessities for mastering today's carbines."

CHAPTER 25

THE TRG-22 –
TOOL FOR A SNIPER

The Finns Have Long Believed That a Conventional Bolt-Action Rifle Promises First-Shot Accuracy

"FINLAND IS A nation made up of super-nationalistic citizens who have been forced to defend their country over the centuries. They have been noted for some of the military firearms they have developed and one of the best is the Sako TRG-22 Sniper Rifle," says Lewis.

He has hunted in the Arctic-edging country, toured the nation's arms factories and come to know the people. As he puts it, "They drink hard, play hard and if pushed, fight hard. The legends regarding what the Finnish ski troops – armed primarily with rifles and submachine guns – did to Russian invaders in the 1930s offer full testimony to their feelings about preserving their nation's boundaries," he says.

In 1939, Russia's communist forces invaded Finland in an attempt to add it to the Soviet Union. The Russians' rapid advances were unsuccessful since the Finns knew their own terrain and took full advantage of it. Russia lost more than 100,000 troops in the attempted invasion. In what has come to be called the Winter War, Stalin decided it was better to negotiate terms with the Finns. The Moscow Peace Treaty between the two nations was signed on March 12, 1940. The Finns had fought the Russian hordes to a standstill.

Today's premiere Finnish bolt-action, magazine-fed sniper rifle, the TRG-22, is conventional in design, but is produced with care that speaks worlds

The Sako TRG-22 sniper rifle, built for the Finnish army is a formidable piece of equipment in the hands of a trained sniper. It is chambered for the 7.62mm NATO cartridge.

The muzzle brake of the TRG-22 is a heavy-duty item that has proved to be quite effective in reducing recoil.

for the craftsmanship of the tiny nation's gunmakers. The bolt and the receiver are somewhat large in comparison with other 7.62mm NATO rifles, but this is due to the forethought that bigger and better cartridges would come along.

That happened and the same basic design now is being used for the TRG-42, which is chambered to handle both the .300 Winchester Magnum cartridge and the .338 Lapua Magnum. Barrel lengths and some other specifications differ for the TRG-42, so this essay is relative to the TRG-22 and will stick to that model.

The TRG-22 has three forward locking lugs with an indicator at the rear that shows the shooter whether the rifle is cocked. In keeping with the lessons learned against the Russians, the safety located on the right side of the receiver is silent when activated. The safety serves three functions: It locks the trigger mechanism. It locks the bolt in the closed position. It blocks the firing pin from the cartridge primer.

Barrel length is just a fraction short of 26 inches with overall length pegged at 45-1/4 inches. The barrel carries four grooves with a right-hand twist for every 11 inches.

The box magazine holds 10 rounds of 7.62mm NATO ammunition. This is a center-feeding detachable type that is designed for reliable feeding. The narrow magazine opening on the receiver offers the unbroken bolt guiding surfaces and causes the bolt to move smoothly. During his visit to Finland some years ago, Lewis had the opportunity to watch local experts load match-grade ammunition. When he fired some of it at a range of 300 yards, he was amazed at the resulting accuracy. Fired from a bench, his five-shot group could be covered by his hand.

Lewis credits his unusually good shoot in part to the steel bipod that is adjustable for height. The bipod also is constructed to allow some degree of movement without the shooter having to reposition it. The stainless steel barrel is fitted with a muzzle brake that must be removed if one wants to replace it with a sound suppressor.

Another factor involved in the rifle's accuracy, Lewis believes, is the two-stage trigger than can be adjusted for pressure and position without having to tear down

The pad can be removed from the buttstock and spacers added to increase the length.

the rifle. The trigger group includes the trigger guard and can be removed as a unit if necessary.

With the trigger group removed, it is possible for a shooter to adjust the trigger to personal requirements. It is adjustable in three directions: length, as well as horizontal and vertical pitch. A hexagonal key is included with instructions on how to adjust the trigger. Lewis, however, was happy with the way the trigger was set – which he estimated to be about 2 pounds – when he was issued the rifle for testing. Trigger pull weight, he learned, is set at the factory at between 2 and 4 pounds.

An earlier version of the rifle, the TRG-21, was equipped with either a wood stock or one made from a fiberglass-based compound. The base of the stock of the TRG-22 is of aluminum where the polyurethane fore stock is attached. The polyurethane butt stock is reinforced with an aluminum skeleton. The receiver is bedded directly onto the aluminum profile. The cheek piece is adjustable with spacers for height and in pitch. The buttplate also is adjustable with spacers. The military rapid-fire model features the CISM stock designed for both right- and left-handed shooters. Sling swivels are included.

The sniper rifle features folding iron sights – front and rear – but the receiver is designed to simplify mounting of a scope or other types of modern sighting devices. The rifle that Lewis fired during his visit was equipped with a variable scope, but he does not recall the manufacturer. Without the scope, the TRG-22 weighs 10-3/8 pounds.

The bolt has an over-size knob that makes it easier to reload if wearing gloves. Considering the fact that the Arctic Circle is almost within spitting distance of the nation's northernmost border, gloves are a must during much of the year. The bolt lift angle for eject-

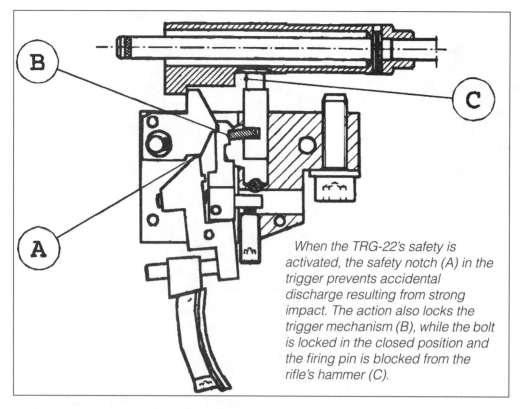

When the TRG-22's safety is activated, the safety notch (A) in the trigger prevents accidental discharge resulting from strong impact. The action also locks the trigger mechanism (B), while the bolt is locked in the closed position and the firing pin is blocked from the rifle's hammer (C).

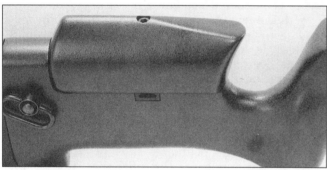

The adjustable cheek piece of the stock adds to the rifle's capabilities as a sniper tool.

Metal work on the TRG-22 is smooth and well done by expert craftsmen. The stock, cast from man-made materials, fits snuggly around the metal parts.

ing a case and loading a fresh round in the chamber is 60 degrees. Bolt throw is 3-7/8 inches.

Lewis did not have an opportunity to fire the rifle with the sound suppressor attached. However, he noted that the suppressor is installed after the muzzle brake and the open sights have been removed. The suppressor is screwed onto the same exterior threads on the barrel used to mount the muzzlebrake.

If a shot is to be fired without noise, subsonic ammunition must be used with the silencer fitted. Subsonic ammo is low in velocity and thus accuracy requires different sighting than with standard ammo. If one is not concerned with the sound created by the bullet breaking the sound barrier, the Sako suppressor can be used with standard 7.62mm ammunition without adjusting the rifle's zero.

Sako engineers suggest that the TRG-22 undergo an annual maintenance check, which is not a bad idea for any firearm.

After cleaning the barrel carefully, remove the metal parts from the stock, then clean the inside of the metal parts and the stock. Screws and pins also should be cleaned. Metal parts and sling swivels should be oiled.

In cleaning the bolt, the Sako folks suggest removing the firing pin first, then removing all old oil from the bolt and the firing pin. The bolt face, locking lugs, extractor and ejector can then be cleaned and checked for damage at the same time. It is important to check the point of the firing pin and its attachment to the bolt sleeve.

The instructions are based on a cold-weather scenario. It is suggested that cold-resistant oil be used to lightly lubricate the inside of the bolt and the firing pin. Other parts that should be lubed are the locking lugs, cocking slope, bolt sleeve locking cams and the cocking piece.

In re-assembly, the firing pin should be checked for protrusion of 1.65mm. With the sights or scope attached, the gun is re-assembled so one can check function. The Sako people then suggest the gun owner go to the range and test the gun. Somehow that sounds a bit like overkill, since the gun then will have to be torn down for another cleaning.

"However, those making up the Sako staff obviously know their rifle and what they are doing. It's tough to argue with success," Lewis notes.

CHAPTER 26

SPRINGFIELD'S TACTICAL M-21

Here's a New Use for an Old Veteran That's Wearing a Whole New Look

THERE ARE A lot of things in the field of military armament that just won't go away. Take the Thompson submachine gun. As a fully automatic weapon of war, it got dropped about the time we ended World War II and gave the military surplus supply of this gun to the Chinese Nationalist Army. However, if you look around, the gun still is being manufactured in a semi-automatic mode.

Other WW II armament frequently recycled in one form or another includes the .30 M-1 Carbine and the .30-06-flinging M-1 Garand. Both are considered classics and only recently Springfield, Inc., has started to reproduce the Garand to its original military specifications, meeting a demand from serious shooters, collectors and those simply touched by nostalgia.

But the rifle that had perhaps the shortest full-scale military life and that still is being reproduced is the M-14, which has been described over the decades as "a full-auto M-1 Garand". That is not so far from true. It was developed by the government-owned Springfield Arsenal to be introduced as the interim rifle between the Garand and what was to come. That ultimately turned out to be the M-16 5.56mm rifle designed by Stoner and introduced originally as the Armalite AR-15.

As explained more fully elsewhere, the M-14 is seeing new life with the Marine Corps, which dug through thousands of them to come up with the 1,000 best. They have been reworked and reconfigured to become the Corps' DMR. At present, they are being issued to explosive ordnance destruction units.

Taking an entirely different tack, the modern Springfield organization, a commercial outfit located in Geneseo, Ill., has made a career of producing two

Fiesta displays the shooting techniques he learned in a military sniper school. He serves as a firearms instructor with his law enforcement unit.

The Springfield Tactical M-21 rifle is a revamping of the venerable military M-14, but looks to be more than adequate in an entirely new military and police role.

items: clones of the Colt-designed M-1911A1 auto-loading pistol and the M-14 rifle.

Recently the company introduced the Springfield M-21, which is chambered for the venerable 7.62x51mm cartridge. There is no evidence that the company tried to sell this to the Department of Defense for any specific role. It is, however, doing an excellent job of showing it off to police departments across the nation as well as civilian shooters, who want to have one of everything in their arms collections.

As a result of a long relationship with Dennis Reese, vice president of Springfield Armory, a branch of Springfield, Inc., Lewis was able to borrow one of the M-21s in order to work it over with personnel of the Island of Hawaii Police Department. Lewis has checked out a number of firearms with the help of Isaac "Ike" Fiesta III, a member of the island's SWAT team.

Fiesta is a veteran of almost 10 years in law enforcement. Prior to signing on to uphold the laws of the land in general and the island in particular, he served for some 10 years with the military. Initially, he was assigned to a forward air control team of the U.S. Air Force. These are the people who get close enough to the enemy to indicate via lasers where the so-called smart bombs of modern warfare should be dropped. In spite of the fact that this was an Air Force unit, those assigned underwent infantry, urban warfare and air-assault training.

Following that duty, Fiesta enlisted in the Marine Corps for a stint with the 4th Force Reconnaissance Company. He trained in deep penetration reconnaissance, which included underwater scuba work and parachute missions.

Due largely to his expansive military training and the money the government has spent in providing same – not to mention the number of current weapons with which he has qualified with the military – Fiesta is assigned to his department as a firearms instructor. Many of the weapons with which he is personally familiar have law enforcement applications.

As soon as Fiesta heard that we were going to run our own tests on the Springfield M-21, he volunteered to help. He had been exposed to the M-14 along the way and thought this particular version might have law enforcement possibilities.

Although an Island of Hawaii police officer, Fiesta continues to train as a deep reconnaissance specialist with a local Marine Corps unit. He earlier served in the Air Force.

Setting up on a weekend in a lava quarry not far from the still-spewing Kileaua volcano, Fiesta's first move was to dismantle the M-21 and inspect it piece by piece. As a result of his exposure through his military years and personal research, he was quite familiar with the history and capabilities of the original Garand M-l and the M-14. Lewis told Fiesta that during World War II, if a serviceman lost – God forbid – or damaged an M-1 beyond repair, they took $112 out of the amount due him on his next visit to the pay table. The price, today, of Springfield Armory's M-21 Tactical Rifle is $2,975.

Someone pointed out that $112 in the mid-1940s probably had roughly the same buying power as $2,975 does today. Thus, the rifle may not be as expensive as one might at first suppose.

However, there are other expenses involved. There was Springfield's version of the military M-2 bipod attached to the rifle. That adds another $161. Also mounted on the M-21 was Springfield's Third Generation electronically controlled 4-14x56 variable scope. Add another $749.

As Lewis jokingly puts it, "At that price, I wouldn't even let someone clean it who hasn't been through armorers' school and been factory-trained!"

In becoming familiar with the rifle, Fiesta found that without the scope, the rifle weighs 11.6 pounds. Part of this weight comes from the SA9121 stock that Springfield developed specifically for this rifle. It is fashioned from walnut and has an adjustablecheek-piece that is controlled by means of a knurled knot positioned on the right sight of the stock. Proper stock adjustment allows the shooter to keep his head

Hawaii Police Officer Isaac Fiesta settles into the stock of the Springfield M-21 during a firing test in a lava quarry. He learned his rifle marksmanship as a Marine sergeant.

aligned perfectly with the scope. There is also more bulk in the pistol grip than in the original M-14 or its M-l predecessor.

A look at the owner's manual told us quickly that overall length of the M-21 is 44 inches. Part of this measurement is due to the 22-inch Douglas Premium custom heavy barrel. Douglas barrel makers have bored the thickness of steel with a right-hand twist that features one turn in 10 inches of barrel length. Reese told Lewis, however, that for an additional cost the purchaser can special order a stainless steel barrel from either Hart Rifle Barrels, Inc., doing business in Lafayette, N.Y., or from Krieger Barrels, Inc., located in Germantown, Wis.

As with the original M-14, the M-21 Tactical model is gas-operated and air-cooled. It has a rotating bolt and fires semi-auto only. The rifle is fed from the standard 7.62mm 10-round box magazine. However, where legal, there is an option that allows purchase of the pre-ban 20-round magazine that is the same as that used in the M-14.

For those who don't trust electronics when it comes to viewing a target, the scope can be left off since the rifle is outfitted with a National Match blade sight up front. Anchored firmly at the rear of the M-21 is a Match-grade hooded aperture sight that boasts half-minute adjustments for both windage and elevation. The sight radius for this setup is 26.75 inches.

Fiesta looks less than pleased as he inspects the impact of his first five rounds with the Springfield M-21, however any one of the five shots would have meant a kill.

A feature that Fiesta and Lewis, as well as others who fired the rifle, found of particular interest was the military-type two-stage trigger that was factory-tuned for let-off at 4.5 pounds. Some shooters probably will contend that this trigger pull is too light, but like beauty, this sort of thing is in the mind of the beholder – or in this case, the user. According to Reese, the M-21 rifle is being used by elite special operations outfits in far corners of the world, but he and his brother Tom see law enforcement as a coming market for their product.

Test firing took place in that lava pit on a sunny Hawaiian morning, with Fiesta, Lewis and Kaminski, the latter's shooting pardner who was there to see how well the firearm worked. A folding table covered with a rectangle of camouflage cloth had been set up on a flat plane of volcanic ash.

Two silhouette targets had been set up at a measured distance of 100 yards. As mentioned earlier, the rifle was topped by Springfield's Third Generation Government Model scope in the 4x14-56 setting. Mounted on the rifle by means of a heavy-duty proprietary mount and 30mm rings, the scope was designed specifically for use with the 7.62mm NATO cartridge, according to Dennis Reese.

Lewis had learned earlier from Reese that the scope carried a target-tracking green-illuminated reticle that helps in finding, then holding on the target in near-dark situations.

Reese says, "The reticle is calibrated for 7.62mm Match ammo and there's an internal bubble level that helps the shooter keep from canting the rifle." This rig adds three pounds to the initial weight of the rifle – the scope weighs two pounds and the mount and rings add another pound. Reese says, "Considering the fact that this scope incorporates a range finder that is operational to 1,000 meters, we figure the extra weight can be pretty much ignored. The rifleman isn't going to lug it that far before he sets up to shoot," Reese explains.

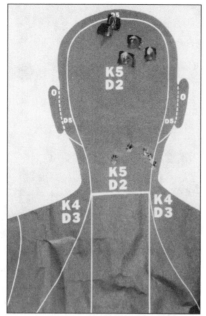

The black blobs in the top of the silhouette cover the initial five rounds fired at 100 yards by Fiesta. The five rounds through the neck comprise his second group. After he found and took care of a loose screw on the mount, he got into serious shooting.

Each of the electronic scopes marketed by Springfield has a spare battery compartment. Elevation and windage adjustments are uninvolved, each click moving the shooter's point of aim one-quarter minute of angle at a hundred yards. For what it is worth, Springfield has seven additional Government Model scopes that range from a 6x40 to a 6x20-56 Mil Dot version.

Lewis had brought along a detailed brochure describing the hows and whys of the scope. Fiesta glanced at it for confirmation of his moves several times before he hunched into the M-21's stock. He took several minutes to assure himself that he had the crosshairs centered on the head of one of the downrange silhouettes. Lewis, Kaminski and several other law enforcement types were standing behind him as he squeezed off his first shot, then cranked up the scope's power to determine how well he had done.

Kaminski was eyeing the target with binoculars and announced, "Head shot right at the top of the cranium."

Apparently, Fiesta had seen the same picture and offered a satisfied nod, as he cranked the magnification back down to 4x and proceeded to squeeze off the remaining four rounds he had initially loaded in the magazine.

As the others looked on, Fiesta removed the empty magazine, checked the rifle's chamber to be certain it was empty, then led the group downrange to the target. Inspection showed that two of the shots were in what would have been the hairline of the silhouette. The other three rounds formed a tight triangle in what would have been the forehead of a baddie.

"There was no doubt in my mind that any of the shots probably would have taken out a felon," Lewis declared later, "but Fiesta wasn't at all satisfied with his performance. The way the bullet holes were placed made it seem to him that he had fired two groups instead of one."

Back at the makeshift shooting bench, Fiesta fiddled with the scope, making slight adjustments, then hunched into the rifle stock once more, while conver-

sation at his rear died. The shooter studied his sight picture for several seconds, then slowly took up the slack in the two-stage trigger for his first shot.

Next came a repeat of the previous performance. Fiesta cranked up the scope to 14x. The rest of the entourage watched as he grinned and offered a satisfied nod. He settled the recoil pad into his shoulder pocket and squeezed off the remaining four rounds, caressing the trigger for each shot, seeming to offer each of them individual care.

Then came another trek across the rough lava wasteland. The changes Fiesta had made in the scope settings paid off. His five rounds all were about 6 inches lower than the first group. All were in the silhouette's neck area. Instead of a group, however, the holes arced across the neck area in a string that measured a tad less than 4 inches. Either of the strings he had fired would have been highly effective in a police combat situation.

"I like the rifle and I like the scope," Fiesta declared later, "but the scope will require some getting used to. Or maybe," he added, "it would take some time for the combination to get to like me. I've had that happen before."

On that note, he began checking the scope and mount more closely than he had earlier. It only took a minute or so for him to find that one of the large knurled screws holding the mount to the rifle's receiver was a trifle loose.

"We had used the instruction manual that came with the M-1A1 scope mount, but hadn't taken one passage seriously," Lewis later said. That passage read:

NOTE: *This scope mount is designed with oversize rails to match and mate to your hardened receiver. Some retightening might be required after the first few uses. In the event tightening is required, be assured it is only temporary. Simply tighten the thumbscrew with a screwdriver.*

The manual also warned not to use Locktite or other adhesives and not to use a file or other tools to attempt to modify the scope mount or the scope mount rail.

Kaminski, who always travels with a tool collection in his truck, found a screwdriver of appropriate size to cinch down the mount. It took several shots to re-zero the scope, but Fiesta's next group shrunk to less than an inch. He was able to smile again.

"That gave the rest of us an opportunity to try the rifle, using a combination of Winchester and PMC ammunition. The latter ammo was loaded with 150-grain boattail Sierra bullets," Lewis says. "Learning about the capabilities of the scope and its sighting system was interesting for most of us. Everyone was impressed with the combo of the scope and rifle."

According to Lewis' notes, no one else fired more than 10 rounds on the downrange targets and no one improved upon Fiesta's performance. It was the general opinion that one who was going to be armed with such a rig should be able to fire several hundred rounds of various brands of ammunition for the sake of familiarity with the piece. This also would give the assigned shooter the opportunity to determine the best possible combination, whether in a law enforcement situation or a military assignment.

CHAPTER 27

FROM VARMINT RIFLE TO SNIPER TOOL

Savage Arms' Model 12VSS Rifle Has Assumed a Whole New Role as a Law Enforcement Tool

"IF THIS RIFLE was chambered for .308, it would make an excellent sniper tool," Lewis said as he looked over the Savage Model 12VSS .22-250 rifle. It was quite different in general overall appearance from any other long gun in the Massachusetts-based company's line. The comment was made on the opening day of the 2000 SHOT Show in Las Vegas.

Bud Fini, who was at that time sales manager for Savage Arms, offered a knowing grin. "Funny you should say that. One of the big southern distributors was just here. He said the same thing and ordered a batch of them chambered for the .308 cartridge," he told Lewis. Today the Model 12VSS Varminter is chambered for .223, .22-250 – and 308 – as standard.

The VSS stands for Varmint/Stainless Steel and it is Lewis' contention that the addition of the .308, while retaining the letter code, means the larger caliber can be devoted to two-legged varmints!

The short-action Savage rifle has an overall length of 47-1/2 inches and weighs approximately 15 pounds without the scope or bipod. When it arrived on his doorstep some weeks after the SHOT Show, Lewis quickly

installed a 3-to-9x variable Weaver scope, using Conetrol mounts and rings. Another addition was the Harris Engineering Model S bipod that is favored today by military forces and most law enforcement agencies.

The 12VSS has an adjustable synthetic stock of full-pistol grip design. This stock was designed by

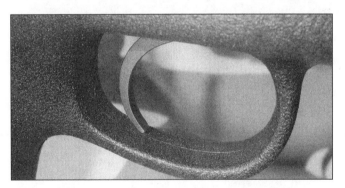

The trigger guard of the Savage rifle is moulded as a part of the adjustable synthetic stock. The measured trigger pull is a trifle over 2 pounds.

The .308 Savage Model 12VSS began life as a varmint rifle, although it was designed by a retired Army major whose primary duties had been in sniper rifle design and marksmanship training.

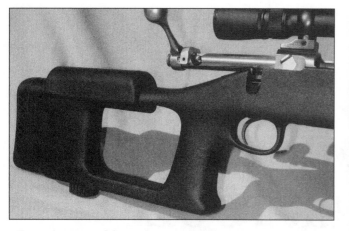

The Model 12VSS stock is ergonomically designed and a pleasure to shoot, with its adjustable cheek piece and thick recoil pad.

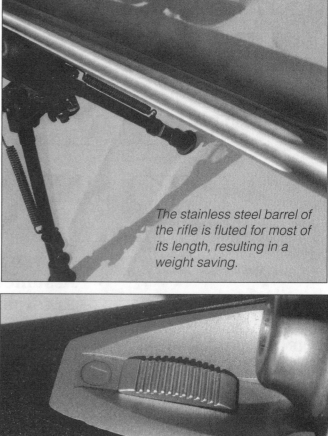

The stainless steel barrel of the rifle is fluted for most of its length, resulting in a weight saving.

Aided by the Harris adjustable bipod, Lewis found it a simple matter to hold the crosshairs on the target in testing the Savage rifle. He was firing Winchester Supreme ammunition.

The easy-to-reach safety of the Model 12VSS is on the tang below the rear of the bolt. When the red dot is visible, the rifle is ready to fire.

sniping expert Maj. John Plaster and produced to Savage's order by Choate Machine and Tool Co. headquartered in Bald Knob, Ark. The retired major was successful in designing a stock that not only was ergonomically comfortable for the shooter but also proved to be a definite aid in holding on target, according to Lewis' report. The trigger guard is moulded as part of the synthetic stock, but it is large enough to allow for a gloved finger.

The rifle's action and the barrel are of stainless steel, with the barrel fluted as an aid to reducing the weight of this sharp-shooting tool. The trigger group is a special order item from Sharp Shooter Supply of Delphos, Ohio.

The trigger is a gem," Lewis says. "When one is ready to fire, there is no creep or travel involved. A little finger pressure and the bullet is on the way. My RCBS trigger-pull scale registered weight of pull at an ounce or so over 2 pounds.

"It should be pointed out that the rifle is marketed without sights, although it is drilled and tapped for scope mounts. If desired, a Picatinny type rail could be installed, if one wanted to use other types of sighting devices," Lewis adds.

Lewis selected Winchester's Supreme Competition .308 ammo as the fodder for checking out the Savage sniper rifle's accuracy. The Competition round carries a 168-grain Nosler hollow-point boattail Match bullet. Mike Jordan, who speaks for Winchester, had some comments on this particular recipe at the time Lewis ordered it.

"The Winchester and Nosler alliance has set new benchmarks within the hunting ammunition category," Jordan noted. "Today, this alliance has evolved into products designed for sporting competition and law enforcement. Our new Match ammo features the J4 competition bullet designed by Nosler. It incorporates the J4 bullet jacket known for extreme concentricity and uniformity. Together, these technologies have resulted in a product with pinpoint accuracy and remarkable consistency."

Lewis and Jordan have known each other for close to three decades and the former never had considered Jordan one to make idle boasts. However, the ballistician's faith in this particular cartridge sounded a bit over the edge.

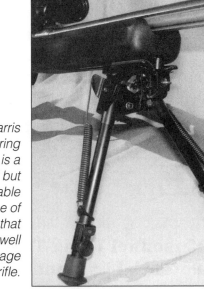

The Harris Engineering bipod is a rugged but adjustable piece of equipment that worked well with the Savage rifle.

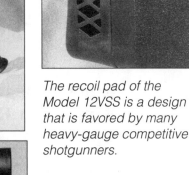

The recoil pad of the Model 12VSS is a design that is favored by many heavy-gauge competitive shotgunners.

In keeping with modern trends, the bolt handle has a large knob that is easily found and grasped even if the shooter is wearing gloves.

At 100 yards, the Savage rifle fired a one-hole group of five rounds, which had a diameter of less than an inch.

The 3-to-9x variable Weaver scope was mounted to the action by means of Conetrol rings and bases. This made a firmly held combination for accurate shooting.

With the scoped and bipodded rifle, ammunition and the other usual shooting paraphernalia, Lewis headed for the range, where he spent half a dozen rounds adjusting the scope for proper zero. Finally satisfied that the scope was on the money, he laid out five rounds of the Winchester Supreme Competition ammo on the heavy-duty cedar bench he favors for serious shooting.

Instead of loading the rounds into the five-round magazine, he chambered one round at a time, settled into the stock and found the small target he had erected 100 yards downrange. He squeezed off that first round, then paused to turn up the scope to 9-power and look at the target. The shot looked good.

He cranked the scope back down to 4-power and loaded the next round, aiming and squeezing it off. He fired the other three rounds without checking the target at greater magnification to determine where the shots were going.

When all five rounds had been fired, Lewis lowered the stock to the cedar, opened the bolt, and then rose to start downrange to his target. The only other person present was his wife.

"He didn't say anything," she recalls, "but as he got closer to the target, I could see he was starting to smile. By the time we got close enough for me to spot what had his attention, his face was covered with a satisfied grin."

There was only one hole in the target, but it was a comparatively large hole. All five of the rounds had grouped together, forming the singular irregular type of pattern that tends to make the day for any serious marksman.

Lewis offered a sigh, as he inspected the diminutive target. "I guess Mike Jordan really knows what his ammunition can do," he muttered, as he handed the target to his wife.

"What do you want me to do with it?" she wanted to know.

"We'll frame it. It's been a long time since I've shot that well!" was the proud reply.

That particular performance of rifle and ammo convinced Lewis that whoever had come up with the idea of turning the venerable Savage Model 12 into a sniper rifle had known what he was doing. This bolt action sells at considerably less than many of the sniper models now on the market. It's a rifle that the average police department could include in its SWAT inventory without creating a heart problem for the civic bean counters. Several military organizations are already looking at the rifle and extensive field tests have been conducted with it.

CHAPTER 28

CALICO'S 100-ROUND CARBINE

Knowledgeable Personnel Think This Novel Semi-Auto Has Potential in Clandestine Operations

"I'VE BEEN INTRIQUED by the offerings of Calico Light Weapons Systems from the time they introduced their first .22 rimfire shooter," Lewis is quick to admit. That also may help to explain why his eyes tend to light up every time he sees a firearm that probably was derived from a star blaster or something else straight out of *Star Wars*.

For those unfamiliar with the company's offerings in the way of firearms, the most unusual feature is a cylindrical magazine that is positioned horizontally atop the firearm's stock and action. In the Third Edition of *The Gun Digest Book of Assault Weapons*, Lewis covered the birth of the Calico 9mm submachine gun. At the time, he believed it would be of interest to the military because of price and design simplicity.

The military powers, however, chose the MP-5 subgun from Heckler & Koch for their contract. That shooter since has been replaced in the tables of organization by the Colt-made M-4 carbine, which fires the 5.56mm NATO rifle round rather than the traditional pistol rounds of subguns.

Since that outing, a lot of things have changed. In those days, Calico was headquartered in California.

Courtesy of an unfavorable political climate, it seemed logical to move. Today, the company is headquartered in Gun Country, namely Sparks, Nev., a suburb of Reno. Ownership and management also has changed. A gent named James Yamas now runs the operation. Since taking over, he has devoted his efforts to producing a semi-auto carbine version of the early submachine gun. In fact, there are two guns that fit that category.

First up was a semi-auto carbine that Yamas and his promotional staff named the Liberty 50. It boasts a cylindrical magazine that holds 50 rounds of 9mm Parabellum ammo. Then there is the item we are discussing here and the one that made Lewis' day. It is the Liberty 100. Its magazine holds two full boxes of 9mm ammo – all 100 rounds.

"I was interested in the Liberty 100 for several reasons," Lewis states. "First off, I felt it had considerable potential as a 'scare gun' for small police departments. All too often, these outfits have only a few officers and little funding for the more exotic types of police equipment.

"While I find the potential of the Liberty 100 more than adequate for a genuine firefight, it could go a

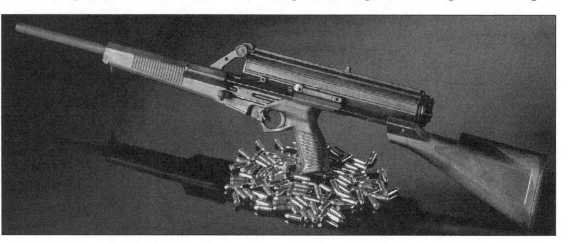

The Calico Liberty 100 is an odd-looking creation, with the 100-round magazine mounted atop the action. Appearance, however, does not affect its firing efficiency.

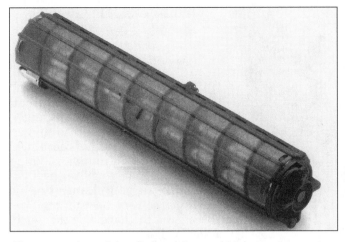

The magazine of the Calico Liberty 100 is transparent, allowing the shooter to have some idea of how much ammo he has left in any given situation.

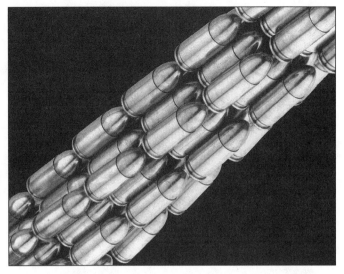

This artist's concept shows the arrangement in which the 9mm cartridges are positioned inside the cylindrical magazine of the Calico Liberty 100.

long way toward discouraging such happenings simply by its appearance in the hands of a police officer. It would be a little like the effect one gets when an officer jacks a round of buckshot into his riot gun. It tends to get people's attention."

The other thing that brought the little weapon to Lewis' attention was called reality. The events of Sept. 11, 2001 have come and gone, although most of the wounds still are unhealed. The biggest manhunt in world history was born with the attack on the World Trade Center, the Pentagon and another flight that was allegedly bound for the White House. .

Just as partisans were supplied with arms during World War II in France, Yugoslavia and other areas, the lightweight Calico carbine, which sells for roughly half the price of one M-16 rifle, could be mass-produced in a hurry and air-dropped to rebels and partisans fighting on our side in the war on terrorism. As Lewis put it, "There are all sorts of possibilities."

We contacted Yamas at his Nevada headquarters and asked for the loan of one of his Liberty 100 models. At virtually the same time, a call was made to Mike Jordan, who handles writer relations for Winchester/Olin's ammo branch. The Liberty 100 and the horde of ammo arrived at Lewis' office in Hawaii only two days apart, thanks to UPS.

Included in the ammo lot were several hundred rounds of Winchester's USA 9mm Luger ammo carrying 115-grain BEB bullets. In addition, Jordan had added several 50-round boxes of Winchester's Super-X recipe, featuring the company's 147-grain Silvertip hollow-point bullets.

The latter had been a specific request in view of Yamas' statement that "This firearm will function most reliably with full metal jacket ball ammunition, but most Calico firearms also will handle semi-jacketed hollow-point ammunition with few or no problems." Lewis had experienced disappointment with several other semi-autos from other makers that made a similar claim regarding hollow-points, but did not live up to the claim. He was looking for proof!

"I should have had faith," Lewis later admitted. "It had been more than a decade since I had fired the Calico 9mm submachine gun. I later looked over my notes on that historic shoot and found that we had used hollow-point ammo from several manufacturers for full-auto fire. If the rounds would work in the subgun, I probably should have been willing to accept the fact that they would work equally well in the Liberty 100." Then he added, "But it doesn't hurt to be sure."

In looking over the Calico carbine and the literature that came with it, we discovered that the Liberty 50, with its 50-round magazine, is cataloged as the Model 915. The Liberty 100, with twice the magazine capacity, is listed as the Model 910.

That would lead one to believe that the 100-shot gun was first up on the production line. We tried to check this out with Yamas, but he was out of the country on other business at the time. We never got back to him.

The helical feed magazine also comes with a loading tool that can handle 50 rounds at a time. To fill the 100-round magazine, one has to go through the loading drill twice.

To handle all this, simply lay the box of ammunition rimmed end down, on the loader's tray, following the simple instructions that come with this tool. The pressure on the magazine spring is released and the first 50 rounds are cranked into the magazine. Engineering arranges for the cartridges to form a helical pattern that aid in feeding.

Should one of the cartridges tumble out of position, stop cranking and restack the misaligned cartridges by hand before continuing with the loading operation. Lewis timed the operation and reported that his best time was just over two minutes to load 50 rounds.

For loading, however, Yamas suggests paying "special attention to the instructions for loading, charging and installing the magazine onto the firearm. Do not over-wind the magazine, this will lead to premature or, in extreme cases, immediate failure of the drive spring and/or components of the magazine."

159

Loading the magazine by hand would be a difficult, tedious chore, but Calico's patented reloading tool makes it easy to crank in 50 rounds at a time.

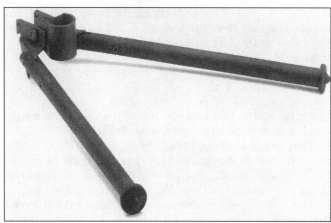

The lightweight Calico can hardly be called muzzle heavy, but the manufacturer also markets a simple, quickly attached bipod for those who might want it.

An easily installed forward handgrip is one of the accessories that the Calico staff has perfected for the Liberty 100.

are delivered with each gun, but it is recommended that this oil be used only sparingly on the bolt as well as the upper receiver during the firing of those several hundred break-in rounds.

Yamas also strongly advises against the use of Tetra gun cleaner or any other strong solvent on the gun. He has discovered the hard way that such applications will damage the finish.

The folks at Calico contend that the effective range of the Liberty 100 is 300 yards, but Lewis thinks its best applications will be at considerably shorter ranges. With that in mind, he set up targets at ranges of 50 and 75 yards. Calico reports that muzzle velocity for the 9mm bullet is in the neighborhood of 1300 fps, depending upon bullet weight, of course.

It was sprinkling the morning Lewis set about checking out the Liberty 100. He had the foresight to erect a portable shelter and bring along a folding table on which to lay the Calico and his ammunition.

I had loaded the magazine earlier at home and attached it to the gun," Lewis said. "Once the targets were set in place, all I had to do was flip off the safety and align the sights. I fired two aimed shots on the target, then triggered three fast rounds. All were aimed at the kill zone on the life-size silhouette."

When he walked down to the target, he was in for a surprise. "I was definitely shook to find there wasn't a single hole in the target. The only proof that I had fired at all lay in the fact, that there was a bullet hole in the top of the PVC target frame," he says.

Walking back to the target, I reviewed the moves I had made in cleaning the gun before I had attached the magazine. I couldn't think of anything I had done that would have affected it. Then I took a hard look at the sights," he recalls.

Lewis discovered that the gun had been shipped with the front sight run down to protect it. On a hit and/or miss basis, he began to adjust the height of the front sight until the bullets were landing in the center of the silhouette.

Should one want to mount a scope on the Liberty 100, this rail device can be clamped around the carbine's magazine and the scope attached to the rail on top.

For the 100-round magazine, we found that completing the recommended 23 turns of the crank resulted in proper functioning of the magazine. However, Yamas also warned that it is not unusual "to have an occasional failure to feed or a misfire due to the bolt not going into full battery." This, he said, "is particularly true of a new gun that is not yet broken in."

In order to avoid or at least minimize such happenings, it is important that the bolt assembly as well as its contact points within the gun's upper receiver be well lubricated in firing the first few hundred rounds.

"After break-in, a light film of quality gun lubricant is recommended on these and other moving parts," Yamas said. Samples of Tetra oil and grease

The Calico organization also produces the Liberty 50, another semi-automatic 9mm carbine carrying a 50-round magazine. Magazines for the two guns are not interchangeable, but most of the other specifications are the same.

This pouch comes in handy when neatness counts or the shooter is a reloader. It is designed for attachment to the ejection port in the bottom of the Calico Liberty 100. It will catch and hold up to 100 expended cartridge cases.

Satisfied that things now were under control, Lewis again aimed at the 50-yard target and fired two aimed shots followed by three rapid-fire rounds. All five shots were aimed at the black outline of the silhouette's head, with the shooter aiming from the standing offhand position.

Of the five rounds fired, four of them were headshots, while the fifth round missed the head outline by about 2 inches. It was hardly championship shooting by Lewis' own admission, "but in a combat situation it would have been a useful group.

"In my mind, there is no doubt that the Liberty 100 would do what it is supposed to do in a clandestine or law enforcement situation.

"In the latter role, I can't help but believe that the awesome appearance of the Calico with that 100-round cylindrical magazine would serve as a deterrent in a good many situations involving suspected felons," Lewis says.

At this writing, the retail price on the Liberty 100 model is listed at $925 on the civilian market. The price of civilian-legal clones of the M-16 rifle go for as much as $1,200 – and most of them can handle magazines loading 40 rounds of 5.56mm ammo.

It seems to us that were our government to get involved in the use of local rebels in such spots as Iraq, the price of the Liberty 100 could be reduced dramatically with a mass purchase and would fulfill the desired mission.

"From what I've seen of the lack of fire control displayed by some of the Arab fighters, the big problem might well be supplying such a force with enough 9mm ammo to keep the guns in operation," Lewis admits. The fact that the 50- and 100-round magazines are interchangeable on the Calico Liberty models might address that problem, if it comes to fruition.

The gun's action is of the retarded blowback design and appears to be similar to that of the highly respected Spanish CETME. The barrel of each Calico is made of heat-treated chrome-moly steel; the receiver is fashioned of prime-cast A-356 aluminum with T-6 tempering. The Calico carbine's safety is built around a rotating sear/striker block, while the stock and handguard are of an impact-resistant, glass-filled black polymer. Because of the design, the weapon is ambidextrous, which Yamas considers a marketing plus.

The sights mentioned earlier are basic, with the rear being the flip type that offers the shooter a choice between an aperture and a rather ragged notch. The front sight is the one that does the work. It can be raised and lowered as required; it also can be moved laterally for windage adjustments. Two knobs adjacent to the rear sight control the sights. One handles lateral movement of the rear sight, while the other controls adjustment of that moveable front sight.

Lewis' evaluation of the sighting system was somewhat philosophical: "They appear to be somewhat crude – but they work!"

Overall length of the carbine is 34.5 inches, while barrel length measures the barely legal 16.1 inches. With the empty magazine attached to the carbine, weight is approximately 7 pounds. A few calculations, however, show that if the cylindrical magazine is carrying 100 rounds of 115-grain 9mm ammo, the weight the user will be carrying is in the neighborhood of 9.5 pounds.

The Nevada-based company also makes a sister weapon for the Liberty 100. It is listed as the Liberty 50 and carries a magazine that loads only 50 rounds of 9mm ammo. Other than the magazines, specifications for the two weapons are virtually the same.

161

CHAPTER 29

THE FIFTIES EXPLOSION

For a Cartridge over Which Last Rites Had Been Read, The .50 BMG Round Shows New Life in Special Rifles

IN CHAPTER 16, Lewis discussed the various Barrett .50-caliber rifles at some length. This Tennessee-based company is not the only gunmaker involved in creating machinery for what has been identified as the world's second-oldest cartridge still in use.

The .50 Browning Machine Gun cartridge is more than 80 years old, having been introduced in 1921 to feed the heavy machinegun designed by the legendary John M. Browning. The gun – and the cartridge – got into production too late to be utilized on the battlefield during World War I. It has, however, seen heavy action in virtually every major conflict, police action and banana war in which the United States has been involved since its introduction.

It also has been used for such chores as starting snow and rock avalanches that might otherwise endanger lives. The Utah Department of Public Safety used the .50 BMG for such purposes for decades.

Nonetheless, the famous old cartridge was on the verge of being declared extinct by the U.S. military powers at the Pentagon a few years ago. A group of

sportsmen, who built their own rifles with which to compete at ranges of up to a mile, kept the cartridge alive. Commercially loaded cartridges are limited in number and many shooters still handload.

For a time, PMC and its marketing arm, El Dorado Cartridge Corp., was producing and selling loaded .50 BMG rounds from corporate headquarters in Boulder City, Nev. The ammunition was being manufactured in South Korea. Several years ago, when Lewis was attempting to test a .50 BMG single-shot rifle for a magazine article, he learned that PMC no longer was selling loaded ammo, but would market new brass to those who wished to handload their own.

Our .50 caliber cartridges are loaded for military machine guns," Larry McGhee, then the PMC sales manager, explained to Lewis. "The rifle shooters felt it was just too hot to be comfortable for those who want to fire from the shoulder."

This policy helped lead to the success of Arizona Ammunition, Inc., headquartered in Phoenix. It is there that owner Jim Schmidt and his crew custom

The Stoner SR-50 semi-automatic .50-caliber rifle originally was announced in 1996, then withdrawn for additional engineering. With a new bolt design, it should go into production in the near future. Note the side-mounted magazine.

If necessary, the barrel of the rifle can be changed almost instantly. In this photo, the magazine is missing from the well on the left side of the action.

load for rifles ranging from the .17 caliber up to and including the .50 BMG. Another source for .50-caliber bullets is a firm called Thunder Cartridge Co., Inc., which also is located in Phoenix. There is talk that the Hornady Manufacturing Co. in Grand Island, Neb., is experimenting with a .50-caliber bullet with an eye to manufacturing it, but we were unable to confirm the rumor at this writing.

With the Pentagon thinking in terms of permanently retiring the .50 BMG cartridge, the Marine Corps took the time to check out the round's potential as a long-range sniper tool. During Desert Storm, Marine heavy weapons units and several marksmen from the U.S. Army were issued Barrett semi-automatic sniper rifles for use against vehicles, ammo dumps and fuel supplies of the Iraqi enemy. The program proved to be a rousing success – and that success has led to a sudden explosion of new .50 BMG rifles being announced by major manufacturers who have military ties. Several smaller manufacturers also are attempting to get into the business by coming up with their own designs.

One of the first to follow the lead of Barrett was L.A.R. Manufacturing, Inc, headquartered in West Jordan, Utah. They came up with the Grizzly Big Boar .50 single-shot, which was immediately

accepted by the long-range sport shooters. (This single-shot bolt-action was reviewed in the 5th Edition of *The Gun Digest Book of Assault Weapons*.)

Knight's Armament announced a semi-automatic .50 BMG rifle in 1996 and it was listed in several editions of The Gun Digest before mention was withdrawn. During a recent visit to Reed Knight's weapons think tank at the Florida site, Lewis had the opportunity to work with the prototype of the gun that has been designated as the Stoner SR-50 Long Range Precision Rifle. This was one of the designs created by the late arms genius Gene Stoner.

Although the rifle has existed in prototype for the better part of a decade, the Stoner SR-50 never has been put into full production. One of the reasons for this, according to Reed Knight, has been the fact that his company has been too busy filling orders for special weapons required by security forces of the United States and friendly foreign nations.

The company also has been involved in a move to new quarters in Titusville, Fla., where it is taking over what once was a missile-manufacturing enterprise of the Boeing Co. According to Knight, the new facilities will offer roughly 10 times the space his company now occupies in what once was a family citrus grove.

A note of interest, however, is the fact that the .50-caliber rifle's bolt has recently been redesigned. According to Dave Lutz, vice president of Knight's Armament, plans are in the mill to begin production of the big bore; it is expected to sell for about $7000 per unit.

Lutz told Lewis, "When the Stoner SR-50 was first announced, we had big-bore shooters sending us

The Robar RC 50F is a folding stock model that has been built on special order for military organizations, but is not in the company's civilian inventory.

The Robar RC 50 shooting machine is a bolt-action repeater with a magazine that carries five rounds of .50 Browning Machine Gun ammunition. The magazine is machined from a block of bar steel.

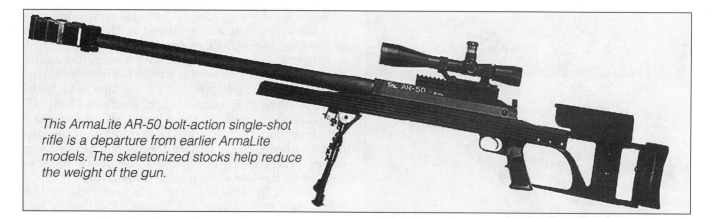

This ArmaLite AR-50 bolt-action single-shot rifle is a departure from earlier ArmaLite models. The skeletonized stocks help reduce the weight of the gun.

deposits for the rifle. With the passage of time, a lot of the deposits – plus appropriate interest covering the period for which the money was held – have been refunded. However, some enthusiasts simply refuse to accept the refund. They are determined to wait until the SR-50 gets into production."

Meanwhile, the Robar Cos. in Phoenix developed a .50 BMG rifle that boasted a folding stock. The gun is still in production, but the folding stock has been abandoned, except for special military orders.

"It was too difficult to produce and there turned out to be little civilian market for the folding stock model," Robert Barrkman, president of the company, told us.

According to Barrkman, the Robar RC 50 system "provides extra-long range, multiple-target engagement with hard-hitting capability using a variety of ammunition."

It has been used in military situations as a counter-sniper weapon at 2500 yards.

This model is the lightest .50-caliber rifle currently available, weighing only 25 pounds with the scope and bipod. Barrkman claims that is also boasts the lightest recoil of any rifle of comparable size, crediting the unique design of the rifle's muzzle brake.

Barrkman says, "The effectiveness of our muzzle brake allows for prolonged and sustained fire without fatigue or physical discomfort. A large number of foreign police, military services, special operations units and many civilian shooters are using this system with great success in a number of roles."

Assuring high-quality performance that has been proven in open competition, the RC 50 action is milled from solid bar stock, using state of the art CNC machines. A bolt-action design, the rifle carries a five-round magazine, which Barrkman says is handcrafted and finished with Robar's exclusive NP3. This finish gives the magazine a corrosion-resistant surface, which requires no lubrication. Coatings used on the metal parts of the rifle have been tested to withstand any climactic condition, no matter how hostile, anywhere in the world. No special tools are required for maintenance.

The RC 50F is the model with the hinged stock. It is 6 inches shorter than conventional .50-caliber rifles, yet velocity is only slightly slower. With the stock folded, the weapon measures a mere 36 inches in length, making it ideal for transportation in con-

Isaac Fiesta, trained as a sniper by the Marine Corps and now part of a law enforcement Rapid Reaction team, did most of the firing of the ArmaLite AR-50 in testing the big-bore weapon.

fined situations such as helicopters, tanks and amphibious assault vehicles.

The folding stock features a unique two-stage hinge system that allows the buttstock assembly to be folded flush with the rest of the gun. The entire assembly is machined from solid steel and has withstood the rigors of typical military operations.

Looking toward both the military and law enforcement market for a big-bore rifle, FNH USA, Inc. has introduced a .50 BMG called the Hecate II in two configurations, one with a supplied sound suppressor. A second model to be called the Nemesis was on the drawing boards at this writing and may well be in production by the time this book is printed.

"The Hecate II is named for the Greek goddess charged with guarding the gates to the underworld," according to James B. Owen, a retired Marine, who is

The wrecked vehicle is barely visible at 200-plus yards. The purpose of the test was to determine how effective the rifle could be on vehicles that law enforcement wanted to stop.

Firing three rounds of military surplus 50 BMG ammo, Fiesta produced an outstanding group.

the manager for training, testing and evaluation at FNH USA. "Hecate was feared by all mortals. It is only fitting that this powerful rifle be named for her. The Hecate II can be used beyond the range of medium-caliber systems with a variety of ammunitions against harder targets."

Lewis concludes, "That sounds like the politically correct way of stating the FNH rifles are designed to knock out enemy supply trains, barricades and whatever else gets in the way."

The Hecate II is a bolt-action repeater. The gun weighs 36 pounds and measures 54.5 inches. With the adjustable stock removed, length is reduced to 43.75 inches. The detachable box magazine handles seven rounds of .50-caliber NATO ammo. The barrel is 27.5 inches in length, carrying eight grooves that make one turn in 15 inches with a right-hand twist. The gun is being marketed with an adjustable cheek piece, a fully adjustable bipod and an adjustable ground spike extending from the buttstock. If the suppressor is added, it increases the gun's weight to 38 pounds.

Owen says the Nemesis will be "a heavy-caliber rifle built around a smaller, lighter system. This platform may be more suitable for tight quarters such as urban environments or where the gun must be packed over considerable distances before being utilized."

The Nemesis prototype is eight pounds lighter than the Hecate II; it weighs only 28 pounds. Like the Hecate II, it is a bolt-action single-shot, but measures only 36.5 inches overall. Chambered for the .50 BMG cartridge, the magazine holds five rounds. Barrel length is 27.5 inches, the same as the Hecate II, has the same eight grooves with one turn in 15

inches and the same right-hand twist. The Nemesis also will carry a fully adjustable bipod and an adjustable ground stake attached to the buttstock. A planned suppressed version will be equipped with a reverse-thrust suppressor, built by Ops, Inc.

There also is a continuing rumor that Heckler & Koch is developing a .50 BMG sniper rifle, but when Lewis checked with the company's U.S. headquarters in Virginia, spokesman Jim Galloway stated that H&K has no such program in the works. So much for rumors.

ArmaLite, Inc., a familiar name to U.S. shooter, also has introduced a .50-caliber rifle listed as the AR-50.

This firm has had a rather odd history. Working with Stoner, the company came up with the original AR-10, the AR-7 .22 rimfire, the selective-fire AR-18, the semi-auto AR-180 and ultimately the AR-15, which became today's military M-16.

After rights to the AR-15 were sold to Colt, Armalite – then located then in Costa Mesa, Calif., – fell on hard times. It would seem that the executives of the company were well versed in firearms production, but lacked marketing knowledge.

Lewis then lived in Costa Mesa and was a frequent visitor to the Armalite plant. As an example of the seeming lack of marketing talent, the company hired a Los Angeles advertising agency to help introduce the AR-7, which had been derived from a survival rifle perfected for Air Force pilots who might be forced to bail out and live off the land.

"The first thing the advertising agency did was to buy only full-page advertisements in each of the fire-

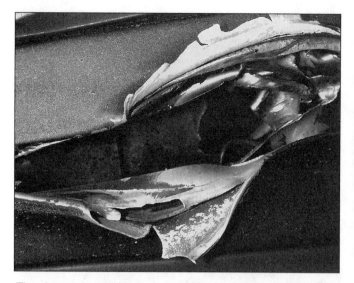

The three rounds fired on the wrecked vehicle passed through the engine block to emerge through a fender on the far side, leaving this mammoth gash in the metal.

Controls for elevation and windage are easily operated as part of the Swarovski 10-power scope that is designed specifically for heavy caliber rifles.

arms journals," Lewis recalls. At that time, he was publishing *GUN WORLD* magazine and was the recipient of one of the full pages.

"That was also the end of the advertising campaign," Lewis notes. "One full page and nothing after that. A successful ad campaign requires a continuing program. I've always blamed the agency – no longer in existence – for its take-the-money-and run approach rather than buying smaller advertisements and running them over a period of time to build interest."

Eventually, the Armalite name and arms designs were sold to an organization in the Philippines. That effort was unsuccessful and a gent named Mark Westrom took over the name. Patent rights to the various Armalite designs had become public domain.

Westrom labored long and hard to bring the company to the level of its present success. He also reworked the company logo to feature a charging lion and the spelling of the company name became ArmaLite.

The AR-50 is a bolt-action repeater that bears no relationship to any of the earlier Armalite designs. There also is word that ArmaLite, now headquartered in Geneseo, Ill., is considering production of a semi-automatic .50-caliber rifle.

Lewis and his crew of working lawmen in Hawaii obtained one of the single-shot ArmaLite AR-50s and put it through its paces soon after it was introduced.

"It took several months to get one of the rifles shipped to me in Hawaii," Lewis recalls. "When it eventually arrived, I discovered it carried an in-place AR-50 Scope Base, which resembles a Picatinny-type rail. With a Harris bipod attached and ArmaLite's one-piece 30mm scope-mounting set, the gun weighed a couple of ounces over 37 pounds," he remembers. The gun arrived in a 62-inch carrying case that could be spread out and used as a shooting mat.

Then came the problem of finding a scope that would withstand the recoil of the .50 BMG cartridge. Lewis called ArmaLite and asked for a recommendation. The company suggested that he try the Swarovski Optik's 11x42 Barrett Model. That meant another call, this one to Swarovski's North American headquarters in Cranston, R.I. Several days later, the scope built for ArmaLite's 30mm rings arrived via air.

Kaminski surveyed the rifle after the scope was mounted. "We gonna knock down mountains?" he wanted to know. Kaminski, it should be noted, is a state law enforcement officer and has a wide acquaintanceship with other police officers and agents on the island of Hawaii. This comes in handy when searching for qualified volunteers to help evaluate a new firearm.

It was decided to find an abandoned car, which could be moved to a canyon-like branch of a lava quarry. The high walls would offer plenty of protection against one of the big bullets going astray. Lewis uses this area frequently on weekends when no quarry personnel are present.

Kaminski managed to bore-sight the rifle before the abandoned vehicle was trucked in and Ike Fiesta, an island police officer and former Marine Corps sniper, was recruited to display his – and the firearm's – talents.

A folding table was set up for use as a shooting bench some 200 yards from the automotive carcass. The scarred surface of the table was covered with green camouflage cloth.

"There had been a degree of difficulty in finding surplus .50-caliber ammunition," Lewis recalls. "I finally located about 60 rounds still in their metal belt links. Using two sets of vice grips, Kaminski was able to break the ammo out of the links for use in the single-shot ArmaLite."

Bore-sighting had not been the answer. The first round fired by Kaminski was about three feet over

A Picatinny-type rail is incorporated as a part of the ArmaLite AR-50 rifle, making it easy to mount a scope or other sighting devices.

The heavy-duty muzzle brake is instrumental in reducing felt recoil when the RC 50 is fired.

The buttpad of the AR-50 rifle is thick and serrated to ensure a solid hold against the shooter's shoulder.

the top of the vehicle, chipping dust from the red lava wall. Adjustments were made to the scope and several rounds of the surplus armor-piercing ammunition soon were slammed into the vehicle body.

The bullet had a muzzle velocity of approximately 2900 fps. The bullet is listed as weighing 730 grains, although military specifications call for an allowable difference of 22 grains over or under the standard. The military surplus cartridges fired during the ArmaLite test were loaded with 235 grains of WC 860, a double-base spheroidal powder.

Without the accessories, the bare rifle weighs 34 pounds, with an overall measurement of 59.5 inches. The receiver is a modified octagonal design that is drilled and slotted for installation of the scope base. The barrel itself is 31 inches in length and is manufactured from chrome moly steel. It carries eight grooves with a right-hand twist of one turn in 15 inches.

The bolt of the AR-50 is of the triple-lug front-locking design, with a Sako-type extractor and an ejector that has a spring-loaded plunger for automatic ejection. Each of these .50 calibers is equipped with Schilen's standard single-stage trigger as well as ArmaLite's exclusive AR-50 muzzle brake.

The ArmaLite folks brag about that particular accessory. "The massive muzzle brake is distinctive and only truly appreciated when you pull the trigger and feel the mild shove of .243-like recoil with a full-charge .50 caliber," is one of the manufacturer's claims.

Lewis found, "The recoil was considerably heavier than any .243 I've ever fired, but it is far from violent. I can't say that for some other .50-caliber rifles I've had the opportunity to fire."

Fiesta arrived fresh from duty and took the time to inspect the AR-50 from stem to stern before he slid onto the edge of the chair positioned behind the makeshift shooting bench. He worked the action, checked the trigger with a nod of approval, then adjusted the buttstock to his own comfort range. He checked out the 10-power scope before pausing to look over several rounds of the military surplus armor-piercing ammo that had been stripped out of the metal belt links.

Finally ready, he loaded his first round, flipped off the over-size Mauser-type safety and pulled the stock into his shoulder to center the crosshairs of the Swarovski scope on a forward area of the junk-quality vehicle.

Fiesta edged the trigger back with quiet care as Lewis watched. As the cartridge exploded, Fiesta continued to stare through the scope, inspecting the hole created in a front fender by the .50-caliber round. Without taking his eye away from the scope, he ejected the spent cartridge case and loaded another round from the row he had laid out earlier. He bolted the new round into the chamber and

Gripping surfaces on the rifle feature a cast pattern that allows for a firm grip without discomfort.

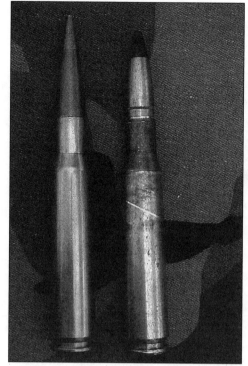

At left is a custom .50 BMG round loaded by Arizona Ammunition using PMC brass. The other round is one of the military surplus rounds carrying the black nose that identifies it as an armor-piercing bullet.

repeated the initial performance. A report of the second round echoed off the walls of the quarry.

"Where did it hit?" Kaminski asked.

Fiesta didn't look around. He was loading a third round.

"It went through the same hole made by the first round," Fiesta said solemnly.

Lewis frankly admits he thought Fiesta was joking, but before he had an opportunity to comment, the shooter triggered a third round, then paused to stare through the scope. He pulled the bolt open and stood up, shaking his head.

"That one wasn't quite as good," he admitted. "Let's go take a look."

After negotiating the rough lava floor of the man-made canyon, the trio paused beside the punished fender. Looking closely, Lewis was glad he had not cast vocal doubts about the first two shots being through the same hole. A slight widening of the puncture on one side verified that there had been two bullets almost on top of each other. The hole made by the third round was less than an inch away.

The trio took turns burning up the rest of the 60 rounds that had cost $4 per cartridge. They were called shots, with shooters taking out the windows, puncturing the engine block.

"What're we going to do with this thing?" Lewis asked Kaminski, when the ammo was gone.

Kaminski looked at the wreck and shrugged. "Take it back where I found it. The county dump!"

The field test was limited to 200 yards only because that was the longest range available in a protected environment. However, it was generally agreed that the ArmaLite AR-50, aided by the attached Harris Series S folding bipod and the Swarovski scope, comprised a combo that was a more than adequate long-distance sniper tool.

"In my mind, there is no doubt that in the hands of a top marksman, this combo could easily take out man-size targets at 1000 yards," Lewis says.

It should be noted that the AR-50 scope base is available in two configurations. The AR500361 model is designed for shooting at ranges from 600 to 1000 yards. The other base, inventoried as the AR500365, is meant for accurate marksmanship ranging from 1000 to 1800 yards.

Later that day, when a forklift was used to raise the battered hulk and place it on the bed of a truck for its trip to the dump, Kaminski found a .50-caliber bullet on the ground where the vehicle had been stationed. It was one of the armor-piercing bullets, which had been fired through the engine block. The bullet was scarred but still intact!

In view of the continuing threat of terrorists, the possibility of more warfare in desert climes and other needs for such long-range sniper-quality armament, it is likely that other companies soon will be coming up with .50-caliber rifles meant for this type of shooting. It will interesting to watch.

CHAPTER 30

THE M2HB: A MIGHTY MAULER

In Terms of Service Years, John Moses Browning's Brainchild Has Been in Military Use Longer Than Any Other Weapon

THE OLD PHILOSOPHY, "If it ain't broke, don't fix it," makes sense to most of us, but this doesn't necessarily apply to the military powers of any country we can think of. In recent years, our own Pentagon has made the mistake several times of introducing a piece of weaponry that turned out not to be as good as the item it was meant to replace.

The venerable .45 Model 1911A1 automatic pistol is a good example," Lewis contends. This gun was used in most of our nation's wars, police actions and international disturbances since World War I. It was originally designed to battle the fanatical Moros in the Philippines after we took that country from Spain in the Spanish-American War. Countless millions of these .45 pistols have been manufactured both for military distribution and later for sale to civilians. It also has been copied by most of the world's gun-making nations over the decades."

But back in the 1970s, it was decided by somebody somewhere that our services needed a new handgun.

After a lot of looking, the Pentagon settled on the Beretta Model 92. As is the usual custom, once in the supply system, it was redesignated by the military as the M-9. This 9mm pistol was the one chosen to replace the more powerful .45 ACP launcher on which millions of servicemen had done their military teething.

Lewis recalls discussing the choice with a Marine Corps general under whom he had served. "Why buy an Italian-made handgun when Colt, Smith & Wesson and Ruger could use the business?" Lewis wanted to know.

The question got him a raised eyebrow from the general, who answered bluntly, "It's a trade-off. We don't need any missile bases in Connecticut!"

It took Desert Storm to raise the realization that there still was a place for the old 1911 design, now close to a century old. There are all sorts of stories about how the M-9 Beretta failed to function during critical moments in the desert sands of Southwest Asia. Pick the story you like best. The result was that several military organizations, including the Marine Corps, sud-

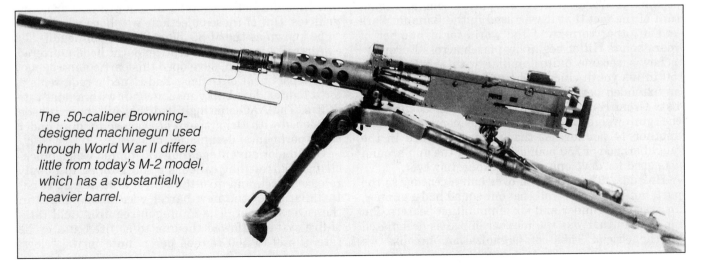

The .50-caliber Browning-designed machinegun used through World War II differs little from today's M-2 model, which has a substantially heavier barrel.

Equipped with a heavy barrel, the M-2 has been most effective in recent campaigns dating back to Desert Storm. A new, faster method of changing the barrel has added to the gun's efficiency.

For cleaning or transport, the M-2 machine gun breaks down into easily handled units. Unloaded, the entire gun and tripod weighs in the neighborhood of 175 pounds.

denly were digging the old .45 autos out of Cosmoline and shipping them by air to the desert battlefield.

More recently, personnel of the Marine Corps' Special Operations-trained Expeditionary Units have been armed with custom-reworked versions of the ancient Model 1911A1. These troops were the first in Afghanistan and they have performed in other trouble spots such as Somalia and Kosovo.

All of which brings us to the subject of the M-2HB machinegun. The late John M. Browning initiated development of this .50-caliber gun in the latter days of World War I. Our general staff had noted that a German big-bore rifle was doing dastardly damage to our tanks and those of our allies on the European battlefields. Actually, Browning did not come up with a working prototype of the desired gun until 1921 in spite of the fact that it was based largely upon his earlier .30-caliber machine gun designs.

The Browning .50-caliber machinegun was introduced officially in about 1925, but according to history, did not become a principle weapon for our Armed Forces until 1933. Today's historians tend to state that the .50 Browning Machine Gun was a product of World War II. They are seemingly ignorant of the fact that it was used in the Banana Wars and in other corners of the world for a number of years before Hitler began his march across Europe.

Lewis became quite familiar with the Browning .50 in his youth since he helped man said model for an extended period during what he refers to as The Late Great Hate. "The thing I remember best is that the gun weighed 84 pounds, the complete tripod another 44 pounds. At that time, I weighed in the neighborhood of 150 pounds. Lugging the gun around was good for developing muscle-tone, however."

He adds, "That was well over half a century in the past, but I seem to recall that our squad had a gunner, an assistant gunner and six ammunition bearers. I'm not certain that was the number of bodies designated by the official Table of Organization, because we always seemed to be short one or more people. At times, our battalion was spread pretty thin."

In the United States, the Browning-designed M-2 was manufactured well into the 1990s and the equipment for turning out the model has not been allowed to rust in storage. More recently, Fabrique Nationale has been producing a European version of the BMG in Belgium for use by some NATO forces.

During the 1970s, all of that discussion about replacing the venerable old M-2 reached a peak, with some powerful individuals calling for a more modern design. The big objection seemed to be that the M-2HB (heavy barrel) was too big and awkward to handle, thus did not lend itself to mounting in armored vehicles. Out of these objections was born what came to be known as the M-85 .50-caliber machinegun.

Aircraft Armaments Corp., an outfit headquartered in Cockeysville, Md, developed this particular weapon. The Department of Defense had issued a requirement for a lighter, less bulky machinegun with a dual rate of fire. The AAC offering filled that bill, having been developed with Department of Defense funding under the experimental designation of T27E2.

One major advantage that was touted was a quick-change barrel that called for the gunner to simply release a lock and give the barrel a 90-degree twist. Installation of the new barrel was accomplished in the reverse order. The Pentagon-required dual-rate-of-fire system allowed the gun to be fired at a cyclic rate of 450 to 500 rounds per minute in the "slow"

Most of the newer M-2 machineguns in use today were manufactured by Saco Defense, a Maine-based arms factory. Note the cleanliness of the gun's machined parts.

The sighting combination of the M-2 machine gun is good for handling targets to 2000 yards and beyond. The firing control is positioned between the gun's spade grips as seen here.

mode. It also could be fired at the fast rate of 1000 to 1150 rounds per minute.

Among other things, the new machinegun featured a time-delay rotating drum that should have won prizes for complexity of design. AAC also had adopted solenoid plungers as part of the design. A number of firearms designers doubted the wisdom of this move. Their doubts seem to have been reflected in the fact that one of the guns literally blew itself up in the late 1970s. Nonetheless, the gun saw action during Desert Storm, the result being numerous reports of the design's failure in actual combat situations.

There are numerous theories and reports as to the failure of the M-85, some experts blaming the ammunition, which used a different powder mix in the .50-caliber cartridge. The Marine Corps was the first service to get rid of the weapon. Meantime, the Marines allegedly were stuck with some 3 million rounds of M-85 ammo, since commanders did not want to fire it in the M-2HB guns that had been brought back on line. Rumor is that the M-85 ammo supply is still stacked in a warehouse somewhere.

There is no doubt that the M-2HB is bulky. Overall length is 65.1 inches, with the barrel alone measuring 45 inches. Weight of the gun and its mount were discussed earlier. The Browning-designed blaster operates by means of the recoil system and offers selective fire from belts featuring disintegrating metal links.

As a crew-served weapon, the air-cooled M-2 can be moved short distances with limited amounts of ammunition by manpower. As issued, the gun has a flash suppressor and a spare barrel assembly. The gun features a back plate with spade grips and a bolt latch release. The M-2 fires from the closed bolt, a definite aid to accuracy, and the AN/TVS-5 night-vision sight can be installed in a matter of seconds.

The usual combat ammunition mix for the M-2HB consists of four rounds of API-M-8 and one round of API-T-M-20, the latter being a tracer. On pre-assigned targets, the tracers often are pulled so they will not reveal the gun's position. Maximum effective range is considered to be 1,830 meters. Maximum range is 4.2 miles. Rate of fire ranges from 450 to 550 rounds per minute. By repositioning several parts, the ammo belt can be fed from either the left or right side, which is one of the advantages of the gun. With standard-issue ammunition, muzzle velocity of the bullet is approximately 2,480 fps. Sights are simple but effective. There is a hooded front sight and a leaf-type is installed at the rear.

With the seeming slow-rate of fire and the traversing and elevating mechanism, the M-2 gained some respect as a sniper weapon during the Vietnam hostilities. Military sources report that the gun was particularly effective when installed at fixed firebases. There, gunners could pre-fire on designated trouble zones and use the data in range cards that would ensure first-round accuracy.

The M-2HB machine gun can handle several types of ammunition, with the M-2 Ball type used for marksmanship training and against personnel as well as light materiel targets. The M-1 tracer round is meant primarily as an aid in observing and adjusting fire. The tracer's secondary purpose is for incendiary effect and signaling. The M-2 armor-piercing round is meant for use against aircraft, light armored vehicles, concrete installations such as pillboxes and revetments as well as other bullet-resistant targets.

The currently manufactured M-8 armor-piercing round combines both armor-piercing and incendiary capabilities, while the M-20 armor-piercing cartridge combines armor-piercing and incendiary capabilities with the additional tracer feature.

This M-2 .50-caliber machinegun is ready for action. The ammo is contained in the plastic box visible on the side of the gun. A special mount is required for use in armored vehicles such as this.

With the cover in the raised position, the inner workings of the ammo-feeding system are revealed. The charging handle for loading the gun extends from the right side.

When loaded with heavy-duty ammo such as the M-903 SLAP round, the saboted bullet can take on light armor. The M-962 SLAP does the same job, but also contains a tracer.

As with other Browning machineguns, timing and headspacing are of major importance when it comes to using this .50-caliber machinegun. If the gunner doesn't headspace the gun before each shoot or after making a barrel change, there is the possibility of a round going off inside the gun. This can damage the gun and possibly injure or kill the gunner and even the assistant gunner. Headspacing and timing gauges are furnished with each gun and are carried by the gunner at all times.

Care also must be taken to ensure that the barrel locking spring is doing its job. If the spring cannot hold the barrel in place, the barrel can turn during firing and lose headspace. Another problem sometimes seen in a combat situation involves chipped or burred threads on the barrel and the barrel extension. This makes it difficult to screw in the barrel. Perhaps worse is the possibility that the gunner thinks the barrel is screwed in properly, but it isn't. This results in bad headspacing. This problem usually can be remedied by using a stone to smooth the burrs or chips.

There are definite sequences for the gunner to follow in headspacing the gun by means of the gauges. Care must be taken to ensure that headspacing is neither too tight nor too loose. Timing, again using the proper gauge, is a matter for the gunner to handle before putting the gun into action.

"In most instances, a well-qualified gunner can accomplish these checks in probably less time than it takes to read about it," Lewis insists, harking back some 60 years. Still in his teens, he observed the performance of the old-timers and marveled at their knowledge of the tools of the military trade. Some of these experts were veterans of World War I and numerous campaigns in between. They knew their machineguns and afforded them the care they thought the weapons deserved.

I recall an old master sergeant named Hoffman, who had a heavy accent," Lewis says. "He had fought with Germany during World War I, then served in the French Foreign Legion in North Africa. Eventually, he made it to the United States and enlisted in the U.S. Army for a hitch. He followed that by entering the Marine Corps. He had more than 20 years in the Corps when I was around him. You'd have thought his machineguns were his wife and mother! With him, the .50 Browning Machine Gun was a love affair!"

CHAPTER 31

HECKLER & KOCH'S 4.6x30mm MP-7

Personal Defense Weapons Keep Getting Smaller, but Fire More Potent Cartridges

THE LAST TIME Lewis talked to the late Gene Stoner, the arms designing genius was attempting to complete the design and prototyping of what he termed a Personal Defense Weapon. Stoner was suffering from a cancerous growth in his brain at the time and was in no mood for long, drawn-out explanations. He died before completing the project.

We will probably never know what Stoner had in mind, but whatever it was, numerous other manufacturers have been attempting to fill the void. First, though, it might be a good idea to decide just what constitutes a Personal Defense Weapon – or PDW, as it is termed in some circles.

"First off, it is a machinegun and it is small and hand-held for operation. Yet, it cannot be termed a submachine gun, because subguns are limited to the use of pistol ammunition, if one chooses to get downright technical," Lewis explains.

"The trend with the Personal Defense Weapon, however, seems to be coming up with a new cartridge that can be fired in a small hand-held weapon, yet is powerful enough to puncture military helmets and pierce many layers of Kevlar body armor," he adds.

FN USA has accomplished this with their P-90, which they choose to call a submachine gun, although it is not. This particular weapon, as discussed in an earlier chapter, fires a new cartridge, the 5.7x329mm and was developed by the parent company, FN Herstal, at its Belgian headquarters.

More recently, Heckler & Koch has introduced its own PDW, a diminutive weapon that fires a bottlenecked 4.6x30mm cartridge. With the buttstock retracted, the weapon measures only 14.96 inches; with the buttstock extended, it's still short: 23.23 inches.

According to H&K personnel, the combo of the MP-7 and the 4.6x30mm cartridge was developed expressly

Jack Lewis found the lightweight, compact MP-7 Personal Defense Weapon easy to handle since much of its design, parts and controls were based upon other Heckler & Koch models with which he is quite familiar.

In looking over the H&K offering, Lewis was impressed with the workmanship on the weapon. It may look like a toy at first glance, but it can be deadly effective.

to provide penetration and lethality that approaches that of an assault rifle with a weapon that is small and portable enough to be carried like a handgun at all times. The MP-7 was adopted by the German KSK, a Special Operations unit, early in 2002. It since has been made available to U.S. military and law enforcement organizations.

Extensive testing has shown that current pistol-caliber handguns and rifles are incapable of penetrating modern body armor such as that worn by former Eastern Bloc special forces. These same vests have found their way into the hands of terrorists and criminals, making conventional pistol-caliber weapons ineffective for defensive – or offensive – engagements.

NATO issued a document, D-29, listing the requirements for a weapon that at up to 200 meters would penetrate the old Eastern Bloc vest, which was comprised of 20 layers of Kevlar and 1.6mm titanium plates. That led to development of the MP-7, a selective-fire design, that can be fired with the extended buttstock or with one or two hands in handgun fashion. According to H&K, "It handles like a pistol, yet allows targets to be engaged like a rifle. A folding vertical foregrip allows the weapon to be fired with excellent controllability to increase hit probability at all ranges."

Tests have shown that with its 7.09-inch barrel, the MP-7 is capable of firing 10-round semi-automatic groups at 45 meters that measure less than two inches in diameter.

This cut-away view of the MP-7 offers an idea as to its design and the mechanics involved in its operation.

HK MP7 Personal Defense Weapon (PDW)

Rotary Locking Bolt Head
Folding Adjustable Front Sight
MIL-STD-1913 Mounting Rail
Optional 24-Hour Q.D. Reflex Sight
Patridge Front Sight
Bolt Group
Patridge Rear Sight
Short Stroke Gas System
Threaded Barrel
Folding Adjustable Rear Peep Sight
Detachable Flash Hider
Buttstock Release Lever (Not Visible)
Ambidextrous Cocking Lever
Finger Guard
Receiver
Rubber Buttplate
Folding Vertical Foregrip
Trigger Mechanism
Ambidextrous Safety/Selector Lever
Locking Pins
Foregrip Release Lever
Ambidextrous Bolt Catch/Release Lever
20-Round Box Magazine
Ambidextrous Sling Mounting Points
Retractable Buttstock
Ambidextrous Magazine Release

Features
Operating Controls
Assembly Groups

For serious business, the MP-7 can be equipped with a scope or a night-sighting device. An extended-capacity magazine will fit into the magazine well and a sound suppressor can be installed quickly.

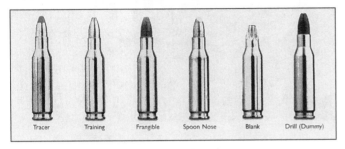

Tracer | Training | Frangible | Spoon Nose | Blank | Drill (Dummy)

Ammunition for the MP-7 is being manufactured with a variety of loads to allow its use in a broad scenario of real-life combat situations.

The forward handgrip folds down to snap into a firm position when needed for action. When not employed, it folds to the rear and can by gripped like the forearm of a carbine. Lewis favored that folded use of the grip.

As an aid to accuracy, the MP-7 fires from a closed bolt, using a rotary locking system similar to that of the Heckler & Koch G-36 assault rifle. H&K engineers say this system is necessary to contain the powerful 4.6mm cartridge. This PDW mounts a 20-round magazine that fits flush into the centrally mounted pistol grip. An optional 40-round magazine is available; when it is installed, roughly half its length extends below the pistol grip.

The basic material from which the MP-7 is manufactured is carbon fiber-reinforced polymer. Metal components are embedded in this framework where needed. Due to its unique gas system, little cleaning is required, but the little gun can be field-stripped within a matter of seconds without any tools.

John T. Meyer, who is in charge of training police departments and others in the use of H&K armament, is quick to point out that all operating controls – including the M-16-type cocking handle, safety/sector lever, magazine release and bolt catch/release are fully ambidextrous.

"A personal defense weapon is only as good as the operator's ability to effectively engage targets under high stress conditions," Meyer maintains. "With this in mind, Heckler & Koch designed the cartridge to defeat today's modern threats, then designed the weapons system around the cartridge."

Meyer insists, "The lethal 4.6x30mm cartridge produces minimally felt recoil – roughly 50 percent of that of the 9mm NATO round. This ensures that multiple hits are easily obtainable in all modes of fire to incapacitate the target through penetration and permanent destruction."

Somewhat tongue-in-cheek, Lewis says, "That particular statement is about as politically correct as any I've ever heard. It circumvents completely the fact that the MP-7 is designed for slaying an enemy!"

Firing from the closed bolt, the gun is gas-operated and features a rotary locking six-lug bolt. The gas system is a short-stroke piston type and does not require gas adjustment The MP-7 fires either semi-automatic or full-auto with a rate of fire of approximately 950 rounds per minute.

Positioning of the trigger and handgrip in relationship to the rest of the firearm make it balanced enough to be used as a handgun. The accessory rail mounted atop the PDW is part of the gun as delivered to buyers.

The gun carries mechanical flip-up sights for ranges up to 200 meters. Both the front and rear sights are mounted on the military standard Picatinny rail on top of the receiver. These sights are adjustable for windage and elevation. All other

The compact design of the Heckler & Koch MP-7 makes it ideal for forced entry work. The powerful bullet, however, could present a penetration problem in urban situations.

Heckler & Koch has developed several holsters that make it possible to carry the MP-7 in much the same way that one would pack a handgun. This one is in current use.

types of sights with Picatinny rail adaptors can be mounted on the rail in addition to the mechanical sights. With the H&K-originated cartridge, the effective firing range is considered to be 200 meters, with maximum range of about 1720 yards. Muzzle velocity is approximately 2460 fps with muzzle energy of approximately 332 foot-pounds.

Heckler & Koch offers a variety of sighting devices as accessories, but the one the test staff seemed to favor was a specially designed 24-hour reflex sight that can be attached in a matter of seconds without tools. This particular reflex model provides a single red aiming dot for around-the-clock use, when the weapon is fired from the shoulder or held at arms' length like a handgun. Meyer reports that his test staff, using the reflex sight, has fired 3.7-inch groups at 100 meters.

Several types of cartridges are available, but the most likely to be used in combat is ball ammunition. The H&K-developed ball ammo cartridge measures 1.52 inches and weighs only .22 ounces. The bullet weight is 26.2 grains, with the hardened steel core coated with copper. A rimless cartridge case is used with the NATO Boxer primer. The gun barrel is designed to accept a sound suppressor.

According to Meyer, the bullet designers used NATO and FBI test protocols to ensure lethality during development of the cartridge. "The 4.6mm ball cartridge employs solid material projectiles produced from steel or copper that retain 100 percent of their weight after penetrating clothing and armored vests as well as auto body panels and windshields."

Meyer adds that using the steel ball bullet guarantees a minimum of 10 to 12 inches of body penetration after the penetration of the enemy's protective clothing or vest. "For special missions, Heckler & Koch has developed subsonic and reduced penetration cartridges, as well as heavy projectiles weighing up to 50 grains. Other available cartridges for the MP-7 include blanks, tracers, frangibles and low-cost training rounds. All 4.6x30mm rounds are intended to be fully non-toxic," he says.

In tests conducted at Heckler & Koch's U.S. subsidiary headquarters in Virginia, 20 percent ballistic gelatin was utilized to get some practical idea of penetration potential. As a starter, the test staff fired the 4.6x30mm round from the MP-7 into an 11.8-inch thick gelatin block. Fired at 50 meters, penetration of the ball ammo round was 11.2 inches in the unprotected block.

The H&K-developed round was fired at 100 meters into a 6-inch thick block protected by a 1.6mm titanium plate backed by 20 layers of Kevlar. The bullet passed through the entire protective panel and made its exit out the far end of the block. According to scientists working the problem, in making its passage, the energy transfer was measured at 115 joules; 85 joules is considered lethal.

In addition to the accessories already mentioned, others include a flash hider, a blank firing attachment, a forearm accessories rail, laser aimers and a cleaning kit. Special carrying devices are available for what Meyer terms "overt and discreet carry of the MP-7."

Lewis tends to agree with Meyer's claim that "due to its lightweight, small size and minimal width (only 1.65 inches), the MP-7 is ideal for VIP protection details while concealed. It seems perfect for drivers, pilots, guards and support personnel who require hands-free carry of their defensive weapon while performing other tasks."

In Lewis' view, the MP-7 provides the combination of handgun-like concealment with the range, penetration and lethality approaching that of a select-fire assault rifle. "That is obviously a useful combination," he believes.

CHAPTER 32

BELT-FEEDING THE M-16

**This Conversion Unit by Jonathon Ciener
Turns This Familiar 5.56mm Rifle
Into a Light Machinegun**

HIRAM MAXIM IS known best for inventing the first successful machinegun. He did it well over 100 years ago, but some of his thoughts and designs still are part of modern weaponry.

Maxim was the first to use the gun's inherent recoil for functioning and operating the gun's internal mechanism. The Maxim machine gun used a belt of ammunition for feeding this full-auto weapon of war. The Maxim invention was used by many nations, most often against each other during World War I as it set the trend for light and heavy machineguns for decades to follow. In fact, it created a whole new category of small arms – the belt-fed machinegun.

"The advantages of a belt of ammunition over the conventional box magazine are many if you want extraordinary firepower," says James, who researched this chapter. The biggest advantage is the continuous stream of fire the weapon can deliver.

Each belt usually contains about 250 rounds and the belts can be hooked together for an unlimited ammunition supply in full-auto fire.

There are disadvantages as well, many of which have limited belt-fed guns to those weapons mounted on tripods and served by dedicated crews. The 250-round belt of ammunition is often heavy and during continuous fire, the gun becomes incredibly hot, often overheating to the point of bending good steel.

The forces affecting a light to medium machinegun are many. Most frequently tripods were used to steady these guns during full-auto fire for improved target engagement. However, tripods add both bulk and weight to an issue that is already overburdened. Then the problem becomes one of moving easily and quickly during the battlefield ebb and flow.

The Ciener belt-fed mechanism can be installed on either semi-auto or select-fire AR-15/M-16 guns; it can be used by either the full-length rifles or carbines. It makes a handy package for an exponential increase in firepower.

The advantages of belt of ammunition versus the box magazine are many, especially if you want extraordinary firepower. Jonathon Arthur Ciener recognizes this with his belt-fed conversion of the standard M-16.

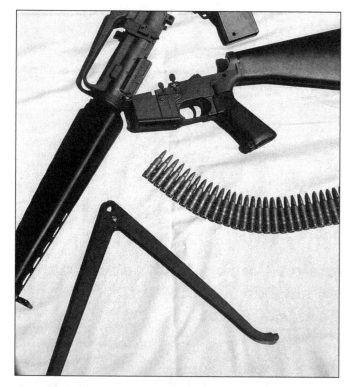

The Ciener conversion requires modifications to the bolt, the upper and lower receiver, and a completely new feed mechanism to move the disintegrating link belt.

Ciener is an innovator located near the NASA complex in Florida. His known specialties include silencers, suppressors and rimfire conversions for many popular firearms.

The lower and upper receivers must be machined to allow clearance for the feed block that is inserted into the lower receiver from above.

The M-16 was the first military service rifle to use the 5.56x45mm rifle cartridge. Criticized for many years as being an ineffective alternative to the hard-hitting 7.62x51mm round, the 5.56mm cartridge proved itself in battles around the world and today it is the NATO standard caliber, and has been adopted by the military forces of most of the Western world.

The .22-caliber centerfire service rifle gained popularity because it was lightweight. Troops can carry far more 5.56mm ammo than they could if armed with the 7.62mm M-14. The .22-caliber M-16 is certainly more controllable in full-auto fire. Additionally, the M-16 was found to be an overall better rifle cartridge for combat in the jungles and forested areas of Southeast Asia.

The small-statured Asian troops – including our allies when there was a South Vietnam – and the soldiers of the Philippines today find the M-16 and its lighter recoiling ammunition more to their liking than the heavy and hard-hitting M-14 and M-1 Garand rifles they had been given previously.

The alternative and lightweight M-1 Carbine was an easy firearm for them to shoulder and carry, but the lethality and wounding capacity of the .30 carbine ball round was immensely inferior to the wound ballistics offered by the M-16 and its then new 5.56x45mm cartridge.

The initial intention on the part of our Department of Defense was to equip all U.S. personnel in Vietnam with the M-16. This was supposed to eliminate the confusion created by an army in the field with sidearms and service rifles firing a host of different calibers. Before the M-16, the U.S. Army had .45 ACP caliber firearms that included the Colt 1911A1 pistol, the Thompson submachine gun and the M-3 Grease Gun, another submachine gun. There also were the M-1 and M-2 carbines chambered for the distinctive straight-walled .30 carbine round, plus the M-1 Garand, the World War II era service rifle chambered for the venerable .30/06 Springfield cartridge. The so-called interim weapon, the M-14, was the temporary replacement rifle for the M-1 Garand but it was chambered in 7.62x51mm caliber.

The U.S. Army and Marine Corps also employed the .30/06-chambered Browning Automatic Rifle – for all purposes a light machinegun – as well as the Browning 1919A4 and 1919A6 medium machineguns in both .30/06 and 7.62x51mm calibers. Bringing up the rear historically was the general purpose M-60 machinegun in 7.62x51mm caliber.

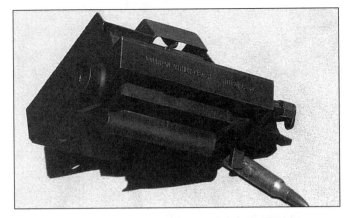

The feed block is a unit made completely in Ciener's facility. It advances the disintegrating metal link belt through a set of fingers activated by the reciprocating bolt.

This connecting rod or shaft is operated by the up and down motion through forces derived from the bolt. The connecting rod turns the fingers that advance the belt of ammunition.

The metal box fastened to the gun via a connection to the bottom of the feeding mechanism contains a compartment for the loaded belt of ammunition. On the far side is a compartment to catch and store the discarded and spent metal links from the ammunition in the belt.

The M-16 replaced the M-1 and M-2 carbines, the M-3 submachine gun, the M-1 Garand and the M-14 service rifle. However, the problem of ammunition compatibility with the M-60 and Browning 1919A4s and A6s remained because the M-16 simply was not heavy enough to replace the light or medium machinegun at the squad level.

This need gave rise to a number of efforts to create a belt-fed 5.56x45mm machinegun to supplement the firepower needed in an infantry squad. Today, that firepower is provided by the excellent FN Minimi, or what the army classifies as the M-249 Squad Automatic Weapon or SAW – but that's today.

A number of ideas were first attempted to supply a belt-fed 5.56mm weapon to answer the firepower requirement at the squad level. Colt made a prototype labeled the CAR 15 Heavy Assault Rifle M-2. It was basically a belt-fed M-16. Problems due to heat build-up plagued its development even though it featured a heavier than normal barrel and a device designed specifically to hold the bolt open between firing bursts. Yet, this gun still fired from the closed-bolt position.

Colt's next attempt at a belt-fed squad automatic weapon was the CMG-2 5.56mm light machinegun. It borrowed a number of features from many different machineguns, but used a cocking and sear design from a Czechoslovakian series of machineguns. It didn't advance beyond the prototype stage.

A belt-fed 5.56mm light machinegun saw service with the Americans in South Vietnam during the war, but it wasn't any of the previously mentioned light machineguns. The light machinegun version of the Stoner 63 system was used by the Navy SEALs.

Stoner, after designing the AR-15, went to work creating an entire system of small arms using many common parts or components. The idea was to have a system that used the same receiver, bolt, gas piston, return spring and trigger mechanism. By interchanging barrels, feed mechanisms and different trigger mechanisms the gun could be transformed from a submachine gun to a service rifle, to a light machinegun up to even a tripod-mounted medium machinegun.

After improvements, the Stoner 63 Light Machinegun was adopted in limited numbers by the Navy SEALs and used in riverine assaults against the Viet Cong. The gun, with 800 rounds of belt ammunition, weighed only 35 pounds and proved decisive in terms of its firepower.

Fitted with a box underneath the receiver to hold the belted ammo, the gun could be handled easily by one man. It was type classified by the military as the Mark 23 Commando, but its use was limited to the Vietnam War.

After that war in Southeast Asia, the U.S. military conducted a long series of trials to select a new squad automatic weapon in 5.56mm and the eventual winner was the FN Minimi. The after-action reports from Operation Desert Storm in Iraq have given the Minimi a good overall review. Thus, the M-249 SAW has established itself as the 5.56x45mm caliber belt-fed machinegun.

The metal box fastened to the gun via a connection to the bottom of the feeding mechanism contains a compartment for the loaded belt of ammunition. On the far side is a compartment to catch and store the discarded and spent metal links from the ammunition in the belt.

The metal ammo box under the converted weapon has two compartments: one for the linked and belt ammunition and a second for the singular metal links once they have been ejected from the gun.

The spent metal links are captured by this chute as the weapon fires and deposited in the ammo box below. This saves time both time and money during training because there are no links left on the ground and they can be easily reused.

Jonathon Arthur Ciener, who resides in Cape Canaveral, Fla., is well aware of the history surrounding belt-fed light machineguns. His conversion for the M-16 rifle is not intended for military deployment at this point. He openly acknowledges the shortcomings of his design. His invention remains an interesting engineering exercise nonetheless.

Ciener started with was the conventional M-16 – or in the case of the photographed sample, a semi-auto AR-15 that he registered and legally converted to full-auto M-16 specifications.

The inventor then made a series of cuts on both the upper and lower receiver to accommodate the feed mechanism for the conversion. Once the cuts were made, the basic conversion unit was installed in the lower receiver.

To do this, the two receiver halves were swung apart much like a traditional double-barrel shotgun, then the feed mechanism was inserted from the top into the lower receiver. The bolt was modified to operate a set of fingers that advance the belt as the bolt reciprocates.

According to James, who checked out the conversion for us, "The problem with this design for military applications is that these fingers are attached to the outside of the receiver on the left side and exposed or open to the elements. Dirt and other foreign materials could easily create a stoppage or feeding problems and malfunctions."

The conversion has other problems as well. James says, "The belts used in Ciener's device were comprised of disintegrating metal links and one of the cuts made to the two receiver halves served as an exit port for the discarded link once the cartridge had been extracted and fired.

"On the bottom of the lower receiver, the feed mechanism had a strut that stuck out the bottom of the magazine well. This strut served as the mounting point for the box magazine holding the linked ammunition. It also contained a compartment to catch and collect the spent links after firing. Ciener admits he did this simply because he grew weary of searching for the discarded metal links after firing a long belt of ammunition."

The metal links are expelled out the right side of the gun and collected by means of a chute that is positioned just below the ejection port. The weapon, once modified for the Ciener belt-fed conversion, will

Ciener demonstrates the firepower that is available from this conversion in a small carbine. A 100-round belt of ammo going downrange is impressive and overwhelming if you are on the receiving end.

Using the ammo-box as a monopod, Ciener was able to demonstrate good accuracy and acceptable reliability with his conversion. Some problems that occurred during the demonstrations were later traced to a bolt of substandard quality. Since then only mil-spec bolts are used.

The hole in the left side of both receivers is closed when the unit is removed and a conventional magazine is inserted.

still accept the normal M-16 magazine and fire it in the conventional fashion.

"M-16s converted to the Ciener belt-fed system still fire from the closed bolt position and operate off the standard gas system of the M-16 rifle," James reports. "The cuts made to the receivers are located in such a way that once the weapon is loaded with the regular magazine, the holes remain closed. The normal load for the system is a 100-round belt and the system can be installed on either semi-auto or full-auto firearms."

During the demonstration given at the Knob Creek Machine Gun Shoot in Kentucky, the first Ciener-converted gun demonstrated a few feeding malfunctions. Closer examination by Ciener revealed a non-mil-spec bolt was the source of the problems. "The bolt was replaced with the appropriately modified mil-spec bolt and the sample gun worked flawlessly," says James, who witnessed the demonstration.

"The increased firepower from a carbine the size of the CAR-15 with this system is dramatic. The bal-

ance point of the gun was not changed and it still was easy to go prone.

"Although Ciener cautions against the systems use for strictly military applications, he did acknowledge some units have been sold to government buyers. However, he would not elaborate on whom or what units had drawn the interest. He did acknowledge that certain law enforcement SWAT teams also have expressed an interest in the system because of the increased firepower and the portability of the entire package," notes James.

One of the features James admits he found endearing during the test session was the ability to capture and retain the spent links from the disintegrating linked ammo. "If you've ever fired a machinegun with disintegrating links, then had to spend the next hour or two trolling with a magnet to collect all of them from the brush, the grass and dirt, you will immediately appreciate this feature. Additionally, it is a cost-saving device, because so few links are lost to the elements," he says.

James thinks the greatest tactical advantage for police applications lies in the fact that the belt is self-contained. Feeding from the box underneath the gun protects the ammo and the integrity of the belted ammo, while maintaining the center of gravity of the entire weapon. It is not unbalanced to the right or left. One of the greatest difficulties with belt-fed light machineguns is how to properly protect the belt of ammo.

Many news photos from the Vietnam War showed soldiers carrying the M-60 ammo criss-crossed about their backs and chests Pancho Villa-style. While visually impressive, it does little to prevent damage to the links or rounds of ammunition. "Placing the loaded belt within its own container under the gun protects it and ensures the system's reliability," James contends.

This system installed on an M-16 rifle or carbine increases the firepower of the weapon to an almost exponential level. Even if it isn't used for law enforcement or military applications, the engineering of the Ciener conversion achieved something the factory Colt effort did not. It worked.

CHAPTER 33

IRON AND IRONY

Development of the Light Machinegun Resembles a Black Comedy of Confusion

HAD IT BEEN written as a comedy, the black irony, direct contradictions and subterfuge involved in the tale of the light machinegun might seem hilarious.

Even the definition often seems to amount to "whatever someone is willing to call a 'light' machinegun." So separating light from heavy, heavy from medium and general-purpose machineguns from everything else becomes an amusing exercise all by itself.

Arms researcher Jim Thompson reports, "Poking around from a variety of scholarly sources for a uni-

form definition of 'light machinegun' resulted in a distillation of a working definition." Here it is:

Light machinegun: A fully automatic, sometime selective-fire support firearm, which can be fired from the shoulder, without a mount (but which may have mounts available); operable by a single man (though often accompanied by one or two assistant gunners). Of the prevailing infantry rifle caliber, it may utilize magazines, belts or both, being capable of burst fire is

The German '08/15 Maxim light machinegun was not lightweight by today's standards. At 39 pounds – plus additional 9 pounds for the drum – the gun required a hefty assistant gunner.

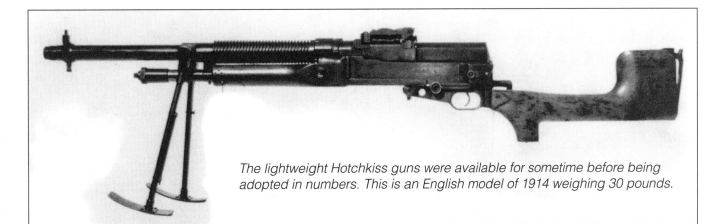

The lightweight Hotchkiss guns were available for sometime before being adopted in numbers. This is an English model of 1914 weighing 30 pounds.

greater than any rifle in such a unit, and which has some capability for sustained fire."

"There are some corollaries and appendices to this rather wordy explanation," Thompson adds. "Generally, since the end of World War I, a light machinegun has had a quick-change barrel and that has come more and more to mean "in less time than it takes to say 'change the barrel NOW'."

All would be neat and clean were it not for the fact that military establishments have, from the very beginning, resisted the light machinegun. They have mercilessly purged it from inventories, often to embrace a new form of the old critter again under some new name, such as Squad Automatic Weapon.

"This is one of the current supremely chic buzzwords of the armament industry. It is also the exact same language under which many early inventors tried to launch their light machineguns," Thompson points out.

"Light is a relative term. In the early days, a machinegun was essentially a water-cooled beast with carriage/mount and gun easily topping 300 pounds. There was no such thing as a 'light' machinegun, save perhaps some new model that used less metal in a water jacket," Thompson explains.

By the end of 19th century, most of the world's great arms works – seemingly always decades ahead of the military officers – realized what a great defensive device the heavy machinegun would become. They also realized that the only way to suppress its great power was to get other automatic firearms fully forward in the combat area in large enough numbers to restore offensive capability.

While the definition of the "light" machinegun has slipped and slid over the past century, the reasons for its initiation have never really changed. These reasons are:

1. The light machinegun had to be at least somewhat less expensive than the heavies of the period, or later, the general-purpose machineguns.

2. The light machinegun had to be much more portable than traditional mounted guns.

3. Rate of fire of light automatics had to exceed or at least be approximately equal to that of the heavy machineguns of the period.

4. While there might be a variety of crew and gunners available, the light machinegun had to be operable by a single man for sustained periods and usable from the shoulder.

5. Light machineguns must use the same ammo supply as the service rifles available, sometimes even the same type of feed device.

6. Whenever possible, the light machinegun or multiples of that weapon should be able to sustain fire for movement support on the offensive.

This now rare Benet-Mercie was a Colt-produced Hotchkiss in .30 caliber. This U.S. Navy version, the Mark II, Model 1, weighed 27.6 pounds unloaded. The United States adopted it in 1909.

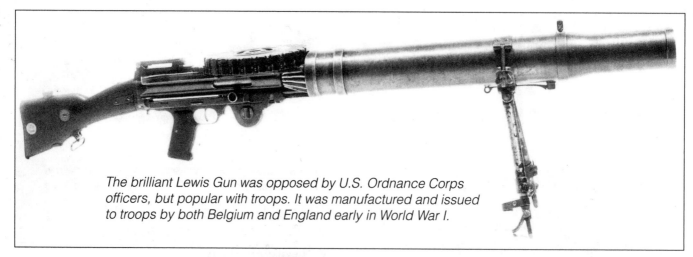

The brilliant Lewis Gun was opposed by U.S. Ordnance Corps officers, but popular with troops. It was manufactured and issued to troops by both Belgium and England early in World War I.

The cooling jacket and internal fins of the Lewis Gun remain one of the best air-cooling systems ever devised. This is a British gun produced in that country in 1918.

The Danish Madsen light machinegun used a long recoil system similar to that of the Chauchat, but detail design and overall execution were far superior. The magazine held 30 rounds. The gun still was widely used in World War II.

Not all light machineguns meet every specification or achieve every goal; many automatic rifles come quite close to the edge of this definition. Indeed, some automatic rifles are described as light machineguns or squad automatic weapons by various authorities, at various times. The French FM 24/29 is such a weapon.

What we will attempt to do in this chapter is to describe some of the capabilities and limits of some of the historic examples of these classic firearms and examine the pressures surrounding them.

"And because it is such a diverse and fascinating story, some of the stranger definitions of 'light' machineguns will be discussed," Thompson points out. "A few of the guns illustrate, once and for all, that a 'light' machinegun, despite all the scholarly definitions, is any apparatus upon which someone is willing to engrave the words!"

Diverse and Contradictory

While the Danish Madsen was probably the first pure light machinegun in the classic sense, the interesting flukes and permutations that were called light machineguns should probably precede the undisputed specimens, if simply to define the extremes of terminology.

The Italian Villar Perosa of 1915 was concocted to provide fire support and even air-to-air gunnery via a totally unusual formula, something never since repeated.

Built by Fiat and Canadian General Electric, the mechanism was essentially twin pistol-calibered, delayed-blowback tubes with 12.5-inch barrels, firing the Italian 9mm Glisenti pistol round. It is roughly the ballistic equivalent of the .380 ACP; the bullets were fired at a rate of 1500 rounds per side – or 3000 rounds per minute. This was one reason the cartridges were usually issued in huge crates containing as many as 100 25-round box magazines. The lack of power and range was such that, in experiments with the rather fragile aircraft of the period, it was rare for the bullets to penetrate the doped fabric skins of the then-contemporary biplanes.

Italy's Villa Perosa twin machineguns fired 3000 rounds per minute, but range was limited and the 9mm Glisenti round was under-powered. The guns were later halved and each half outfitted with a stock to be used as a submachine gun.

The Browning Automatic Rifle was never considered a machinegun, but late models featuring quick-change barrels made it close in terms of tactical use.

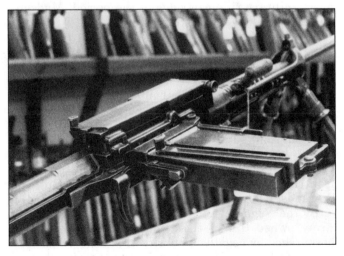

The Italian Breda Model 30 was set up for rapid barrel change even in the dark, the system being copied from the German MG-42.

In Africa, the British armed trucks of the Long Range Desert Group with mainly obsolete but reliable weapons. The upper gun is a standard infantry Lewis model. The lower gun is a captured Italian Fiat.

In the Alpine Theater, the pistol bullets often did not retain enough energy to do much more than bruise Austrian soldiers through their heavy winter clothing. However, the Villar Perosa was not a deadend. It became one of the first submachine guns, when split in half, fitted with a pistol grip and buttstock. It was truly light, quite sleek and easy to handle. It weighed only 15 pounds and was only about 21 inches long. Oddly, however, in its original form the spade grip made it quite awkward to fire from the shoulder.

During World War II, the United States decided to furnish infantry units with a formidable sustained-fire capability. A version of the .30 caliber M-1919A4, to which was added a substantial bipod, buttstock and pistol grip was issued primarily in weapons companies. Thus was generated the M-1919A6 light machinegun. It weighed 32.5 pounds without ammo and was a package that could deliver its 550-600 rounds per minute with considerable accuracy and sustained-fire capability.

"Perhaps the greatest advantage to the '19A6 was that it retained full tripod capability and used the same belts as the standard '19A4," Thompson says.

In the Beginning

The American-owned French firm, Hotchkiss, was one of the first international arms firms to whole-heartedly embrace air-cooled machineguns, but not entirely because of the weight savings. Indeed, many of their air-cooled guns weighed considerably more than liquid-cooled weapons of the period, with their water jackets full.

Hotchkiss had correctly foreseen that coolant might not always be in adequate supply and that soldiers faced with cooling their guns or having sufficient water for drinking might not always decide to feed their weapon. They also perceived the hoses and condensation cans of the water-cooled guns as weaknesses.

By 1898 or so, Hotchkiss engineers had crafted useful machineguns weighing as little as 21 pounds,

The first light machinegun designed and produced by the Japanese was the Taisho 11. It drew concepts from both the Hotchkiss and Browning, but employed a unique hopper feed that handled stripper clips or loose rounds.

The only pure light machinegun issued to U.S. troops in World WarII was the Johnson Model of 1941. Many innovations of the recoil-operated weapon have been copied worldwide.

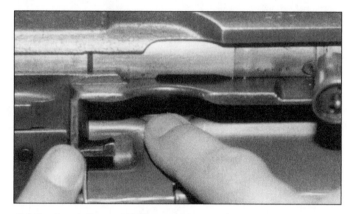

While the Johnson light machinegun's magazine was positioned on the left side, the magazine could be reloaded from the right side of the gun without removal.

all of them still employing the rigid feed strips in place of belts or box magazines. All of these early Hotchkiss guns – and virtually all their designs – used carefully thought-out gas operating systems. It would be some years, however, before these guns would begin to sell in numbers.

"Military ordnance officials of the time resisted the machinegun and many were still not quite sure about the repeating rifle. Many armies still preferred to mount their Maxim machineguns on high, wagon-wheeled mounts not much different from ancient Napoleon cannon, with heavy bronze traverse adjustments and multiple elevation locks," according to Thompson's research. "Their perceived job was much like artillery, and they looked like cannons. But this was all changing," he notes.

Scholarly military journals of the era suggested that the spreading "infection" of the machinegun would greatly complicate logistics, crippling ammunition supplies. However, a series of small wars culminating in the Russo-Japanese War of 1904-05 demonstrated that automatic fire could paralyze an offensive movement. The old myth that the bark of the machinegun was worse than its bite, useful only against "primitives", was proven wrong. Military visionaries began to dig around for a way to restore their own offensives.

The Early Classics

Denmark's Madsen of 1902/04 was the first light machinegun to be manufactured and sold in quantity. Like the later French Chauchat and the classic Browning Auto 5 shotguns, it was a long recoil design. Weighing about 22 pounds, it generated a rate of fire of 400-450 rounds per minute.

The Madsen employed a conventional yet durable set of magazines, usually in 25- 30- and 40-round versions. A few guns were manufactured with much heavier barrels and water-cooled pieces –now extremely rare – were also sold. A few later guns were fitted with optional belt-feed mechanisms.

In time, almost every country in the world owned and used Madsens, though they were never adopted as first-line weapons by any major power. Thirty-one countries ordered Madsens with many other nations simply ordering off-the-shelf commercial versions. Photos exist of German, French, Austrian, Japanese and Italian troops deploying the guns in combat; the chamberings produced were comprised of virtually every military rifle cartridge of the period. Madsens were produced well into the 1950s.

The light Hotchkiss guns finally began to develop some market about 1910, though most ordnance experts disliked the semi-rigid feeder strips. Both the French and British armies referred to these as "portable" or "flexible" machineguns. The United States produced its own at Colt – the Model 1909 Benet-Mercie machine rifle in .30/06 caliber, for issue in the U.S. Navy.

Thompson found that the light Hotchkiss guns are usable from the shoulder, but he believes they are awkward to balance with a full feed strip "and very front heavy when not actually being fired. But," he concedes, "they were sturdy and accurate."

By the beginning of World War I, the United States Army owned 670 of these machineguns. They were besmirched by negative publicity in Pancho Villas 1912 raid on Columbus, N.M., when American troops claimed they could not operate them at night. Jokes began to circulate about these being the daylight machineguns.

The Japanese Type 99 light machinegun may have been the best design of World War II. Note that the gun was fitted with a bayonet.

The Czech-manufactured ZB-26 light machinegun boasted a stable quick-change barrel. This particular gun saw service on the Chinese mainland around 1927.

However, it was an obvious training problem, since no other operator of the Hotchkiss variants had any special difficulty with nocturnal operations.

The Lewis Gun, however, has come to be considered the ultimate early light machinegun. Based loosely upon a design by Samuel Maclean and O.M. Lissak, it was refined and detail redesigned by retired Col. I.N. Lewis.

"The Lewis apparatus is a wonder of complexity and wisdom," Thompson says. "A great deal of very precise fitting in manufacture and exhausting industrial specification control is vital to its completion. One expert once remarked that the Lewis was so fancy, it was a wonder that it ever worked."

Ironically, the same man conceded that the gun not only worked, but worked beautifully. There were hundreds of potential causes of stoppage, most of which boil down to ammunition problems and the introduction of too much dirt.

Produced in Canada, this .303 Bren Gun Mark 2 was manufactured in 1943 and was the most common light machinegun in British Empire service by the end of World War II.

A major problem was that the Lewis was brutally expensive. In 1916, when a decent automobile could be purchased for $500, the government procurement price for a Lewis Gun was at least $1000.

The standard feed mechanism for the infantry Lewis was a 47-round drum. Though primarily for aircraft, a 96-round unit also was available.

Although made at times in other calibers, almost all surviving Lewis guns are chambered for the .303 British or U.S. .30/06 cartridges. Guns – mainly prototypes – were made initially by Automatic Arms Co., with production guns manufactured by Savage in the United States, although Colt and others worked on various aspects of the aviation versions. Great Britain, Belgium and, ultimately, France and Russia produced Lewis guns.

Thompson's research turned up a bit of interesting information. He says, "Although for decades the Soviet government insisted they seldom used and never produced Lewis machineguns, it has recently been discovered that they built them well into the late 1930s. The Soviets also used them as ancillary armament on transport and bomber aircraft throughout World War II. This makes the Russians some of the largest and surely the last users of the Lewis."

Ground versions of the Lewis generated 550 rounds per minute of cyclic rate, and extensive experimentation has proven that the elaborate air-cooling system was virtually the only such air induction and exhaust setup that actually worked in that era.

By far the most fascinating sidelight of the Lewis Gun saga, though, is the vicious opposition of various U.S. Army Ordnance officers to Colonel Lewis and his gun. This existed to the extent that the horrible Chauchat was actually deemed superior. As a result, this excellent, accurate infantry weapon got into the hands of American troops only very late in World War I.

The Chauchat Model of 1915 was, like the Madsen, a long recoil design in which the entire mechanism, including the barrel, reciprocates fully to a length slightly longer than the cartridge, with every firing cycle.

This export Bren Gun was built in Canada for wartime export to China. It was chambered for the 8mm Mauser cartridge. This Mark 2 was the basis for the 7.62x51 NATO version is still in use in the United Kingdom.

Evolved from a medium-caliber Frommer design, the original specification might have become the very first assault rifle, but the French opted to adapt the weapon to their full-power 8mm Lebel round. To accomplish this and keep costs down, it was decided to loosen all the metallurgical and measurement specifications. In addition, the magazine was opened up on the sides, so cartridges could be easily counted. These were three fatal modifications to the original idea and guaranteed the Fusil Mitrailleur Chauchat Sutter-Ribeyrolle-Gladitor 1915 – called the CSRG by U.S. troops – would not work reliably for very long.

"The Chauchat weighed about 19 pounds. This so-called Gladiator did, however, get military authorities accustomed to the idea of issuing large numbers of automatics to infantry. With what the troops came to call the ShoSho, they had to have plenty of guns to make sure some would be working if the enemy showed up," says Thompson.

The German military was convinced that any light machinegun they fielded in quantity would have to be versatile. And they wanted a serious sustained-fire capability. Both their Parabellum and Dreyselight machineguns were successful, but were never truly light or very mobile.

The '08/15 Light Maxim, at least, came close. At 40 pounds or so, with water, the light '08/15 pumped out its rounds at a solid 450 per minute. While standard Maxim belts could be used, the shorter versions were usually tucked in the box drums for mobile attack.

Dug in, these light guns could use standard Maxim condensation cans, hoses and pumps, but rarely did.

The '08/15 light machinegun was 56.5 inches long, and there were those who thought it was too awkward for use in a spirited offensive. However, in the Spring Offensive of 1918 – coupled tightly to the then-new submachine guns – the Maxims proved the big men who handled them could move and move fast. The trouble was that the early successes came, literally, too fast and the Germans could neither exploit nor reinforce.

"The '08/15s were rugged, durable, reliable guns and vast quantities were sold postwar all over the world. The were frequently rebuilt and rigged as elaborate anti-aircraft rigs and, surprisingly, many saw use in Russia during World War II against the sons of their original owners. These guns were employed mainly in the multiple-gun mounts used for anti-aircraft applications," according to Thompson's findings.

Between the Big Wars

When The War to End All Wars was finished, it was time to study the lessons learned. First, it was accepted that offensives had cost entirely too much. In short, the ancient philosophy that attack was the only real business of soldiering was stood on its ear.

While there were many answers that would be developed, the importance of the portable machinegun was one that was immediately obvious.

Czechoslovakia had achieved independence from the by-then dissolved Austro-Hungarian Empire and set out to develop wealth by marketing weapons worldwide. Czech designer Vaclav Holek combined many time-tested features with a new, single-twist, quick-change barrel system. In 1926, he introduced the light machinegun that would be the standard for the 20th century.

Properly called the ZB/Vz 26 and 30, this creation was a gas-operated, supremely smooth mechanism in which tremendous testing and design effort were applied to spreading metal fatigue. It was the first – and not far from being the last – truly modern light machinegun.

At 20.3 pounds, early literature claimed the design for the gun was established to be "no more than twice the weight of a standard service rifle", while offering a rate of fire of 500 rounds per minute. Though the mechanics of the ZB/Vz are derivative, the combination was unique and the rapid barrel change requiring only a twist of the wrist greatly increased the gun's sustained fire capability.

Thompson has found that, "Tremendous attention was paid to balancing the weapon. The original stick-like bipod, similar to that of the old Maxim '08/15, was quickly replaced with a design that improved the balance factor. Used later on other Czech models and Bren guns, the design became the prototype for virtually all modern bipods.

The German MP-44 was the rifle that changed everything. It was the first medium-calibered assault rifle to take to the field. Other nations eventually copied the basic design.

"From the moment this series was introduced, every army that contemplated using light machineguns went back to the drawing board," Thompson insists.

This Finnish-made RPK is used in much the same role as the light machinegun. Many still are in issue in the Finland's armed services. Moves are being made to convert it to the newer Russian small bore loadings.

Having purged light machineguns from U.S. service, American ordnance gurus kept trying to beef up service rifles. This is the M-14A1 with a civilian scope. The ultimate answer was the Squad Automatic Weapon, a buzz term of the 1990s. However, it amounts to the reincarnation of the ancient light machinegun.

Italy developed its Model of 1930, a sleek, competent gun, with an even better barrel-change setup. The Japanese combined features from their older guns, plus the Lewis and the ZB/Vz, and rapidly came up with their Model 96 6.5mm. A bit later, they introduced the Model 99 in 7.7x58mm chambering, which some authorities think may have been the best overall light machinegun of the period. The French adopted their 24/29 machine rifle, which some people call a light machinegun, and which almost fills the bill.

The Soviets Degtyarev series was very much an upgrade over their motley collection of Hotchkiss and Lewis guns, but went back to their standard heavily rimmed 7.62x54R cartridge. This particular round demanded a flattened-out, pan-style drum magazine of 47 rounds. The DP 1928 was 51 inches long, and weighed 20.5 pounds. These guns have shown up recently in Afghanistan.

The British did the wise thing and simply adopted their own version of the Czech weapon in their own .303 loading, thus beginning the Bren series," Thompson points out, adding, "The last Bren incarnations still serve in diminishing numbers in many places, now mostly in the ubiquitous 7.62x51mm NATO chambering."

U.S. ordnance experts had decided – probably wisely – not to utilize a light machinegun, instead incorporating more of the Browning Automatic Rifles. They persisted in referring to all air-cooled versions of the .30 Browning .30 caliber as light machineguns despite the fact that most were useless without mounts. The late M-1919A6 was the only one remotely capable of shoulder fire, however, and the only version of that long-lived series which fulfills even part of the classical, scholarly definition.

Melvin Johnson, one of America's many little-known and little-appreciated firearms' designers, began marketing a unique light machinegun in the 1930s. It mounted its 20-round in-line magazine horizontally on the left side and, unusually for a light machinegun, semi-automatic fire was available. The magazine could be topped off from the right side.

The Johnson machinegun's sights, general layout and balance features have all been copied on many firearms since, most notably the German paratrooper rifle, the FG-42. Most guns featured a high rate of 750 rounds per minute, a low rate of 450.

The Johnson guns were recoil operated. Generally, they were not as accurate as the BAR, but they were only 42 inches long, weighed less than 13 pounds and were popular with the Marine Raiders, reconnaissance Marines and Army Rangers who were their primary users.

Production of the only service version of the Johnson, the Model of 1941, wound down at Johnson Automatic, Inc., by the end of 1944, but it was produced later in Israel as the Dror.

It wasn't just the end of the Johnson, the media declared at the time, it was the end of the light machinegun. At least, it was supposed to be the end of it in the United States.

Re-enter the LMG

Just as the submachine gun is supposed to be dead, but keeps cropping up everywhere, the obituaries for the venerable light machinegun appear to be grossly exaggerated.

Though the German introduction of the assault rifle and the general purpose machinegun have frequently been seen as a new era in infantry armament in which only one or two firearms would equip whole army divisions, that revolution has never quite happened completely.

In the last full-power rifle period, the FAL, M-14, G-3 and others kept spawning versions much like the old light machinegun, such as the FALO series and the H&K-21, but no one wanted to call them light machineguns.

When the M-16 and Kalashnikov were supposed to be the "pure" infantry weapons in much of the capitalist and communist blocs, everyone wondered from where the serious offensive firepower would come. The result was that spin-offs of the reduced-power rifles with heavier barrels kept cropping up.

Finally, worldwide, in the now-dominant, medium calibers and sometimes in the old rifle calibers, whole new support weapons are called Squad Automatic Weapons. They are sneaking into supply systems, carrying fourth- and fifth-generation box-and-belt can-style magazines, which look very much like miniatures of the old '08/15 magazine of World War I.

"And though their mission is the same as that of the ancient portable Hotchkiss, it is politically incorrect and imprudent to call them light machineguns," Thompson points out in his best tongue-in-cheek fashion. "After all, aren't light machineguns obsolete?"

CHAPTER 34

THE RATTLING STEN

Cheap and Simple, This Submachine Gun Had Many Critics; The Gun is Still Around, Most of Its Critics Are Not

MORE THAN 4 million British Sten 9mm submachine guns were manufactured in Great Britain and Canada in varying configurations during World War II. In spite of that, the gun garnered little respect from those who carried it in combat. Its looks may have been the greatest cause for criticism. As Thompson puts it, "The thought that always springs to mind when looking at an early World War II specimen is that it is sleazy and even weak, although neither is entirely true." Nonetheless, those assigned to go into combat with the firearm often referred to it as the Woolworth Special, the Plumber's Delight or the Stench Gun.

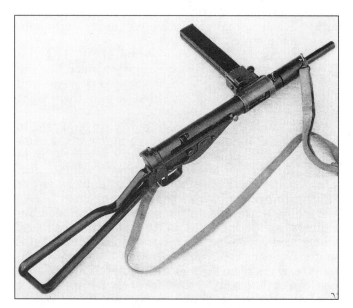

The Sten Mark 2 submachine gun cost the British government roughly $10 in U.S. money to produce. Several million were produced and used by numerous foreign countries against the Germans. It is still employed in some Third World nations.

"Studs" was a term used in the manuals for almost all non-trigger controls on the early Stens. Knurling sometimes was used or the parts were made relatively ergonomic by means of beveled edges or grooves, but generally, the Sten exuded a look and feel of mediocrity or worse.

Oddly, the United Kingdom's troops did not have a viable subgun in their military inventory when the war burst into fiery actuality. With Hitler's threat of invasion of England proper in 1940, the British arms industry sought desperately to fill the void. Citizens were being armed with sporting rifles begged from American hunters and target shooters. As a result, what was designated as the Sten Mark 1 9mm carbine was hurriedly introduced in early 1941. There is no doubt that it was simple in design and that it was cheap to produce. In 1941, the cost to the British government was in the neighborhood of 10 U.S. dollars.

There were problems with the early guns and the British soldiers to whom they were issued had little faith in the product. The 32-round single-column magazine was cheaply made and tended to jam. This problem eventually was solved in part by loading only 30 rounds. Using the magazine rather than the stock as a forward handgrip was another cause of jamming. This hold tended to bind the magazine and disrupt the feeding system. Roughly 100,000 guns were designated as the Mark 1. The Mark 2 is the most common Sten; more than 2 million units were made during a three-year period.

The Mark 2 was smaller than the original, but still suffered some of the same problems. To avoid jams, 30 rounds became standard in the 32-round magazine. The model also was made in a silenced version that was designated as the Sten Mark 2S. This one was produced with an integral silencer and was used to equip the British Commando units. Actually, it was recommended that the gun be fired with single rounds, since

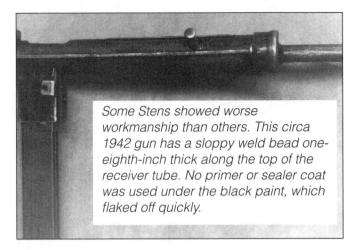

Some Stens showed worse workmanship than others. This circa 1942 gun has a sloppy weld bead one-eighth-inch thick along the top of the receiver tube. No primer or sealer coat was used under the black paint, which flaked off quickly.

The superior care taken in the production of Canadian Sten guns is obvious in this photo. The finish on the gun is clean as is the overall metal work.

anything faster wore out the baffles and even damaged the sound suppressor. However, the Mark 2S remained in service until after the Korean War.

Canadian-made guns were better made and some parts – the shoulder stock struts, for example – were made of heavier stock. Some were better machined than others with weld slag excised in visible places," Thompson says, adding, "Most of them, though – especially the Mark 2 versions – were merely tossed out the factory doors as soon as they were complete."

Thompson's research indicates that all Stens were in 9x19mm chambering and all were pure blowback guns. Any magazine other than the standard 32-round unit is rare and most were purely experimental. Likewise, any Sten that is not selective fire is either experimental or has been modified. The selective-fire switch was always a push-through type located just below the safety slot cutout. Pressing from left to right engages the "R" setting which stands for "repetition". Pushing the switch from right to left brings it to the "A" setting – automatic.

Thompson's belief is that the "most important single accessory for the Sten was the magazine loader. Heavy magazine springs tended to make compression of cartridges difficult to load by hand toward the end of the process. This is one more reason why only 30 – sometimes 28 – cartridges usually were loaded.

All of the magazines projected to the left and were never intended to be used as grips. The magazine catch is positioned at the rear of the housing and is pressed to release the stick-type magazine.

Thousands of the guns were dropped to partisans behind the lines who were fighting the Germans. In later years, what Thompson considers "this most primitive of submachine guns" was copied in factories and even small workshops in Germany, China, Denmark, Israel, Indochina and Belgium. It was not a case of these countries liking the gun, it was simply because the gun could be simply produced with minimum tooling and gunsmithing talent.

The primary British producers of completed guns were British Small Arms and the Royal Ordnance factories. However, hundreds of small subcontractors produced most of the parts. The gun drew the first part of its name from the first initials of the designers' names

"S" from R.V. Shepperd and the "T" from H.J. Turpen. The last two letters came from the fact that the early guns were produced at Royal Arsenal at Enfield.

Turpen, credited with being the gun's principal designer, had reduced the blowback mechanism to its most fundamental form, using a heavy bolt and a single, robust coil return spring.

The Mark 1 Sten used a collapsible vertical foregrip, which was nothing more than a simple rod activated by a weak hinge. There was a brace grip ahead of the trigger housing and a brace piece welded into the skeletonized buttstock.

The cost factor had a great deal to do with the mass production of the Sten. As Thompson puts it, "At a time, when a typical light machinegun cost half as much as a house, the Sten cost less than a substantial meal for two at a descent restaurant."

History shows that the guns were so cheap – and numerous – that during World War II if one malfunctioned in the field, it usually was tossed beneath the wheels of a truck or a tank. That saved going through the extensive paperwork of sending it to the rear for repair. Far less administrative effort was involved in writing it off as "lost or destroyed in combat."

The Mark 2 version has been called the definitive Sten. It was produced in a skeleton frame butt version and also in what has been called a rod version; the latter's stock was a single strut on which was mounted an elliptical plate.

However, in the 1942 version of the Mark 2, the flash hider and foregrip were no longer installed. Like the Mark 1, the guns made in that era bore sloppy coats of paint. Some were painted black, some green and others beige. It seemed to be a case of what paint colors were available in a then-desperate country.

While some units such as the British Royal Marines preferred the Thompson and the .45 ACP cartridge, the British army stuck with the 9x19mm, the cartridge favored by the German enemy. It was a wise move, since the so-called Luger caliber was coming to be accepted by most of Europe.

More important perhaps was the fact that the 9mm cartridge was cheaper to manufacture than the .45 ACP, lighter in weight and there was the continuing possibility of using rounds captured from the enemy. Thompson notes that "Virtually all of the military handguns and submachine guns of any merit that were produced in the West after 1921 used this round. Oddly, the Germans initially viewed the Sten as noth-

This is the left side of the Sten's predecessor, the Lancaster, which was a direct copy of the German army's Bergmann MP-28. The only difference was that to the Lancaster fittings had been added to mount the British Lee-Enfield bayonet.

ing more than junk, but eventually copied it with a vertically mounted magazine, issuing it as the MP-3008."

It was the Mark 2 Sten that was responsible for what Thompson refers to as what might be "the most famous single jam in firearms history."

Reinhard Heydrich, Storm Trooper governor of Slovakia and Moravia, was considered by many to be the most dangerous man in the Nazi hierarchy. He was admittedly a brave man, but also was an efficient and totally ruthless officer and administrator – good reasons for the British to mark him for assassination.

A well-equipped and trained team of Czech assassins was air-dropped into the area, where the men spent some time studying this particular Nazi's movements and habits. They finally set up their kill zone at a stop sign near Heydrich's headquarters in Prague.

History shows that the trap was sprung on May 17, 1942, when the designated Czech assassin approached the Nazi staff car in which Heydrich was seated. The Sten was aimed at the officer at close quarters. When the trigger was pulled, there was only a click. The subgun was recocked only to deliver another click.

Luckily – but unluckily for the Nazi general – another of the assassins tossed a #36 Mills bomb, a potent hand grenade, into the passenger's lap. Badly wounded, Heydrich died on June 4, 1942, from an infection caused by the grenade.

The Gestapo recovered what was supposed to be the assassin's weapon some months later. According to official reports, the failure to fire was caused by compressed magazine lips.

Throughout the war years and after, Stens still were being dressed up and refined, efforts being made to weed out the defective magazines and parts.

The two manufacturers continued to roll out versions of the Sten. The Mark 3 was the one most often found in the hands of British troops. With limited materials at hand, it was a variation of the Mark 1. However, the barrel jacket and receiver were a single piece formed from a sheet steel tube. The gun's magazine housing was fixed. A guard in front of the ejection port was meant to keep the shooter's fingers from entering the opening. Most of the Mark 3 guns had a tubular buttstock almost identical to that of the Mark 1. This particular version was produced both in Great Britain and Canada during 1943-44.

That was about the time that the designers got fancy and produced what they called the Mark 4A and Mark 4B. Approximately 2200 of these variations were produced with the intent of issuing them to special units. This product suggested that someone was thinking ahead. The design was similar to that of the Mark 2, but the skeleton stock of the Mark 4A was tooled to fold forward beside the barrel housing on the side away from the protruding magazine. The pistol grip and trigger were positioned directly behind the vertical magazine port. The Mark 4B was much the same design as earlier Stens. Both, however, were equipped with flash hiders.

At first appearance, the Sten Mark 5 looks like a somewhat aborted Thompson submachine gun. This probably was based upon he fact that British paratroopers were armed with the Thompson and favored it. Thus, in 1944, the Sten appeared with a wood stock and handgrip. Installation of the latter required that the trigger mechanism be moved forward. The initial run of the Mark 5 also featured a front handgrip in the style of the Model 1928

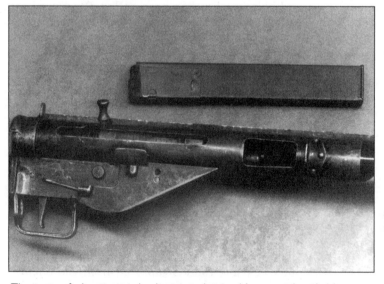

The use of sheet metal, cheap paint and low-grade wire in construction lowered confidence in the capabilities of the Sten variations. This is a Mark 2 with its 32-round magazine. Thompson found that this one made in England worked well.

Thompson, but this addition broke easily and soon was dropped from the design.

The Mark 5, which was equipped to carry a bayonet, was replaced among British forces by the Sterling subgun in 1953, but still was being made in the United Kingdom into the 1960s.

The last version of the gun – which British children referred to as the tinny – was the Mark 6, which was the Mark 5 with a sound suppressor attached. According to Thompson, "The gun actually was a modified Mark 2S, with the wood furniture of the Mark 5." Only minor numbers were produced before the Sten line was replaced totally by the Sterling L-34.

In spite of the lack of affection for the Sten by those who had to use it, the Danish Madsen M-45 and M-46 subguns, the designs of Sweden's Karl Gustav and even the U.S. Army's M-3 all borrowed from the Sten design. In our opinion, all were just as ugly as the original. For the most part, the M-3 was unpopular with the troops to whom it was issued.

On the other hand, the Sten's compact dimensions made it easily concealable for partisans and others operating behind enemy lines. A legend born of World War II has it that partisans in Europe produced a bicycle that used Sten gun components as its frame and crossbars, the gun thus being hidden in plain sight!

Physical specifications for the various Sten models varied greatly, but all were equipped with the 32-round stick magazine and carried barrels that had a six-groove right-hand twist – except for a few Mark 2s, which had two-groove barrels.

The magazines on all of the Sten models projected horizontally to the left, allowing the shooter to maintain a low silhouette in shooting from the prone position. On all models, the magazine catch was at the rear of the housing and was simply pressed to release the 32-round stick magazines.

Later issues had what Thompson refers to as "fixed barleycorn sights" and were adequate for getting on target. On the earlier guns, sights seemed to consist of an indentation in the receiver and what resembled an ordinary iron nail sticking up from the front of the barrel.

Cyclic rate of fire for all was in the 550-600 rounds per minute category, except for the silenced M-2S and the M-6. Rate of fire for the M-5 was 600 rounds per minute; that of the M-6 was 550 and that of the M-2S was 450 rounds. Muzzle velocity for all except the two suppressed models was clocked at about 1,250 fps.

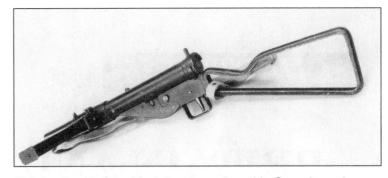

This particular Sten Mark 2 was produced in Canada and illustrates what could be done with the gun with proper attention and materials.

Arms researcher Pat Fisher fired this Sten Mark 2. He found that this particular gun had a distorted extractor and a slightly weak magazine spring, but it functioned perfectly as long as the magazine was held firmly to the rear.

While it has been some four decades since the British armories turned out the various Sten models, they still seem to be prevalent in a number of Third World countries and often are issued by today's warlords to arm their private armies. There also have been several reports in recent years of the Sten being used in political assassinations.

CHAPTER 35

BRITAIN AND THE BREN

By Way of Czechoslovakia, This Light Machinegun Has Proven Its Worth for the United Kingdom

BRITISH FIREARMS USED to seem boring. They always looked ugly and seemed primitive. Back in the 1960s, many made a presumption that the .303 rimmed British cartridge, pounding its 175-grain bullet downrange at more than 2,400 fps was just flat inaccurate, brass life was terrible and everything was just plain bad. How these people manage to blunder through and win wars must be a mystery to the whole world. Their engineering, many believed, was just silly, their ballistics odd, and much of what was tried, including old Webley and Enfield revolvers, seemed right on the edge of useless.

How time and experience change perspectives!

In the late 1960s, when dealers acquired Canadian surplus Bren guns, the shooters' views started to change. At that point, some high-quality, late issue-ammunition was also available.

The Bren's top-mounted magazine, which had seemed ridiculous to many Americans, allowed prone shooting with ease and the offset sights – a no-no among American designers – proved to be no problem at all.

"The guns shot like match rifles," recalls Thompson. "Everything immediately fell quickly under the hand, as if designed for the clumsy. One could change magazines without leaving battery. Try that with a Browning Automatic Rifle sometime! Also, the brass

The British Bren originated from this is the Czech-produced VZ/ZB26 light machinegun. It had a long barrel and a flash hider.

The Czech Connection

Most shooters knew the Bren from films and literature, but it was the easy handling that impressed most of them. Besides, the murky Eastern European origins of this "British" firearm were intriguing.

"At the height of the Cold War murky was a word that was applied to anything from the communist bloc and all those languages, which we find difficult to pronounce," Thompson explains. "In truth, the origins of the Bren were clear as a bell and very much the product of an industry, which, from the '20s and '30s, went through changes in government from democratic to fascist to communist, then back to democratic again, then recently to partitioned status. However, this industry has never been anything but creative, aggressive, innovative and perceptive.

"Even in the communist days, the Czech arms industry and primarily Ceskoslovenska Zbrojovka Brno – called BRNO or simply ZB – was every bit the competitive export and manufacturing venture any capitalist country would have been proud of to the point of chest-pounding. It still is."

How directly the Bren's origins are related to the Czechs is hinted at when one sees the cover of an arms book written by Maj. Frederick Myatt and published in England in 1980. Inside the front cover is a color photo of what is obviously an early Bren gun, but marked on the receiver's left side is: CS. ZBROJO-VKA, A.S. BRNO. On an inside page is another photo, this one of a Bren with a finned barrel. Obviously Czech-built, this gun was referred to as one of the tool-pattern guns transferred to Enfield in 1933.

These are some of the very first Bren guns, nominally inch-pattern, in the collection of the Weapons Museum at the British School of Infantry in Warminster, England. The Czechs apparently delivered many more guns and a great deal of tooling as well.

"That the British, with their distaste for privately owned firearms, chose to retain these for so long is remarkable," Thompson says. He adds, "But the Bren is a special gun, with a very special tradition. It was the finest light machinegun of World War II.

"The Czech guns are part of that tradition and really are the self-same firearm. Because Czechoslovakia disappeared in 1938 – oddly and ironically due primarily to British maneuvering – the Czechs seldom used their own designs in combat. Many others, including the Germans, did.

"These two branches of a common tree comprise a wonderful story and some brilliant engineering. Between the lines lies a startling tale of the British swallowing some pride."

But some side notes first:

The Czech model from 1926 is viewed here from the front end. The flash hider was somewhat crude by present standards.

This Canadian-produced Mark 2 Bren was manufactured for the Chinese market and sported a straight magazine. This one actually reached China and was captured by U.S. troops in Korea in 1951.

lasted nicely. Shooters and collectors began to study these treasures from north of the Canadian border."

Shooters had been testing two quite different weapons. Enfield made the British Brens early in World War II. Canadian-built Inglis Mark 2s allegedly were manufactured from about 1942. Searching through the literature another fact was discovered: These guns and their systems were neither British nor Canadian in design, but Czechoslovakian.

This is the Canadian-produced Inglis Mark 2 Bren, with a simplified rear sight. Note the curved magazine, which was designed to handle the British .303 cartridge.

Those who compare the Browning Automatic Rifle and the Bren are in a classic apples-and-oranges situation. The BAR was an automatic rifle weighing 5 to 7 pounds less than the Bren. The BAR was without a quick barrel interchange or top-mounted magazine at that time, but it was issued in far greater quantity. It was no more a light machinegun than the heavier Bren was an automatic rifle. Both were excellent weapons.

The Bren had far better sustained fire capability, which was boosted further still by its fast barrel swap capability, but it could never be as mobile or independent as the BAR.

Both guns had some factors in common: tactics around their combat roles were superbly well developed and they were both extremely accurate. Aussies and New Zealanders who used both found it hard to choose between them. That the Bren and the ZB still see duty in various parts of the world, though in diminishing numbers, is a testament to their designers.

In the 1920s and 1930s, light machineguns were a vital part of what everyone was trying to do: avoid the carnage of another static conflict like World War I.

World War I light machineguns were a mixed bag. There was the so-called light Maxim '08/15, a water-cooled, belt-fed bruiser that weighed 31 pounds, without ammo or water. The mount added another 51 pounds. There was the Hotchkiss light series, excellent strip-fed guns in various calibers. In almost infinite variations, most weighed around 22 pounds, but were expensive to produce and awkward to use in the field.

There were others – the Madsen and the Chauchat – long recoil designs, basically obsolete, albeit the Madsen gave good service in the field. The best of the leftovers from the so-called Great War was, of course, the Lewis Gun, an efficient design, which relied on drum magazines.

The Lewis, weighing 26 pounds, was both labor-intensive and complicated. All these guns saw some service in World War II and most were decent firearms. However, they generally lacked quick-change barrels, easy reloads in the dark or under adverse conditions and a general sleekness of design. Worse, most were not as mobile – aka: lightweight – as the planners of newer tactics wished.

The modern Czech arms industry was born at basically the same time as the country and developed not merely to service domestic needs. Upon the foundation left by the old Austro-Hungarian Empire, the Czechs built formidable factories and were determined to lead the world.

"This effort required designers," Thompson points out. "Vaclav Holek and Anton Marek quickly went to work on a system which, with a few refinements, might have become the world's first general purpose machinegun. However, the Praga Model 24, a belt- and box-fed piece, was somewhat too complex and expensive for the market, evincing much of the complexity of manufacture and maintenance that made the Lewis obsolete. Oddly, the ZB26 (or ZB 26 or ZB.26, all of which are imprinted on various guns) is commonly known in Eastern Europe as the Model 24, which it actually never was."

A new gun in the 20-pound range, the Model 24 went back to basics and directly addressed the shortcomings

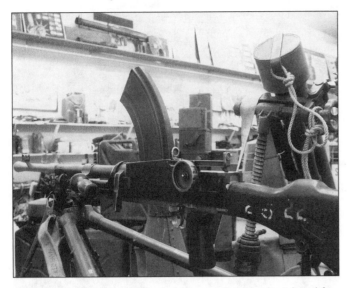

This circa 1941 Bren Mark 1 is mounted on its tripod for infantry support. Note the elaborate drum sight, the sturdy handle and the barrel nut grip.

Looking forward from the gun's stock, it is obvious that the rear sight is offset. Note the size of the magazine release and the general configuration of the sight.

of all its predecessors. The fine-edged division among the moving parts and the spread of stress was brilliantly executed. A long, sturdy stainless steel gas cylinder ran under the barrel, starting just aft of the muzzle. The gas piston also was of stainless steel to eliminate corrosion and obviate the need for cleaning in the field. Springs were designed in such a manner that breakage was unlikely and the guns usually continued to work even with snapped springs.

Field-stripping was quite simple. Controls were large and easy to find by feel; this was particularly true of the barrel nut grip and the magazine catch. Everything was designed to be found easily with a gloved hand or in the dark. In fact, some versions of the ZB26 and the ZB30 enlarged the trigger guard hoop for use with thick gloves. And the top-mounted magazine was

intended to allow reloading without the gun being jockeyed about and therefore off-target.

Field-stripping for checking, lubrication and cleaning were simplified. The receiver-locking pin was shoved out and the frame group withdrawn. The entire slide, gas cylinder and bolt assemblies came out the rear of the receiver. The barrel then was removed with the nut grip handle. Turned to the right, the barrel slid off frontward. Then the buttplate catch was pushed and the two buffer springs removed. Comparing this with the stripping sequence of the Lewis Gun immediately makes one aware that the Czech method tended to simplify training. This was an intended result.

"Within two years of the design's introduction, almost every country in the world was at least testing the ZB guns," Thompson reports. "Many nations had ordered either the standard item or their own slightly modified version."

The Model of 1930 was visually identical to the Model 26, but was a slight improvement. The Model 26 bolt did not ride directly on the piston, as is the case for the ZB30 and the Bren. Instead, the bolt was cammed into the locked position by an enlarged rear section of the piston/slide assembly. The Yugoslavian ZB20J is the ZB30, but often with an enlarged trigger guard and a heavily knurled section on the barrel just ahead of the handle. Both are accommodations for gloved hands.

All these guns are selective fire, controlled by a switch on the left that is positioned just above the trigger guard.

In an aside, Thompson points out, "Every designer is a copyist to some extent. There was little to nothing that could be patented as absolutely new on the ZB guns, but the combination and applications are unique. The ergonomics of the controls were masterful at a time when the term 'ergonomics' was not yet concocted. Even the huge sight adjustment drum is one of those small details, which combine to demonstrate the pure genius of Holek and his team."

By the mid-1930s, 24 countries had standardized some form of these elegant, new light machineguns, and many others nations – with or without authorization – were copying features of the guns or the entire design.

Almost as an afterthought, the British included the Models 26 and 30 in their trials, and results were astounding. Nothing else was even close. By 1933, Holek's team had completed modifications necessary for use of Britain's sloped, heavily rimmed .303 cartridge. The prototype series called the Lehky Kumomet ZGB33 – perhaps 10 to 25 guns – were shipped and Czech engineers were packing for work at Great Britain's armory at Enfield.

Cosmetically, the guns are only slightly different, the most obvious change being the forward-curved magazine required by the fat rim of the British cartridge. The Brits also insisted that the barrel be shortened to bring gross length to 45.5 inches, just an inch or so longer than a typical Lee-Enfield. A rather prominent cone-shaped flash suppressor was also incorporated.

A butt-leveling fitting and rear sling attachment are part of the setup when the Bren Mark 1 is tripod-mounted. Note the traverse control in lower left of the photo.

The huge controls of the Bren Mark 1 make it easy to find the sight and the barrel nut grip even in the dark.

The gas cylinder was shortened and the port moved much closer to the receiver, while the definitive British version eliminated the finned barrel. The British version was in inch pattern rather than metric, although many parts would directly interchange. Thus, the Mark 2 in 7.92mm circa 1943 or so was a slightly revised VZ30 with the Bren gas system.

"The gun's name was a stroke of inspiration, simple and memorable," Thompson notes. " 'Bren' is a simple combination of the city where the gun was designed, Brno, and the city where the British weapon would be produced, Enfield."

By July 1938, guns were being produced at the rate of 300 weekly in the Enfield works. Just barely in time, the guns began to reach cavalry units first, then the infantry and finally the specialists, although the old Hotchkiss and Lewis guns still saw considerable service in France in 1940.

Meantime, also in 1938, the Germans had seized control of Czechoslovakia and introduced the original versions of the guns into their services, especially the Waffen S.S./Verfugungstruppe, who gleefully accepted these supremely reliable weapons as Maschinegewehrs 26(t) and 30(t), the letter suffix describing the German word for the county of origin.

The Germans continued to produce the guns, as well as to export them for hard currency. The gun was also being manufactured at the same time in other countries in Europe, Asia and the Middle East.

The Guns in Combat

The British Army issued the Bren much as it had the Lewis Gun: two guns per platoon. However, this ratio improved, even doubling late in the war; in some specialist organizations the issue per unit was much higher. Some non-infantry outfits never had Bren guns at all, but armored units frequently added Bren Carri-

ers – small tracked personnel and equipment haulers – to their total firepower. Special magazines and mounts for anti-aircraft applications became common issue, though they saw less use after about 1943.

The Chinese army, the various warlords and even the Chinese communists used and even built both the Bren and the ZB. However, these guns usually were chambered for the German 7.92x57 loading, far more powerful than the British .303 round.

The Kuomintang (Nationalist) government of China never really ruled the entire country, and was so corrupt that many weapons were actually stolen or sold on the open market before delivery. Nevertheless, the Chinese front was where the Japanese army deployed most of its personnel and took tremendous losses.

The ZB and the various derivatives fought well, surviving into the Korean War. As late as the 1980s, Defense Intelligence manuals still carried the notation with these weapons that "if in good condition and with a supply of ammunition, these are extremely reliable and very accurate weapons, fully the equal of any modern equipment." The shortened Mark 3 and Mark 4 worked well, too, although they saw almost no service.

British tactical technique called for moving Brens rapidly, usually on the flanks. Most often a Vickers or two provided support and suppressive fire, while the riflemen and the Bren gunners moved forward. Tripods were frequently used when troops were on the defensive, although digging in a Bren Carrier with a Vickers or two on the flanks, was a formidable and common alternative. The Bren fired at less than half the cyclic rate of the German general-purpose guns, especially the MG42, but the Bren was far easier to use from the hip or shoulders and it was never necessary to fiddle with belts or saddle drums.

"The ZB and the Bren were the end of the line for the light machinegun, but the line drags on in diminishing numbers," Thompson states. "Designed to be

This Bren Mark 1 is equipped with all the British furniture, including the butt-level/grip device. It is mounted on a tripod in the anti-aircraft configuration.

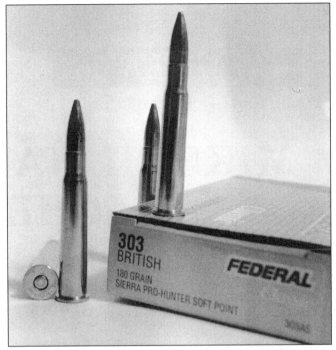

Quality-made commercial ammo works well in the Bren, but the rim must be loaded ahead of the next lower cartridge or jams can result.

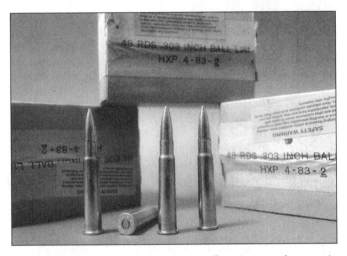

High-quality ammo such as these Greek-manufactured .303 British cartridges will vastly improve performance of the Brens. Such ammo was difficult to find 40 years ago, however.

used with minimal training, and built around the instincts of ordinary men, they are easy to use, if not so easy to carry.

"Except for their uncanny accuracy, shooting these guns is uneventful and almost automatic after the first time," Thompson says, adding that the same can be said for cleaning and maintaining them. Thompson notes, "Recoil is subdued and flash seldom obscures the sight picture. From the prone position, only chatter is encountered and there is virtually no muzzle rise due to their superb balance. This is somewhat better on the ZBs, with their longer barrels, than on the Bren. There is never any complicated fumbling with drum magazines or feed strips,

although Bren magazines for the old .303 cartridge must be carefully loaded to avoid rim jams."

In semi-automatic mode and prone positioning, many top shooters have shot groups with a ZB30 that would win most local high-power rifle matches. Some have done almost as well with short bursts in the full-automatic mode.

The L4 series Bren, chambered for the 7.62mm NATO cartridge, survives in non-infantry units throughout the former empire. New chrome-lined barrels are issued, the flash hider is the more modern bar-style and the ejector, extractor and magazine are clones of the 7.92 Mark 2 versions. New magazines are for 20 and 30 rounds.

"The British guns were continually simplified beginning in about 1940, losing the wonderful drum sight rather early, then various bits of the buttstock furniture along the way. The shoulder brace was first abbreviated, then eliminated altogether," Thompson notes.

The ZB survived as a new item in Czech Merkuria catalogs well into the 1950s. Some Middle East countries seem to have acquired and issued new guns well into the 1970s. Many of these were of recent Czech manufacture, but were chambered for the old British cartridge.

"These magnificent and cosmopolitan guns were never really replaced, though like the old soldier, they seem to be fading away," Thompson laments.

CHAPTER 36

MIKHAIL KALASHNIKOV'S MACHINEGUNS

Best Known and Remembered for Developing the AK-47, This Designer Had Other Successes

IN THE WORLD of firearms, any time that the name of Mikhail Kalashnikov is mentioned, invariably it is in regard to the former tank crewman's invention of the AK-47 rifle. This design, in its various clonings, has come to be recognized as probably the most widely known and used instrument of warfare manufactured since the club and the spear.

It is true that Kalashnikov gained personal fame and recognition through the development of the AK-47 and the later versions that followed. What generally goes ignored is the fact that his first assignment in Soviet Russia as a designer was to come up with a machinegun. In 1942, the Soviets were seeking a design for a new 7.62mm light machinegun. Sergeant Kalashnikov was one of several people chosen to pursue this need.

One of the requirements for the new light machinegun was that it should weigh no more than 15.5 pounds and should be capable of practical aimed fire of not less than 100 rounds per minute. The design created by Kalashnikov featured short recoil with the barrel recoiling inside the jacket. The gun's

bolt locked and unlocked by means of a cam track that engaged with a lug in the receiver.

Trials were held on three different designs and eventually the prototype developed by another designer was chosen, but by 1943, the Russians had adopted what is now the familiar 7.62x39mm round, a short cartridge that had been designed originally for assault rifle use only. The whole project had to be reconsidered and the design chosen earlier never got into production.

The Korean War was fought with surplus weapons turned over to the North Koreans by Russia and even the Chinese communists. Much of this armament had been used effectively in World War II, but by this time the Kalashnikov AK-47 had been adopted throughout the Soviet army. Thinking was that a light machinegun needed to be developed to fire the same round.

It would seem that the development of a machinegun from the design of the AK-47 should be no great task, however, Soviet Russia's new light machinegun was not unveiled until 1966. It was called the RPK, the K standing for Kalashnikov, as the designer.

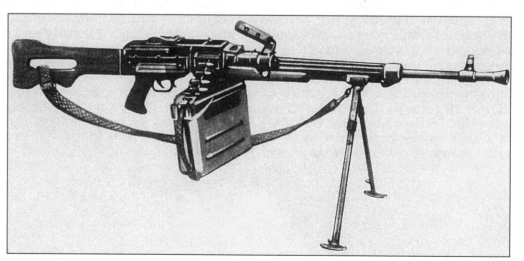

The Russian-made PKM is a lighter version of the PK designed by Mikhail Kalashnikov. The PK had a great number of machined parts; the PKM is made up largely of stamped steel parts, especially in the feed system. It also has a lighter fluted barrel than the original.

Mounted on a tripod, the PKM becomes the PKMS. This particular specimen is part of Knight's Armament's collection. The boxed ammunition belt is not attached to this gun.

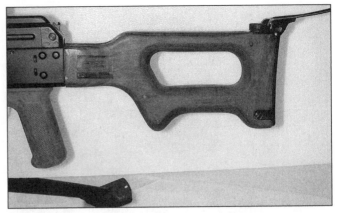

The stock of the PKM is somewhat crude in appearance when compared to recently introduced light machineguns. Wood instead of plastic has been used for the buttstock, the handgrip and the gun's carrying handle.

Originally, this gun had a fixed stock, but it was not long before a folding buttstock was substituted for paratroopers and similar special troops. It also was not long before other nations began to copy the design. For example, Yugoslavia did an almost direct steal of the design, but chambered its production for its own 7.62x51mm and 7.62x57mm cartridges. These Yugoslavian rifles were built primarily for export, but the effort came to an abrupt end when civil war engulfed that nation.

Note has been made that a plus for the RPK was the fact that a number of parts from the AK rifles were interchangeable with the machinegun. U.S. ordnance experts quickly discovered that it was possible to pull the bolt from an AK-47 rifle and install it in the workings of the light machinegun. The RPK, incidentally, was issued to troops with two magazines. One was a box type that held 40 rounds; the other was a drum design with a capacity of 75 rounds.

As might be expected, the original AK-47 design was updated to eventually become the RPK-74, another light machinegun. For all practical purposes, the RPK-74 was the same as the rifle, except that it had a longer, heavier barrel, a larger magazine and was fired from a tripod. Perhaps the greatest difference between the newer guns and the older versions was the fact that the Russians had developed a new cartridge they designated as the 5.45mm, the Soviet answer to NATO's 5.56mm round.

While Kalashnikov apparently was involved directly in design and development of all of the Russian guns that had a K in their titles, it is understood that his own favorite efforts were those in what has come to be known as the PK Family. Among Russian-designed weapons, this general-purpose machinegun probably is second in the number of guns that have been created around the world. Chambered for the Russian 7.62x54R round, this particular design was adopted by all of the communist countries associated with the now dead Warsaw Pact. The design also was virtually pirated by some nations that definitely were not communistic. The gun has been manufactured in Bulgaria and Romania and is licensed for production in Communist China as that nation's Type 80.

Kalashnikov – like other arms' designers including Stoner – tended to stay with a basic system once he had developed it and found that it worked as wanted. Thus, the Russian designer used the same basic mechanism for his machinegun design that he had featured in his other weaponry. His 7.62x54R general-purpose machinegun is a gas-operated automatic type. As with previous designs, it features a rotating bolt contained in a carrier driven by the gun's gas piston.

The innards are primarily standard Kalashnikov, but the designer did adopt features that he had observed on weaponry by other European designers. For example the piston that is necessary to drive the belt feed system of the Czech-made VZ-52 is incorporated, as is the trigger mechanism that was found originally on the earlier Degtyarev RPD. The basic belt feed system seems to have been copied from another Russian designer's work.

The design decision that still puzzles many present-day arms experts is why it was decided to chamber the PK family for the rimmed 7.62x54R Mosin-Nagant cartridge. This particular round had been introduced in 1891 for use in bolt-action military rifles and was loaded originally with a 150-grain spitzer bullet. Adopted later by China and Finland, the cartridge remains in use by Russian troops. These days, it usually is listed as the 7.62x54 Russian round and no doubt is the oldest military cartridge in continuing service, although it is followed closely by the .50-caliber Browning Machine Gun cartridge.

Since the various versions of the PK design are listed as having an effective range of 1000 meters, the long range and power of the bullet no doubt had much to do with the decision to use what amounts to an antique cartridge.

The PK model is selective fire, carries a 30-round box magazine and measures 45.6 inches in overall length. Unloaded, the gun's weight is a respectable 19

The rear sight of the PKM is an intricate, well-machined piece of equipment when compared to the stamped areas of the receiver. The same rear sight is used on all PK variations.

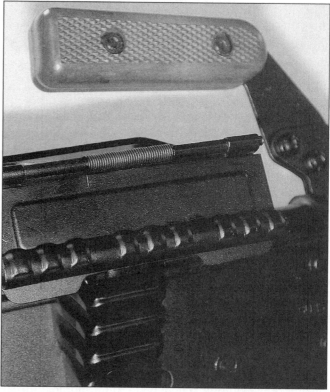

The checkered wooden carrying handle is attached to the PKM mechanism by an arrangement of strap metal. This is inexpensive to produce, yet does its job.

pounds, 14 ounces. Rate of fire is set at approximately 700 rounds per minute from the 25.9-inch barrel. The bore features four grooves with a right-hand twist. Tests by U.S. Army personnel have shown that muzzle velocity is approximately 2700 fps, offering a muzzle energy of some 3000 foot-pounds.

The Russian military still issues the PK arms in various forms and designations. The standard PK is a bipod-mounted weapon that is composed of a combination of machined steel and stamped parts. The PKS is the same gun, but has been rigged to fire from a tripod or even as an anti-aircraft weapon. Next comes the PKT, which has been reworked for mounting in armored vehicles and even tanks. The more recent PKM is an updated PK that has been outfitted with a lighter barrel. Rather than machined parts, most of the feeding mechanism, the receiver and some other parts are stampings, thus reducing the cost of production.

The PKMS is the PKM mounted on a tripod, while the PKB is the same gun except for the spade grips, which have been installed to replace the standard stock.

Anti-Russian guerrillas captured thousands of the guns during the Soviet Union's misadventure in Afghanistan in the late 20th century,. These irregulars then turned the PKMs against the uniformed hordes that were attempting to back a communist regime in this Mid-Eastern nation. Not surprisingly,

many of those same guns captured from Russian gunners have since been used to plague U.S. troops who were ordered to Afghanistan as part of the continuing battle against terrorists.

In researching material for this book, Lewis had the opportunity to work with a tripod-mounted PKMS, which is included in the collection at Knight's Armament. He was impressed with the simplicity of the gun's design. Like Kalashnikov's AK-47, it obviously has been designed for mass-production as low cost.

"There is none of the expensive machining that one sees on more sophisticated infantry weapons," Lewis notes. "At the same time, the gun no doubt is highly effective in a combat situation. That lack of frills probably makes all of the guns in the PK family simple to produce today in Third World countries, where appearance is less important than unskilled workers being able to produce a working firearm rapidly and at minimum expense," he adds.

In checking out the PKMS, Lewis worked with Lutz. He found that field-stripping the gun can be accomplished rapidly and without tools. Re-assembly is just as rapid. If a part breaks and a replacement is on hand, the gun should be out of service no more than a few minutes. It doesn't take a trained armorer to keep the gun in shooting condition.

The several variations of the PK utilize a belt box that attaches to the bottom of the firearm. This makes a neat, efficient-looking package. However, in most of the photos of Afghan guerrillas and dissidents of other nations, it would appear that the belt

The front sight of the PKM appears somewhat crude. The sight proper can be screwed up or down in order to achieve the desired zero. The protective wings are purposely bulky to guard the sight during rough-and-tumble movements in a combat environment.

The flash hider of the PKM is reported to be reasonably effective. Its size does little to affect the overall weight of the machinegun.

box is little used in such circumstances. Ammo-filled belts are fed directly into the mechanism.

Most important from a combat point of view is the fact that all of the variations are rigged for quick barrel changes. The bores of all the guns are chromed as an aid to accuracy.

In changing the barrel, the gun must be unloaded and the belt removed. The feed cover is raised so that the barrel can be unlocked. There is no handle on the barrel on most models, so a lot of care must be taken in handling a hot barrel, according to Lutz.

In an instant, a new barrel is positioned and locked in place, the gun is reloaded and the gunner is back in business.

A review of the way the weapon functions is probably in order at this point. The PK carries a slide to which the gas piston is attached. The bolt carrier also is mounted on the slide, which has a pair of cam grooves that serve to actuate the belt feed unit. As the bolt moves forward, a pair of claws closes over the rim of the cartridge. When the gun is fired, the slide is driven rearward and the claws pull the cartridge from the belt and place it into the bolt's feed lips positioned on the bolt face. The fresh round then is forced into the chamber from which the fired case already has been extracted and ejected.

As the bolt moves forward to chamber the fresh round, the cam path, which is part of the slide, moves the next cartridge forward, ready to be caught by the matched claws as the bolt closes. This is the general procedure of all the guns included in the PK family. All of the variations fire at a rate of approximately 700 rounds per minute.

These firearms are in use not only in Russia today, but as indicated earlier, are part of the armament of various nations – friendly to the U.S. and otherwise.

However, in the mid-1990s, it became known that the Russian armories had come up with what was considered a new gun. They called it the 6mm Unified Machine Gun. It is assumed that this was a move to match the U.S. force's M-249 5.56mm squad assault weapon.

To date, little information has been made available regarding this particular Russian model. However, it is reported that a slightly modified PK action is the heart of the product. Weight has been reduced to slightly more than 14 pounds and the gun has been outfitted with a longer, heavier barrel than on the earlier PK variations.

At this point, the new 6mm machinegun is not in general issue to Russian troops.

However, claims out of Moscow are that the cartridge has been developed with newer, more powerful propellants to give the gun an effective maximum range of up to 1500 yards.

CHAPTER 37

THE .32 ACP MODEL 61 SKORPION

Some Say the Cartridge Is too Small to be Effective; Several Assassins Would Disagree

THE CZECH-DESIGNED AND manufactured Model 61 Skorpion is a .32 ACP machine pistol that represents a high state of the art in miniaturized submachine guns. It was introduced in the early 1960s and was exported to several countries – particularly in Africa – as a police and military weapon. It also found a place among several terrorist gangs and with professional assassins.

According to some U.S. Government sources the VZ ("Vzor" or Model) 61 was issued for a time as a sidearm for company grade officers in the Czechoslovakian army, replacing the pistol for that purpose.

"If this is true," says Steele, "it demonstrates the foresight of Czech experts, since the U.S. Army had not replaced the venerable .45 auto with an equally compact, high-firepower weapon."

During the search for a new Army sidearm, several were appraised informally, including the VZ-61, the Ingram M-11, the Heckler & Koch VP-70 and what the Colt called its .221 Arm-gun. The Beretta 9mm M-9 was the ultimate choice.

A number of articles have been written about the VZ-61, most of them condemning the choice of the .32 ACP chambering, calling the bullet "an ineffective man-stopper." Steele believes that the Czechs probably adopted this caliber to standardize with potential market countries rather than for its ballistic efficiency.

"Surely it is inadequate as a pistol caliber," Steele says, "but it is uncertain what cumulative effect multiple hits with even so small a bullet would have on a human target. Sykes and Fairbairn of the pre-World War II Shanghai police force maintained that the additive shock effect of such bullets hitting almost simultaneously could equal the effect of a larger bullet.

"The idea seems to be that a second shock wave would be produced in the body before the first had subsided." Steele contends, "This is an effect not usually produced by a pistol due to the time lag between shots. I would not defend the .32 ACP cartridge as a man-stopper on these grounds, but I would point out the differences of a pistol caliber fired from a submachine gun."

He says, "Understandably, these benefits of the subgun depend on hitting the target more than once.

The original VZ-61 featured a bright-colored wood handgrip. Note the eyelet at the bottom of the grip for a lanyard or sling swivel.

The swinging wire stock was considered a weak point for the Skorpion VZ-61, but we found it works better as a brace, shooting with the arm fully extended rather than being fired from the shoulder.

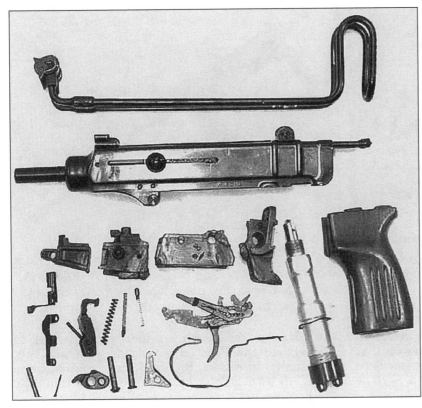

Design and construction of the VZ-61 was relatively simple. It was a favorite assassination weapon for the women members of Italy's left-wing Red Brigade.

The .32 ACP round appears to have two principle advantages besides exportability. It is easy to silence, a fact that is a prime consideration in choosing an assassination weapon. The .32 caliber ammo also is lightweight and convenient to store or even carry.

Steele and others have found that the VZ-61 is extremely accurate due to its closed-bolt design, its adjustable open sights and the light, crisp trigger pull. Since its weight seems to vary from 2.8 to 3.5 pounds, shooting it is something like firing a .22-caliber rimfire cartridge from a Smith & Wesson N-frame revolver.

"With its shoulder stock in place, I found the VZ-61 to be effective to about 200 meters, but it actually was designed for close-range defense work. The wire stock often is criticized as being too short; its primary purpose, however, is not to be used as a shoulder stock at all," Steele says.

"The stock should be held along the top of the right forearm by the left thumb, while the left hand grasps the right wrist. This position sounds more complicated than it is. It is extremely stable and effective for close-range firing from either eye or hip level," he adds.

This use of a forearm brace antedates Colt's so-called Arm-gun, which was designed as an "individual multi-purpose weapon." That particular effort was developed at Elgin Air Force Base in Florida well over a decade ago and barely got beyond the prototype stages.

The open rear sight on the VZ-61 is an L-shaped leaf graduated for 75 and 150 meters. The selector lever on the left side of the frame utilizes international symbols, using numerals rather than letters. The stamped-in zero means the gun is on safe; the numeral 1 indicates

As an experiment, I fired a 10-round clip from an under-arm position at a 7-yard silhouette. Five of the bullets struck the target.

"I have found the VZ-61 to be most accurate and effective when fired in two-round bursts, but the 10-round experiment was meant to duplicate the probable response of an untrained gunner to a close and dangerous target. Due to recoil characteristics, not all full-size submachine guns could keep five rounds on the target!"

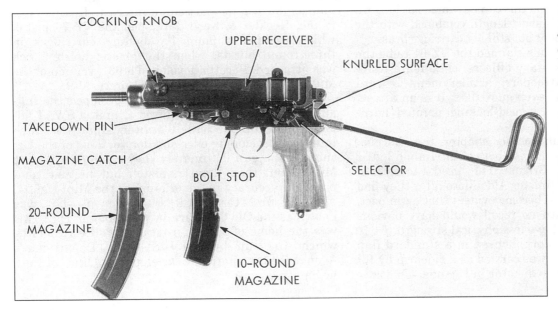

The sales brochure aimed at U.S. sales carried this photo of the VZ-61 Skorpion to identify the various exterior features of what has been classified as a submachine gun, a machine pistol or both.

COCKING KNOB

UPPER RECEIVER

KNURLED SURFACE

TAKEDOWN PIN

MAGAZINE CATCH

BOLT STOP

SELECTOR

20-ROUND MAGAZINE

10-ROUND MAGAZINE

Armitage Arms marketed this U.S.-manufactured clone of the VZ-61 as the Skorpap, thus getting away from the registered Skorpion name. It was short-lived.

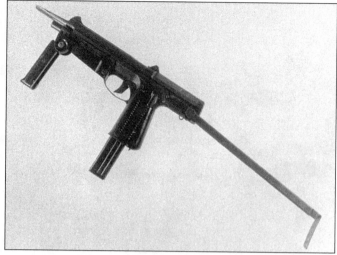

A competitor of the Skorpion for military interest was this Polish PM-63 machine pistol, which was chambered for 9mm Makarov. Cyclic rate was 600 rounds per minute.

semi-automatic; and 20 marking refers to magazine capacity. All 20 rounds can be fired full-auto with that setting. This numerical system, incidentally, has since been adapted for export weapons by Heckler & Koch as well as several other companies.

On a technical note, the folded length of the VZ-61 Skorpion is 10.6 inches; with the wire stock extended, length becomes 20.2 inches. There also are options, which include a sound suppressor, scope, hip holster, a shoulder holster and 10- and 20-round magazines. A recoil buffer in the butt is designed to slow the rate of fire from 840 rounds per minute to a more manageable 750 rounds per minute. Needless to say, perhaps, the weapon's light weight dictates extremely short bursts to minimize recoil-induced shot dispersion.

In testing the Skorpion, Steele found that the stock can be held to the shoulder, but "this will change the point of impact from that made when the weapon is used at arm's length. This is due, of course, to the difference in sight picture."

The wire stock also can be held in the under-arm position, but Steele found this can be somewhat hazardous due to the stock's short length combined with the upward ejection of spent but still hot cartridge brass.

Czech advertising has claimed the VZ-61 to be the ideal firearm for military officers, chauffeurs, tank crews, pilots, paratroopers, artillerymen, forward observers, police and even guerrillas. It is an attractive production with a good-looking painted hardwood handgrip.

As suggested in an another chapter, the Skorpion was a favorite of female members of the Italian leftist terror group, the Red Brigade. They used it to assassinate former Prime Minister Aldo Moro after they had kidnapped him. It had become evident that a compact, full-auto weapon with no recoil would have obvious appeal to those who have less physical strength.

As a matter of history, housed in a standard flap holster, the Skorpion was carried as a sidearm by Idi Amin when he was the dictator in Uganda. On some-

one his size, the Czech machine pistol looked no larger than the PPK on a German general's belt. Eventually, of course, the genocidal Amin was run out of his own country by the army of Tanzania. No one knows what happened to his Skorpion.

The M-61 has been found as far afield as Ghana, but its principle home was the Czech forces as a sidearm for officers, tank crews, police and gendarmerie. It was seen in use in television coverage of the 1969 riots in Prague on the anniversary of the Russian occupation. The version issued to police could be equipped with a sound suppressor.

"The .32 ACP chambering, of course, was not Soviet standard and the guns were made in that caliber for foreign markets. The VZ-61 also was designed to handle the 9mm Parabellum and other calibers, but it is rarely seen in other than .32 ACP," Steele reports.

Perhaps due to the Vietnam War and other guerrilla conflicts, there was a resurgence of interest in machine pistols in the 1970s. The Soviet Stechkin and the Ingram M-11 saw some use. In China, the Mauser 96 was of particular interest. In this time frame, Heckler & Koch developed the VP-70 pistol, which could fire 9mm Parabellum cartridges in three-round bursts, when the plastic holster/stock was attached. Beretta developed a 93R version of the M-92, which had become the U.S forces' M-9.

Moving into the 1980s, Glock developed the full-auto 9mm M-18, which acquired a limited SWAT following. Meantime, Israeli Military Industries was intent on developing ever-smaller versions of the Uzi submachine gun. Ultimately they came up with the Micro-Mini, then the Uzi pistol, but neither compared for accuracy to the original or the Mini-Uzi.

Steele first tested the Skorpion in what was known as the Old Car Barn in Washington, D.C. This was the home of the International Police Academy, which was run by the U.S. State Department's Agency for International Development/Office of Public Safety.

This Virginia police officer checks out the Heckler & Koch VP-70 machine pistol in the 1970s. It fired a three-round burst, the holster being attached as a stock. It was another attempt to duplicate the Skorpion.

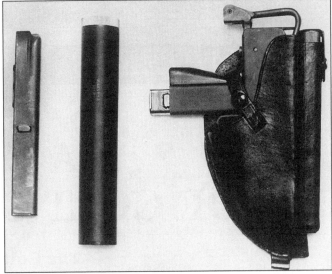

Gordon Ingram's M-11 .380 machine pistol gained fleeting interest in the late 1960s as a possible Skorpion competitor. In an early 1970s holster, it is seen with an extra magazine and sound suppressor. The M-11 fired from an open bolt, which made it lack accuracy.

"Range training was conducted in the basement by Ellis Lea and other instructors," Steele recalls. "A few years after that, the organization was disbanded, as it became common knowledge that it was a front for the CIA."

Steele tested a number of guns on that range. It was there that he found the upward ejection of the spent case from the Skorpion was noteworthy for knocking down some of the ceiling baffles. "This may be why placement of an upper ejection port is rare on submachine guns," Steele suggests. In spite of this, he found the Skorpion to be "extremely accurate with a target-level trigger and little recoil. It was most accurate for me, when fired either semi-auto or in two-round bursts."

The Czech-made Skorpion M-61 is a simple blow-back type with a heavy bolt compressing two recoil springs. The front of the bolt telescopes over the barrel, thus minimizing overall length. Interestingly, the magazine feeds in front of the trigger guard like a submachine gun or the Hammerli sport pistols. The bolt has dual retraction knobs on either side of the receiver, making the weapon ambidextrous.

The pistol grip carries an inertia plunger recoil buffer, which is meant to lower the cyclic rate of fire. "This is always a potential problem with machine pistols, with their light recoil," Steele notes.

"The buffered rate of fire is as high as 840 rounds per minute, but without the device, the rate could easily exceed the 1200 rounds per minute of the Gordon Ingram's MAC-11," Steele adds.

The Skorpion that Steele tested in 1970 had been borrowed from the Foreign Science & Technology section of the U.S. Army. At that time, only a couple of ZB-61s were known to be in this country.

"It was one of the most enjoyable subguns or pistols I have ever shot," Steele recalls. "It is too bad that its non-standard caliber and Soviet bloc manufacture made it simply a curiosity during that era. Actually, it was far ahead of its time. With its light caliber, excellent trigger and good sights, it could put rounds into an opponent's breadbasket before he could unlimber his service pistol."

This approach follows the same principle as the security staff for El Al Airlines using .22 LR pistols with which they can wound a hijacker several times before he can get off a shot. To get this repeat hit capability out of the 9mmP would require a pistol weighing from 6 to 12 pounds in order to handle the recoil between shots. The other answer would be to incorporate a burst control device, but Steele thinks that even the three-round burst from the lightweight Heckler & Koch VP-70 is too many.

This report would not be complete without mention of the fact that an outfit called Armitage Arms produced a stockless clone of the M-61, which was marketed in the United States into the 1990s. This was chambered for the 9mm cartridge. Still another company, Murkuria, manufactured and sold the Skorpion design in the 1980s, including a .380 ACP version that carried a straight stick-type magazine. Efforts of these companies were far from successful.

Whether or not the VZ-61 should eventually achieve large sales in Third World nations, it will remain a monument to Czech small arms designers. This machine pistol and other innovations such as the Bren machinegun and the ZK-576 submachine gun have become models for designers in America, Britain, Israel and elsewhere around the globe.

CHAPTER 38

A CASE
OF COLT CONFUSION

The Colt Commando and the Same Maker's Model 635 Submachine Gun are Not the Same Gun!

"**I'VE NOTICED THAT** a number of firearms writers tend to confuse the Colt-made Commando model with the Colt M-635 machinegun. The Commando is pretty much an AR-15 with the barrel shortened and the buttstock converted to a telescoping type. It has been called a submachine gun, but technically that is not true," Lewis points out.

"Traditionally, subguns have been designed to fire pistol ammunition. The Commando, as a miniaturized clone of the AR-15/M-16, fired the standard NATO rifle round, the 5.56x45 M193 cartridge. The Colt M-635, while based upon the same design, is a true submachine gun in that it fires the 9x19mm Parabellum cartridge.

Let's take a quick look at the Colt M-733 Commando. As a cut-down AR-15, it was designed specifically for jungle combat and encounters in close quarters. It was designated initially as the XM-

177E2 and was made by Colt Industries. It had its disadvantages in that the shortened barrel resulted in a lot of blast and flash when fired. This was remedied by adding a rather lengthy flash suppresser.

The clean, unencumbered lines of the Colt submachine gun are suggestive of efficiency. Those who used it in combat situations have found it to be a real performer.

Both of these guns are the Colt M-635 9mm submachine gun, but the lower gun is equipped with a barrel-length sound suppressor developed by Knight Armament of Vero Beach, Fla.

Colt Manufacturing, following the reorganization of what had been known as Colt Industries, manufactured the 9mm Colt subgun. On this particular model, an action inherited from the older company has been used to create the gun.

Were it not for the 9mm magazine protruding from the reworked magazine well, one would thing he was looking at the receiver of a standard M-16 rifle. This approach was cost-effective for the manufacturer and the buyer.

The left side view of the Colt submachine gun makes it rather obvious that the 9mm had been adopted from the workings of the M-16 military rifle.

The rear sight of the subgun is positioned atop the carrying handle the same as with the M-16 rifle. It is a flip-type allowing sighting at two different battle ranges.

Retired Marine Lt. Col. David Lutz, now a vice president of Knight Armament, checks out co-author Jack Lewis (right) on the Colt submachine gun. The subgun is part of the company's extensive arms museum.

Results of tests and actual combat observations showed that the Commando did not offer the same accuracy as the standard AR-15/M-16. The fact that in firing the standard 5.56mm NATO rifle ammo, not all of the powder was consumed before the bullet left the muzzle of the little gun was blamed for the difference. At the short ranges for which it was designed specifically, however, it proved satisfactory.

Overall length of the Commando with the butt extended is 31 inches; with the butt telescoped, length is reduced to 28 inches. Length of the barrel is 10 inches, featuring six grooves with a right-hand twist. It can be fired with both 20- and 30-round detachable box-type magazines. Unloaded, the gun weighs 9 pounds, 9 ounces. Muzzle velocity is reported to be in the neighborhood of 3000 fps; the gun has a cycle firing rate of 750 rounds per minute.

"Prior to the introduction of the Colt Model 635, Colt Industries went through a reorganization and became known as the Colt Manufacturing Co.," Lewis notes. "The Colt 9mm submachine gun was

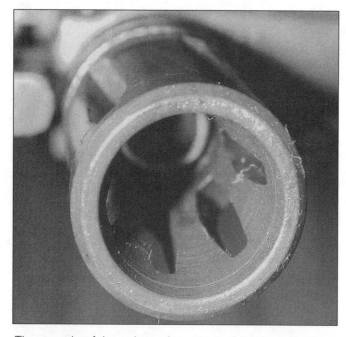

The muzzle of the subgun is protected against damage by the flash suppressing unit.

As is obvious here, standard M-16 parts were used in building the Colt M-635 submachine gun. The M-16 magazine well was blocked to handle the 9mm stick-type magazine.

This submachine gun used in checking out its capabilities on the range was not equipped with a sound suppressor and carried the standard M-16 front sight and flash reducing unit

introduced in 1987 and was quickly adopted by the U.S. Marine Corps, which had not had a submachine gun in its inventory since the demise of the Thompson. Further acceptance soon followed with orders from the U.S. Drug Enforcement Agency as well as numerous law enforcement entities."

There are those who say that while the 5.56mm Commando has been called a clone of the AR-15/M-16, the Colt M-635 is simply a clone of the Commando. There is no doubt that much of the technology was drawn from the improved M-16 rifle. In fact, the Marines liked the fact that controls and operation of the subgun were the same as for the M-16. Since every Marine is trained with the M-16 during boot camp, it was believed that training with the Colt submachinegun would be a simple matter.

If one looks at the magazine well of the Colt subgun, it becomes instantly obvious that the model was adopted from the M-16. The well is that of the full-size rifle, but has been blocked off to handle the smaller 9mm stick magazines.

With the telescoping butt extended, overall length of the M-635 is 28.74 inches, more than two inches shorter than the Commando. With the butt compressed, the length is reduced to 25.59 inches – still more than two inches shorter than the Commando. In spite of this, the barrel of the Colt subgun is longer than that of the Commando, measuring 10.5 inches. It also has six grooves and a right-hand twist.

Muzzle velocity of the Colt 9mm is considerably below that of the Commando, being measured at approximately 1000 fps, but the cyclic rate is higher at 900 rounds per minute from either the 20- or 30-round stick magazine. Unloaded the 9mm tips the scales at 5 pounds, 11 ounces.

There is no argument that the Colt 9mm utilizes the configuration and even the basic body of the M-16 rifle. The little subgun fires from a closed bolt in the same fashion as does the rifle, the action remaining open after the last round is fired. Utilizing M-16 technology, the buttstock of the 9mm tends to be more rigid when extended than that of the predecessor Commando model. Operation of the action is based upon the blowback principle.

The M-635 later was relegated to armories by the Marine Corps and replaced by the Heckler & Koch MP-5 9mm subgun, which was said to be more versatile. More recently, however, Marine reconnaissance units and elements of the military police have been ordered to turn in their MP-5 models, which have been replaced by still another Colt product, the M4 Carbine – yet another clone of the AR-15/M-16. What goes around obviously comes around, even in the military!

CHAPTER 39

FIRST LOOK: THE U.S. NAVY'S EXPERIMENTAL EX 45

This Weapons System, Still in Its Development Stages, Shows Great Promise for the Future

MILITARY COMBAT ALWAYS has been a matter of communications as well as weaponry and leadership, but in recent decades, communications – and denying communications access to the enemy – seem to have become increasingly important. Sometimes, the old ways turn out to be better – but not all that often.

During Desert Storm, the U.S. Air Force worked mightily to deny the Iraqi armed forces use of communications. When the telephone lines and radio capabilities were knocked out by Air Force bombers,

the Iraqis continued to get their messages through by a system first proven during World War I: motorcycle-riding couriers. This turned out to be a frustrating situation for our flyers. There was discussion that pilots should start strafing motorcyclists. That idea was dropped in a hurry since efforts were being made to protect the desert nation's civilian population, many of whom also rode motorcycles.

All of which brings us to the matter of the U.S. Navy's EX 45, an experimental weapons system now under evaluation and study. The development of this unit has been the responsibility of a scientist named Steve Cannon at the U.S. Naval Surface Warfare Center in Louisville, Ky.

Scientists from U.S. Naval Surface Warfare Center prepare the M-2HB .50 BMG machinegun for remote firing during a demonstration at Marine Corps Base Hawaii. The remote operation is handled by the prototype EX 45.

In a fully enclosed Humvee combat vehicle, a Marine gunner operates the joystick setup that controls the gun he cannot see. He watches the situation on a television screen in front of his position and maneuvers the control until the crosshairs are on the target.

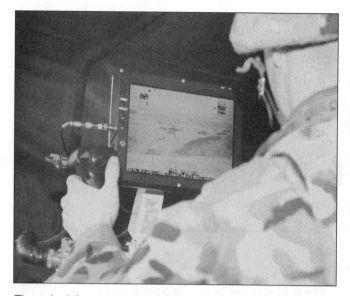

The television camera attached to the machinegun as part of the EX 45 unit can be moved by remote control to survey an area for likely targets. The gun is controlled in the same way.

Smoke issues from the muzzle of the M-2HB machinegun as a hidden gunner fires it by remote control.

Lewis learned of this prototype system when it was demonstrated in September 2002 at Marine Corps Base Hawaii across the island from Honolulu. Exactly 50 years ago Lewis was assigned to the base as the public information officer.

Earlier, the EX 45 had been unveiled at the government's Multi-Agency Craft Conference in a non-firing presentation. There also had been live-fire demonstrations of the system at the Marine Corps Base in Quantico, before representatives of the Navy, Marine Corps and Coast Guard, as well as a number of science and technology advisers attached to military units. The next demonstration was at Fort Knox, Ky., for the U.S. Army.

The intense interest shown by various military entities in the EX 45 thus far lies in the fact that it is a remotely controlled weapon. According to Navy scientists Steve Cannon and Ashley Johnson, the system is unique in the fact that it offers the ability to detect, identify, illuminate, deter and engage threats at great distances.

According to Johnson, assigned as the civilian science adviser for Marine Forces, Pacific, headquartered at Camp Smith, Hawaii, the system can do all these things, even piercing diverse weather conditions as a stand-alone system or as part of a larger defense strategy.

To date, the system has been operated successfully with the M-2HB .50 caliber machinegun, the Mark 19 Model 3 grenade machinegun, which fires a 40mm explosive round, and with the GAU-17 7.62mm Gatling gun. Rate of fire of the M-2HB is 500 rounds per minute with a muzzle velocity of 2,950 fps. The GAU-17 is a modernistic clone of the historic Gatling gun and boasts a firing rate of 6,000 rounds per minute with a muzzle velocity of 2580 fps. The Mark 19 M-3 launches explosive grenades at 375 per minute with its muzzle velocity measured at 795 fps.

Comparison of these statistics alone should suggest that there is a great deal of versatility built into the EX 45 weapons system," Lewis suggests.

The gun and the attached mount are set up in a chosen position that offers a good field of fire on the designated target; the gunner is stationed some distance away. At the Hawaii demonstration, the gunner was hidden in an enclosed Humvee, which was only about a dozen yards from where the gun and its instrument-loaded mount were positioned on a 7-ton military truck. However, Cannon told Lewis that the distance between the actual gun and the operator had been lengthened to approximately 600 feet in some earlier tests. Range to the target was approximately 1000 meters.

"If fiber optics were used, there is no telling how far the separation between the gun or guns could be and still be controlled by the gunner," Cannon declared at the demonstration showing the same enthusiasm a father might show for a touchdown-scoring son.

"The engineering prototype to which the gun is attached is lightweight and multi-purpose and can be mounted on any existing shipboard Mark 16 stand if it's to be used at sea," Cannon explains. "It is adaptable for unique applications and is stabilized by two axis gyros. Remote firing utilizes optics that are attached the mount."

The EX 45 has elevation and sensor drives that allow the gun to be driven off bore sight, thus allowing the user to use the systems optics in a non-threatening manner. The separate drives allow the super elevation of the ballistic solution to be incorporated, while maintaining the line of sight at all zoom levels.

Additionally," Cannon is quick to point out, "the EX 45 can be driven by an off-mount sensor such as the Mark 46 optical sight, the phalanx system or even a ship's radar."

In the demonstration conducted at Marine Corps Base Hawaii, the EX 45 firing system included an M-2 .50 machinegun followed by the Mark 19 40mm grenade machinegun. In each test, the gunner was seated in an enclosed Humvee with a small television

The gun and its mount are positioned on the bed of a 7-ton military truck for the firing exercise. The white rectangle on the distant hill is the target. A civilian Navy Department technician sits behind the prototype EX 45 as a precautionary measure during the demonstration. He also is charged with reloading and charging the gun when necessary.

Although firing, the gun is traversing to the white target shown in upper right by remote control. The gun currently must be loaded and charged by humans, but work is under way to develop a system where the gun will be loaded and charged automatically.

screen in front of him. In each hand, he held what resembled the joystick used on early aircraft.

"As nearly as I could determine, one stick involves vertical movement of the gun's muzzle, the other deals with elevation," Lewis reports. On a more scientific level, the baseline sight attached to the mount is day-color television with a zoom lens. This involves use of an uncooled FLIR (which translates to "forward-looking infra-red") and an eye-safe laser rangefinder. Sensor options and enhancements include longer-range optics; an image-intensified night TV camera; and uncooled and cooled FLIRs.

According to scientists Cannon and Johnson, day sensor performance is good out to a maximum of approximately 1500 meters. Detection of targets by means of the FLIR setup is greater than 500 meters.

Using both day and night sensors combined with the ballistic solution – where the bullet is going to land, to simplify the scientific jargon – allows the gunner to be on target with his first burst of fire. Using the joysticks and viewing the self-adjusting television screen, the gunner is able to pick his targets, then put the gun into action immediately.

As a precaution, Cannon or one of his staff sat behind the gun and the mount mechanism during actual firing. The Navy scientist was quick to point out that this is not a necessity, but in a situation where there are civilian onlookers, it is believed best to have someone close to the gun in the nearly impossible chance that something should go wrong.

"I watched this safety guard, if that's what he's considered, closely. At no time did he do anything other than observe what was happening downrange," Lewis reports.

According to Johnson, the U.S. Navy already has similar remote firing systems, but none as compact and versatile as the EX 45.

The actual system – less the weapon involved – is relatively lightweight, but one of the challenges at the Louisville center is to reduce the size of the unit, thus making it easier to transport.

The EX 45 Lewis had an opportunity to study at the time of this particular demonstration was a one-of-a-kind prototype, but Johnson contends the cost of producing the unit on a large-scale basis will be economical because it combines existing technology and weapons.

With proper communications linkage, one operator can handle several guns all from the same position. At present, the gun must be loaded and the weapon charged by hand. Another challenge is to create a means by which the gun can be loaded and charged automatically without the gunner or anyone else becoming involved. A feed link to the bridge of a ship or to an in-the-field military organization is being developed so that the officer-in-charge will have situational awareness.

According to Cannon, the fiber optics link currently is being introduced in large ships and eventually will be modified for use in ground-warfare situations. He also wants to develop programmable zone scanning as well as an autotracker with automatic ballistics correction.

Within the size and weight constraints of the system, Cannon's goal also is to introduce the EX 45's use in weapons currently in development. His staff of scientists also is working on a split screen so that the operator – as well as "higher headquarters" –can monitor multiple systems to view that so-called "big picture".

Also in development is a unit called the Raptor. This is a helmet-mounted display, which allows the gunner to view the action without having to look at the screen. This waterproof system is powered either by existing lines or batteries. It is an LCD unit with a 1.44 million-dot display. Other goals involve motion detection by image processing and further upgrades of the day camera and the night-use FLIR.

At the Hawaii demonstration, Marines and members of other branches of the armed services took turns firing the EX 45 by watching the video screen, then using the joystick arrangement to bring the crosshairs onto the target. One Marine likened it to playing a lethal video game.

When asked how he sees the EX 45 system being used in a combat situation, Johnson gave it a bit of thought, and then said that one of the best missions for such a system could be to guard American embassies around the world. He suggested that a unit could be placed at corners of the buildings and controlled safely from within the embassy complex.

"The only problem with embassy use as I see it lies in the fact that Marines assigned as security to such installations have not been allowed to defend them in recent years," Lewis says. "In Saigon, the embassy was evacuated, in other situations, embassy personnel – including the Marine guards – have surrendered on orders of our State Department and even been taken as prisoners."

Lewis sees communications as the key to any remote systems. "Whatever comes about, maintaining communications will be a continuing problem for this and other remote weapons systems. If so, I guess there is always that motorcycle."

As for an assault role, he says, "It's always nice to have heavy fire being laid down on an enemy before the grunts are ordered to move out. When that heavy fire comes about, the enemy invariably retaliates by trying to knock out the machineguns. With remote operation, the effort would be a trifle safer for the gunner, at least, but it seems to me that a self-destruct device should be attached to the guns so that they could be destroyed if the positions are overrun. In my day, allowing the enemy to capture a machinegun was a court martial offense for the machinegun platoon leader!"

CHAPTER 40

COMBAT SHOTGUNNING 101

New Needs are Calling for Upgrading the Scatterguns Lawmen and the Military Have Used for a Century

WHAT HAS COME to be called the patrol shotgun has been grandfathered into law enforcement since the late 19th century. The pump gun, in particular, has become so ubiquitous that it is authorized in law enforcement agencies that have forbidden submachine guns, rifles and, in some instances, even high-capacity pistols. So far as we can determine at present, no one has suggested smart-gun technology for shotguns (a contradiction in terms, since "smartness" has not added to accuracy, reliability or combat effectiveness in civilian firearms – just political control).

The question is how to make the old pump gun design – introduced more than a century ago – perform in modern police work. The first and oldest trick is to shorten the barrel for maneuverability inside and around vehicles. The typical barrel length for personal shotguns is the legal minimum 18 inches. For the SWAT or narcotics entry gun the departmental standard is 14 inches, a length that usually demands agency, rather than personal, ownership.

Steele's research found that the most common brands and models in police pumps at present are the Remington Model 870 and the Mossberg 590; both of the 12-gauge persuasion.

"Occasionally other styles appear, like the refinished, folding-stocked Ithaca Model 37s now carried by some traffic officers of the Los Angeles Police Department on their motorcycles," Steele notes.

"After the North Hollywood bank shootout of several years ago, the Los Angeles Police Department authorized slugs for issue shotguns. However, for standard-issue guns – minus rifle sights – slugs are of marginal utility. The slug provides greater penetration, range and stopping power than #00 buckshot, but its accuracy potential is minimal without a rifle-sighted weapon. In recent days, the LAPD's M-870s have come to be fitted with open sights and tactical slings," he says.

Sophisticated slugs such as the sabots and Brennekes are available, but standard Foster-type slugs are sufficiently accurate and powerful, while remaining cheap enough for serious practice. A department can get along well with reduced recoil slugs and #00 buck for duty, while using #7-1/2 birdshot for training. Specialized less-lethal loads for tactical situations include the MK Ballistic beanbag and the Ferret CS barricade round, a tear gas projectile. Other special purpose loads are too numerous to list here.

Shotgun Retrofit

The venerable Ithaca Model 37 still sees limited use with LAPD. In the late 1960s, the New York City Police Department's Stakeout Unit also used the Ithaca M-37. Cut down fore and aft, it was meant to supplement the stakeout unit's M-1 Carbines and pistols.

Jim Cirillo, probably the best-known veteran of the New York City Stakeout Unit, used a shortened Ithaca M-37 on several occasions. In one case, he was concealed behind a curtain when a pistol-armed robber suddenly turned toward him. Jim put a one-ounce slug into the felon's head from 18 inches. The effect was so dramatic the medical examiner initially mistook the entrance wound for an exit.

This is the vintage Remington M-870 riot gun. A slide-action model, it chambers a 12-gauge shell or slug. It is typical of the patrol shotguns that now are being phased out of service in place of more tactically oriented versions.

This Benelli 12-gauge is equipped with a standard stock. It is close to the design recently adopted by U.S. Armed Forces.

This Mossberg M-500 with a Vang Comp barrel makes an accurate combination for police work.

A law enforcement-only 14-inch barrel is mounted on this Benelli entry gun.

The gunsmith at the Gunsite Training Center in Arizona has an excellent reputation for retrofitting sporting shotguns into combat tools. Other experienced gunsmiths, like Jim Wilson in Brunswick, Ga., also can rework individual pump or semi-auto shotguns.

By selecting a common and basically sound design, like the Remington M-870, a company can make a few inexpensive changes that radically improve the gun's performance. This is precisely what Scattergun Technologies, now a division of Wilson Combat in Berryville, Ark., has done. For something like $170, Scattergun Technologies can rebuild and refinish an old riot gun into a Parkerized, polymer-stocked wonder, with a five-year warranty. You can also choose more options such as extended magazines, abbreviated stocks and quality rifle sights.

Other options on Scattergun Tech's currently made Patrol model include a high visibility, fluorescent, non-binding ABS nylon follower, a three-way adjustable sling with mount and swivel, the jumbo-head safety for use with gloves and rifle sights.

"If one chooses to go this fix, the shotgun's front bead is replaced by a chrome-molly steel post and ramp, with a luminous tritium insert that is a great aid in a low-light situation," Steele says. The rear sight is a chrome-molly steel assembly with a counter-bored ghost ring aperture. A supplied Allen wrench adjusts the Trak-Lock rear sight for changes in both elevation and windage.

The Patrol model retains the standard 18-inch barrel. Scatter Gun Technologies' FBI Model is similar, with the addition of a tactical foregrip that includes a light. The Standard Model has the tactical foregrip with light and adds a magazine extension. The Border Patrol Model has the magazine extension, but retains the standard foregrip. The Scattergun Tech Military Model is the same as the Border Patrol, except that a bayonet lug for the M-9 survival bayonet is added.

Scattergun Tech also produces several entry gun variations. The Entry Model is like the Patrol version, but with a 12.5-inch barrel and a Tac-Lite. The Border Patrol can be had by proper agencies with a 14-inch barrel. Add a Tac-Lite and it becomes the Professional Model. These all are classified as "Short Barreled Shotguns" by Bureau of Alcohol, Tobacco and Firearms (BATF), while stockless weapons are in the "Any Other Weapon" category. Scattergun Technologies produces several of the latter.

Examples of stockless entry guns, all produced with 12.5-inch barrels, made by Scattergun Tech include one called the Concealment 00 Model. The Concealment 01 adds a vertical foregrip. The Model 02 uses a Pachmayr pistol grip, while the 03 features a tactical foregrip with its safety hand sling. Included on the O3 version is a 5000-candlepower light. As one jokester put it, "The theory here may be, if you can't shoot 'em, blind 'em!"

"My own experience with stockless shotguns tells me they are formidable tools for threat management such as altering a suspect's thinking, as well as being far more powerful than service pistols," Steele states. "However, accuracy is limited to about five yards with loads limited to buckshot. I have found that stocked entry guns are far more versatile."

New Thinking on Scatterguns

Rather than retrofit, some agencies have adopted a new weapon to replace those aging Remingtons or Ithacas. At the forefront of this movement is the police department in Burbank, Calif., and its range-master, Larry Nichols.

Nichols, a retired Marine master sergeant, wanted an ambidextrous shotgun; one that was more accurate, with less recoil than current car guns. What he adopted

In what he calls his "Sneaky Pete" mode, David Steele demonstrates the use of the Border Patrol model. It is the M-870 Remington that has been modified by Scattergun Technologies.

During the Vietnam unpleasantries, this was called the "rice paddy prone" position by GIs. It resembles the squat seen among older Asians holding conversations with one another.

The kneeling position allows a lower profile and better use of cover than some other positions. The offhand arm position is used for speed on moving targets.

Standard transition without a sling calls for one to place the shotgun under the left arm, drawing the handgun. In this case, a SIG P226 is being drawn from Uncle Mike's nylon holster.

Under different sets of circumstances, the pistol backs up the shotgun and vice versa. Being used are the SIG P226 and the Scattergun Technologies-modified Remington 870.

ees found the long wood stocks (designed for the average 5-foot 8-inch male) punishing. Accuracy with bead sights and #00 buck was indifferent and limited pretty much to 20 yards.

In contrast, the upgraded Mossberg 590 Model provided an ambidextrous tang safety, ghost ring sights, extra ammo in the stock and a more convenient 14-inch barrel. Combined with reduced-recoil slugs, training and confidence improved, according to records maintained by Nichols.

"Instead of leaving these shotguns in their patrol car, so many officers wanted to carry the Mossberg on every call that management eventually had to specify where, when and how many shotguns could be taken to locations," Steele says.

These days when someone calls Nichols and asks if his agency issues patrol carbines, he answers, "Yes." When they ask what caliber, without hesitation he answers, "Seventy-two." That's the equivalent caliber of a 12-gauge slug.

Without the political and community relations hassle of adopting a patrol rifle, he has equipped every car with a precision shoulder weapon effective out to 100 yards.

"Personally," Steele says, "I like the latest high-tech assault rifles, submachine guns and machine pistols, but in most of the search warrants I've served, I was looking over the sights of the most conventional .38s, 9mms and 12 gauges. In the State of California, the legislature pushes gun control on police agencies just as it does on the general public. While I might prefer an AR-15, the Heckler & Koch MP-5 or FN P90 on certain assignments, my Scattergun Technologies Border Patrol 870 is accurate, powerful, politically correct and, as I have found, far more intimidating than any service pistol."

was a Mossberg M-590, with a 14-inch Vang Comp barrel, ghost ring sights and the Davis Speed-Feed stock. This setup can be used with buckshot, but the standard load is a reduced-recoil Foster slug, which has an effective range from point-blank to 100 yards.

With the exception of the barrel made by Hans Vang, most of the design features of the Nichols-designed Mossberg LE-14 590GS shotgun have been incorporated into the currently cataloged Mossberg M-590AI Compact Model. Buckshot ammunition and slugs featuring reduced recoil are available from several manufacturers.

As seems the case with most departments, in the past the Burbank Police Department had problems teaching recruits to use shotguns. Left-handers didn't like the cross-bolt safety. Small-stature train-

CHAPTER 41

TRISTAR'S
TACTICAL PHANTOM

This Turkish-Made 12-Gauge Import Shows
Real Promise as a Combat Long Gun

AS LEWIS RECALLS, it was the late Bill Ruger who once told him, "There are damned few new gun designs, just revisions of what has worked best."

"I learned early on to listen to what Mr. Ruger had so say," Lewis quickly admits, "for he had forgotten more about firearms design than most of us are ever going to know. Chances are some of that knowledge, unrecorded elsewhere, went with him at the time of his passing."

Thus, when Lewis opened the heavy-duty carton in which the Tristar 12-Phantom HP was delivered by UPS, he quickly noted some similarities between this Turkish product and Remington shotgun designs that have been in the public domain for several decades.

The Phantom HP model was introduced in 2002 and is listed in the 2003 GUN DIGEST as a scatter-gun meant for military and police use. This particular category is a somewhat exclusive listing, since it covers only two pages in the 558-page volume and includes only eight manufacturers and importers.

It should be noted that Tristar introduced a sporting model of the Phantom in 1999. It has much more the look of the old Remington model than does this later law-and-order version. The owner's manual that came with the HP model was actually written for the sporting model and contained a photo of it in appropriate four-color so one could see that this particular gun carried a walnut stock and forend.

The 12-gauge Phantom HP, chambered to handle shells measuring up to 3 inches, has a 19-inch barrel and is a fraction over 39 inches overall. The gun is gas-operated and carries a buttstock and forearm cast from a heavy-duty black synthetic. Metal parts have a heavy blue-black finish that tends to be scratch-resistant. According to the GUN DIGEST listing, it is equipped with a bead front sight, but that was definitely not the case with the model shipped to Lewis for testing and presentation in this tome.

The front sight on this particular shotgun was a blade set on a sturdy ramp with an inset brass bead offering quick reference when fitted into the notch of the adjustable rear sight. Lewis' first thought was that the combat-type sights must have been added after the shotgun arrived at the importer's Kansas City headquarters. However, a call to Marty Fajen at Tristar determined that the sights were made and installed at the Turkish factory.

Two screws requiring the use of a small Phillips' screwdriver for adjustments control the rear sight. The screw that must be adjusted for elevation is atop the sight, while a screw mounted on the sight's right side adjusts lateral movement.

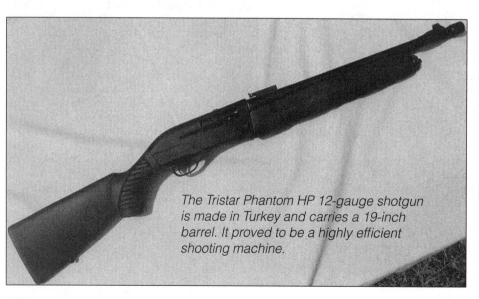

The Tristar Phantom HP 12-gauge shotgun is made in Turkey and carries a 19-inch barrel. It proved to be a highly efficient shooting machine.

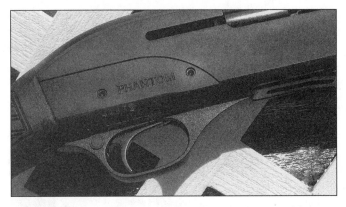

The trigger of the Turkish-made shotgun is a positive instrument with virtually no creep. Let-off was measured at approximately 6 pounds.

Positive gripping surfaces on the pistol grip and the forearm of the shotgun are cast into the heavy-duty material.

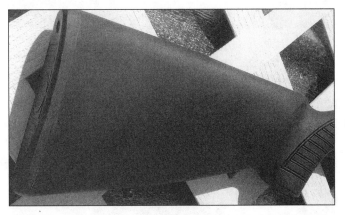

The rear sling swivel stud is mounted on the bottom of the buttstock. Design of the stock is comfortable for the average shooter.

The sturdy front sight of the Phantom HP has a brass bead incorporated for easier sighting.

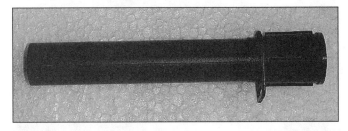

A furnished accessory is the heavy-duty plastic magazine extension, which allows two additional shells to be loaded in the magazine.

The front sling swivel stud is attached to the shotgun's magazine tube cap.

The tubular magazine holds only three rounds, but there is a plastic extension that can be installed to the magazine tube to allow five rounds to be loaded. Lewis' objection to this installation was the fact that the magazine tube then extended beyond the end of the barrel. When loaded with three rounds in the magazine, he thought the balance of the scattergun was ideal, but the weight of the extension and the added two shells stuffed up forward tended to make the gun somewhat muzzle heavy.

In addition to the screw-in cylinder choke, three other chokes – improved, modified and full – are included with the gun, as is a wrench for changing them. However, for combat-type shooting, it was decided to stick with the installed cylinder choke.

Using the RCBS Premier trigger pull scale, Lewis learned that let-off was just below six pounds. Actual weight of the gun, unloaded and sans the magazine extension, was 6.75 pounds.

Considering the short length of the shotgun, it seemed an ideal weapon for brush fighting. That approach called for help again from Fukui of the Island of Hawaii Police Department. When Lewis described the Phantom HP shotgun, Fukui was eager to give it a try. The two of them had worked together on other firearms test projects, along with Kaminski, another State of Hawaii law enforcement agent.

The buttplate of the Phantom HP is of soft rubber, but there is obvious recoil, when firing slugs. A thicker pad would be beneficial to the shooter.

In addition to the cylinder choke installed at the time the gun was delivered, three other chokes – improved, modified and full – are included with the Phantom HP model.

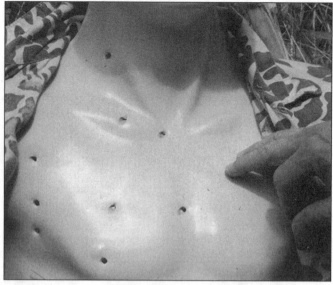

In spite of the interference by heavy brush, all nine pellets of the buckshot pierced the chest area of the plastic dummy used as a target.

Fukui spotted the second dummy 10 seconds after the first and fired what would have been a lethal round in an actual confrontation.

When cruising around in Hawaii's tropical jungles in search of marijuana farmers and associated felons, Fukui usually carries a light submachine gun of his own design, but on occasion he favors a shotgun.

Fukui, Kaminski and Lewis gathered on a Sunday morning in an abandoned lava quarry that they often used. One feature of the site was a stretch of jungle along a road leading into the canyon-like quarry. Marijuana growers had often used the trail to pack out their crops on foot. Over the years, Fukui had been involved in more than one chase along its length.

The trio decided to test the Tristar first as a jungle gun, since it's short length obviously led it to such use. Lewis and Kaminski arrived at the site early and set up a trio of three-dimensional dummies that were covered in surplus camouflage clothing and well concealed. The test for Fukui would be to follow the now overgrown trail until he spotted the first dummy. He was to fire on that plastic felon, then continue on until he spotted the other two and fire one round each on them. Like Lewis, he thought the gun handled better without the magazine extension.

"If I can't do the job with three rounds, I'm probably dead anyhow," the police officer said wryly.

The gun was loaded with three rounds of Remington Express 00 buckshot and trio decided to stick with the cylinder choke already installed in the muzzle.

Prior to this exercise, Lewis had taken time to check the velocities of the various loads on his chronograph. The Remington load out of the 19-inch barrel was traveling at 1,076 fps at 6 feet from the muzzle.

Chad Fukui chose to fire off the hood of his personal vehicle while testing the Phantom HP in an abandoned lava quarry.

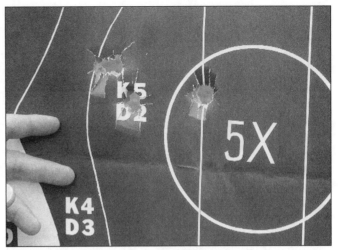

The three-round group was fired with Lightfield sabot slugs, which can be fired in either rifled or smoothbore shotguns. They are imported from Hungary.

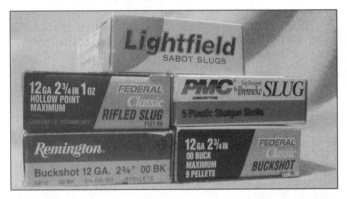

In testing the Phantom HP, buckshot and slugs from several different manufacturers were used. All performed relatively well in the short-barreled scattergun.

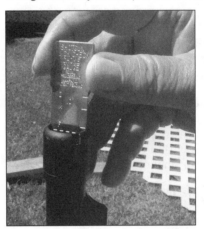

An early check on the tube installed in the gun barrel showed it was a cylinder choke. The metal gauge is marketed by Brownells of Montezuma, Iowa.

On Lewis' signal, Fukui started down the overgrown trail, edging carefully through wild cane, hanging vines and other jungle flora. He had been told that all three shots would be timed from the first shot.

Fukui moved approximately 20 yards down the trail before the first shot sounded. The second shot came nine seconds later, then it was 22 seconds before the shooter located the third target and squeezed off his third round.

Kaminski was following close behind the shooter and noted that the three plastic dummies from Law Enforcement Targets in St. Paul, Minn., had been so well hidden and camouflaged that the shooter was within 15 yards of each before he spotted it.

"It's relatively easy when no one's shooting back at you," Fukui said as he inspected one of the targets.

With the results recorded, Fukui was sent for a walk on a nearby road, while Lewis and Kaminski rearranged the targets. The same sequence was to be followed, but this time with Federal's Classic 00 rounds. As with all of the shells used in this test, length was 2-3/4 inches. Lewis' earlier endeavors had

shown that the .33-inch pellets were traveling at 1107 fps out of the 19-inch barrel.

The second trip down the trail was somewhat anti-climactic. Fukui cut 4 seconds off his original time and all of the pellets would have been deadly in a real-life showdown.

The second segment of the Phantom HP test took place nearly half a mile away in the worked-out lava pit. These days, manufacturers of both ammo and shotguns are advertising that a 12-gauge slug can put down an enemy – or a deer, if that's your target – at 100 yards.

A standard paper silhouette target was erected in a flat area in the man-made depression that was protected on all sides against stray shots. The exercise began at 50 yards as a means of getting the shotgun more or less zeroed.

Fukui fired three rounds into the silhouette at this range, using an off-hand stance. All of the slugs penetrated the chest area. In this instance, the ammunition used was from PMC, which was loaded with a Brenneke-designed slug. Eldorado Cartridge Co. of Boulder City, Nev., imports this ammunition from Italy. According to the importer, "The wad is attached permanently to the rear of the 1-ounce slug,

With the shotgun's iron sights properly zeroed, the Phantom HP put one slug into the 5X ring, the other two in the adjoining K5 area. The black tape at the top of the target and the holes in the white area mark earlier rounds fired in the zeroing process.

assuring a tight gas seal for maximum velocity and accuracy. It should be noted that Lewis had chronographed this round, too, through the barrel of the Tristar gun to come up with a reading of 1562 fps.

Moving back to the measured 100-yard mark, Fukui decided that he needed a good rest for this part of the exercise. He moved his personal vehicle into position so he could shoot off the hood.

Three different brands of ammunition would be used for this shoot: PMC, Federal and saboted rounds manufactured in Hungary and marketed as Lightfield by the Slug Group of New Paris, Pa.

Braced on the vehicle hood, Fukui aimed and squeezed off the three PMC rounds with a pause of no more than 3 seconds between shots. Kaminski was observing the target through field glasses and announced that the rounds were high and to the right.

A walk down to the target showed that all three rounds had ended in the white paper. Three inches higher and they would have been off the target completely.

Back at his shooting post, Fukui used a Phillips screwdriver to adjust for both windage and elevation, then loaded up once more. The original plan had been to use the rest of our PMC ammo to get the shotgun sighted properly at that range, but the sky was clouding up and we were going to get a downpour within minutes. The trio decided to try the rifled slugs manufactured and marketed by Federal Cartridge Co. of Anoka, Minn. The manufacturer claims that "the Federal Classic rifled slug with a proven hollow-point design and single-piece wad delivers consistent performance, improved accuracy and reduced felt recoil in smoothbore shotguns."

As before, Fukui chose the chest area of the target as his aiming point and triggered off his three rounds.

A wrench also is included with the Tristar Phantom HP for use in changing choke tubes.

"Well, it looks some better," Kaminski ventured, lowering the field glasses. He handed them to Fukui, who took a look. Lewis followed up with his own inspection.

"You need to do a bit more sight adjusting," Lewis told Fukui who was already busy with the screwdriver. That second three-round group had still been in the white area of the target but lower and closer to the actual silhouette.

When Fukui was satisfied with his adjustments, Lewis handed him a packet of Lightfield Hybred sabot slugs. As mentioned, these are made in Hungary and may be fired in either rifled or smoothbore shotguns. However, the maker insists that when used in smoothbores, they should be fired only through cylinder or improved cylinder guns. There also is a warning that they should not be fired in guns with 3-1/2-inch chambers.

A trajectory chart on the back of the box shows that at 50 yards, the 1-1/4-ounce slug will be 2.41 inches high out of a 30-inch barrel, but at 100, it will be on target. In his earlier checks, Lewis had chronographed the load at 1356 fps.

"I just hope the manufacturer's self-assurance rubs off here," Fukui muttered as he again positioned himself over the auto hood and leaned into the gun. As before, he wasted little time in triggering off the three rounds. This time, Lewis had his eyes glued to the binocular cups.

"You're in there," he announced. He started to hand the binoculars to Fukui who shook his head. It was starting to drizzle but he didn't care.

"This I have to see up close," he told Lewis and Kaminski.

The trio trotted downrange to inspect the three holes in the chest area of the target. One round had penetrated the 5X ring, while the other two were in the K5 area. All three rounds could be covered by the shooter's hand.

In spite of the drizzle, Fukui started to remove the target with care.

"What're you going to do with it?" Lewis wanted to know.

"I think I'm going to bronze it," Fukui said with a grin.

CHAPTER 42

THE M-1014
COMBAT SHOTGUN

It Has Taken More than Two Decades of Acute Bureaucracy but There Finally Is a New Scattergun for U.S. Armed Services

THE MODEL 97 Winchester slide-action shotgun was a game getter for years before they began to shorten its barrel and call it a trench gun. Thus, the gun made a name for itself as a combat arm in World War I. That success also led to international agreements limiting the use of shotguns in warfare. Those rules, however, did not preclude the scattergun in some situations including guard duty and defense. In the days when the rules were laid out, no one had given much thought to terrorists. Times change.

While the search has been on for the new armed services scattergun, the various elements have been using the products of at least three different arms-makers. Contracted for and issued during the last 20-odd years have been the Mossberg 500, the Remington 870 and the Winchester 1200. Now it looks as though these scatterguns will go the way of the Model 97 trench gun, ending up in museums or in the hands of arms collectors.

After all those years of testing, changing specifications, rejecting models and leaving the combat troops to wonder what was going on, the Benelli M-4 Super 90 semi-automatic shotgun finally has been chosen by the Joint Services Small Arms Program as the new model to be issued eventually to all of our Armed Services. That decision was made in February 1999,

but it wasn't until late in 2001 that the first of the guns came off the production line. As a result of a $2.8 million contract with Benelli and partner Heckler & Koch, initial production – nearly 4,000 guns – was being issued to Marine Corps units around the world by mid-2002. Benelli manufactures the shotgun in Italy, while H&K handles importation and servicing through its facilities in Sterling, Va.

Marine Cpl. Charles N. Double was the armorer charged with care of the first dozen M-1014 shotguns to arrive at Marine Corps Base Hawaii. These guns were issued to the base's military police.

The M-1014 combat shotgun now being issued to U.S. armed services is designed to stay in action regardless of the combat situation.

Corporal Double holds the heavy-duty plastic silhouette that was punctured by slugs and buckshot during the demonstration of the gun's capabilities.

The corporal thought that the cheek piece of the M-1014 is a bit overdone and tends to bruise the shooter's cheek. However, two other stocks are available and interchangeable for the shotgun.

Jack Lewis had an opportunity to check out the new combat shotgun. The Picattiny rail mounted on the receiver accommodates a variety of sighting devices. Lewis, however, approved of the ghost ring sights on the weapon.

Issuing some of the first of what has been designated as the M-1014 shotgun was what took Lewis to Marine Corps Base Hawaii, a beautiful installation on Oahu's Kaneohe Bay. During World War II, the installation had been a Naval air station and on December 7, 1941, Japanese aircraft attacked the base on their way to Pearl Harbor. Kansas Tower, the air traffic control element atop a high hill, still bears the imprint of Japanese bullets.

At the time of Lewis' return, the military police for the base had been issued the first dozen M-1014 shotguns. As other guns arrived, they eventually were to be funneled to tenant units such as the 3rd Marine Regiment.

A three-man team from the Marine Corps Systems Command, headquartered in Quantico, was ordered to Kaneohe along with the new shotguns. This trio put the initial recipients through the instructional paces ranging from use and tactics to weapons care and gunsmithing.

One of the graduates of this mini-course, Cpl. Charles N. Double, a native of Salem, Ohio, was selected to check out Lewis on the shotgun. The armorer for the base's headquarters battalion, Double was quick to state that he never had fired any shotgun in a combat situation, but he had taken a lot of rabbits with the family 12 gauge back in the Midwest.

"The thing I noticed with this shotgun is that the recoil with slugs and buckshot is not as heavy as I expected it to be," Double told Lewis. The M-1014 accepts either 2 3/4 - or 3-inch shells.

A well-groomed and prepared young man who had been a Marine for three years, Double kept it simple and led Lewis through the various functions, as well as disassembly and assembly procedures.

Lewis tends to agree with Double that the extreme contours of the adjustable cheek piece could use some redesign work.

This photo showing the interior of the shotgun's chamber reflects the excellence of the machining done on the weapon.

The buttpad of the M-1014 is plainly marked to show that Benelli manufactured the gun in its Italian plant.

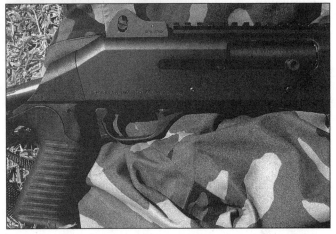

The pistol grip and forearm is of polymer reinforced with fiberglass. The bolt handle can be removed for use as a tool in cleaning the gas system.

Then came instruction in the proper technique for firing the new scattergun. Double pointed out that the Quantico team had him and the other selected personnel fire the gun at only two ranges, 7 yards and 26 yards. However, the Benelli-made gun has a Picattiny rail for mounting a scope. Double reported that killing accuracy with a gun so outfitted has been accomplished with slugs at 100 yards.

"For indoctrination, we each fired 65 rounds on 13 targets," Double explained. "We also learned that one is expected to score with a minimum of five 00 pellets on a silhouette target at 40 yards." Such 2 3/4-inch shotshells invariably carry nine pellets.

During the extensive testing conducted by Marine Corps Systems Command marksmen at Quantico, the average number of hits per round was 6.4 pellets at the 40-yard distance.

When firing slugs at 7 yards, the wadding tends to stick in the target," Double added. The target was a full silhouette made of heavy-duty black plastic. It can take a great deal of punishment before it begins to disintegrate.

The first thing one notes is the telescoping stock that allows varying adjustment of five inches. With the stock telescoped, overall length of the shotgun is 34.9 inches; with the stock fully extended, length becomes 39.9 inches. Length of the barrel is 18.5 inches with a fixed modified choke. An optional 14-inch barrel also is available for combat use.

Lewis did not have an opportunity to weigh the gun, but weight unloaded is approximately 8.5 pounds, according to Double.

To ensure semi-automatic fire, the operating system is gas-operated and regulated automatically. This involves a twin operating system that features dual gas ports, pistons and cylinders. These have been developed to meet the stringent operational and functional requirements for the combat shotgun. (With slight changes, the same shotgun still is available to civilians under its original factory designation, the Benelli M-4 Super 90.)

"The operating system is self-cleaning to a degree. It is unaffected by fouling and requires little or no maintenance," Double told Lewis, obviously quoting from his standard lecture. "The system is self-regulating for the cartridges of varying length and power levels. It has been found to function reliably under all environmental conditions with both short and long barrels."

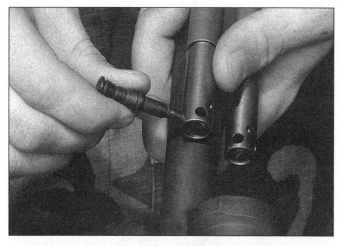

The bolt handle of the M-1014 shotgun is utilized in adjusting the new shotgun's dual gas systems.

Using the bolt handle and a cartridge rim, the Benelli shotgun can be field-stripped for cleaning or repair. Disassembly takes only a matter of seconds.

The ghost ring rear sight is adjustable for elevation by use of the slotted screw on the forward end. A similar screw positioned on the right side of the sight controls lateral adjustment.

The corporal did warn, however, that if low-power, "less-than-lethal ammo such as bean bags are used, ammunition must be cycled manually, using the bolt handle."

The shotgun's bolt handle is a doubly important item. It not only activates the gun, but also doubles as a tool needed to remove pins so the shotgun can be disassembled and reassembled. Three differing modular buttstocks also are available for the weapon. There is the telescoping stock, plus an optional, easily installed or removed pistol grip stock and a semi-pistol grip. The modular assembly group approach allows the shotgunner to exchange the barrel and buttstock without tools.

"I am a more or less recent convertee to the so-called ghost ring sights and found them excellent on the new military scattergun," Lewis reports. "According to Corporal Double, the ghost ring sights on this particular gun have been improved specifically for use in low-light situations.

"I learned also that rear sight protection strength has been increased by a special heat-treating process. This sight set-up is adjustable for windage and elevation without tools. Sight radius for the shotgun, measures 23.7 inches."

Back a few paragraphs we made mention of the receiver-mounted Picatinny rail that has become a feature with many military small arms these days. This rail allows the mounting of all sorts of sighting devices, including night-vision units and close combat optics. Double also pointed out that no matter which of these units might be mounted on the MIL STD 1913 rail, the iron sights still can be utilized.

The tubular magazine is fashioned from a heat-treated steel alloy. It can handle seven rounds of 2 3/4-inch ammo or six rounds of three-inch magnums. The adjacent barrel has two rings that are designed to provide the shotgun with better rigidity. As explained, the purpose of this rigging is to allow the barrel to offer the best possible ballistic performance.

In the action, Benelli's traditional locking system includes a milled mechanical guide for the rotating bolt head on the barrel extension. The shotgun also has a revised bolt cam designed for higher reliability in adverse conditions such as low temperatures, mud or whatever else nature can throw at us in combat.

The firing pin of the M-1014 has been redesigned from the original Benelli to be lighter. A new firing pin spring improves safety should the shotgun be dropped or handled roughly.

This shotgun is designed to be ambidextrous, and the safety button has been increased in size for better visibility and to allow the shooter to activate it while wearing gloves. This button, Lewis learned, can be reversed by an armorer to accommodate left-handers like himself. The shell release lever system allows release of a round in the tubular magazine onto the shell carrier during loading. It also is used to lock the bolt to the rear when the weapon is empty. Positioned for ambidextrous actuation by the shooter's non-shooting hand, the bolt release allows the bolt to travel forward during loading.

Among the things Lewis noted were the finishes on the gun's external parts. Benelli reports that steel parts are coated with a heavy phosphate, while aluminum parts are hard anodized. Such treatments, black

The front sight of the M-1014 is welded to the gun's barrel. The band surrounding the magazine tube and welded to the barrel is meant to improve accuracy with slugs.

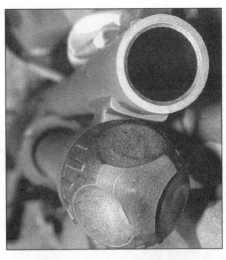

The barrel of the combat shotgun has been manufactured with a fixed modified choke to handle slugs and buckshot.

HECKLER & KOCH,INC.-STERLING,VA.-MAD

U.S

The enlarged safety button at the rear of the trigger is adequate for shooters wearing gloves. The shotgun is made by Benelli but marketed by Heckler & Koch.

12 GA. 3" – FOR 2 3/4" OR 3" SHELLS
READ OWNER'S MANUAL BEFORE USING GUN

The warning and shotshell designation stamped on the barrel of the combat shotgun are the same as those on the civilian-available M-4 Super 90 model.

in color, make the gun "durable, corrosion resistant and non-reflective," the manufacturer insists.

Someone obviously was thinking in terms of combat efficiency, in designing this Benelli offering. According to Double, average time to fieldstrip the weapon is 36 seconds; average time to clean and lube it is less than 10 minutes; and average time to load is 11.5 seconds. Probably most important of all is the fact that the shotgun has been designed to fire in excess of 10,000 rounds without requiring overhaul. Only time in a combat environment will determine the validity of that statement.

Lewis hoped for an opportunity to wring out the M-1014 at the 40- and 100-yard ranges. It didn't happen. Double was the only armorer on duty at the time and already was behind in his work. Lewis had to settle for the targets shot at 26 yards.

"The photos should offer an idea of how efficient this new shotgun can be!" Lewis declared later. "I wish I'd had one in Vietnam. A lot of other folks I know probably feel the same."

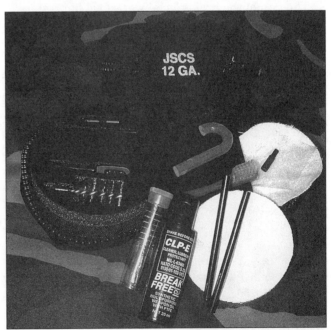

A compact cleaning kit is included with the shotgun. It can be carried in a pocket or in the pack. It has the materials needed for field cleaning and for checking the gun's bore.

CHAPTER 43

THE SEMI-AUTO SHOTGUN AND YOU!

Scatterguns Have Been Among Our Police and Military Armament for a Century and More, but There's a New Wrinkle

THE SHOTGUN HAS been a tool used by lawmen and soldiers since before the turn of the century. Back in the days when the West was truly wild, it was the short-barreled side-by-side with twin hammers and triggers that accompanied the guard's six-gun along most stagecoach routes. It was such a blaster that Doc Holliday carried at the O.K. Corral when he sided with Wyatt Earp in putting down the Clantons.

The gun of the professional waterfowl harvesters at the turn of the century, the Winchester Model 1897 slide-action, became a favored weapon for trench warfare during World War I.

What Campbell calls the sporting load is not acceptable for any type of law enforcement work.

Law enforcement and the military personnel have been happy with the slide action for more than 80 years. It has only been in recent years that they have considered upgrading their buckshot launchers to semi-automatics.

There is a reason for this. Even in the hunting fields, there were any number of early semi-automatic shotguns that failed to function for one reason or another. As a result, a lot of people just didn't trust them.

"I was talking about hunting leopards once with the late actor, Lee Marvin, back in the 1970s," Lewis recalls. "When it came to going after a wounded cat, he said he would never take a semi-auto. He wanted something over which he had control when it came to cranking a fresh round into the chamber."

This seemed to be the attitude of a lot of folks, including the law enforcement and military brass that make the decisions concerning ordering and paying for the armament.

"However, the attitude changed considerably almost 20 years ago, when the armed services began looking for a semi-auto that would stand up under combat conditions," says Robert Campbell, a veteran police officer. For the armed forces, led by the Marine Corps, the switch to the semi-auto became a reality with the official introduction of the Benelli-made M-1014 combat shotgun in late 2001.

Despite a great deal of interest in carbines and selective fire weapons, the shotgun remains the peace officer's friend," Campbell claims. Taking a longer look at history, he is quick to point out that "smooth-bore muskets stuffed with what were termed buck-and-ball loads often were used on the long-ago battlefields. These loads consisted of a large lead ball, usually ranging from .69 to .72 caliber in size, rammed down the barrel to lie ahead of several smaller buckshot balls.

Thumbing a shell into the magazine from the kneeling position presents no great problem.

The reloading techniques used by bird hunters and other sportsmen seldom are used in a combat situation.

"In time, other weapons were developed to fire large loads of shot. The blunderbuss was one such weapon. In European countries, this gun was carried as a coach gun, with the idea that it gave the shooter the chance to connect with the holdup man or other adversary from the coach seat, a bouncing, imperfect platform."

History shows that early shotguns tended to be heavy shooting tools that were difficult to manufacture. However, demand as always called for progress. In the early part of the 19th century, a gent named H. Allen introduced a shotgun that weighed only 5.75 pounds, although it carried two 30-inch barrels. There were others, including Sharps, a firm noted for big-bore rifles that produced a shotgun in 1853 that was considered the best-balanced scattergun of that early era. By the time the 1867 Remington was introduced, centerfire shot shells in brass cases had become popular even though expensive.

The Roper, introduced in 1866, was one of the first single-barrel repeating shotguns. The receiver was cast from brass to incorporate a hinged door that opened to a box magazine. The shells were fed from this magazine. In the same era came the Spencer slide-action scattergun. A single-barrel, it was outfitted with a second trigger that could be pulled to re-strike a shell that did not fire on the initial pull.

During the Great Depression, the 12-gauge Model 97 was still popular with law enforcement types. The Browning A-5 seems to have been favored by early Federal Bureau of Investigation agents who were after such infamous folk figures as John Dillinger, Baby Face Nelson, Pretty Boy Floyd and dozens of others who were making careers of bank robbery and kidnapping.

In more recent years, other slide-actions that have found favor with the military have been the Remington 870 and the Mossberg 500 series. In most instances, a vast number of police departments have followed the lead and adopted the same models. "There was plenty of discussion concerning the slide-action shotgun versus the semi-auto even before the interest of the military began to lean to the latter," Campbell recalls. "In fact, I am aware of at least one police agency that adopted the semi-automatic and quickly reversed itself and went back to the slide-action gun."

If one gets in too great a hurry in the reloading sequence, he may suddenly feel his fingers have turned to thumbs. It takes practice and time.

Campbell explains, "There are many reasons for favoring one or the other, but one thing seems to remain basic: While a clean, well-maintained semi-auto shotgun may be fully reliable, a dirty auto is a lot less dependable than a dirty pump gun!"

That does not mean there are no complaints from officers and trainers concerning the slide-action. There are. Campbell reports all too often police shotgun training is compressed into a much shorter time period than is desired. "As a result, some officers do not have a great deal of confidence in the shotgun and it is a tool that is under-utilized."

A majority of the nation's police departments – not to mention the military – has gone to semi-auto handguns in recent years. Based on this, several law enforcement firearms' trainers think that officers also should adopt semi-automatic shotguns. These trainers think that the difference in operation between the handgun and the pump-action scattergun can be confusing to an officer in a tense situation.

"Training officers still point to the death of a state trooper in Oklahoma in 1978, who short-cycled his shot-

Here Campbell uses the weak hand to drop a shell into the open chamber. This is not difficult with a modicum of practice.

gun under stress," Campbell reports. "These trainers rationalize that the trainee who has been trained with semi-auto handguns may well fire his pump shotgun in a tight situation, then forget to cycle it for the next shot.

"Some say that such a likelihood is the result of poor training, but there also have been situations where officers carrying handguns with no safety such as the SIG or the Glock have forgotten to flip off the safety on the shotgun in a tense situation."

There is little doubt that the human brain is probably the most important component involved in self-defense and any police action, but Campbell believes that the semi-auto shotgun has some definite advantages.

"I have to agree with most of the firearms trainers I know who insist that when the semi-auto is adopted, special tactics and skills have to be fine-tuned, maybe even reworked," he says.

An obvious advantage of the semi-auto shotgun is less recoil. Whether gas or recoil-operated, the gun's action soaks up a certain percentage of the backup against the shooter's shoulder. That means follow-up shots should be faster and more accurate.

"With a semi-auto, the double tap becomes a viable option," Campbell says. "Wyatt Earp was a believer in the shotgun and he always fired both barrels as insurance when involved in a deadly encounter. Of course, in those days, there was always the possibility of a dud round in one barrel. Though a mighty weapon, the shotgun can hardly be termed infallible even now."

For this book, Campbell took it upon himself to inspect several semi-auto shotguns with an eye to training officers using such firearms in teaching. He found the auto shotgun easier than the slide action to unload during administrative handling.

"There are other advantages as well," Campbell believes, adding, "Like most weapons systems, advanced training is needed to capitalize on these advantages. Under stress, fine motor skills tend to deteriorate. The auto-loader offers excellent continuity of fire during such critical incidents."

Campbell contends that one of the worst mistakes officers make with the pump gun is to perform what he calls "the Hollywood Shuck". This involves taking the shotgun from the shoulder, working the action, then returning it to the shoulder.

"No one's arms are too short to hold the slide-action on the shoulder when ejecting the spent shell and feed-ing a new round into the chamber. Actually, that shoulder offers enough resistance to help in working the action. Using the recoil of the fired pump gun as it rises, one can easily work the action quickly and vigorously. With a semi-auto gun, there is no such problem."

During his comparisons, Campbell conducted a reliability test of the auto shotgun. "I have fired the Beretta shotgun a great deal," he explained, "but wanted to confirm my belief that it would function as advertised and prove reliable with light loads. To add to my knowledge, I fired two boxes of Winchester's light trap loads carrying #7 1/2 shot. The Beretta emptied the three-round magazine – plus one in the chamber – without a problem until all 50 rounds were gone. There may be those who question my use of light loads, but I have found they are great for training officers who have little experience with shotguns."

Campbell recalls that a number of years ago, his grandfather, W.R. Williams, a top small game shooter with his Winchester Model 12, decided to trade it in on a Remington Model 1100 semi-auto.

"I attempted to show him that my Mossberg 500 was just as fast as his new Remington. I never did show him up, but we agreed that both were quite similar speedwise when it came to triggering off shots."

During his more recent investigations, however, Campbell matched the semi-auto Beretta 12 gauge against his personal High Standard pump gun; the latter was the veteran of long years in police work.

"Actual stopwatch and electrical-timer checks of the two guns showed that the guarded agreement between my grandfather and myself that both actions were pretty much the same when it came to rapidity of firing turned out to be somewhat out of order."

The time between two shots – what Campbell calls "the split" – was in the .5- to .7-second range for the Beretta. His timing tests showed that the pump gun was slower, averaging .7 to .9 seconds.

"For practical purposes, however, speed is virtually the same if one is going to take care to register good hits," he says. "The peace officer cannot be satisfied with the sportsman's few pellets that end up in a target. A law enforcement agent had better center his hits. In short, either system, using buck shot or slugs, should do the job in well-trained hands."

Campbell found the auto-loading shotgun easier to use when attempting to shoot from behind cover. Fir-

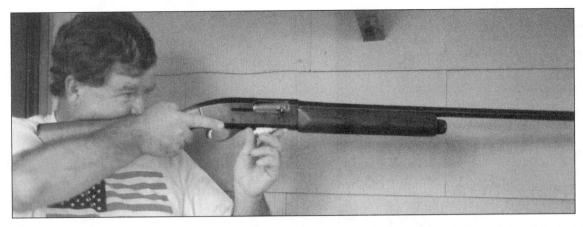

Campbell considers this one of the smoothest of all loading positions: Eyes on the target, the weak hand thumbs a round into the shotgun's magazine.

ing from beside a patrol car, from the prone or from an uncomfortable, off-balance position, he thinks the auto-loader has definite advantages.

Campbell says, "When using a shotgun in combat, reloading is rarely required, but it is a skill that should be practiced.

"The pump gun is topped off easily during a fire-fight by speedloading. One simply grasps the shot shell and uses the forefinger to shove the shell into the magazine tube.

"The Beretta, I found, is slightly more compli-cated. I had to depress the bolt release to free the carrier for reloading. However, with the Beretta, if the gun runs dry, the bolt locks to the rear. One knows the gun is empty."

In the system developed by many departments' manual of arms, after the bolt locks to the rear, one simply drops a shell into the chamber and presses the bolt release, keeping it under tension with the support hand, while reloading with the other.

"The hand position is simple," Campbell points out. "The firing hand is used to load the auto, while in the case of the slide-action, the weak hand is used to reload. These drills are suitable to one action type or the other and should be practiced extensively with the individual officer's duty shotgun."

Campbell fired a quantity of Quik-Shok slugs through the bead-sighted Beretta. With the same ammunition, his High Standard was sighted perfectly at 25 yards. The Beretta turned in what he considered good performance, the slugs cutting a ragged one-hole pattern at 10 yards, although 3-inches high.

"Using buck shot, 20 yards is about the maximum for adequate accuracy," he points out, "although hits out to 100 yards can be made with slugs."

While some officers favor tang safeties such as those on the Mossberg 500 line, Campbell thinks that the simple safety located just ahead of the Beretta's trigger guard is a fine option. He has used the Ber-etta extensively while wearing his recently issued Hatch gloves, which he says, "offer excellent protec-tion for the officer's hands, but do not impede manip-ulation with any firearm.

"The small bolt release of some shotguns can be difficult to manipulate with gloved hands especially

in cold climates," Campbell adds. "This has to be con-sidered not only when choosing a shotgun, but when training with it."

The standards of the National Institute of Justice call for handguns to be able to fire as many as 300 rounds between cleanings, according to Campbell. "The shotgun should be able to do that. In fact, I am aware of a number of shotguns in law enforcement service that have never been cleaned."

In his own experience, however, he has found that performance of the semi-automatic shotgun becomes increasingly sluggish before it begins to malfunction.

"If an officer is going to make his patrols with a semi-auto shotgun, it should be kept in a case. There is just too great a chance of contamination if the gun lies naked in the trunk of the cruiser." For his own purposes, Campbell has adopted the lockable Soft Safe made by W. Waller and Son, Inc., in Grantham, N.H.

"This case affords many advantages for the working officer," he states. "One plus is the fact that the case is heat resistant. It also is available in several colors. For myself, I chose the bright red number, since stud-ies show that color denotes danger to most people.

"The Waller folks spent many months working with the FBI in coming up with this product."

Campbell's conclusions include the fact that the semi-automatic shotgun seems to be increasing in popularity with major police departments as well as the military. "But there still are the small depart-ments with limited budgets," he notes. With the adoption of the pistol-caliber carbine by many agen-cies, the older shotguns are seldom slated for replace-ment, especially since the semi-auto models are considerably more expensive than the pump actions. After all, the Remington 870 complete with a police magnum action and rifle sights can be purchased for less than $300.

Campbell's chief belief is that models should not be mixed in a department. Duty shotguns should be all pump action or all semi-auto so that training and use involve only one set of operational sequences, not two that can offer the distraught officer mixed sig-nals in a firefight.

CHAPTER 44

FABARM'S TACTICAL 12-GAUGE

Here's Another Semi-Auto Shotgun Aimed at Making Rapid Fire Even More Rapid – and More Accurate

"I'LL NEVER CARRY my 11-87, again!" vowed Chad Fukui, a lieutenant with the island of Hawaii's Police Department, following an extensive shooting session in a field of unattended sugar cane. The gun involved was Fabarm's 12-gauge Tactical Model, which is marketed in the United States. by Heckler & Koch.

All it takes is a glance to recognize the fact that this shotgun probably was created as a result of the Pentagon's efforts to come up with a new 12-gauge semi-auto shotgun to replace the hodgepodge of slide-action guns that have been purchased for military use over the years.

This particular shotgun didn't make the Pentagon's cut. The contract was awarded to Benelli – another Italian company marketed on U.S. shores at this time by Heckler & Koch. However, there are sizeable markets these days for tactical shotguns other then the armed services. Law enforcement agencies across the nation are coming to realize that the armament used in the days of Al Capone doesn't meet today's needs. When the bad guys have better armament and ammunition than those defending the law, it's time to take a long, hard look.

In a number of missions designed to put a permanent crimp in the Polynesian drug scene, Fukui carried a submachine gun of his own design, which was built for him by a Maui gunsmith. On others jobs, he preferred a shotgun and carried the same familiar Remington Model 11-87 12 gauge for years.

"We thought we'd give you a chance to see how the other half lives," Lewis joked, as Fukui continued to fondle the black gun. Lewis, Fukui and Kaminski had just completed the cane field exercise and were impressed with the performance of the shotgun. But let's go back to the beginning.

Fabarm is an old Italian firearms company that has concentrated primarily on sporting shotguns with a complete line of semi-auto, slide-action and over/under models over the years. More recently it has become involved in the law enforcement market and the possibilities of interesting various military organizations – foreign and domestic – in its products.

The company has created several of what it calls Security Shotguns, all based upon the basic design of their FP-6 slide-action design. However, the Tactical model is the first Fabarm semi-automatic to be developed with the express purpose of using it against felons or terrorists.

The Fabarm Tactical is designed to function reliably with all standard 12-gauge shotshells without

Although a host of accessories are available for the Fabarm Tactical shotgun, the bare-bones gun carries a Picatinny rail for mounting scopes or other sighting devices and a flip-up front sight.

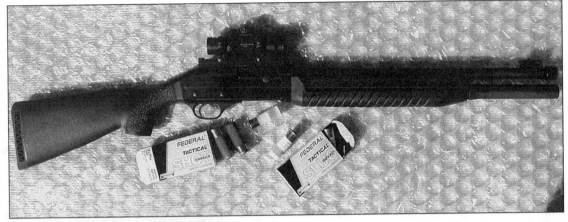

For the exercise described in the text, the Fabarm shotgun was outfitted with a Redfield red dot electronic sight. Slugs and buckshot fired were Federal Tactical loads.

The Redfield electronic sighting device was a plus in conducting the shooting exercise. It allowed the shooters to get on target rapidly.

adjustment be they the light 2 1/2-inch tactical loads or the most powerful 3-inch slugs and buckshot loads.

The gun uses the proven gas operating system that has been successful in the company's sporting models. Note is made that there are no action parts contained in the buttstock to change the center of gravity, when the shotgun is fired. According to Heckler & Koch spokesperson John Meyer, "This allows the Tactical Semi to stay balanced – and stay on target when firing." He added that the Tactical Semi accepts many of the same accessories as those manufactured for the FP-6 pump shotguns.

Other than the heavy-duty fitted case in which the gun was shipped from Virginia, there were no other accessories included, unless the included changeable cylinder choke is listed in that category. However, it was already mounted on the threaded outer barrel when it arrived.

The Tactical Semi features a Tribore, chrome-lined 20-inch barrel and a receiver made from something called Ergal 55 alloy. The free carrier allows a shell in the chamber to be replaced without emptying the whole magazine. A folding stock is available, but

the crew had settled for the fixed-stock version, which is cast from a tough grade of black polymer. The standard magazine carries five rounds of 3-inch shotshells. The gun came to us, however, with an optional magazine extension, which allowed eight rounds to be loaded.

Overall length of this tactical tool is 41.2 inches and weight – unloaded – scales at 6.6 pounds. Metal parts carry a non-glare matte finish. There is a flip-up front sight and a Picatinny rail for mounting scopes or other sighting devices. One of the options offered is a ghost ring rear sight. This is an item Lewis has come to favor and he regretted not asking Heckler & Koch's marketing arm to include one of those with the package. As it was, Kaminski installed the Redfield Electronic Sighting Device (ESD) listed as their Model 800624, which is marketed with rings for attachment to the accessories rail.

The ESD obtained from Redfield had a matte black finish to match that of the shotgun. Another ESD model, the 800624, is silver colored as are the rings to fit it. The shooter has a choice of four different reticle patterns, which include the centered red dot, red crosshairs, crosshairs with a circle in the center and a dot within a circle. Lewis and company had chosen the simple red dot configuration.

The shooter can dial in dot sizes of 4, 8, 12 and 16 MOA. Overall length of the Redfield EDS is 5.5 inches and weight is 6.5 ounces. The device works equally well on shotguns, rifles and handguns.

Lewis has made a recent study of such long-ago experts as Sykes and Fairburn, who contended that lots of small bullets could be more effective on a villain than perhaps one large bullet.

Following the lead of the military, law enforcement seems to have adopted the .223/5.56mm cartridge and the armament that goes with it. When this round was first used in Vietnam, troops complained that the bullet often failed to penetrate heavy brush, coming apart if even hitting a small twig. Efforts have been made to solve this problem, but this brings us back to the fact that most military and law enforcement rifles carry magazines that hold no more than 30 rounds.

"The combat shotgun with an extended magazine has some definite advantages, when it comes to pay-

When not in use, the rugged front sight lies flat against the top of the barrel of the Fabarm shotgun.

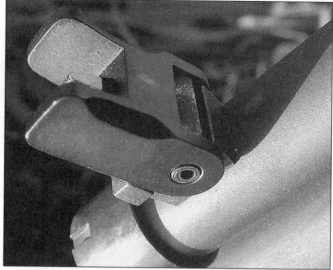

The efficient design of the flip-up front sight has heavy protective ears on each side so that the sight itself is not likely to be damaged.

load," Lewis insists. "If loaded with a combination of buckshot and slugs, the tactical shotgun can induce a lot of bleeding at short ranges."

The sugar industry on the island of Hawaii died a lingering death some two decades ago, but uncultivated fields of sugar cane covering broad expanses of acreage still dot the island and make good test sites.

Used in this particular test was a combination of two Federal products. One was the ammo maker's tactical rifled slug, which is 2 3/4 inches in length and carries a high-power 1-ounce Hydra-Shok slug. This slug features helical ribbing for smoothbore shotguns and carries a hollow-point. This missile has a muzzle velocity of some 1600 fps. At 25 yards, the longest range at which they would be shooting, muzzle energy is something over 2500 foot-pounds.

The other round utilized for this particular experiment was Federal's tactical buckshot in #4 size with 27 pellets to each round. Length of this shell also is 2 3/4 inches and diameter of each of the pellets was .24-inch. Muzzle velocity out of a 30-inch barrel has been measured in the neighborhood of 1300 fps.

Lewis and Kaminski both had fired the shotgun after the former had zeroed it at 25 yards for slug use. Fukui was not allowed at the test sight until after Lewis and Kaminski had hidden a bad-guy target in the sugar cane growth at 25 yards.

Once ready, Fukui was ordered to load a buckshot-filled round, followed by a slug, then another buckshot load and another slug in that order. The last of the five rounds was another buckshot load.

Fukui then was stationed at the 25-yard mark, told to find the target hidden in the cane and turn loose on it. Using the Redfield red dot sight, he soon found evidence of the hidden target and began to fire from the offhand position. All five rounds were expended in approximately 6 seconds.

The next part of the exercise was on the same type of target, which was hidden among the cane stalks at 15 yards. The same combination of shells was used:

The Federal 1-ounce slugs fired at 15 yards cut clean holes in the head of the paper villain. Note the tear in the lower right-hand corner, where the plastic wad from the shell made its own entry.

two slugs and three alternating buckshot rounds. Fukui raised the flip-up front sight, saying he would align it with the red dot in the Redfield USD. He then squeezed off the five rounds in almost exactly the same time he had used on his initial string.

The third round of shooting was at 10 yards, where it was possible to see more of the target than in the earlier sequences. The magazine was loaded

On the target fired on at 10 yards, one slug went through the nose, the other through the eye. Above the eye is a tear showing where the round's plastic wad passed through. Note the numerous buckshot penetrations.

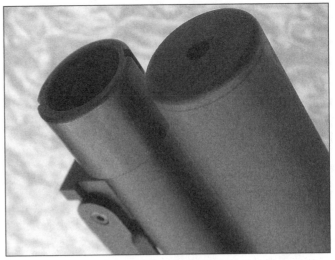

The cylinder choke, which is installed on the Tactical shotgun, is an exterior screw-on type that fits threads cut in the gun's barrel.

The cocking handle attached to the gun's bolt is heavy-duty and ergonomically designed for fast action.

with the same recipe as the earlier two strings and Fukui did his usual workmanlike job on the target.

In going into the sugar cane growth to remove the targets, it became obvious that at each of the three ranges, the #4 buckshot had pierced the cane stalks to continue on their way. The stalks were inspected closely, some of them virtually shot in two, but there was no evidence of the syrup-heavy cane stopping passage of the shot.

One by one, the now heavily punctured targets were removed, marked with the date and the range, then rolled up and taped for later inspection and conclusions.

As this exercise was concluded, Fukui picked up the Fabarm Tactical shotgun from the tailgate of Lewis' truck, hefted it to his shoulder and eyed the battered sugar cane growth through the sighting device. That's when he decided to "never carry my 11-87, again," adding, "I gotta have one of these!"

That night, with the targets spread out on the floor of his office, Lewis counted shot holes in each of them. He believes his findings are interesting, but is quick to admit he considers them non-conclusive.

On the target hidden at 25 yards, the three buck-shot-loaded shells dispensed a total of 81 pellets, but there were only 25 holes in the target. On the printed figure, 11 of the pellets had left ragged keyholing perforations. Two of them were in the left arm and the others were on the target, but had not scored on the subject. None of the holes were beneath the subject's waist. On the same target, one of the 1-ounce slugs missed the subject, cutting a hole through the

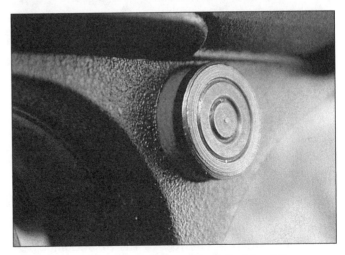

A quick glance at the safety on the left side of the gun just behind the trigger should be enough to tell the condition of the piece. When the red band shows, the gun is read to fire.

The forward sling swivel installed on the shotgun is functional and is positioned at the forward end of the stock.

The sling for the shotgun runs through this inset in the gun's pistol grip.

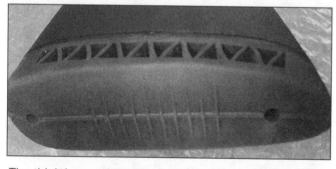

The thick buttpad on the rear of the stock is part of the reason that the Fabarm Tactical shotgun offers relatively light recoil even with slugs.

target a quarter-inch from his right ear. The other slug, which Fukui later said he thought was fired first, was in the subject's hairline and probably would have been fatal. Seven of the 25 buckshot pellets were in the subject's head area.

At the 15-yard distance, the same number and combination of shells were fired. Of the 81 buckshot pellets contained in the three rounds, 33 were in the target's torso area, with 9 pellets on the paper but not in the target area. Both slugs resulted in headshots

The loading gate must be pushed to the rear before more rounds can be loaded in the magazine.

The foregrip of the shotgun is ridged so that a firm grip can be achieved without the use of checkering.

and the plastic that followed the slug apparently got as far as the target, cutting its own ragged hole.

At the 10-yard marker, there were 54 pellets in the target's torso area, with 11 of them below the subject's belt. Only three rounds punctured the paper surrounding the target area. One slug went through the target's eye and the other hit what would have been on the bridge of the felon's nose. Both of these holes were ragged in shape, testifying to the fact that the plastic wads must still have been attached to the slugs when the target was hit.

When the counting had been done, Lewis called Fukui and asked, "Where were you aiming with your shots?"

"At where I thought the target's head should be," was Fukui's answer.

"That's where you aimed with the buckshot, too?"

"Yep. All of the rounds, except on the last target. On that one, I aimed for the body. Why the question?" the lawman wanted to know.

"It's not important, but we're missing a lot of lead. By aiming at the head with the buckshot, a lot of the pellets must simply have sailed over the top of the target."

There was a moment of silence before Fukui muttered, "That's something to remember."

As indicated, this exercise in cane blasting can hardly be considered scientific, but it may supply enough information to show that the Fabarm Tactical Model would make a worthy addition to any police armory.

CHAPTER 45

RUSSIA'S TACTICAL SHOTGUN

The Saiga-12 Is Based on Kalashnikov's Venerable AK-47 Rifle Design, Using the Same Simple Gas System

"WHEN I OPENED the box carrying the Saiga-12, I thought at first glance I was looking at a heavy-barreled AK-47 assault rifle," admits Lewis. "Actually, the piece was – and is – a 12-gauge shotgun, but it became obvious that much of Kalashnikov's design thinking had gone into development of this one, too."

A little research reveals that what European American Arms markets in the United States as the Saiga-12 originally was designed as what probably was the world's first accepted semi-auto combat shotgun.

Unlike the United States and most other countries, the Russians never have made any attempt to rework an acknowledged sporting scattergun into an assault tool. Instead, of thinking in terms of pump-action guns descended from the Winchester Model 97 – the original World War I trench gun – the Russians had decided on a semi-automatic designed specifically for assault missions. Originally, what now is marketed as the Saiga shotgun was issued to Russian troops chambered for the .410 round. Thus far, no one has come up with understandable reasons for the decision to issue

so diminutive a bore for combat use. More recently, the gun has been produced in 20 and 12 gauges as well. Among other things, it utilizes the same gas system as the AK-47 rifle.

The Saiga-12 is marketed in the standard fixed-stock version, which we tested for this book, as well as in a folding-stock variation that is listed as the Saiga-12 S.

The importer, European American Arms Corp., headquartered in Sharpe, Fla., offers a choice of guns with changeable chokes. However, the gun Lewis received carried no barrel threads for such choke variations. It was bored with a cylinder choke and obviously was meant to handle buckshot and slugs as its primary diet.

Since our test staff was suffering from an acute shortage of enemy troops to assault, it was decided to look at the Saiga-12 in the role of a police tactical shotgun. One of the more important law enforcement uses of a shotgun has to do with removing locks or hinges from doors when attempting to serve arrest warrants on those who don't really want to be served. With this in mind, Lewis rounded up the front door

The 12-gauge Saiga-12, imported from Russia by European American Arms, was tested with Federal 1-ounce Tactical slugs shown with the same manufacturer's Tactical No. 4 buckshot. The test crew considered the shotgun short on bells and whistles but a tool that is capable of doing its job once the shooter learns its workings.

Left: Ace Kaminski, a member of the test team, is ready to fire Federal Tactical slugs at the redwood front door that has been staked in place with rebar. His target is the lock on the door at 15 yards.

Right: Kaminski's shot hit the lock on the door, the 1-ounce slug passing through two inches of seasoned redwood to exit on the door's backside. Note the dent in the door knob caused by the passing slug.

Joshua Wills. As a law enforcement officer for the State of Hawaii, Kaminski has been involved in a number of armed-entry door-opening escapades. He pointed out that most times the use of a shotgun on either the lock or the hinges of a door is a rather close-range operation. The shooters decided to fire on the lock and the doorknob of the well-seasoned redwood door from a range of approximately 15 yards.

Kaminski used lengths of iron reinforcing rod to hold the door in position. The rods then were pounded into the rocky soil and stapled to the sides of the door. Lewis shook the door and questioned whether the rods would be sufficient to keep a 1-ounce slug traveling at more than 1000 fps from knocking down the door. Kaminski promised there would be no problem.

The shooters wanted some idea of where the slug would print before the test so they erected a paper target and Kaminski fired five rounds of Federal Tactical 12-gauge slugs on the figure of a bad guy. At 15 yards, the five holes formed a pattern that measured roughly five inches center to center, but they were roughly a foot to the right of and four inches below where the shooter had been aiming.

There is no firm evidence that Kalashnikov had much to do with the sights. The rear is a fixed-notch type, but included with the gun at the time of delivery was a drift tool. With this tool and a hammer from Kaminski's ever-present toolbox, he was able to move the rear sight on a tap-and-shoot basis until he was able to punch holes in the center of the target. The front sight is a simple, almost crude post that seems to have no easy means of adjustment.

"Had the gun belonged to me, I would have given serious thought to filing down the front sight to raise the point of impact on the target," Lewis says, adding, "but manufacturers take a dim view of amateur gunsmithing on the products they are attempting to sell.

"One also has to take into account the fact that people hold their heads differently on the stock of a gun,

from an old house that was being demolished and had it hauled out into the hills not far from where he lives.

Gathered to experiment with the shotgun were Kaminski, Lewis and the Lewis' 14-year-old grandson,

Left and Right: Jack Lewis tried his hand with the shotgun, firing a round of Federal Tactical No. 4 buckshot, then five rounds of PMC's Brenneke-designed 1-ounce slugs. All of his shots were high and to the right, but the slugs grouped well enough to create a single large hole in the wood.

A search in the vicinity of the shot-up door produced the metal door handle, which had been blown apart by the slug. A close look indicates that the misshapen slug is stuck in the remains of the handle.

It was necessary to use a drift tool to move the rear sight, which originally caused shots to print to the right on the target.

The front sight of the gun is fixed and appears not to be adjustable. Jack Lewis says he would opt for replacing existing sights with a ghost ring sight system or installing a scope. Scope mounts are available from the importer.

The barrel of the Russian-made gun carries a cylinder choke, which worked well with the slugs from both PMC and Federal. The same model also is available from the Florida importer with changeable chokes.

thus getting varying sight pictures. I've found the same true for scopes. What is zeroed for one shooter may not be zeroed the same for myself or others."

There is a scope mount available as an accessory, but the importer had not included one with the gun, so the testers were limited to use of the attached iron sights.

Kaminski was first up and managed to put his first round through the square lock mechanism, but missed the lock entirely with the next two rounds, driving the slugs through the two-inch thick doorframe.

Lewis had brought along a single five-pack of PMC ammo loaded with 1-ounce slugs designed by Brenneke. The information on the box claimed they have a velocity of some 1600 fps. He loaded all five rounds into the Saiga's magazine, snapped it into the magazine well and stepped up to the firing line.

In a clocked five seconds, all five rounds were fired off-hand at the brass-plated doorknob that still was intact. None of the slugs hit the knob or even the lock, but the group made by the five rounds was something to brag about. The five Brenneke slugs had taken a hole out of the door panel that measured about three-inches wide and four-inches high.

"If we were simply firing for group damage, I'd be proud of that," Lewis says.

The magazine was reloaded with five rounds of the 1-ounce Federal Tactical slug load, then 14-year-old Joshua Wills, an experienced deer hunter, was handed the gun. He confidently stepped up to the 15-yard marker, which was nothing more than a line drawn in the lava ash with the toe of a boot. The safety lever on the left side of the gun is large and positive. The teenager had no problem flipping the lever down to put the gun into firing mode.

This young deadeye hit the doorknob with his first shot, then put the second shot into almost the same hole that had been created by Kaminski's early shot through the lock mechanism. His third round went into the redwood frame below the lock.

"I think Kaminski and I both were jealous," Lewis said later. "The kid knows how to shoot, but the fact that he wasn't worried about the sights and the other things Ace and I had been considering might have had something to do with his shots. He was concentrating on the target, not what might be wrong with the firearm."

Lewis found the balance of the Saiga-12 beyond reproach and the fact that it weighed only 6-1/2 pounds made for easy swinging, if that became necessary. Each of the three chamberings of the Saiga model is available with barrel lengths of 19, 21 or 22 inches. The shotgun we had drawn for this test was the 19-incher. With a barrel of that length, overall measurement of the shotgun is 40 inches. The metal parts of the gun are a muted black that tends not to reflect light.

The stock and forend are cast from a tough polymer material also in the traditional black. Both the forend and the pistol grip have cast-in checkering that is comfortable to grip, yet offers good holding qualities.

The Russian proofmarks on the receiver of the Saiga-12 are clearly evident. The shotgun is based upon the design of the AK-47 assault rifle. This particular shotgun design was issued originally to Russian troops in .410 bore.

The plastic magazine for the Saiga-12 holds five rounds of Federal Tactical rifled slugs. The gun also is available from the importer with an eight-round magazine.

The trigger guard of the Saiga-12 appears to be a piece of strap iron that has been bent in a jig, then screwed to the gun's action. However, it is large enough to allow one to reach the trigger when wearing thick gloves.

The gun is available with either a five- or eight-round polymer magazine to handle 2-3/4-inch shells. The magazine the testers drew with the gun was the five-rounder. No one liked it at first because the plastic lug on the front of the unit must be matched to another lug in the gun's magazine well. The first few tries for all three of the shooters left a bit to be desired as far as speed was concerned. Eventually, with a bit of practice, each member of the test crew was able to tilt the magazine in to make the proper match and snap it into the locked position without trouble.

The trigger is positive and reacts nicely in spite of the fact that the trigger guard appears to be nothing more than a length of strap iron that has been bent to proper proportions in a jig, then screwed to the receiver. A plus is the fact that the guard is large enough that the shooter could get a gloved finger to the trigger with no particular trouble.

The gun incorporates a bolt block safety. When the safety lever is in the full up position, any movement of the bolt is blocked, the bolt is covered and trigger movement is blocked at the same time. When the bulky safety lever is shoved to the down position, the bolt is fully exposed and free to move. The gun will fire when the trigger is pulled. The bolt's cocking handle extends from the right side of the receiver and is long enough so that drawing the bolt to the

rear should be no problem even if the shooter is wearing heavy gloves.

According to the manufacturer, some of the Saiga-12 guns are available with a hold-open feature for the bolt, but this was not the case with the gun tested. It's one of those refinements most of us have come to expect and all three shooters thought it would have been a plus for this particular firearm.

The Saiga gas system is one that can be set for either magnum or lesser loads. To make the change, one must press down on the gas nut's locking detent. This is located at the forward end of the gas piston assembly and is positioned just beneath the gun's front sight. To choose the proper gas force, one must rotate the gun nut clockwise until it no longer moves, keeping the detent depressed at the same time. One then must rotate the gas nut in a counter-clockwise direction until stopping at either the marked Position 1 or the similarly labeled Position 2. Position 1 is designed for light loads, while Position 2 is meant for heavy loads such as buckshot or slugs of the type we had been shooting.

The receiver and action of the Saiga-12 are fashioned from some type of ordnance steel, but the safety lever, the upper receiver dust cover and the gas tube are stampings of lighter metals. The upper receiver cover is held in place by a release latch, with a detent that must be depressed before the dust cover can be removed for further disassembly of the shotgun.

Lewis learned following the field test that the scope mount for the Saiga-12 is available from the importer as an accessory. Were he going to use the shotgun in a combat environment, he would either replace the existing sights with a ghost ring setup or install a scope.

"Most of us tend to get caught up in our enthusiasms for the bells and whistles that go with a lot of modern-day firearms, both military and civilian," Lewis concludes. "However, we have to keep in mind that the AK-47 from which this shotgun is derived was designed – and used – as a relatively uninvolved killing machine. It is simple in design, easy and cheap to produce and deadly effective in combat. The same probably can be said for the Saiga-12 shotgun."

CHAPTER 46

COMBAT AMMUNITION TODAY

Coming up with the Most Effective Load Has Become a Continuing Race Between the Good Guys and the Bad

"**KEEPING UP WITH** developments in present-day ammunition is a daunting task. There are conflicting claims of performance beyond the realm of anything available in the past – and some of the claims do in fact appear to be true," reports Campbell.

For this chapter, however, all we have to present are the facts. Campbell, an experienced police officer and ballistician, has fired the ammunition discussed here in no small quantity.

"While ballistic testing in materials designed to mock flesh – dare we say it, the human body? – was undertaken, I have no illusions concerning effectiveness," Campbell says. "Perhaps a cartridge will work as designed. Ballistic gelatin provides only a rough estimate of the capabilities of a cartridge/bullet design despite the faith put in it by the uninitiated.

"I have done a lot of reading and found the writings of Dr. Martin Fackler, Gene Wolberg and Vincent DiMiao compelling. They present science, not hyperbole and offer little in the way of magic bullets. Some handgun cartridges, of course, are more effective than others, but compared to a long gun, the weak .38 and strong .45 tend to be more alike than they differ."

Campbell conducted a series of simple tests of the ammunition mentioned in this review. He chose individual samples and soaked them in water, oil and solvent, respectively, for two days. Those that did not fire after this initiation were examined no further.

Modern service ammunition offers better performance and reliability than anything previously available.

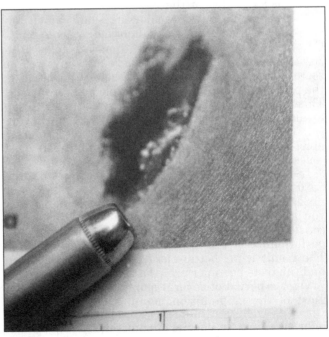

Wound ballistics is an exact science with predictable conclusions, Bob Campbell contends.

Among the older cartridges are the Winchester 125-grain JHP (left) and the same maker's 158-grain LHP.

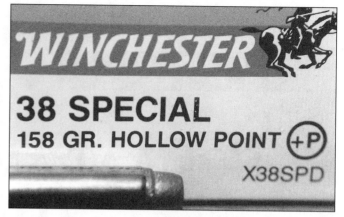

A highly developed service cartridge, Winchester produced this one in +P .38 Special for the Federal Bureau of Investigation.

Texas Ammunition Co.'s products include the .45 Super. Note the mushrooming of the Hornady XTP bullet, which is loaded by this company.

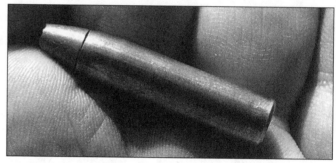

The .45 Super Tactical load by Texas Ammunition carries a 185-grain JHP-XTP bullet for its deadly performance.

He also chambered chosen samples in auto pistols, cycling each cartridge a dozen times. If the bullet bumped into the chamber butting the feed ramp, the load was not tested further.

"Numerous so-called wonder loads and much foreign-produced ammunition will not meet this testing," Campbell says. "Reliable ammunition with good integrity is needed for service use. These tests involved no secret sources; no shadowy figures were involved in the program. My results are verifiable and repeatable. This makes them less exciting than some reports now available, but they are factual. Take your own counsel. The ammunitions that passed our test are reliable, accurate and show a full powder burn in most cases. This means little muzzle flash.

"Some of the loads generate more recoil than standard calibers, and one should consider his or her needs in this regard. If you need a .45 Super pistol, you know who you are. After the tests, I carefully considered my results. The reliability, accuracy and performance of the cartridges were uniformly good. The result is far better than I would have expected had the tests been performed a generation ago."

Over a period of several months, Campbell tested most of the ammunition manufactured for general issue, as well as a number of specialty rounds that offer an option for special circumstances. Any special procedure needed to make the most of these loads was carefully logged.

Service Ammo in the New Century

"Choosing ammunition for the service handgun is a difficult task," Campbell points out. "Today we have a bewildering choice of loads for five service calibers: the 9mm Luger, the .40 Smith & Wesson, the .357 SIG, the .45 ACP and the 10mm. The .38 Special and .357 Magnum are far from being dead, but these days neither is seen with any great frequency in law enforcement situations.

"Some law enforcement instructors feel the most important attribute is the ability to control a handgun, so they will vote for the 9mm Luger. Those who favor penetration against vehicles choose the .357 SIG. The FBI has conducted the majority of research concerning handgun ballistics over the past few years. Thus, the FBI has isolated the main components of bullet-wounding ability. While there are those who argue with the FBI program, this agency has facts and science to support its findings.

"One arms writer insists that the FBI has placed too much reliance on penetration. With 11 of the last 13 police shootings in my data basis involving felons behind vehicles, it would appear the FBI approach is correct."

The FBI's recognized wound mechanisms for handgun ammunition are:

1. Penetration: If the bullet does not reach a vital organ, it is useless.

HANDGUN TEST RESULTS

(F stands for Fragmented)

CALIBER	LOAD	VELOCITY	PENETRATION (in inches)	EXPANSION (in inches)
.380 ACP	96 gr. Winchester SXT	889 fps	9	.55
.380 ACP	88 gr. Silvertip	934 fps	6	.60
.38 Special	158 gr. WW LSWCHP	768 fps	13	.52
.38 Special	110 gr. Silvertip	807 fps	6	.52
.357 Mag	125 gr. WW JHP	1423 fps	12.5	.60
.357 Magnum	WW 145 gr. Silvertip	1340 fps	14	.78
.357 SIG	Federal 125 gr. JHP	1352 fps	14	.68
.357 SIG	Cor Bon 115 gr. JHP	1515 fps	9	.56F
9mm Luger	100 grain Hirtenberger	1393 fps	24+	.355
9mm Luger	Federal 115 gr. JHP	1156 fps	9.5	.68
9mm Luger	WW 115 gr. +P+	1307 fps	7	.75
.40 S&W	Federal 155 gr. Hydra-Shok	1150 fps	13.5	.66
.40 S&W	Federal 180 gr. Hydra-Shok	978 fps	15	.75
.45 ACP	Remington 185 gr. +P	1139 fps	11	.56F
.45 ACP	Hornady 200 gr. XTP +P	1044 fps	15.9	.67
.45 ACP	Black Hills 230 gr. JHP	899 fps	14.5	.70
.45 ACP	Federal 230 gr. Hydra-Shok	866 fps	12.5	.76

Veteran police officer Robert K. Campbell unloaded on this target with a variety of ordnance, including MK slugs, which performed well.

2. Permanent cavity: The bullet must do damage as it travels through tissue.

3. Temporary cavity: This is the shock wave created by a bullet passing through tissue.

4. Fragmentation: Bullet fragments can produce complex wounds.

Penetration is needed to carry the bullet through light cover and even heavy clothing. If a handgun projectile shows less than 10 inches of penetration in the ballistic gelatin test, its chances of performing well in a variety of situations are slim.

Campbell used the standard gelatin mix and a Competition Electronics Chronograph during his testing. He insists that any interested individual can repeat his tests. He also states he expects their results to be much the same as his own.

Campbell used seven different handguns in making his determinations. They were:
Walther PPK .380 ACP,
Smith & Wesson M-60 .38 Special,
Smith & Wesson Model 19 .357 Magnum,
CZ 75 9mm,
Glock 22 with a Bar Sto .357 SIG barrel,
SIG P229 .40 S&W,
a rather ancient High Standard 1911 chambered for the .45 ACP.

Texas Ammunition

"Among the ammunition I have been most impressed with in testing is some from Texas. As many of us remember, the late Tom Ferguson teamed with reloading guru Dean Grennell, was instrumental in the development of the original .45 Super cartridge. I cannot tell you the esteem in which I held that man," says Campbell.

Today, Texas Ammunition, operating out of Ballinger in the Lone Star State, produces some of the best .45 Super ammunition on the market, although the developers of the .45 Super have licensed a few other firms to market this load. However, the company also has recognized a need for more powerful ammunition for standard .45 autos. The .45 Super brass is thicker in the head than standard .45 ACP brass, but remains the same in length – .900 inch. Texas Ammunition produces a Tactical loading which moves the Hornady XTP bullet out at tremendous velocity. Campbell has fired several hundred rounds with what he terms "good results."

A 22-pound WC Wolff recoil spring is recommended. He also added a Hartts recoil reducer to his personal High Standard .45. Campbell says, "These

HANDGUN	LOAD	VELOCITY	GROUPING
High Standard 1911	TA 185 gr.	1210 fps	2.0 inches
Glock 21	TA 185 gr.	1222 fps	2.9 inches
Springfield 1911A1	TA 185 gr.	1187 fps	3.0 inches
SIG P 220	TA 185 gr.	1156 fps	3.2 inches
High Standard 1911	TA 200 gr.	1071 fps	1.5 inches
Springfield 1911A1	TA 200 gr.	1089 fps	2.6 inches
High Standard 1911	TA 230 gr.	945 fps	2.25 inches
Glock 21	TA 230 gr.	999 fps	2.6 inches
Wilson Combat CQB	TA 230 gr.	976 fps	2.0 inches

Tactical loads performed well in a Glock 21. However, the SIG P220 is just too light. In my tests, the SIG's high bore axis allowed too much slide velocity, outstripping the ability of the magazine to feed. In a quality 1911, these loads are dynamite. Loads in 9mm and .40 S&W also are offered, but the .45s are representative of Texas Ammunition at its best."

For accuracy, Campbell tested the Texas Ammunition in three bullet weights at a range of 25 yards. Above are his findings:

Tungsten Powder Bullets

The use of projectiles fashioned from tungsten powder is among the more interesting approaches in law enforcement efforts. For this report, Campbell admittedly borrowed heavily from the skills and knowledge of the staff of Northwest Custom Projectile of Moorhead, Minn., makers of these bullets. "And rightly so," Campbell admits, "They are the experts. I am knowledgeable, but only the reporter in this instance."

According to the NWCP staff, the advantages of these bullets are many, including the following: These bullets can be used where a lead-free environment is specified. They also can be utilized with a heavier than normal bullet weight with conventional rifling. This means they can be used as subsonic loads for silenced weapons. The maker's standard bullets can be used in a shorter, more dense package for better powder efficiency. The company's claim is that with more freedom in moving the center of balance of the bullet, accuracy can be improved, as well as delivering "high energy to a target and enhancing penetration."

Campbell found, "Tungsten is dense and it is a truly tough metal, but in powdered form, it can be fabricated into a shape useful as a firearms projectile. For a given volume, tungsten is almost twice as heavy as lead. A bullet with the same shape and bearing surface will weigh approximately 1.7 times as much as a lead core bullet. Northwest Custom Projectile's .30 caliber tungsten core bullet weighs 250 grains, but carries the same length and appearance of a 168-grain .30 caliber bullet. The long bearing surface is the same.

"Research has shown these heavy bullets can be stabilized in standard rifle barrels. Special rifling or a different rate of spin is not needed. One of the more interesting Norwest Custom Projectile offerings is a 250-grain .308 diameter bullet with a 40-grain soft lead tip. This bullet is a subsonic varmint load with explosive action in the nose. The powdered core breaks up quickly on contact with hard resistance, making for safety in densely populated areas."

Northwest Custom Projectile also offers more or less conventional bullets that give excellent accuracy in Campbell's personal rifles. Their rifle ammo has the appearance of .308-diameter jacketed expanding bullets, but the custom quality of manufacture shows. Below are some of the combinations Campbell tried and the results he got. All were five-shot groups fired at 100 yards.

BULLET	POWDER	VELOCITY	GROUPING
NWCP 150 gr.	47 grs. AA2495	2776 fps	1.0
NWCP 165 gr.	39 grs. AA2015	2298 fps	1.6
NWCP 165 gr.	43 grs. AA2520	2402 fps	1.0
NWCP 165 gr.	47 grs. AA2520	2607 fps	1

Hornady's Urban Legend

With the issue of more and more 5.56mm carbines to law enforcement personnel across the United States, it became obvious that a new type of ammunition was needed. Military ball ammunition was not acceptable and neither was the thinly jacketed soft-point ammunition designed for varmint shooting. What was needed was a bullet that expanded on striking a body. Such a bullet should break up readily when hitting solid resistance in order to limit danger to the public, yet is should offer acceptable light-cover penetration.

"That was a tall order, but one which the Hornady TAP has met," according to Campbell. "It is a police round that is designed to perform well under varying circumstances."

Campbell has been able to test the Hornady ammunition extensively and likes what it does. "My only concern," he says, "is that the 75-grain projectile is a little slow for the caliber, but I found that it performs acceptably in ballistic gelatin testing.

"I was recently able to do a fresh test with the newest production TAP ammunition in two AR-15-type rifles. Accuracy was sterling. In firing more than 500 rounds, there were no failures to feed, chamber, fire or eject. When firing, it was obvious the ammunition was treated for a low flash, a big plus for police work."

Campbell fired this ammunition at 50 yards, a greater distance than that at which 99 percent of police gun battles take place. All groups were of five rounds. The Colt HBAR rifle used carried a 20-inch barrel. The Bushmaster also fired in testing had a barrel length of 16 inches.

LOAD	VELOCITY	FIREARM	GROUPING
55 gr. TAP	3077 fps	HBAR	1.0
55 gr. TAP	2959 fps	Bushmaster	1.9
60 gr. TAP	3055 fps	HBAR	1.25
60 gr. TAP	2933 fps	Bushmaster	1.8
75 gr. TAP	2655 fps	HBAR	.76
75 gr. TAP	2599 fps	Bushmaster	1.5

TAP ammunition is also offered in 9mm, .40 Smith & Wesson and .45 ACP calibers. "In pistol calibers, I found TAP performed with excellent accuracy and was on the long end of the penetration scale," Campbell reports. "With the growing trend toward controlled penetration, these rounds should prove popular for law enforcement needs."

Powermax

Powermax ammunition is offered by Aeagle Ammunition, a company headquartered in Salem, Ore. According to Campbell, "This company is not noted for ammunition on the weak side. The company goal is to give officers and qualified civilians the most powerful ammunition possible for a given caliber."

The .25 ACP, .32 ACP, .380 ACP, 9mm Luger, .45 ACP, .40 Smith and Wesson and various revolver cartridges are included in the product lineup. For purposes of this review, Campbell selected the heaviest 9mm Luger loading and tested it in three handguns. The average velocity was 1383 fps, although one handgun recorded 1401 fps. Penetration of 14 inches in ballistic gelatin and impressive expansion to .83 caliber – a solid inch in one case – was recorded.

"If I were carrying a 9mm handgun, this would be my first choice. Believe it!" Campbell says.

In conducting tests of the ammunition produced by the Oregon organization, Campbell selected the Beretta Elite 92, the CZ 75 and the SIG 226. All were five-shot groups fired at 25 yards. Here are his findings:

HANDGUN	VELOCITY	GROUPING
Beretta Elite 92	1390 fps	2.2
CZ 75	1401 fps	1.9
SIG P 226	1365 fps	2.0

MK Ballistics

The shotgun is perhaps the most versatile weapons system in existence and those going into armed combat must be aware that this is what it is: A weapons system.

"Slugs are fine," Campbell thinks, "but one must remember that they are derived from 18th century technology. MK Ballistics, located in Hollister, Calif., offers a special slug, their QB, which is manufactured from an exceedingly dense material.

"Slug penetration is normally far inferior to that of the .30 caliber rifle, a fact that is surprising to many

MK Ballistic Systems' marking load can be used to mark fleeing vehicles for quick identification.

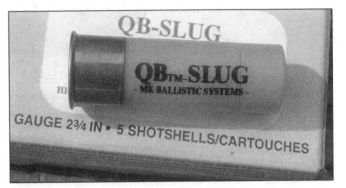

The MK Ballistics QB Slug load is designed to take out vehicles or knock the hinges off of heavy doors before entry.

MK Ballistic Systems also manufactures a shot shell loaded with rubber buckshot for use in situations where less lethal weaponry is required.

investigators,"Campbell notes. "The QB slug, however, offers rifle-type penetration from a shotgun. It is accurate for normal duty to 50 yards, and burns clean."

MK also offers various sizes of rubber buckshot and other non-lethal loadings, as well as a special door buster that takes the hinges off a door without penetrating the door itself.

Campbell adds, "My favorite from MK is their paint marker. It is offered in various colors, presumably for marking get-away vehicles. MK is perhaps the most popular specialty shot shell maker, with an excellent reputation. If you cannot find a suitable special purpose load there, it cannot be found – or even imagined."

CHAPTER 47

SSK'S SUBSONIC
.500 WHISPER

J.D. Jones Has Come up with What May Well be the Ultimate Suppressed Combat Cartridge

J.D. JONES, who operates SSK Industries out of the smallish town of Wintersville, Ohio (population 4,100), is a long way from his beginnings in the business world, where he was a mid-level executive in the auto-building industry.

Along the way, he became involved in handgun hunting and became a noted authority and author regarding that sport. He also developed a reputation as a handloader and as an experimental ballistician.

It was back in the mid-1970s that Jones took on the chore of developing a special subsonic cartridge for a writer friend. This led to other experiments in subsonics that eventually was coupled with interest in their use for special operations by the military and as a tool of law enforcement agencies.

All of is this based on the fact that if a bullet exceeds the speed of sound, it will create a sonic sound that verges on the explosive. Millions of service personnel who have worked the target butts on rifle ranges are fully familiar with the fact that a bullet passing overhead offers an explosive sound that is

J.D. Jones, a long-time shooting enthusiast who made it a career, is the developer of the Whisper subsonic cartridge in its various calibers. He also has converted various arms to handle the unusual cartridges in addition to developing sound suppressors used with the weapons.

virtually as loud as that issuing from the firearm just triggered some hundreds of yards away.

The speed of sound varies, depending upon environment, altitude, temperature, etc. Basically, the speed of sound is 1,087.5 fps at sea level and at a temperature of 32 degrees Fahrenheit. Any bullet moving faster than the speed of sound can be a giveaway in a combat situation. This is true even if the weapon being used to launch the bullet is outfitted with the most modern sound suppressor.

Jones' interest in subsonics eventually led to his being assigned by the Jet Propulsion Laboratory in Pasadena, Calif., to develop a .50-caliber cartridge that would have extremely low velocity when fired. After some thought and experimentation, Jones was able to combine a 750-grain Browning Machine Gun bullet with the case for the venerable .50-70 Government cartridge. The case had been a military black powder standard that was adopted by the U.S. military in 1866. It was the first centerfire cartridge to be adopted by the U.S. Army. The cartridge worked up by Jones now is produced commercially as the .50-70-750.

Intrigued by the possibilities – not to mention the challenge – Jones continued his investigations into the field of subsonic ammunition. His experiments eventually included development of a subsonic round that used the case of the M-1 Carbine cartridge. This was the beginning of the series he calls the Whisper. Caliber in this instance was .300.

Jones soon switched to using the brass for the .221 Fireball cartridge that had been developed initially by Remington for a single-shot handgun the company produced. Jones selected this particular case because it would fit the magazine of the M-16 military rifle. To make this cartridge workable, he had to blow out the neck of the Fireball case to accept a bullet with a diameter of .308-inch. Thus, the .300 Whisper was born with case dimensions of 7.62x36mm. After a

With a new upper receiver built to handle the cartridge, Jones reworked this military M-16 rifle to handle the .50 American Express cartridge, another subsonic. It is effective in this rifle to 300 yards.

The reworked .50 American Eagle II M-16 suppressed rifle has a Jones-developed single-shot upper receiver to handle the 700-grain ball bullet. Velocity has been measured at 1000 fps.

One of the smaller Whisper calibers is the .338. This rifle was built on a Winchester Model 70 action to handle the subsonic cartridge. The camouflage on the stock is a vintage pattern known as French Lizard.

good deal of additional experimentation with various bullets, Jones settled on the Sierra Matchking bullet weighing 240 grains. This one had a hollow-point boattail configuration.

With the problem of sonics more or less solved, Jones launched into an investigation concerning the cartridge's capabilities in a submachine gun and with sound suppressors. Today, Whisper cartridges are available in a number of calibers and bullet weights. Jones and his staff have developed an upper receiver for the AR-15/M-16 rifle that will handle the subsonic .300 Whisper cartridge. This is being marketed by Jones' SSK Industries. He also has worked out an arrangement with Peter Pi, honcho of Cor-Bon Ammunition, to load and market all of the Whisper calibers on a commercial basis.

"Subsonic velocity in all calibers is still 1040 fps," Jones explains. "A silenced Whisper 300 in the M-16 rifle is quieter than Heckler & Koch's MP-5 submachine gun firing a 9mm cartridge. In a single-shot or bolt-action rifle, the Whisper 300 sounds about like a .17-caliber air rifle. A silenced high-velocity rifle such as a .308 sounds about the same as a .22 magnum pistol being fired."

"J.D. and I have been friends for going on 40 years," Lewis says. "During that time, I've never heard him offer the theory that bigger has to be better, but some of his experiments and developments appear to be built around that particular approach."

All of this brings us to the .500 Whisper, which may seem like a return to that original creation for the Jet Propulsion Laboratory several decades in the past. Not true!

The .500 Whisper is based upon the Weatherby .460 Magnum cartridge case, which has been shortened by Jones and necked up to .50 caliber. This particular Whisper caliber was developed at the request of the U.S. military and involves a dual-purpose round. The idea was that the cartridge could be used for sniping purposes on targets out to 300 yards and also could be utilized for long-range harassing fire against enemy troops up to 3000 meters.

This particular assignment required a bit of rethinking. The case of the .300 Whisper carries just enough powder to drive a relatively heavy bullet at a velocity that is just below the speed of sound. Experimentation has shown that to be silenced, a bullet cannot leave the muzzle at the speed of sound or anything beyond that.

At the other extreme, it became obvious that for the .500 Whisper to deliver bullets on a target at 3,000 meters, there would have to be sufficient powder in the case to send the bullet that distance with any degree of accuracy.

As originally conjured, the .500 Whisper was to carry an explosive charge in the nose of the bullet that would function much like a hand grenade upon contact with a target or even the ground. The .460 Weatherby case was shortened to 2.25 inches so that the bullet could be crimped in the cannelure of the .50 caliber military cartridge yet still fit into the magazines of certain rifle models manufactured by Sturm, Ruger and Weatherby.

The Ruger Model 11 Mark II and Weather Mark V rifles were chosen initially for the strength of their actions and the fact that both were built to handle large-caliber cartridges. One of the test rifles reworked by

This side view of the Accuracy International rifle displays the intricacies of its design. The lengthy sound suppressor covering the barrel is a product of J.D. Jones' SSK Industries. The scope is Leupold & Stevens' Mark IV model.

Sako's TGRS action was used to build this rifle to fire the .510 Whisper, which has the same ballistics as the 500 Whisper. The rifle is mounted with a Leupold & Stevens Mark IV scope.

Jones utilized a Ruger magnum action, but a 26.5-inch bull barrel replaced the original. Diameter of the barrel at the muzzle was 1.25 inches. Equipped with a Pachmayr synthetic stock, the outfit weighed 16 pounds.

Like the other Jones-devised calibers, ammunition for the .500 Whisper is available from Cor-Bon Ammunition. The firm now is headquartered in Sturgis, S.D., where there is plenty of available real estate nearby for experimental shooting.

More recently, Jones has come up with still another round in the .500 family. This one is the .510 Whisper and has the same ballistics as the .500. However, the case for this cartridge is modified from the .338 Lapua. Jones also has converted a number of other rifles boasting strong actions to handle his behemoth rounds. Single-shots that have proven accurate include the Accuracy International rifle, which is sturdy enough to withstand the pressures of any .50 BMG projectile, according to Jones. Firing a 750-grain bullet in the .510 Whisper case, this rifle shows a muzzle velocity of 1040 fps.

Jones and his crew also have reworked a military rifle to become what they call the .50 American Eagle II M-16. Carrying a sound suppressor, this shooting machine launches the bullet at 1000 fps and has an effective range of 300 yards. What Jones has come to call the American Eagle II is a cartridge based upon the .50 Action Express cartridge.

"Both cartridges carry the letters AE on the headstamp," Jones explains, adding that the American Eagle II rifles are outfitted to be subsonic only.

"Nothing subsonic matches the .500 Whisper for downrange accuracy," Jones declares. "The 750-grain bullets are the most practical, although 900-grainers are at the top end of what is available these days.

"In addition to cutting down the .460 Weatherby case and opening it up to .50 caliber, the rim must be rebated to standard magnum dimensions so that the bolt doesn't have to be reworked. Neck reaming is a requirement to ensure uniform neck tension.

"Overall length of the seated 750-grain bullet is the same as a loaded .460 Weatherby or the .416 Rigby," Jones explains. "Both the Weatherby and Ruger rifles convert easily to handle this caliber."

In working with the .500 Whisper, the ballistician has found that the most accurate subsonic load combination is 44 grains of IMR powder behind the 750-grain Thunder Cartridge Co. bullet. This bullet manufacturer makes match-grade bullets from solid brass. It has been found that this combination creates a muzzle velocity of approximately 1,030 fps. In a recent test, Jones fired four of these rounds at 100 yards for a group that measured only .46-inch, center-to-center.

"Subsonic or otherwise, the .50-caliber group stays under an inch, if the rifle is fed decent ammo," Jones claims. He adds, "Surplus government-issue bullets are good for little other than load development and plinking. They just aren't very accurate.

"The .50 caliber can do a lot of things other calibers can't, if the right bullets are chosen. At 951 fps, my 500 Whisper rifle penetrated the side of a Kevlar military helmet, and then went on to cut off a 9/16-inch bolt on which the helmet was mounted. With that kind of penetration, it is possible to take out large vehicles, radar units and even disable missiles. Fuel dumps can be fired using tracers and one can create a lot of mischief without making more noise than a cough!"

Jones' experiments have shown that subsonic bullets don't expand on impact. Generally the bigger and heavier it is, the more lethal the bullet will be. This is true of the Whisper calibers. However, tumbling bullets create wounds far out of proportion to their diameter.

Jones also has developed a .300 Whisper-firing submachine gun that he says, "renders obsolete any pistol-caliber submachine gun. Accuracy and control are simply unmatched by any other subgun."

A number of law enforcement agencies and military organizations now are using one or more of the Whisper rifles, but Jones refuses to identify these organizations. "I'm just not going to talk about it," he says.

CHAPTER 48

MODERN POLICE BALLISTICS

Civilian Law Enforcement Often Adopts Weapons Of Military Origin, but Makes Ballistic Changes

IN THE UNITED STATES, it is not at all unusual for civil authorities to adopt military weapons for use by law enforcement agencies. The Colt Single Action Army revolver is a prime example, as are the Beretta 92 9mm pistol, the M-16 rifle and others.

The Colt Single Action Army sixgun was initially issued to the U.S. Cavalry, but later became the preferred sidearm of hordes of frontier lawmen. Some lawmen still carry it. No sooner had the U.S. Department of Defense decided on issuing the Beretta model than law enforcement agencies across the nation began purchasing the same model.

At the other extreme, elements of the U.S. military also use shooting tools that many think of as civilian weapons. An excellent example of this is the shotgun.

"I found it amusing that many of us spent our youth sporterizing military bolt action rifles for hunting whitetail deer, then saw the our armed forces militarize the Remington 700 for use as a sniper tool," says law enforcement agent Robert Campbell.

There is a tradeoff, of course. In most instances, the civil authorities must tailor the weapon's support gear and ammunition to meet the requirements of urban actions – not to mention political demands. In numerous instances, ammunition changes are made in order to enhance terminal performance and to prevent ricochets and over-penetration.

This civilianization effort often involves the use of an expanding bullet, usually a hollowpoint in pistol ammunition and a softpoint for rifle cartridges.

Black Hills offers excellent choices in their .223/5.56mm ammo lineup.

In firing from behind cover, the 5.56mm rifle offers excellent accuracy. Bob Campbell contends that thus armed, the cop on the spot has a fighting chance.

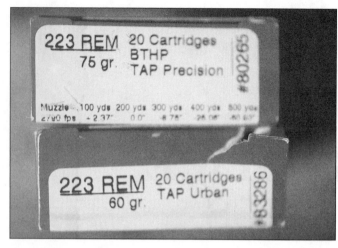

Bob Campbell praises the efficiency of the .223 Remington bullet - also known as the 5.56mm - in its heavier weights for police work. The 40-grain bullet, he feels, is too light to afford required penetration in a police shoot-out.

"The military forces, of course, are forbidden to use expanding ammunition in warfare, although this rule has been relaxed in recent times when it comes to actions against anti-terrorists action," Campbell points out. "With Saddam Hussein gassing Kurds and Arafat allowing the bombing and butchering of children, a lot of citizens now seem to see little point in a free state disregarding the highly developed resource of commercial expanding ammunition."

In a number of recent situations, ammunition has been developed primarily for use in the war on terrorism. As an example, the German Blunt Action Trauma round – perhaps better known by its acronym as BAT – was developed to not only cause instant incapacitation in the human body, but also to inflict immediate deflating damage to vehicle tires. The thought was that most terrorists escaped the scene in vehicles, so the BAT was designed to excise a piece of the tire in order to stop the vehicle quickly.

In other cases, ammunition has been over-developed. As an example, the 40-grain 5.56mm bullets developed for the AR-15 rifle have proven to have too little penetration for use in an anti-personnel role.

"While highly touted by some individuals who are for the most part unqualified to make ballistic recommendations, these loads are best left to the varmint fields," Campbell says. "This was first brought to my attention as a young police officer who became a dis-

ciple of Chief Dick Fairburn, a respected lawman and ballistician of the past.

"The tests conducted in ballistic gelatin and described by Fairburn in law enforcement literature are verifiable and repeatable, the true test of a science scientific. In my own gelatin tests, I have attempted to meet the same standard as Fairburn. A careful reader can duplicate anyone's published gelatin test, including those conducted by factory ballistics personnel. I have found that so-called secret sources or studies that cannot be independently verified are suspect at best," Campbell states.

The first part of this report features the performance of top quality 5.56mm ammunition. The 5.56mm rifle has found a solid place in America's police arsenal, for good reason. The guns are widely available, as well as being highly developed, reliable and accurate.

The cartridge also has many preferred qualities. It is not prone to ricochet, does not produce great recoil and, most of all, is effective in a combat situation be it open warfare or law enforcement. The 5.56mm cartridge produces a void in tissue when fired at close range. The effect is often immediate.

"It is true that the cartridge quickly loses effectiveness at long range, but this matters little to the police marksman. Virtually all law enforcement face-offs are close- range situations. Most police gunfights take place within a range of no more than 100 yards, but the 5.56mm is at its best as an entry weapon or patrol carbine," Campbell has found in his years of enforcing the law. "Heavier calibers are better suited for precision hostage rescue, especially if intermediate obstacles must be defeated.

"However, the 5.56mm rifle is a wonderful urban environment tool. It offers less penetration than the average law enforcement pistol, making it safer for the uninvolved population. In fact, this safety factor is two-fold. Only seldom will more than a handful of rounds be fired from the rifle, because it is easier to use well. Practical accuracy has greatly improved some of the law enforcement armament of the past, including issue pistols. The police carbine is here to stay."

Campbell has come to believe that there is a move toward use of heavier than normal 5.56mm bullets. The 69- to 75-grain bullets are indeed more accurate and penetrate light cover better than the .40- and 55-grainers. But are they more effective? Time will tell.

Below are the facts born of Campbell's tests in ballistic gelatin. It should be pointed out that expansion listed is approximated. About half of all bullets fired

BRAND	WEIGHT/ TYPE	VELOCITY	PENETRATION (in inches)	EXPANSION (in inches)
Black Hills	75 gr. JHP	2720 fps	13.9	.50
Hornady	75 gr. TAP	2698 fps	13.0	.51
Black Hills	68 gr. MATCH	2667 fps	12.0	.44
Winchester	64 gr. JSP	2667 fps	12.5	.46
Federal	55 grain JSP	2991 fps	10.0	frag
Federal	55 grain JSP Tactical	2887 fps	17.0	.48

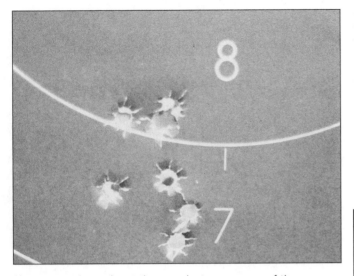

If one wonders about the combat accuracy of the .223/5.56mm round, this group fired at 100 yards should offer a positive answer.

with the exception of the Federal Tactical loads suffered fragmented bullets.

Campbell believes that these recorded results shows that the standard 55-grain JSP is effective, but that the heavier bullets retain a degree of authority. The 5.56mm will take out most bulletproof vests. The Federal Tactical load is a special-purpose round, which gives the 5.56mm more penetration for special circumstances.

Accuracy Testing

"Accuracy testing is problematic," Campbell admits, explaining, " I set my competition Colt HBAR up in a MTM rest. I was totally careful with each load tested, firing four five-round groups with each type of bullet. I allowed the rifle's barrel to cool between test firings.

"On occasion, this particular rifle has turned in 1-inch groups at 100 yards. With loads it likes, it may group slightly less. At the other extreme, it seldom strays beyond the 2-inch grouping with quality American ammunition."

Campbell says that for what they are worth, the results of his accuracy tests are shown below. However, he cautions, "The most accurate load in my gun may not be the best load for your own 5.56mm rifle, but odds are it will not be a real dog, either." All rounds were fired at a measured 100 yards.

LOADS	GROUP SIZE
Black Hills 75 gr.	.9 inch
Hornady 75 gr. TAP	1.1 inch
Hornady 55 gr. V Max	1.1 inch
Black Hills 60 gr. JSP	1.2 inch
Black Hills 68 gr. Match	1.25 inch
Black Hills 52 grain Match	1.25 inch
Winchester 64 gr. JSP	1.25 inch
Remington 55 gr. JSP	1.25 inch
Black Hills 55 gr. JSP	1.3 inch
Federal 55 gr. Tactical	1.4 inch
Remington UMC 55 gr. FMJ	1.4 inch
Handload Sierra 55 gr. JSP/Accurate powder	1.5 inch
PMC 55 gr. FMJ	2.35 inch

"Based upon these five-round groups, I am beginning to believe I cannot hold closer than 1.25 inches at 100 yards," Campbell says. "Nonetheless, all of the premium loads tested were more than accurate enough for defense and police duty."

This is part of Bob Campbell's arsenal for duty use. Choices include a .40 S&W Glock, a Colt .38 Super auto and a 9mm Uzi. He favors the wood-stocked .223 carbine in the field.

The hole through a side window of an auto suggests that the .223 bullet doesn't do much damage. However, the bullet went through the windows on both sides of the vehicle.

The author's contention is that V-Max bullets of 55 grains are fine for police work, while the 40-grainers are best left to the varmint hunters.

The next step in Campbell's determinations was to learn whether the major loads were accurate enough for hostage rescue at 50 yards. For this, he fired the two most accurate and the least accurate from his 100-yard testing.

LOADS	GROUP SIZE
Black Hills 75 grain	.69 inches
Hornady 75 grain	.72 inches
PMC 55 grain	1.65 inches

At a distance of 25 yards, Campbell fired three rounds of Federal Tactical 55-grain ammo into a Nine Dog target. Two of the bullets went through the same hole. The third bullet opened the group up to .5 inch.

"The 5.56mm has made the grade for police work," in Campbell's opinion. A lot of other officers agree with him.

The .45 ACP bullet is big and slow but it performs more impressively on auto glass than the smaller rifle calibers.

CHAPTER 49

HUSH, HUSH!

Here Is a Type of Extreme Performance Ammo That Meets a Lot of Law Enforcement Needs

CAMPBELL CONSIDERS HIS primary expertise to be in the field of ammunition. An advanced handloader, he understands well the physical properties of bullets and gunpowder.

We asked him to check out the recently introduced 9mm HUSH cartridge manufactured as part of its Delta Precision line by Custom Cartridge, Inc., of Goleta, Calif.

"This was no weekend test," he says. "It involved hundreds of rounds of ammunition and a good deal of test materials. All of my results are repeatable and verifiable. That is the true test of science. Shadowy figures and unconfirmed reports are not acceptable when choosing what may be lifesaving equipment. Every test I undertook can be set up and repeated by those who might be interested."

According to the manufacturer, the HUSH cartridge is the result of years of combined engineering, physics, chemistry, ballistics and quality manufacturing. In different forms, it is considered suitable for both defensive action and assault work.

The HUSH rounds carry a lead-free, highly frangible bullet, which is shaped and alloyed for different purposes.

"Looking at standard types of ammunition, there are some shortcomings that show why the HUSH-type round is needed," Campbell notes. "For example, a bullet with a full metal jacket has low stopping power, tends to over-penetrate and is prone to ricochet. The hollow-point requires high velocity and sometimes fails, acting like the FMJ bullet under certain conditions. It also can expand too quickly.

"The pre-fragmented bullet requires high velocity, often exhibits low accuracy and is expensive. I have found it unreliable in some instances due to light bullet weight and an unconventional pressure curve. This particular type of bullet also fires to a radically different point of aim than do typical service loads.

As for the frangible bullets, most of them require high velocity if they are to perform well."

The HUSH cartridge has been developed in several distinct performance levels. Campbell thinks that careful study of the differing levels should give

It is Bob Campbell's contention that the HUSH cartridge fired in his 9mm Luger CZ 75B autoloader has acceptable combat accuracy. This rapid-fire three-shot group was fired at 20 yards.

Visual inspection of the HUSH 9mm cartridge shows that Custom Cartridge, Inc., the maker, has maintained excellent quality control.

Low lead content in bullets is the coming thing even with law enforcement. Campbell found that these Custom Cartridge loads were safer in testing than many types and brands he has used over the years.

The 100-grain 9mm Luger hollowpoint used in his tests offered good results, Campbell says. Packaging from the maker is clearly marked.

the shooter a feel for the one that fits his particular needs. The manufacturer's ratings are arranged so that the higher the level number, the more penetration can be expected.

Level 00 – Campbell's tests show that this cartridge has shallow penetration with great disintegration properties. He recommends it for soft targets; it offers excellent bystander safety.

Level 0 – This cartridge has the same properties as the Level 00, but offers only partial disintegration.

Level 1 – Here we have low penetration and what Campbell describes as hyper fragmentation.

Level 2 – Cartridges loaded at this level feature moderate penetration accompanied by more fragmentation.

Level 3 – For combat use on soft to medium targets, this round offers moderate penetration.

Level 4 – This round offers hyper penetration on soft to hard targets with no fragmentation.

Level 5 – This is a match-grade target load that offers no splashback on a steel backstop.

Campbell reports, "My testing confirmed that HUSH indeed performs within the parameters specified by Custom Cartridge. On loads for which they claimed 10-inch penetration in ballistic gelatin was capable of a neat trick. With a 20-inch block of gelatin, I found I could shoot a HUSH round through each end of the block and the cavities would meet in the middle. This proved to be the case time after time.

One of the differences with this ammo is that the various grades have different muzzle velocities. Depending upon the level chosen for the 9mm Luger HUSH round, velocity ranges from 1,050 to 1,450 fps with a 100-grain bullet.

"Even at the top end, this is not particularly hot for the 9mm. With a 115-grain +P+ load, I achieved 1,380 fps on a regular basis. Of course, the HUSH round does not rely primarily upon velocity, but upon bullet design to do its job. I found the Level

0 – listed by the maker as HUSH 1.0 and rated at 1050 fps – especially pleasant to fire in full-size 9mm pistols."

Factory tests, of course, are done with special equipment and it is these readings upon which man-

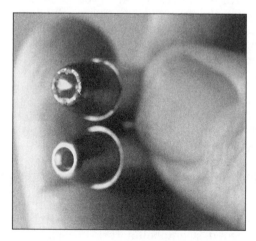

The HUSH cartridge at bottom is compared with the standard Gold Dot hollow-point. The HUSH bullet is of a synthetic material.

ufacturers base their claims. For example, Custom Cartridge claims 1050 fps for the HUSH 1.0 rounds. Campbell, firing a CZ 75 9mm with the same round had a velocity reading of 1042 fps. When the cartridge was fired from the Beretta Model 92, the reading rose to 1061 fps.

Campbell says, "The factory claim for the HUSH 1.2 – the Level 2 round – was 1250 fps. Again using the CZ 75, the round scored 1237 fps for me. In the Beretta, the velocity rose to 1266 fps. The HUSH 1.4 cartridge hits along at 1450 fps, according to factory

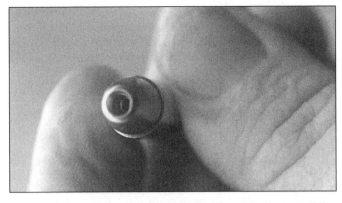

The HUSH hollow-point, viewed at this angle, leaves little doubt as to its efficiency in a combat situation.

Considered something of an ultimate test in law enforcement, the HUSH cartridge gave a good account of itself, when tested against automotive windshield glass. Bullets were fired at extreme angles to test effectiveness.

figures. In the CZ 75, my chronograph logged it at 1,441 and at 1,469 in the Beretta pistol."

Regarding performance capabilities, Campbell points out that an important consideration regarding HUSH ammunition lies in the fact that while all loads fragment upon striking hard resistance, several of the available loads will penetrate body armor. "That would have been a boon to officers involved in the North Hollywood shootout of several years ago, where the bank robbers were wearing armor, but such ammo also demands tight discipline and control."

Campbell has found that conducting a large-scale test outside of a laboratory – firing into mixes of gelatin and auto bodies – can be confusing if one does not have a program on which to base procedure.

"However, I have tested thousands of rounds of handgun ammunition in this manner," he adds. He found that "the HUSH high-penetration rounds are true performers, cutting through clothing and armored vests, but fragmenting upon truly hard resistance. The loads designed to fragment immediately do just that."

One of the rather obvious uses for this cartridge is in air marshal work. A major Southern California law enforcement agency undertook testing the HUSH cartridges against an aircraft body. When fired into the inner wall of the cabin at an angle of less than 30 degrees, the bullet penetrated the inner wall but not the outer shell. In fact, no sign of impact could be found on the outer wall of the alloy aircraft skin.

A one-gallon plastic jug filled with water then placed in front of one of the aircraft's passenger windows. The HUSH round did not penetrate the window. Then this window was shot at a 30-degree angle. The internal plastic window was breached, but not the outer window. A 9mm hole appeared on the inner window, with a cavitated bulge in the outer window. No fractures were in evident in the window, however. In firing directly at the window, both inner and outer panes were breached. Of course, when flying at 30,000-plus feet, differences in pressure might well create a different story.

This particular police agency also tested HUSH on gelatin blocks, firing at 10 feet. The gelatin was covered with clothing of various thickness and materials. The HUSH bullet passed through the clothing

and traveled 10 inches into the gelatin. A .308 rifle was fired in the same fashion on this test target and penetrated 12 inches.

During his testing, Campbell gave careful consideration to a number of claims that the manufacturer makes for its pet cartridge. Here are the claims and Campbell's conclusions:

Low Muzzle Flash – Low muzzle flash is a product of careful loading and full powder burn. This means little muzzle signature at night – at most, a warm, orange flash and little unburned powder. Campbell found that the HUSH cartridge lived up to the claim.

Low Recoil – This factor usually depends upon use of a lightweight bullet; Campbell found the HUSH round "pleasant to shoot, even in the .40 S&W caliber with muzzle velocity of 1350 fps."

Positive Function – In several hundred rounds, Campbell experienced only one failure – a failure of the cartridge to feed fully. He thinks this probably was "due to the low recoil impulse of the CZ 75 I was using. More powerful loads probably are the best choice for law enforcement use."

Consistent Reliability – Campbell experienced extremely low velocity and consistent accuracy.

Match-Grade Accuracy – "Fired in rifles, the cartridge probably has such accuracy," Campbell thinks, adding, "In my handguns, the HUSH was on the high end of accuracy testing results."

One-Shot Stop-and-Drop – "I had no opportunity to shoot animals with this load," Campbell says, "but an educated guess is that it will work well."

Reduced Ricochet Hazard – "This is qualified and confirmed. Bystander injury potential is clearly reduced by using this load," Campbell says.

Less Maintenance – The bullet is lubricated, which makes for clean shooting. "This ammunition burns with extreme cleanness," Campbell notes. "The spent cases were as clean as new ones."

Less Wear – The bullets are lubricated and are not rated +P. "Common sense tells us these rounds are not as hard on the gun as are the heavier service loads," Campbell concludes.

Returning to the matter of accuracy, Campbell points out that "HUSH handgun ammunition probably will not be used at long range. At short ranges, precision shooting is required in hostage rescue operations as is firing with a civilian presence in the immediate vicinity of the target.

"Also, felons may be behind cover, offering only a small part of the body as a target. HUSH is more than accurate enough for general defense and special team use," he says.

To back up this observation, Campbell ran more tests. All were five-shot groups and were fired from a braced barricade position. Group measurements were center-to-center of the most widely spaced bullet holes.

Firing the 9mm HUSH round the five-round groups fired with a SIG P226 measured .8 inch at 7 yards, 1.4 inches at 15 yards and 2.3 inches at 25 yards. At the same distances, group measurements for the Beretta 92 were 1 inch, 1.9 inches and .3 inches respectively. For the CZ 75B, the 7-yard group was .8, at 15 yards, Campbell managed 1.75 and the 25-yard group had a center-to-center measurement of 2.5 inches.

To substantiate manufacturer's claims for its ammo, Campbell also fired five-round groups at the same ranges, using HUSH .40 S&W ammo. The first gun up was a Glock Model 22 with a Jarvis Custom barrel. Group measurements were 1 inch at 7 yards, 1.25 at the 15-yard mark and 2 inches at 25. Firing a SIG P229, group sizes were 1.25, 1.5 and 2.25 inches for the three respective ranges. A Smith & Wesson Model 99 didn't do quite as well. Respective group sizes for the three distances were 2, 3 and 4.1 inches.